THE WORLD THROUGH LITERATURE

The World
Through Literature

edited by

CHARLTON LAIRD

Essay Index Reprint Series

BOOKS FOR LIBRARIES PRESS
FREEPORT, NEW YORK

STANDARD BOOK NUMBER:

8369-1359-0

LIBRARY OF CONGRESS CATALOG CARD NUMBER:

77-99639

PRINTED IN THE UNITED STATES OF AMERICA

TO

ARTHUR E. CHRISTY

(1899-1946)

PROFESSOR OF ENGLISH, UNIVERSITY OF ILLINOIS

WHO PROPOSED AND PLANNED THIS BOOK

PREFACE

A book of this sort incurs obligations, as anyone will know who has endeavored to put together a coöperative work, especially a work which, of its nature, must be done for the love of the job if it is to be done at all. The obligations incurred by this volume are not the less because the editing has extended over some five years. Suitable contributors were hard to find; not many critics in the United States are competent to discuss Arabic literature, for instance, and of those few not all are fluent in English. People who have these unusual competences are likely to be so busy with previous involvements that they can not find time to do an exacting essay, and even if they promise to do so, the editor may find that they disappear in the direction of Beirut or Pusan, called by urgent duties. Some of the chapters have been assigned as many as three or four times before an essay was prepared which met the standards we have tried to maintain for the book. The finding of a suitable contributor, furthermore, was a long process, requiring many exploratory letters and sometimes months of negotiation.

For patience and help in all this, the collector of these essays is indebted to more people than he can list here, but he hopes his creditors will accept this statement as intended for them personally. Many people, who could doubtless ill spare the time, have written long letters in answer to appeals, mentioning possible contributors and reviewing their qualifications. These benefactors should feel they have a part in the book. The editor is especially indebted to those contributors who prepared their essays to meet the first deadline, and then because some chapters had to be reassigned, found that their promptness was rewarded only by having their essays incarcerated in the editor's files. For their patience and consideration, much thanks.

Several who have helped must be mentioned by name. The late Prof. Arthur E. Christy planned the volume, and upon his death the National Council of the Teachers of English undertook the completion of the manuscript and accepted sponsorship of it as one of the Council monographs. Throughout the preparation of the book the Council has maintained editorial supervision over it. In this connection particular thanks are due W. Wilbur Hatfield, secretary of the Council, Robert C. Pooley, chairman of the publications committee during most of the editing of the book, and Max J. Herzberg, his successor during the final crucial months. They have been helpful beyond the duties of their offices, and understanding in ways which make an editor's life easier. The manuscript was read for the Council by Professors Horst Frenz, Indiana University; Lennox Grey, Teachers College, Columbia University; and Henry W. Wells, of the Faculty of Philosophy in the same institution. Their suggestions have been many and helpful. Thanks are due, also, to the University of Nevada through its Research Committee, which financed necessary travel by the editor.

C.L.

INTRODUCTION

This symposium was conceived by the late Professor Arthur E. Christy, who was a missionary at heart and a scholar in practice; readers are likely to find that it reflects the duality of its conception. There has probably never been a time when the lives and the happiness of mankind have seemed to depend more directly than they do today upon understanding and sympathy, understanding which knows no political barriers and sympathy which endeavors to transcend them. This book should make its modest contribution to those ends. It may also be read for more philosophic purposes. Professor Christy planned the volume in the hope that, if thoughtful essays dealing with the great literatures were laid side by side, the implied comparison might reveal a good bit about the way men write, and incidentally about the way men live and what they are. With that in view, specialists in thirteen great literatures were asked to write the most penetrating statements they could about the fields of their special study, and the results are here presented for comparative purposes.

To a considerable degree, this duality in the book is likely to lead to its being read by two different sorts of people. Some potential readers would willingly comprehend the whole literary output of man, if that were possible, with a view to probing more deeply into art and mankind. This book should give them suggestions and guidance. These readers are not likely, however, to read a book calculated only to remind them that men are brothers under the skin and neighbors except for the fence. There are readers of this latter sort, and they constitute an extremely important portion of mankind, but they are not usually intrigued by the mental labor which entices the scholar or the philosophic critic. If this volume, then, is to serve the needs of two widely differing sorts of readers, perhaps something more might be said about each of these supposed uses of the book, or the uses to which two different sorts of people may possibly be expected to find for it.

First, the hope that it may promote understanding. Why, if one wishes to understand in order to sympathize, should one read literature? Because art is the whole approach to life, the rounded approach which combines man with his world and his life, and literature is the art which uses the medium most understandable to most people, language. There is certainly much to be said for analysis, and science makes excellent use of the method, but there is also much to be said for synthesis, the other basic means of expression. It is the method of art, and we are likely to find in literature a better approach to any culture, to the whole culture —the individuals, their beliefs, their hopes, their ideals, their knowledge, their past and present—than through any other avenue. This is surely one of the great utilities of literature, if literature must be reduced to utilities. For instance, we in America will be slow to believe, while we have Tolstoy and Dostoevsky, that the Russian people want the kind of world which the Russian leaders, at this writing, seem to wish to promote. Anyone who reads even so much as the essay in this book concerning the literature of Japan will have the basis for a more sympathetic approach to the Japanese people than has been formerly held in this country.

Now for the second supposed use of this volume, that if this book is anywhere near so good as it should be, it says a great deal, and a great deal that is significant, about mankind, human nature, and culture. It was Professor Christy's hope that each of the contributors would endeavor to extract from the critical writings of the people concerned a coherent statement of their thought, temper, and essential nature. This intent has not been equally achieved in all chapters, partly of course because of the preferences of individual contributors, but partly also because of the nature of the materials which they have considered. Clearly, an analysis of this sort could be made for the classical Greeks.

Plato and Aristotle were uncommonly self-conscious and self-analytic, and we have enough classical speculation to think about classical ideas with some confidence. The reader will find that Professor Benham, seeking the classical ideals, has restricted himself very closely to the writings of the classical critics. Professor Radin, on the other hand, endeavoring to penetrate to the essential nature of primitive literature, had no such advantage. Civilized men have known very little that is reliable about folklore until recently, and primitive people, though they knew a great deal about their surroundings, knew very little about themselves. Professor Radin has been forced to rely largely upon modern anthropological studies, and of necessity often upon his own studies, and has produced an essay which is likely to become one of the standard statements about the mind and art of early man. Other contributors have varied, for cause, from the norm. Professor Morgan has advanced an interpretation of the German character which is likely to be viewed with abhorrence by many Germans. Professor Huse, dealing with French literature, has attempted no such comprehensive statement, but has studded his essay with finely and deeply cut bits of criticism. Professor Buck concerned himself with the elucidation of essential Hindu concepts; Professor Jurji, I believe quite rightly in view of general ignorance of Arabic literature in the Western world, has given more attention to shifting Arabic ideals and ambitions.

There are obvious omissions in the book, most of which reflect the purpose of the volume. The line had to be drawn somewhere, although it is too much to expect that all readers will approve the drawing of the line. Readers may ask why a chapter is devoted to the Scandinavian Peninsula and none to the Balkan Peninsula. There would have been justification for considering Celtic, Dutch, Swiss, and other bodies of writing. Subjects for the chapters were chosen by Professor Christy, and accordingly represent his judgment; there might have been other good selections, but his is at least defensible, and given the restrictions mentioned above, I personally doubt that it could have been improved

greatly. The smaller literatures were omitted because shortening
chapters sufficiently to provide space for minor bodies of writing
would have assured articles suited to encyclopedias, not critical
essays. There are already many good articles in encyclopedias.
Where original plans had envisaged combining several literatures, contributors sometimes found the combination inexpedient;
Polish and other middle-European literatures were omitted, for
instance, because Professor Posin despaired of describing one
stream of Slavic writing significantly if he were to ramify his
attention among the various Slavic streams. Celtic was omitted
because it has usually been closely associated with British literature; similarly, reasons could be advanced for the other omissions.

But the most obvious omission was deliberate, and had nothing to do with printing costs. There is no chapter on writing
in English. The reason, of course, is that the book is intended
mainly for readers of English, who might be supposed capable
of thinking about British and American literature without reading any more about it, and thinking at least as well as they would
be likely to think about Chinese literature even if they read a
great deal about it. Accordingly, if anything is to be said in this
symposium for writing in English, apparently it must be said by
the editor. I shall not endeavor to compress any summary of the
nature of writing in English into the few pages which may seem
appropriate to an introduction, the more because I am aware that
contributors have experienced understandable difficulty restricting an adequate estimate to a chapter. Conciseness, pushed too
far, can approach poverty. A few suggestions, however, may not
be out of order.

By common consent the language of Chaucer and Shakespeare,
of Melville and Mark Twain, comprises one of the great bodies
of writing in the world, and no space need be spent in eulogy.
Neither need we labor the point that writing in English is so
extensive and varied that a thoughtful critic should find many
revealing approaches to it. I shall mention only three, and I shall
choose these because they seem to me uncommonly suggestive,

and because I am not aware that they have been given the attention they deserve.

The first concerns British literature. I know of no other body of writing which might serve so well as "a literature," as a typical example of its genus, as an evidence of literature as a cultural phenomenon, as a laboratory model of what literature is. We need not accept all of Spengler's theses concerning culture to recognize that most great societies have risen from barbarism, and given time and opportunity, have experienced a series of changes, many of which fall into recognizable patterns, and which lead eventually to a complicated and sophisticated culture. Nor would many of us doubt that changes in culture are reflected, more or less adequately, in the literature of the time and place. For few peoples, however, has the literature been preserved for all stages of culture from barbaric times to a sophisticated and industrialized society. I know of no other which has preserved the whole sequence of acculturation, and which is at all comparable to English in its quantity, range, and excellence.

In the great Chinese literature, for instance, which staggers by its bulk scholars who are accustomed to thinking in Western terms, there is nothing culturally early, nothing that antedates the products of the School of Confucius, writings of an uncertain age, but reflecting an advanced society. Of Egyptian we have almost nothing. Greek has little but Homer that is notably earlier than the Golden Age. Italian literature sprang from the decaying body of Latin, and even French, which offers a very fine run of cultural change, has nothing significant earlier than the *Chanson de Roland* that dates well into the second Christian millennium.

English literature, on the other hand, has no great breaks from *Beowulf* to T. S. Eliot. Anglo-Saxon includes one of the few genuine extant epics, a respectable body of lyric verse, the fragments of a lay. The early extant works were composed *ca.* A.D. 700, and they embody extensive materials that are clearly much older, out of the fens of barbarism and the wolds of the Teutonic heroic age. From that time until today there has never been a great period on the Island of Britain which was not celebrated by many competent writers, never any long period without writers of notable stature. Some of them, like Geoffrey of Monmouth, used other tongues than English; he was born to Welsh and wrote Latin. John Gower wrote a long work in each of English, Latin, and French, hoping thereby to assure his reputation against the ravages of time and the shifts of linguistic fashion. But if one accepts Anglo-Norman and Anglo-Latin as parts of British literature, which they certainly are, the preserved writings of the English people provide a remarkably fine survey of the whole growth of a literature, the record of the artistic and intellectual expression of an important people from barbarism to community planning.

Now for my second suggestion, which concerns the literature of the United States. It is, so far as I know, unique, and curiously enough because it is a typical example of just what British literature is not. Most literatures, like British, are the result of a long tradition, a considerable portion of which is native. American literature has no native roots at all. It has no barbarism, no middle ages, no renaissance. It has a brief colonial and pioneer period, a brief transition period, a sophisticated-socialized period, and that is all. Most people living in the United States have some ancestors who were not here a century ago. The culture is a European culture, imported and established in a land where it had no native soil. This tradition was altered, and sometimes altered extensively, by the frontier, by the slave-holding South, by culture patterns like that provided by the cowboy-cattle country, but basically it remained a culture brought in by the people who arrived in ships, people who had little community and less sympathy with the Iroquois, the Sioux, and the Athapascans who were the native Americans. Thus the literature of the United States is the great example of colonial letters. There have been others. No doubt there was a colonial literature in Abyssinia; interesting things have come from colonials in Indo-China; there is a very healthy and growing literature of Australia and of several other areas.

Nonetheless, the literature of the United States is the only colonial product which has as yet become one of the major literatures in the world of its day.

My third suggestion, which concerns the writing of both the United Kingdom and the United States, is this: The world seems now to be involved in a broad social shift, and this is better reflected than elsewhere by writings in English, because Britain and the United States have been and are the leaders in this change. I am suggesting that we are now in a great Middle Age, the transition from the Age of Individualism to whatever kind of world grows from our present trends toward more socialized living. I am suggesting that the periods of history and literature to which we are accustomed in Western criticism and scholarship—the Medieval Period, the Renaissance, the Reformation, the Age of Reason, and the like—are not major periods at all, but minor though important subdivisions of a great period which rose with the decay of the Roman Empire, was the dominant fact in the Western world for a millennium or two, the time being dependent upon the area one elects to consider, and is only now in process of fundamental change.

I call this long stretch of time the Age of Individualism because the importance and the power of the individual seem to dominate it, and its end comes with the shift from the individual to society. During this period work was done by the hands of individuals, inventions came from the brains of individuals, travel was on the feet of individuals or by beasts of burden which were subject to individual wills, people lived mainly in individual and self-supporting units, government was run by individuals for individuals, the church existed to save the individual soul, and the whole period came to its climax in the eighteenth century with the exaltation of the individual reason, and during the romantic movement with the exaltation of the individual man.

The Age of Individualism had scarcely reached its height, however, before it was shifting into what I am trying to call the Great Middle Age, and the shift seems to have begun more than elsewhere in Britain, and to be led at the moment, at least in some respects, by the United States. We no longer make goods by hand, and this is the great fact of modern Western society. We have changed our means of production and our means of earning a living, and this change—along with others which have accompanied it, whether or not they were caused by it—a change which began with the industrial revolution and has led from the spinning wheel to the assembly line, seems to be fundamental for the Great Middle Age and for the age to come. Less and less do inventions come from individuals; what one man could have developed atomic energy? We can still walk, but many of us find that most of our traveling is done with the help of machines, and many of these machines could not conceivably be made by an individual, or even be operated by an individual. The shift of population is away from the self-supporting croft and the self-defending manor, to the city in which no man can feed, clothe, defend, or even move himself, at least not so far as to reach his day's work. How many dwellers on Long Island could get to an office in Manhattan if they had to rely upon walking and swimming? The ideal government is no longer founded upon obedience to a prince and does not exist for the exaltation of a nobility. Democracy has changed all that in principle, and to a degree in fact. Churches are relatively less concerned than they used to be about saving individual souls, and more concerned with social solidarity. No scientist can do much alone. Even art, perhaps the most individualistic of all man's activities, moves toward socialization. Reading is no longer the favorite pastime; it has been superseded by looking at some kind of animated pictures, and whether this is done at a cinema or at home before a television set, it is highly coöperative both in its production and its appreciation. The pictures to be observed can be produced only after an elaborate coöperative effort involving the arts, and the results can be indulged in only in concert with thousands or millions of other human beings. A printed book, of course, represented some coöperative effort, and even books are more coöperative than they used to be, but compared with a multi-million dollar moving picture even the most elaborate book represents a homey and highly individualistic performance.

Thus it seems to me that the great fact of Western civilization in recent times, say the last century or two, has been a pervasive shift away from individual living toward a life in which the individual finds himself involved in and submerged by activities which are socialized and coöperative. This shift seems to have started among English-speaking peoples, and on the whole to have developed more consistently among English-speaking peoples than it has in other great linguistic or cultural areas. Nor is this all. The change, whether impelled by the machine or by influences more difficult to identify, seems to be spreading over the world. The disturbances in China and Russia are surely somehow related to this shift, and they may perhaps be best described as the disruptions concomitant with the efforts of great peoples to adopt socialization too rapidly. Nor are these changes limited to the larger countries; they are coming in an orderly way in Scandinavia, and apparently in Turkey; in a less orderly way in Ecuador and Malay. There are great changes throughout the world, and the changes seem to follow a pattern. This pattern can be the most extensively and intimately observed, I believe, in the writings of English speakers.

So much for English, and for some of the ideas which might be developed in a chapter concerning it. For English and the literatures here surveyed, the reader will doubtless prefer to make his own comparisons as he reads, and this is the purpose of the volume. The opinions expressed by individual contributors are, as a matter of course, their own. There has been some effort to restrict observations, particularly as to matters which may be conceived to approach fact, to statements which are documentable or are widely accepted among critics of the literature. Any such ideal can scarcely be achieved equally among all circumstances, nor is uniformity entirely desirable. The more significant the question, in considering life and letters, the less the likelihood that there can be any non-controversial answer. As someone has observed, peace on earth is scarcely the aim of literary criticism, and when the contributors are at their best, their conclusions are most likely to be open to dissent.

C.L.

CONTENTS

I

Primitive Literature

PAUL RADIN
KENYON COLLEGE

The nature of primitive man, the primitive mind, and primitive art reveal one of the world's most interesting problems, for in studying the creative desire in primitive man we are presumably studying whatever made civilization. He would be an audacious anthropologist who would assert he knows more about this subject than does PROFESSOR PAUL RADIN, who brings to the discussion a background based upon years of study in the field, a wide knowledge of both early and sophisticated literature, and a questing mind which has always sought the significance back of his research. His research among the Winnebago has made that people one of the most understood primitive groups, and his general command of his material has found expression in such books as The Story of the American Indian (1925), Primitive Man as Philosopher (1927), Indians of South America: The American Museum of Natural History, Science Series (1942), and The Road of Life and Death (1945).*Through a long life he has made the intricacies of the primitive mind and primitive esthetics his peculiar province as has no other living American. He is visiting professor at Kenyon College, and for the last two winters has been lecturing in Switzerland and Sweden. His home is in Berkeley, California.*

Primitive Literature

NATURE AND EVOLUTION

A N ALMOST universal belief among students of literature
holds that the word *literature* means what its etymology
implies, namely, that which is written. Not a few anthropologists
subscribe to this view. Yet if we reach our judgment on the basis
of specific criteria, as assuredly we must, then that which when
written, instead of recited, meets these criteria is literature. It is
not the absence of writing, however, which, I suspect, has led
scholars and laymen alike to deny to the productions of aboriginal
man the right to be called literature, but something else. Underneath their attitude lies a series of assumptions, expressed or un-
expressed: first, that oral composition in some fashion or other
specifically circumscribes form and subject matter; and secondly,
that literature cannot develop until a people has reached the stage
at which it has either evolved for itself or can profitably borrow
from someone else a system of writing.

Other assumptions too, we shall see, are involved. For this
reason it will be best to examine briefly how the term *literature*
has been used by different students of the subject. This procedure is the more imperative because definitions hitherto suggested have either minimized or neglected aspects of the subject
which are prominent in preliterate civilizations and seem destined to play an important rôle, on another level to be sure, in
the future.

The term literature is notoriously resistant to definition and
treacherous after it has ostensibly been defined. Mr. T. C. Pollock[1] recently noticed the difficulties and confusions in the many

[1] *The Nature of Literature* (Princeton, 1942), pp. xiii-11.

3

definitions that have been attempted. If his definition is not more satisfactory, and if his discussion of those of others does not carry conviction, the reason is easy to determine. He has arrived at his definition by treating literature as an isolated unit, as something on its own. In such an approach he is, of course, today in distinguished company, in the company of those who, as Philip Henderson has well said, maintain "that beliefs and external interests in a poet are an obstacle to the free practice of his art and who say that poetry and painting should express nothing but itself." [2]

Mr. Pollock is clearly a relativist, and although he insists that he is merely trying to avoid the pitfalls of value-definitions, actually he is rejecting them. Yet a value-definition must be made; and is, in fact, inevitable when treating of literature, particularly that of aboriginal peoples. It can have little validity unless it is made with reference to the social order of which it is always an integral part and of which it is everywhere the outcome. Two questions must consequently be posed and answered before we can fruitfully and meaningfully proceed with our inquiry. For whom has a given literature value? Whose way of life, whose thoughts and feelings does it express? I am provisionally including in the term every type of poetry and prose, good and bad, and irrespective of its purpose and functions.

Let us begin with the great ancient historic civilizations of Asia, Africa, and Europe. There we know precisely what part of the total output has been labelled literature, and what not, and why. It includes only that which had value for an infinitesimal portion of the whole population. It reflected the thoughts and feelings of this minority only. Nor was what has been preserved in writing selected because it conformed to specific literary criteria, good or bad; although manifestly, only individuals with great literary gifts could have composed some of the hymns, incantations, and prose narratives which have come down to us.

All these civilizations rested upon stratified class societies, with

[2] *Literature and a Changing Civilization* (London, 1935), p. 2.

the ideologies which emerge from and accompany such societies, and the compositions preserved naturally reflected these ideologies and dealt with the interests of the small minorities in control. Accordingly we must not be surprised to see their literature concerned overwhelmingly with religion, with the affairs of state, and with the fortunes and achievements of kings, nobles, and officials.

The earliest significant contributions of the ancient civilizations of Asia and Africa were cast in the rhythms and special language of verse. It was in verse, predominantly, that the achievments of kings and heroes were later extolled. Prose played a smaller rôle, although a much greater one than appears to most of us who are taught to regard the written literatures of Greece, Rome, and modern Europe as the norm.

Roughly speaking, from 3000 B.C. to 600 B.C., the relative ratio of religious to profane literature in these civilizations remained practically the same. After that, and mainly in Europe, for a period of approximately one thousand years, this ratio changed significantly in favor of profane subject matter, only to be overwhelmed then, for almost another thousand years, by a literature dealing again predominantly with religious material.

I need not point out what unwarranted and at times absurd inferences have been drawn, and for that matter still are drawn from these facts, both as to the nature of true literature and the evolution of literary forms. Any history of Greek literature will indicate what these inferences are and it is a significant fact that even so great a mind as Wilamowitz-Moellendorff succumbed to them.[3]

That there existed in ancient Egypt, Babylonia, and India, compositions which were not officially accepted and consigned to writing yet which represented the thoughts and feelings of the overwhelming part of the population, we know. Indeed we have excellent evidence for believing that more was rejected than accepted; that, in fact, many categories of compositions were dis-

[3] *Die Griechische Literatur und Sprache* (Berlin, 1905), pp. 1-236.

carded just as they were discarded, many centuries later, in
China. Nor must we assume that here either literary criteria
alone determined what was thus excluded. We do know one
thing, however, that what was eliminated, namely, the whole of
oral literature, was stigmatized as inferior and worthless because
it represented the output of socially inferior classes, of groups
who were felt to be uncouth, unsophisticated, and underdeveloped. The existence of this oral and traditional literature was at
all times recognized, yet even when it played a rôle in determining the subject matter of written compositions, as at times it did,
it was at best regarded as a source for true literature and no more.[4]

We can form some idea of what categories and types of composition must have been present if we examine the literatures of
Babylonia and Egypt where writing was adopted early, or those
of India where special conditions existed for the perpetuation of
a directed and circumscribed oral tradition. In the case of Egypt
we have by no means negligible indications for the existence of
such poetry and prose. Take, for example, the excellent lyric
poetry included in the famous *Dispute with his Soul of One
Who is Tired of Life, The Story of Sinuhe, The Story of the
Ship-wrecked Sailor,* and *The Instructions in Wisdom.*[5]

[4] There are few books on comparative literature which pay much attention
to aboriginal peoples. The work of A. S. Mackenzie, *The Evolution of
Literature* (New York, 1911) is rendered useless for my purposes because of
the author's acceptance of many of the outworn and completely discredited
clichés about the mentality of preliterate peoples. By far the best treatment,
although it is incidental to the authors' main interests, is that found in the
great work of H. Munroe Chadwick and N. Kershaw Chadwick, *The Growth
of Literatures* (London, 1932-1940) 3 vols. The Chadwicks are among the
few historians of literature who have clearly understood the significance of
the oral literatures of the great historic civilizations and evaluated them properly, thus laying the foundations for obtaining a proper perspective in ap-
proaching the study of the oral literatures of aboriginal peoples. The peoples
they have selected for treatment are, however, unfortunately, the Tartars,
Polynesians, Northern Bantu, Galla, Tuareg, and Yoruba, who present highly
special problems.
[5] Adolph Erman, *The Literature of the Ancient Egyptians* (New York,
1927), pp. 86ff., 35ff., 54ff. Cf. also Gaston Maspero, *Popular Stories of
Ancient Egypt* (London, 1915).

All these compositions have been preserved in highly sophisticated forms, reinterpretations, and reworkings. Yet they undoubtedly represent examples of subject matter and of literary forms which must have been current among the great mass of Egyptian peasants, a subject matter and, to a certain extent, forms which can be duplicated in the oral literature of aboriginal peoples today. Similarly, for instance, no amount of secondary reinterpretations, embellishments, and reinterpretations can possibly disguise the fact that not a few of the Sumerian hymns preserved in writing must originally have been modelled on personal lyrics composed among the people at large.[6] The same holds for the ancient Semitic magical incantations.[7] Granet and Waley have shown how many pure rustic love songs are embodied in the Shih Ching.[8] The situation in India was, as mentioned above, a very special one, but it has unusual significance for the problem of how elaborate and sophisticated a literature can be which has developed and been perfected without the use of a script.[9] Among other things it demonstrates how effectively a class-caste structure of society can operate in preventing whole categories of composition from being perpetuated whether writing exists or not. For an understanding of Polynesian literature, for example, which is entirely oral, this is of paramount importance.

However, welcome as are the hints and suggestions from Egypt and Babylonia concerning the oral literatures that preceded and were contemporaneous with the written literatures of these coun-

[6] Stephen Herbert Langdon, *Tammuz and Ishtar* (Oxford, 1914), pp. 10f., 13ff.

[7] B. Campbell Thompson, *Semitic Magic* (London, 1908). The best general treatment of Sumerian, Babylonian, and Assyrian literatures, although somewhat antiquated, is still Otto Weber, *Die Literatur der Babylonier und Assyrer* (Leipzig, 1907). For more recent treatment of Sumerian literature, cf. Samuel Nathan Kramer, *Sumerian Mythology* (Philadelphia, 1944) and the appended bibliography.

[8] Marcel Granet, *Festivals and Songs of Ancient China* (New York, 1908), and Arthur Waley, *The Book of Songs* (Boston and New York, 1937).

[9] For the questions involved, cf. Chadwick and Chadwick, *op. cit.*, vol. II, pp. 459-625.

tries, they unquestionably give a totally inadequate picture of the nature and the full extent of the oral literatures these civilizations must have possessed.

It is here that the oral literatures of aboriginal peoples have relevance. What, for example, is the range of their subject matter? Did they deal with the whole or with only part of life? Was a given literature the possession of the whole group or of a small minority within this group? What variety of forms did their verse or prose-narratives take? How much dealt with religion and magic, and how much with strictly lay matters? What directed selection has taken place, and have some portions been stigmatized as superior, others inferior? Finally, and this is possibly the basic question, to what extent do the various and divergent social structures of aboriginal peoples, with their divergent economies, interfere with the emergence of artists and the attainment of literary craftsmanship?

The answers to these questions can be given immediately. From them we obtain the following picture. In all aboriginal cultures where our knowledge is even moderately satisfactory, Polynesia and certain portions of Africa excepted, we find both poetry and prose, each with distinctive forms and dictions; we find a range of subject matter embracing the whole of life, and an audience including the entire community. Everywhere, the societal structure has placed its impress upon the products of the literary craftsman, yet nowhere has it interfered significantly with his freedom of expression or his craftsmanship. Everywhere we find this literature firmly integrated with music and dance and with every aspect of social existence.

These answers do not provide us with a definition of literature. But we will have made progress by having increased the body of facts to be considered, and extended the limits within which a definition must lie. Moreover, they strengthen and reinforce what we have stressed before, the impossibility of considering any form of artistic expression, more particularly literature, apart from the societal framework within which it has developed.

Bearing in mind what we have now discovered for aboriginal oral literatures, and knowing what we do about the great historical literatures, we can perhaps hazard a definition. It makes no claim to originality. Literature is the formal communication, through language, of an esthetic experience whose content and form are conditioned by the structure of the society in which it has developed. This holds as much for the writings and the critical pronouncements of thinkers and poets like T. S. Eliot, I. A. Richards, Cleanth Brooks, Allen Tate, and John Crowe Ransom, as it does for thinkers and poets in aboriginal civilizations. The esthetic, it is vital to remember, is, as Dewey has so well pointed out, "no intruder in experience from without, whether by way of idle luxury or transcendent ideality, but . . . the clarified and intensified development of traits that belong to every normally complete experience." [10] Such an experience can no more be projected into a vacuum than it can be created within a vacuum. No supremely creative artists can exist unless, at the same time, there be a vitally responsive and actively participating audience. And, ideally the audience should comprise the whole population, never a special fragment of it.

However our difficulties have only begun. What standards are we to use in judging the relative greatness either of an individual poem, of a prose narrative, or of a literature as a whole? T. S. Eliot, for instance, insists that "this greatness cannot be determined solely by literary standards." [11] What this non-literary constituent element is, however, he never tells us. Presumably it is, in part at least, identical with the use of literature for moralistic purposes and as a vehicle for the expression of ideas, both of them, as we know, aspects of literature against which such able critics as Ransom and Tate protest vehemently. For the latter such uses represent contaminations of literature as an absolute and pure art. If the strict uses of Ransom and Tate were valid,

[10] John Dewey, *Art as Experience* (New York, 1934), p. 46.
[11] *Essays Ancient and Modern* (New York, 1936). He adds, correctly enough, "We must remember (however) that whether it is literature or not can be determined solely by literary standards."

there would indeed be few masterpieces in European literature, and practically none at all among aboriginal peoples.

Yet it is not merely the members of the school to which these two distinguished poets and critics belong who hold such views. They are, strangely enough, implied, although confusedly, in the statements of anthropologists like Malinowski and philosophers and historians of ideas like E. Cassirer. What is involved here is of fundamental importance, centering as it does around the whole question of function *versus* form. Both Ransom and Malinowski are "functionalists," if you will, but in entirely different fashions. For Ransom, I take it, a great literary masterpiece will function only when a properly prepared audience is present to receive it. That audience must always be small. For Malinowski, it is the complete functioning of the oral literature of aboriginal peoples, the fact that it must be valid for all alike, which prevents it from ever becoming true literature. For Cassirer, on the other hand, the inherent mythical thinking prevents aboriginal man from ever functioning maturely or developing a true literature.

But let us return to the problem of what overall criteria are to be employed in assessing the greatness of a literature. Assuredly, the answer must be that its greatness will depend upon the extent to which it has as its main object the developing and the intensification of consciousness, the imaginative apprehension of life both for the poet as well as for his audience.[12] In aboriginal societies such an intensification of consciousness and imaginative apprehension of life did obtain, and if I. A. Richards correctly defines the function of poetry,[13] the prerequisite conditions for the existence of excellent poets and great literatures are present. What we would like to know then is this: were there individuals in aboriginal societies endowed with the gifts to express this

[12] Herbert J. Muller, *Science and Criticism* (New York, 1943), pp. 39, 41.

[13] *Practical Criticism* (New York, 1929), pp. 319ff. "Poetry," he there states, "translates into its special sensory language a great deal that is given in the ordinary daily intercourse between minds by gesture, tones of voice, and expression . . . There is no gap between everyday emotional life and the material of poetry. The verbal expression of this life, at its finest, is forced to use the technique of poetry; that is the only essential difference."

imaginative apprehension of life? But before we turn to that
question we must first examine certain assumptions and presuppositions which bar the way to a proper understanding of aboriginal man's literary achievement.

SUPPOSITIONS AND THEORIES

Of the many viewpoints and presuppositions which constitute
a bar to the proper understanding and appreciation of aboriginal
literature, I shall discuss only a few. I shall ignore the scientifi-
cally discredited theories of racial superiority and inferiority, although they do, consciously or unconsciously, permeate much of
the thinking of most Western European scholars. In some ways
far more dangerous and treacherous than these theories is the
postulation of a mythical mentality, of a group-mind, of the inadequacy of aboriginal languages, or the supposed metaphorical
character of their vocabularies.

This is not the place to discuss these latter theories at length,[14]
and I shall confine my remarks to a minimum. Let me begin by
saying that there is no justification for any of them. Why when
so much careful work has been done since Boas' time on aboriginal languages, especially on those of North America, philosophers like Lévy-Bruhl, Cassirer, and others, not to mention psy-
chologists and sociologists, still persist in their willful naïveté, is
difficult to understand. Suffice it to say that all modern students
of language are agreed that every language has the grammatical
apparatus and the vocabulary for expressing fully and accurately
whatever it is asked to do. Each language will obviously not
achieve expression in the same manner nor with the same grammatical apparatus. Manifestly, likewise, every language will select and emphasize certain categories for formal expression and
omit others. This does not mean, however, that what is thus

---

[14] For a full discussion, cf. Paul Radin, *Method and Theory of Ethnology*
(New York, 1933);—*Primitive Religion* (New York, 1937), and, for a
later treatment, *Winnebago Hero Cycles,* in *Indiana University Publications in
Anthropology and Linguistics* (1948).

omitted does not exist or cannot be rendered. Aboriginal languages vary tremendously in their structure and in the nature of their vocabulary.[15] Some may seem poverty stricken in certain directions as compared with, say Greek and English; yet in other equally important directions, Greek and English will seem poverty stricken when compared with them.

The same holds for the often repeated statements concerning the essentially metaphorical character of aboriginal languages. It makes very little difference whether metaphor is used in an essentially derogatory sense to imply a primitive mentality as H. Werner[16] does, or in an appreciative sense as Philip Wheelwright[17] does. Werner's view need hardly be considered. Wheelwright deserves comment because of the by-products of his attitude. He agrees with Shelley that, "in the infancy of society every author is a poet," interpreting this statement as the expression of aboriginal man's mythical mentality. Although he does not use this term with Cassirer's implications, his comments deserve specific quotation. "There are two outstanding respects," so he states, "in which primitive language, and specifically spoken language, tends to be poetic, or at any rate to have a natural kinship with poetry: first, in its manner of utterance, its rhythms and euphonies; second, in its manner of reference, in the delicacy and associative fulness with which it refers to various aspects of the all-encompassing mystery . . . The metaphorical character of primitive language . . . consists of its tendency to be rather manifoldly allusive; it can be so, because of the varied associations with which communication within a closed society has gradually become charged; and it has a semantic necessity of being so . . . Owing to such referential plenitude the language of primitives

[15] Franz Boas, *Bureau of American Anthropology*, vol. I, Bulletin no. 40 (Washington, 1911), *Introduction*; Edward Sapir, *Language* (New York, 1921); and Leonard Bloomfield, *Language* (New York, 1933).

[16] *Die Urspruenge der Metapher* (Leipzig, 1919). Cf. also Rich Thurnwald, *Die Psychologie des Primitiven Denkens* (Berlin, 1918).

[17] "Poetry, Myth, and Reality," in the symposium ed. by Allen Tate, *The Language of Poetry* (Princeton, 1942), pp. 3-33.

tends to employ paradox freely; it makes use of statements contradicting each other and of statements contradicting an experientially accepted situation." [18] Most of what Wheelwright says here is wrong as a matter of actual fact. His approach itself, however, is infinitely more penetrating and correct than that of most professional anthropologists.

For some anthropologists, however, it is not the inadequacies of the languages or a mythical mentality which has prompted them to deny the existence or, in fact, the possibility of true literature among aboriginal peoples as it is the manner in which, they feel, the unwritten verbal output functions. The most famous and certainly the most articulate proponent of this viewpoint is Malinowski. Because he has had considerable influence on theorists in the field of literature I shall discuss mainly what he has to say.[19] Malinowski contends that "language in its developed literary and scientific functions is an instrument of thought and of the communication of thought." [20] In its primitive function, and that is what we find among aboriginal peoples, he insists, it is a mode of action and not a counterpart of thought. Myth and song are, among them, consequently, so inextricably intertwined and interpenetrated with utilitarian activities that they can never partake of the nature of a true fiction. The demands of life on these lower economic levels, so runs his argument, effectively stifle and overwhelm any artistic stirrings which assert themselves.[21] No true prose literature exists at all, only myths. Moreover, these myths are not symbolic but, rather, a direct expression of their subject matter. "What we find," he adds, "is simply a narrative resurrection of a primeval reality, told in satisfaction of deep religious wants, moral cravings, social submissions, assertions, even practical requirements . . . It is not an idle tale . . .

[18] *Ibid.,* pp. 14-15.
[19] Largely because of his essay, "The Problem of Meaning in Primitive Languages," which appeared as a supplement in C. K. Ogden and I. A. Richards, *The Meaning of Meaning* (New York, 1945) pp. 296ff.
[20] *Ibid.,* p. 297.
[21] *Myth in Primitive Psychology* (New York, 1926), pp. 18-19.

not an intellectual explanation or artistic imagery but a pragmatic charter of primitive faith and moral wisdom." [22]

The correctness of this definition, amazingly enough, was challenged in the very book to which Malinowski contributed his essay. Indeed it is the outstanding merit of the newer school of literary criticism from Richards and Eliot to Brooks, Tate and Ransom, that it has, by implication, shown the complete inadequacy of such a view. Eliot, I feel confident, would not exclude from the realm of literature Malinowski's "narrative resurrection of a primeval reality" and the "satisfaction of deep religious wants." On the contrary, he would contend that these must form the very basis for great literature. The question he might ask is whether this can be achieved in aboriginal societies. What Malinowski and all the functionists always forget is that the utilitarian and magico-religious functioning of many poems and prose narratives was frequently secondary; that these poems and prose narratives were composed first and had originally no connection with the uses to which they were subsequently put. This is a phenomenon for which we have many instances in the history of European literatures. The functionalists seem to assume, likewise, that because a given poem, for instance, has been composed for a specific purpose or function, this fact by itself will interfere with its artistry. However, the question to determine is obviously not this at all but, rather, whether a real artist has composed a poem and whether in form and content it conforms to literary standards. [23]

If the professional anthropologists are thus in doubt, we must not be surprised to find students of general literature and of folklore skeptical. The famous Finnish folklorist, Antti Aarne, [24] for

[22] *Ibid.*, p. 19.

[23] In justice to Malinowski, let me add that he does in one passage of *Myth in Primitive Psychology* state that, "myth lends itself in certain of its forms to subsequent literary elaboration and . . . in other of its forms remains artistically sterile." (p. 88) Unfortunately his functionalist position prevented him from doing anything with this perfectly correct insight.

[24] *Leitfaden der vergleichenden Maerchenforschung,* Folklore Fellows Communications, 1913, no. 13, p. 14.

instance, contends that even the *Maerchen* cannot be expected among aboriginal peoples. At best we can expect to find legends (*Sagen*), and legends are simple narratives possessing no artistic traits and having no artistic import.

The same attitude is encountered in the well-known work of R. Petsch,[25] although his treatment has also been markedly affected by a vague psychological evolutionism. In its main outlines it is close to the attitude of Malinowski.

For both, manifestly, true literature must be pure. There must be no entangling alliances with the utilitarian and practical. The justification is in both instances the same; namely, that utilitarian adhesions distract the author from his primary creative effort and introduce disturbing and disruptive mundane factors into what should always remain an aesthetic-spiritual activity. For Malinowski that which has prevented true literature from developing is, we have seen, the interpenetration of myth and poem with all the activities of the community, with what he chooses to call its living reality. For Petsch much more is involved. To him, as to so many sociological theorists and students of comparative literature, the thinking of aboriginal peoples is primarily analogical and "mimetic" and is completely under the domination of mentally autonomous mythological and magical schematisms.

For Cassirer, likewise, the languages of aboriginal man are adequate only for the description of direct and unmediated sensory impressions, impressions which must be reproduced in all their multiplicity and meticulous detail. Language, he contends, is so inextricably attached to this function of depicting the concrete happening and its sensory image that all attempts at generalization are thereby rendered impossible.[26] In the place of generalization we have multiplicity, an exuberant development of

[25] *Wesen und Werden der Erzaehlerkunst* (Halle, 1934).
[26] Cf. his *Die Begriffsform im mythischen Denken* (Berlin, 1922); *Philosophie der symbolischen Formen;* pt. 1, *Die Sprache* (Berlin, 1923), *Das mythische Denken* (1925); *Language and Myth* (New York, 1946). Reference should, of course, also be made to the discussion of the language of aboriginal peoples in the famous work of L. Lévy-Bruhl, *Les Fonctions mentales dans les sociétés inférieures* (Paris, 1910), ch. IV.

expressions for a particular activity in all its manifold differentiations. Not only can aboriginal peoples consequently not objectify their thought, they cannot properly form abstract notions.

If these contentions were true then there would indeed be little possibility of encountering among aboriginal peoples what we all agree is the essence, if, indeed, it is not the primary function of literature; namely, to recreate out of the discreet facts of the world around us an imaginative synthesis for our pleasure and our delight.

Opposed to the above views, at least in theory, is that of Boas[27] and of those who have been influenced by him. Boas unfortunately formulated his views in a very loose and at times contradictory fashion. To say, for instance, that "the investigation of primitive (prose) narrative as well as poetry proves that repetition, particularly rhythmic repetition, is a fundamental trait," [28] is not very helpful.

At bottom Boas was and remained a folklorist, although he did, after a fashion, recognize the existence of true literatures among aboriginal peoples. One point of marked difference between their literatures and ours he finds in the manner in which the contemporary scene is reflected without deviation in the narratives of aboriginal peoples, and, for this, he suggests an explanation. What makes for lack of agreement between the actual conditions of life and those depicted in our narratives is the pronounced social stratification of our society. "This brings it about," he states, "that the various groups represent, as it were, different periods of development." [29] This generalization has, however, proved to be quite erroneous. It was based primarily on the tribes of the north-

[27] "Stylistic Aspects of Primitive Literature," in Franz Boas, *Race, Language and Culture* (New York, 1940), pp. 491-502.

[28] *Ibid.*, p. 491.

[29] *Ibid.*, p. 497. Cf. also Franz Boas, *Comparative Study of the Mythology of the Tsimshian Indians*, Bureau of American Ethnology, Annual Reports, vol. 31 (Washington, 1909-1910); and for a completely different area, Clara Ehrlich, "Tribal Culture in Crow Mythology," *Journal of American Folk-lore*, L(1937), 307-408. Her results, however, have been questioned in part by R. H. Lowie (personal communication).

west coast of Canada and the Pueblo Indians of the Southwest. It holds for few other tribes in the Americas[30] and is completely contradicted by the prose literatures of the rest of the aboriginal world. The contemporary scene is reflected to varying extents, depending upon the particular genres involved, in all literatures, and much the same situation exists in aboriginal societies. In fact, what is to be explained in the narratives of the northwest coast of America and the Pueblo Indians is rather why no deviations exist, and not the reverse.[31]

If Boas' generalizations were correct it would mean a societal determinism which would effectively prevent all developmental sequences,[32] and it would play directly into the hands of those scholars who postulate, for all aboriginal peoples, a static and unchanging culture. Boas certainly did not subscribe to any such view in general.[33]

Boas' generalizations have been accepted by a number of later anthropologists, notably by Ruth Benedict. Her remarks about the Zuñi indicate that both she and Boas are speaking as folklorists, not as students of literature. At bottom, they are really not so far removed from Malinowski when he says, "[myth] is obviously also a narrative and thus has its literary aspect . . . which . . . should not be completely neglected. Myth contains the germs of the future epic, romance and tragedy." [34]

[30] For the Navaho, Boas' generalization has proved incorrect. Cf. K. Spencer, *Reflections of Social Life in the Navaho Origin Myth, University of New Mexico, Publications in Anthropology*, no. 3 (Albuquerque, 1947).
[31] The northwest coast examples themselves invalidate Boas' conclusions, for a pronounced stratified society is found among these Indians.
[32] "The only exceptions," he insists, "are found in periods of an unusually rapid change or of disintegration." Boas, *op. cit.*, p. 497. He is thinking here, however, only of the conditions after contact with Europeans; i.e., either the direct result of European penetration or such secondary consequences as the reflection of the mixed culture of the West African coast on the modern Negroes of Angola.
[33] On p. 498 of the same article he says, "These remarks relating to literature do not mean, of course, that in other respects of life, ancient customs and beliefs may not persist over long periods."
[34] Malinowski, *op. cit.*, p. 80.

TYPES AND CHARACTERISTICS

Now that we have cleared away some of the underbrush of presuppositions preventing a proper approach to our subject, let us turn to the literatures themselves.

Despite the distribution of aboriginal peoples over the five continents, the often contrasting environments in which they live, the totally different ways in which they are organized socially and economically and the many mutually unintelligible languages they speak, their literature possesses two traits in common. All of it is transmitted orally, and poetry always appears in a musical framework. Have these two facts any implications? Let me begin with the first.

Of the oral literatures which preceded and accompanied the written literatures of the great historic civilizations, we have already spoken. Of far more value than the scant information these latter afford are the living oral literatures of Europe and Asia recorded so diligently for the last one hundred years. The best examples are, perhaps, the Russian and Yugoslav.[35] When we compare the latter two with the oral literatures of aboriginal peoples[36] we find among the known aborigines no diminution in the number of literary forms but, on the contrary, a marked increase. Some forms are identical although the majority, naturally, are distinct. When we compare these oral oboriginal literatures with those of ancient India, however, we find a different picture. Although poems can be found comparable in a general way to those of the *Rig-veda*, no collection even remotely comparable in extent or so well integrated exists anywhere among aboriginal peoples, the Polynesians possibly excepted. The same holds true for such prose

[35] Chadwick and Chadwick, *op. cit.*, vol. II, pp. 3-456.
[36] Because of the difficulties inherent in discussing so large and diverse a mass of material, I shall frequently fall back upon what I can personally control. Actually, of course, for the demonstration of the thesis of this essay a half-dozen cultures are quite adequate.

works as the *Çatapatha Bramana* which is more than three times the size of the *Iliad*.[37] Nor does there exist anything comparable to the long heroic verse epics like the *Mahabharata*, the much earlier *Iliad* and *Odyssey* and the much later *Cid, Chanson de Roland*, and *Nibelungenlied*. All of them certainly owe the form in which we know them to the influence of the adoption of writing. But this fact by itself would manifestly not account for their existence. The ancient Egyptians, Hebrews, Chinese, or Japanese never developed verse epics despite the adoption of writing. Two factors, it would seem, are essential for their appearance, a caste or stratified structure of society and an Heroic Age;[38] not, of course, the vague "heroic" period described in so many aboriginal origin myths. For aboriginal civilizations these conditions were fulfilled only in the case of the Polynesians. Interesting in this connection, however, are the approximations to epics—they are no more than that—in prose among the Pueblo Indians and the Navaho. Both possessed what might be termed a true heroic age, more particularly the latter. Neither possessed a stratified social structure.

The evidence at our disposal would suggest that, on the whole, writing is the determining factor. And this would appear to be confirmed by the appearance among the Hawaiians, after the introduction of writing, of such prose epic-narratives as the *Laieikawai*[39] and of *The Twins*[40] among the Winnebago.

Writing introduced one fundamentally new element, privacy.

[37] Some Sanscrit scholars do not accept this and believe that writing was in use for literary purposes quite early despite the total lack of evidence to the contrary. However the consensus is that given above.

[38] The standard work is H. M. Chadwick, *The Heroic Age* (Cambridge, Eng., 1926). Cf. also his subsequent treatment in Chadwick and Chadwick, *The Growth of Literature*, vol. I. To be consulted likewise, are Cecil Maurice Bowra, *Tradition and Design in the Iliad* (Oxford, 1930); M. Rhys Carpenter, *Folk Tale, Fiction and Saga in the Homeric Epics* (Berkeley, 1946); and Erich Bethe, *Homer, Dichtung und Sage* (Berlin, 1914).

[39] M. W. Beckwith, *The Hawaiian Romance of Laieikawai, Bureau of American Ethnology, Annual Reports*, vol. 33 (Washington, 1919).

[40] Paul Radin, *The Myth of the Twins* (Santa Fe, 1915, privately printed).

That aboriginal authors clearly possessed some type of privacy before is clear. Thurnwald,[41] for instance, speaks of Buin authors secluding themselves in the forest in order to be undisturbed. Other examples will occur to all experienced ethnologists. But the privacy which developed with writing is fundamentally different. It was a new and sustained kind of privacy, one which pushed the audience far into the background and which encouraged, in the artist, the illusion that he was free from the restraints imposed by such an audience. In aboriginal societies, be it remembered, the audience was both commanding and demanding and expressed its disapproval in clear, unmistakable, and what we would regard, disturbing terms.

Only where writing is in use can I, consequently, conceive of such artificial, individualistic, and conglomerate literary forms as the *Iliad, Odyssey,* and *Mahabharata,* as we know them today, arising and being perpetuated. No audience in the prewriting periods would have listened to them long or tolerated the liberties they took with accepted lays and themes. Bethe[42] is undoubtedly correct then when he contends that the author of the *Iliad* and *Odyssey* utilized one lay, *The Wrath of Achilles,* and expanded this lay by combining with it a number of others current in his time. These lays were strictly comparable to the *byliny* and the *narodne pjesma* of the Russians and the Yugoslavs, to the songs used by Lönnrot when, in 1835, he "composed" the *Kalevala,* and to the tales and legends which Firdausi used to write, in verse, the great Persian epic, the *Shah Nameh,* even though early poets may have handled lays less deliberately than did Firdausi.[43]

Epics manifestly attempt to organize and integrate diverse materials—folk-tales, myth, legend, historical events. One of the conditions making this feasible was apparently the possession of writing. However, with this sole exception, there seems to be no indication that writing added any other fundamentally new forms

[41] *Profane Literature of Buin,* Yale University Publications in Anthropology (New Haven, 1936), no. 8, p. 6.
[42] Bethe, *op. cit.,* vol. I, pp. 1-30.
[43] Cf. the English translation by J. Atkinson, London, 1892.

or, by itself, led to the production of better poetry or better prose narratives.

The second of the traits common to all aboriginal literatures, is the musical framework in which verse is set. We know, of course, that this was characteristic of lyrical poetry among the ancient Greeks till far into the fourth century B.C., and of many other literatures of the ancient world. No one has ever contended that, in these early literatures, the music interfered seriously with the words of the poems, the two always being regarded as independent. Yet for aboriginal poetry, on the contrary, the assumption seems to be that there the fusion of music and words is of some special and inextricable nature, and that the words were inherently unimportant and secondary. The evidence at our disposal, and it is enormous, makes it quite clear, however, that this "mystic" fusion is no more true for them than it was for the Greeks. The real difference in the two instances seems to reside in the apparent absence of meters and rhyme in the overwhelming number of aboriginal cultures. I say apparent because practically no thorough studies have been made of the subject. European meters certainly exist nowhere. Among the Greeks these presumably antedate the *Iliad* and the meters of the *Rig-Veda* certainly were known before the *Rig-Veda* itself was consigned to writing. The important question to be answered then is, when were poems composed without any regard to a musical framework, and why? Since this happened within three centuries after the adoption of writing in both Greece and India, writing must have played a significant part in this divorce.

The main general difference, then, between the literatures of the great historic civilizations and those of all aboriginal peoples is the absence of writing and the invariable enclosure of verse in a musical framework.

To indicate, however, what features aboriginal literatures do not possess is surely only a preliminary step in the characterization of aboriginal literature. What are its positive traits? Let me begin with the prose narratives.

While it is not my intention here to enter into any discussion of folk-tales among aboriginal peoples, a few remarks concerning the statements of professional folklorists and anthropologists are in order.[44] It is a strange fact that the folklorists who have done so much for the study of the European *Maerchen* and have shown that it represents a true literary art-form with a long and varied history, should still be so uninformed and should still so completely misunderstand the aboriginal folk-tales. A. H. Krappe, for instance, who has written a major work on folklore, questions seriously "whether the Ethiopians (Africans) or American Indians are at all capable of the sustained effort required by the ordinary fairy-tale with its string of adventures." [45] The members of the famous Finnish school are no better. But if a *Maerchen* is, as Krappe states, a type of popular fiction with no ulterior purpose, if it is simply a melodrama with few protagonists, a faultless hero, no evolution of character and no traces of any philosophy, idealistic or other, then it can safely be said that no art-form as simple and underdeveloped as this exists among aboriginal peoples.[46] If the latter have no *Maerchen* it is then because their civilizations are too sophisticated to possess them.

As to the distinctions so frequently insisted upon between myth, legend, and *Maerchen*, they have little inherent value. For those, however, who feel compelled to make them I recommend the brilliant and suggestive little book of J. A. K. Thomson, *The Art of the Logos*.[47] *Logos*, Thomson tells us, meant originally, "What is said." *Muthos* had the same meaning in Homer. Logos can be divided into what is true, what is untrue, and to that to which we cannot apply the ordinary canons of truth and falsehood. This threefold division corresponds to history, to deliberate

[44] For the latest treatment of the folk-tale, cf. the important book by Stith Thompson, *The Folktale* (New York, 1946).

[45] Alexander Haggerty Krappe, *The Science of Folklore* (London, 1930), p. 3.

[46] *Ibid.*, pp. 3ff. and William Reginald Halliday, *Indo-European Folk-tales and Greek Legend* (Cambridge, Eng., 1933), pp. 6-7.

[47] London, 1935. For his purely sociological interpretation, cf. Malinowski, *op. cit.*, pp. 17, 33.

fiction, and to what, for lack of a better term, must be designated as a product of "unconscious fiction." They do not appear as pure types. "It is theoretically possible," Thomson continues, "to have a story, popular and traditional, which shall preserve a series of historical facts in their historical order . . . Incomparably more common [however, than pure types] is the intermediate type of story, which borrows from the other two and yet transmutes what it borrows into something quite its own. It has truth but not the truth of history; it has an element of fiction but not the fiction of the novelist . . . The moment you grapple with a typical Logos you find it changing in your hands. What was fact turns to fiction, what a moment since was myth is now legend. The legend imperceptibly passes into folklore or fairy-tale." [48]

Now, if one will look into most representative collections of aboriginal narratives labelled folk-tales or myths, it will be apparent at once that this is a thoroughly false designation and that they fall, roughly, into three groups. The first, and generally the smallest, approximates to what Thomson calls "unconscious fiction" in the realm of religion and custom, that is, to his myth and *Maerchen*. This is the closest we get, as a rule, to what is customarily called folk-tale. It is a very mixed type of folk-tale at that and usually quite superior artistically to the European myth and *Maerchen*. The second and, by far the largest, consists of what is basically deliberate fiction, but where the plot and the subject matter are still somewhat closely tied to the folk-tale; and the third, the smallest but by no means the most insignificant, consists of novelettes, semi-romances, romances, etc., representing completely recast, remodelled, and expanded plots, secondarily using folk-tales and folk-tale materials. They are of the same category as the stories found embedded in Herodotus and the Greek romances, but of a far more mature type.[49]

Owing, unfortunately, to special circumstances such as the

---

[48] Thomson, *op. cit.*, pp. 20, 21.
[49] For a discussion of these in Herodotus, cf. Thomson, *op. cit.*, and W. Aly, *Volksmaerchen, Sage und Novelle bei Herodot und seinen Zeitgenossen* (Goettingen, 1921).

directed selection on the part of most professional ethnologists and folklorists based on many factors[50] over which they have little control, as well as the unwillingness on the part of aborigines to impart information,[51] published collections tend to be quite unrepresentative of the literatures as a whole.[52] Novelettes, romances, historical and semi-historical narratives, orations, gnomes, dramas, and that vast body of literature Chadwick designates as antiquarian learning, in short, all that might be designated as contemporary literature, is rarely included. It goes without saying that this neglect of contemporary literature does not represent a native attitude. I think it can be safely stated that for every volume of folk-tales published there exist a half-dozen volumes of contemporary literature which is uncollected and unknown.

Difficulties of a far greater kind have interfered with the securing of a proper record for poetry. The necessity for recording the music was, of course, one of the major ones. However, what has led more particularly to a distortion of our perspective is the enormous number of song-poems obtained in connection with rituals and magico-religious practices. These vary all the way from meaningless doggerel to poems of great beauty. Sometimes they have been completely subordinated to the magico-religious practice in question and have little artistic merit; at other times, they have not been thus overwhelmed. Among most aboriginal peoples all types are found.[53] As an example of a song-poem of considerable merit, let me quote the following charm for rain.

My dracaena, let the great storm come,
A great storm, surf rushing both ways.

[50] Primarily three: their general ignorance of the native languages, lack of time, and the belief that most of the narratives were folk-tales.

[51] Because many of the narratives were regarded as sacred and secret.

[52] The narratives dealing with origins, whether of the world in general or of specific rituals, form a class by themselves.

[53] Cf., for example, James Mooney and Franz M. Olbrechts, *The Swimmer Manuscript, Bureau of American Ethnology, Bulletin* no. 99 (Washington, 1932), pp. 170-179, and Walter William Skeat and Charles Otto Blagden, *Pagan Races of the Malay Peninsula* (London, 1906), vol. II, 294ff.

My dracaena, let the lightning flash,
Let the thunder sound on the far horizon,
Let the thunder sound on the near horizon,
Lightning speed hither, waters of Maramara,
Strike hard the source of the waters of Maramara:
Strike and tear out where the great rocks go deep,
Sweep down thence the great banyan,
Drag it to the far horizon,
Let it overshadow darkly the great sharks.
O red dracaena leaf, what is that? a great storm
Roaring and pressing down:
Roaring and dragging out the trunk of the great Fata,
Carrying down the landslip from the great river,
Carrying its trunk to great Mara. [54]

NON-RELIGIOUS POETRY

Many monographs written by the most estimable anthropologists give the impression that aboriginal peoples possess very little but religio-magical poetry. Nothing is farther from the truth. Most ethnologists simply do not collect any other kind of poetry. Thus, from the reading of Malinowski's books on the Melanesian Trobriand Islanders one might get the impression that no other type of poetry existed there. Yet Thurnwald collected a vast amount of lay poems from Buin, one of the Solomon Islands, a people with a culture very similar to that of the Trobriand Islanders.[55] He found an astounding number of different types and subtypes. Let me enumerate them.

The first type consisted of dirges with various subtypes, one employed when a man is bewailing the death of his father, another that of a relative on his mother's side, another if it is his brother's death, and still another if it is his wife's. Still another subtype is used if the author is a woman and is bewailing her

[54] Charles Eliot Fox, *The Threshold of the Pacific* (London and New York, 1925), p. 101. Cf. also the philosophic hymn used as a magical incantation among the Maori, quoted in Radin, *Primitive Man as Philosopher*, p. 323.

[55] Cf. Thurnwald, *op. cit.*, and also Thurnwald, *Lieder und Sagen aus Buin in Forschungen auf den Salamo Inseln* (Berlin, 1912), vol. 1. Even more amazing is the material collected by G. Maurice Léenhardt, *Documents Néo-Caledoniens* (Paris, 1932), especially pp. 255-276.

sister's death, and a sixth, if lamenting that of her husband. The second general type of song is used in connection with a concert of pan-pipes. There are innumerable subtypes, dealing with such subjects as fights, glorification of the accomplishments and deeds of the family, vilification of the deeds of opponents, etc. The third main type consisted of love poems. The Buin term for this type means "whirling water," and these poems are so designated because the manner of rendering them is interpreted as resembling the water in a whirlpool. A fourth type consists of poems composed only by women. Their form and subject matter are strictly circumscribed. The subjects are, for instance, the death of a chief, the presentation of a chief's son to his father's confederate friend, a boy's initiation into garden work, the introduction of girls at a festival, gibes on unpopular men, and poems for a marrying couple while they stand on the sacred pig. A fifth type is concerned exclusively with one subject, the presentation of a pig for a feast, and a sixth with the completion of a new drum.[56]

Let me give two typical examples, a lament and one concerning a frivolous love episode.

LAMENT FOR A WOMAN[57]

The Introduction

Why has Ku-gui, the chief of the world beyond and the creator of the sun, destroyed this old woman? There are so many old people who are lame. This one was always active. Why should the crabs dispute with each other for this prey? Why should she disintegrate in the waste?

Address to the Body

Your son would have carried you like a child, on his shoulders. When I, your father's female relative, visited you in Kugumaru, did I not advise you to take the rain-mat with you? But you despised

[56] Thurnwald, *op. cit.*, pp. 4-5.
[57] *Ibid.*, p. 9. The author, a woman, is supposed to be lamenting the cremation of a woman, her aunt, who while fishing in a river for crabs, was caught in the suddenly rising waters caused by a tropical downpour and drowned.

my words, and you said, "A rain-mat is needless in the big forest; I shall stay there in a house of leaves like a witch." You could have been saved by your son.

A LOVE ADVENTURE[58]

Introduction: The Complaint

Did I not hear it from the messenger's mouth that I shall come to another spear (i.e., village-district)? When I arrived at that chief's hall, Togora, I said, "This witch said, I should come to that row of betel-palms northward." But I came in vain.

Address to the Woman

You had said, "Be at that row of betel-palms there, man!" I am here now. But you got a basket full of red shell necklaces, and for them you give your love to another one. I did not call you up from the sleeping house, it is you who persuaded me, the red parrot, through messages you sent from inside your sleeping house. I did not want you. I thought, you have been given away to that pretty spear (man of another village). When rain came from a black cloud, from the south down the road I started cursing you.

The same multiplicity of song-poem types can be duplicated practically everywhere, even among the supposedly simplest tribes, like the African Bushman, the natives of the Andaman Islands and the Australian aborigines. However I do not wish to contend that all aboriginal peoples are equal in their poetic achievement. What I am trying to point out is that among all of them, without any exception, the composing of poems was an art with old traditions, set rules, and special diction just as was prose. For examples I must refer the reader to the small anthology I have included in *Primitive Man as Philosopher.*[59] I cannot refrain, however, from giving here a few additional poems from the Eskimo to illustrate the degree to which aboriginal poetry gives evidence of an imaginative apprehension of life and a highly developed craftsmanship.

[58] *Ibid.*, p. 11.
[59] *Op. cit.*, cf. pp. 103-151, 212-226. Excellent material from North America is to be found in Natalie Curtis, *The Indians' Book* (New York, 1907).

I [60]

Eyaya—eya,
I find again
The fragment of a song
And take it to me as a human thing.
Eyaya—eya!

Should I then be ashamed
Of the child I once bore,
Once carried in my *amaut*,
Because there came news of his flight
From the dwellings of men?
Eyaya—eya!

Ashamed I may be,
But only because he had not
A mother flawless as the blue sky,
Wise and without unwisdom?
Now the gossip of others shall teach him,
And ill repute follow that teaching.

I should indeed be ashamed,
I, who bore a child
That was not to be my refuge.
I envy instead all those
Who have a host of friends behind them
Beckoning on the ice
When they have taken leave at a merry feast before starting.

Alas! I remember a winter
When we set off from the island.
The air was warm
And the thawing snow sang under the runners.
I was as a tame beast among men.

But when the news came
Of the killing, and of the flight,
Then the earth became a mountain peak,
Its summit needle-pointed,
And I stood trembling.

[60] This song-poem was composed by a woman whose son had killed a man and was living as an outlaw. It is taken from Knud Johan Victor Rasmussen, *Across Arctic America* (New York, 1927), pp. 164-165.

II [61]

I am filled with joy
Whenever the dawn rises over the earth
And the great sun
Glides up in the heavens.

But at other times I lie in horror and dread
Of the creeping numberless worms
That eat their way in through hollowed bone
And bore eyes away.

In fear I lie, remembering:
Say, was it so beautiful on earth?
Think of the winters
When we were anxious
For soles to our footwear
Or skins for our boots:
Was it so beautiful?

In fear and in horror I lie.
But was I not always troubled in mind,
Even in the beautiful summer,
When the hunting failed,
And there was dearth of skins
For clothing and sleeping?
Was it so beautiful?

In fear and in horror I lie.
But was I not always troubled in mind
When I stood on the sea ice
Wretched beyond measure
Because no fish would bite?
Or was it so beautiful
When I, flushed with shame and dismay
In the midst of the gathering,
And the chorus laughed
Because I forgot my song and its words?
Was it so beautiful?

Say, was it so beautiful on earth?
Here, I am filled with joy
Whenever the dawn rises over the earth
And the great sun
Glides up in the heavens.

[61] This and the three following poems are from Rasmussen, *op. cit.*, pp. 264-266 and 353.

But at other times
I lie in horror and dread
Of the creeping numberless worms
That eat their way in through hollowed bone
And bore eyes away.

III

There is fear
In the longing for loneliness
When gathered with friends,
And, longing to be alone.
Iyaiya-yaya!

There is joy
In feeling the summer
Come to the great world,
And watching the sun
Follow its ancient way.
Iyaiya-yaya!

There is fear
In feeling the winter
Come to the great world
And watching the moon
Now half-moon, now full,
Follow its ancient way.
Iyaiya-yaya!

Whither is all this tending?
I would I were far to the eastward.
And yet I shall never again
Meet with my kinsman.
Iyaiya-yaya!

IV

The autumn comes blowing;
Ah, I tremble, I tremble at the harsh northern wind
That strikes me pitilessly in its might
While the waves threaten to upset my kayak.
The autumn comes blowing;
Ah, I tremble, I tremble lest the storm and the seas
Send me down to the clammy ooze in the depths of the waters.
Rarely I see the water calm,
The waves cast me about;
And I tremble, I tremble at thought of the hour
When the gulls shall hack at my dead body.

This last is a sacred song-poem, and according to Eskimo theory can only be composed during the silence and darkness called *karrt-siluni*, literally, "the time of waiting for something to break," which precedes every festival. It is then when "everyone is striving hard to think fair thoughts (that) songs are born in the minds of men, rising like bubbles from the depths—bubbles seeking breath in which to burst." [62]

In addition to individual song-poems there are likewise to be found, widely distributed song-poem sequences. An unusually interesting example of such a sequence is found among the Besisi of the Malay Peninsula.[63] It consists of at least thirty song-poems, each of which, originally, had a definite position. Their subject matter is somewhat miscellaneous but deals, primarily, with animals and plants.

Longer poems, say of thirty or more lines, with profane as opposed to sacred subject matter, have a much more limited distribution. They are largely confined to Malaysia, Polynesia, Micronesia, Melanesia, and Africa. The situation in Africa is not always clear. Such longer poems certainly existed among the Bantu-speaking peoples and the peoples of West Africa. In fact, there is reason to believe that the former at one time possessed what approximated to heroic epics. Conditions there were favorable for their development. Elsewhere in the aboriginal world, with the exception of the Eskimo and some sporadic examples among the Indians of the northwest coast of Canada, long poems are conspicuous by their absence.

Many of them are dramatic in character, with a number of individuals participating[64] and frequently have a chorus. Cho-

[62] Rasmussen, *The Eagle's Gift* (New York, 1932), p. 70, quoting an old Eskimo woman.

[63] *Op. cit.*, pp. 147ff. Cf. also the charm-songs used in connection with the erecting of a house among the Malays of the Malay Peninsula, in W. W. Skeat, *Malay Magic* (London, 1900), pp. 146-147. Cf. also F. Densmore, *Chippewa Music, Bureau of American Ethnology, Bulletin* no. 53 (Washington, 1913), pp. 67ff.

[64] For unusually good examples cf. Léenhardt, *op. cit.*, particularly the poems entitled "La Victoire des Mea," pp. 253ff. and "La Mort du Chef," pp. 485ff.

ruses are also very common among the Polynesians[65] and the
Bantu. Other examples are to be found in the song-duels quite
common in Melanesia, in the northwest coast of Canada, and
among the Eskimo.

Long poems of epic type exist, as we have already pointed out,
only among the Polynesians.[66] But poems of "epic" length with
a religious subject matter are encountered everywhere where complex rituals exist.[67] They rarely occur, however, with peoples
whose economy is non-agricultural.

DRAMATIC TYPES

Over a very large area of the aboriginal world poetry is frequently combined with prose narratives. Far more restricted in
the range of their distribution, however, are the short dramatic
interludes of poetry and prose that are found among the Bantu.
These consist of two parts, one sung and the other narrated. The
portion sung is by far the more important and is much freer in
style than that which is narrated. It can be either a monologue or
a dialogue and it must always have a chorus.[68] Thus, in effect, we
are here dealing with lay dramas.

To this same mixed type, of course, belong all ritualistic performances, long and short. Whether to call them dramas or not
is largely a matter of terminology. It seems impossible to deny
that designation to the rituals of many secret societies where the

[65] Cf. the famous "Death-talks" or "Dirges" and the drama-poems in William
Wyatt Gill, *Myths and Songs from the South Pacific* (London, 1876), particularly "The Drama of Ngaru" and "The Ball-thrower's Song," pp. 188ff.,
238ff., and 273ff.
[66] The most easily available examples are to be found in *Memoirs of the
Bernice Pauahi Bishop Museum* (Honolulu, 1919), vol. VI, pt. III.
[67] Cf. for the American Indians, Ruth L. Bunzel, *Zuni Ritual Poetry,
Bureau of American Ethnology, Annual Reports*, vol. 43 (Washington, 1932),
pp. 615-835; Alice G. Fletcher, The Hako, *A Pawnee Ceremony*, same series,
vol. 22 (1912); and Francis La Flesche, *The Osage Indians*, same series, vol.
36 (1919).
[68] John Torrend, *Bantu Folk-lore from Northern Rhodesia* (London, 1921).
Cf. particularly "Kapepe, the Little Feather," pp. 97-145, and "How Thick
the Bush is Today," pp. 156-157.

ritual is conceived of as being the reënactment of the origin of that society and where there are actors with specific rôles.[69] More difficult to place, however, are perhaps the dramatic rituals connected with the curing of disease. They are to be found everywhere in some form or other. Frequently there are four *dramatis personae* involved in such a ritual, the patient, the doctor, the unseen audience of spirits, and an audience playing the rôle of chorus. The patient, the doctor, and the chorus-audience will change with every performance, but the highly stylized subject matter and framework is always present. Take, for example, the following Eskimo curing-séance:[70]

SHAMAN. I ask you, my helping spirit, whence comes the sickness from which this person is suffering?

PATIENT. The sickness is due to my own fault. I have but ill fulfilled my duties. My thoughts have been bad and my actions evil.

AUDIENCE. Let her be released from her offense!

A short intermission

SHAMAN. She is not yet released from her evil. It is dangerous. It is a matter of anxiety. Helping spirit, say what it is that plagues her?
She is not yet released. I see a woman who seems to be asking for something. A light shines out in front of her. It is as if she was asking for something with her eyes, and in front of her is something that looks like a hollow. What is it? What is it? Is it that, I wonder, which causes her to fall over on her face, stumble right into sickness, into peril of death? Can it indeed be something which will not be taken from her? Will she not be released from it? I still see before me a woman with entreating eyes, with sorrowful eyes, and she has with her a walrus tusk in which grooves have been cut.

AUDIENCE. Oh, is that all? It is a harpoon head that she has worked at, cutting grooves in it at a time when she ought not to touch anything made from parts of an animal. If that is all, let her be released.

[69] Cf. Paul Radin, *The Road of Life and Death* (New York, 1945).
[70] Knud Rasmussen, *Observations on the Intellectual Culture of the Caribou Indians* (Copenhagen, 1930), pp. 133ff.

SHAMAN.   Now this evil is removed, but in its place there appears
            something else; hair combings and sinew thread.
PATIENT.   Oh, I did comb my hair once when, after giving birth to
            a child, I ought not to have combed my hair; and I hid
            away the combings that none might see.
AUDIENCE.   Oh, such a trifling thing; let her be released.
SHAMAN.   Return to life. I see you now returning in good health
            among the living, and you, being yourself a shaman, have
            your helping spirits in attendance. Name but one more
            instance of forbidden food, all the men you have lain
            with though you were unclean, all the food you have
            swallowed, old and new offenses, forbidden occupations
            exercised or was it a lamp that you borrowed?
PATIENT.   Alas, yes, I did borrow the lamp of one dead. I have
            used a lamp that had belonged to a dead person.
AUDIENCE.   Even though it be so, let it be removed. Let all evils be
            driven far away, that she may get well.

True lay dramas are not of very wide distribution. The Polynesians had them at one time and certain Melanesian peoples
have them today.[71] In North America the Hopi seem to have
converted an old ritual-drama into a profane one.[72] These lay
dramas must be carefully distinguished from pantomime performances even when they are as elaborate as those of the native
Australians.

Let me now turn to three types of composition among aboriginal peoples which deserve special treatment, satire, orations, and
gnomes. I shall have to confine my remarks to a minimum. I think
it is best to use the term *gnome* instead of *proverb*, for the latter
has come to imply something simple and primitive.[73]

HUMOROUS AND GNOMIC GENRE

I know of no tribes where satires and formal narratives
avowedly humorous have not attained a rich development. Ex-

[71] Francis Edgar Williams, *Orokaiva Society* (Oxford, 1930), pp. 237-257;
————, *The Drama of the Orokolo* (Oxford, 1940).
[72] Loomis Havemeyer, *The Drama of Savage People* (New York, 1916),
pp. 202ff.
[73] Cf. the excellent discussion of gnomes in Chadwick and Chadwick, *op. cit.*,
vol. I, 337-403; III, 705, 825ff., 883, 892ff.

amples of every conceivable form are found, from broad lampoon
and crude invective to subtle innuendo and satire based on man's
stupidity, his gluttony, and his lack of a sense of proportion. At
times this satire may attack the most sacred things in a culture,
as is the case in the Winnebago Trickster Cycle.[74] These satires
are composed both in prose and poetry. They include the satire-
duels common in many Melanesian tribes, among the Eskimo,
and among the Indians of the northwest coast of Canada. Nor
should we forget that throughout the aboriginal world there are
numerous stories associated with the adventures of a buffoon-
hero. These tales have often undergone very little secondary
literary reinterpretation and are probably among the oldest in
the world.[75]

We come now to oratory. Most of us think of it as though it
represented a natural gift of aboriginal man. We have all heard of
the speeches of American Indians with their "spontaneous"
metaphors and their figurative language. It will therefore come
as a surprise to many to know that orations are, among them, and
probably everywhere else, the most artificial of all aboriginal narratives; that no narratives are more fixed in form and content, and
that the metaphors, similes, etc., are all frozen and never spontaneous. This applies to all types of oratory. Their number and
their special traits are legion.[76]

Gnomes (proverbs, maxims) are so generally associated with
simple peoples that it has been forgotten that Aristotle thought
fit to devote considerable attention to them in his *Rhetoric*. For
him they were statements either relating to universals con-

---

[74] Cf. Paul Radin, *Winnebago Hero Cycles*, *op. cit.*, *passim*.

[75] The best treatment, limited, however, to the Greek-Romance literature, is
still H. Reich, *Der Mimus* (Berlin, 1903), vol. 1, pt. 1. For a later but much
shorter treatment cf. Allardyce Nicoll, *Masks, Mimes and Miracles* (New
York, 1931), pp. 17-79.

[76] The various historical societies have published innumerable ones. For
orations in the original languages with translation, cf., for the Pima, Frank
Russell, *Bureau of American Ethnology, Annual Reports*, vol. 26 (Washington,
1909) and for the Winnebago, Paul Radin, same series, vol. 32 (1923). For
the Melanesians, cf. G. Maurice Léenhardt, *op. cit.*, pp. 313ff.

cerned with the objects of human actions and with what was to be chosen or avoided with reference to them, or, in a broader sense, statements relating to the properties and characteristics not only of mankind in general and the various classes of mankind, but to those of other beings, objects, natural phenomena, etc. as well.[77] The characteristic difference between the two is that, in general, the latter type is rarely capable of being converted into precepts. Both kinds exist in great abundance in aboriginal civilizations, although they are developed meagerly, if at all, in the Americas.

The gnome is a very old art-form everywhere. Apparently, however, it very early lost most of its old vitality in the great historic civilizations. This was not so for aboriginal civilizations, particularly those of Africa and Polynesia. In Africa it still functions today in all its vigor, both as a special type of literature of unusual artistry and as a social, legal, and moral force. It has, in Africa and Polynesia, attained a perfection in form and content to which very few indeed of the gnomes of Europe can even remotely compare.[78]

From this essentially cursory summary of the prose and poetry of aboriginal peoples a few facts emerge clearly: first, the similarities between aboriginal oral literatures and the written literatures of the western world have been greatly underestimated, both as to subject matter and as to the art-forms, secondly, the contrast between the literatures of these two worlds has not been rightly evaluated. Basically, that contrast lies along three directions: the interpenetration of the arts of literature, music and dance; the full functioning of literature, that is, its close and dynamic relationship to all social experience and activities; and, last, the preservation of old art-forms. To some scholars all these three traits are clear signs of primitiveness and lack of artistic maturity, particu-

---

[77] Chadwick and Chadwick, *op. cit.*, p. 377. Cf., however, the whole chapter on "Gnomic Poetry," *ibid.*, pp. 377-403.

[78] Many collections of gnomes have been published. Perhaps the best study of a particular group is that of George Herzog, *Jabo Proverbs from Liberia* (London, 1936).

larly the last. That these traits occur in the archaic epochs of certain literatures is unquestionable; that they persisted into the mature periods of other literatures is, however, equally true. The question to be answered, however, is not how archaic is the form in which a poem or prose narrative has been cast, but how great is the artist who has composed them and how adequate is his craftsmanship? To this we shall accordingly turn.

COMPOSITION AND ITS CONDITIONS

Oral literatures have thus far been discussed in terms of their content and of those aspects of their form and structure which can be detected without any knowledge of the languages in which they are composed, without reference, in short, to what is admittedly basic for even the more elementary appreciation and enjoyment of any literary work. To this latter aspect, no outsider, even if he has a fair knowledge of a given tongue, can possibly do justice. Nor is the best of the material an ethnologist obtains always sufficiently authentic and accurate to make a proper appraisal even if he were so qualified.

That diction, beauty of expression, a particular patterning of sounds meant as much to author and audience in aboriginal cultures as they do among us, all those who have had any intimate knowledge of such cultures can testify. It is naturally not easy to obtain precise information on such matters, but every ethnologist must have been told repeatedly what individual in a given group is a good raconteur and why, whose diction is preferable to another's, who is an innovator in the use of words and diction, who is a classicist and formalist.

Let me give one experience of my own. Among the Winnebago Indians of Wisconsin and Nebraska I asked one of my informants in what the superior excellence of a particular individual's manner of telling a given folk-tale or novelette lay. The answer was given immediately. It lay, was the reply, not simply in the fact that he was narrating an accepted and traditional version, but in the fact that he was using words and phrases so that they meant precisely what they were supposed to mean, without any equivocation being possible and without the presence of any extraneous allusions and overtones. This theory of the *mot juste* differs, of course, in different types of narratives, and admittedly only superior artists attained it among the Winnebago as among ourselves.

These last few comments on language and diction bring us to the all-important question of authorship. I think we can safely dismiss all theories of communal authorship.[79] The evidence at our disposal today proves overwhelmingly that poems and prose narratives are composed by individuals, no matter how communal the setting in which they are composed. Nor is there any reason for believing that at any time in the history of the world it has been otherwise. Nothing, indeed, has caused so much mischief as this assumption and the oft-repeated German dictum *das Volk dichtet*.

But granting the existence of individual authorship, to what extent, it may then be asked, do the various types of society encountered there and the idealogical superstructures reared upon them, limit or constrain an author and determine his subject matter, possibly also his form? The answer is that they do so somewhat to the same extent as among ourselves. Where one finds democratic and essentially communistic clan structures or democratic non-clan societies the only constraint exercised is that imposed by literary traditions. Deviations from tradition were frowned upon and discountenanced by the custodians of the past but no more so than they were discountenanced for English literature by a literary historian like George Saintsbury for instance. In a civilization where no writing existed these deviations from the accepted literary tradition stood little chance of survival. Some

[79] For the classic discussion of this theory cf. Francis Barton Gummery, *The Beginnings of Poetry* (New York, 1901), and the excellent critique of this theory in Louise Pound, *Poetic Origins and the Ballad* (New York, 1921).

deviations, of course, did, thereby laying the basis for new styles and new treatments. There was no punishment meted out to those who attempted new experiments. Rebels existed in every group and, as we know, expressed their rebellion in subtle ways, particularly in satire.

As far as freedom of literary expression was concerned, with the possible exception of the Polynesian caste societies and certain portions of Africa where a highly stratified society existed —although even there this is doubtful—artistic freedom was to be found everywhere. If a man cared to try a new style, to reorganize completely and reinterpret a traditional pattern, if disapproval and derision mattered little to him, that was his affair.

Considerable variability existed in the conditions for literary expression. In aboriginal democratic societies poems were sometimes composed to order. In the two Americas, however, no such specialization occurred. In parts of Melanesia, apparently, it did,[80] although even there it was not common. Where a highly organized priesthood or stratified societies occurred, specialization was common and important, and the subject matter frequently imposed. This, however, did not prevent the more or less "official" poets from composing on other subjects nor did it imply the absence of non-official poets.

Where there was a monarchical or semi-monarchical type of government, as in parts of East and West Africa, with "courts," etc., a very special situation obtained, although it may be of comparatively recent origin. The two most widespread types of poetry found there, however, the elegy and the panegyric, are unquestionably very old, at least as old as the monarchies, and that means probably six to seven hundred years.[81] But it is really quite erroneous, I feel, to regard any of these native African literatures as aboriginal in any true sense of the term except perhaps mar-

[80] Thurnwald, *op. cit.*, p. 6.
[81] Some of the material has been brought together and commented upon for the Northern Bantu and the Yoruba by Chadwick and Chadwick, *op. cit.*, vol. III, pp. 569-649.

ginally.[82] This holds particularly for their poetry. In prose narratives there seem to be types of subject matter and styles that unquestionably antedate the rise of the monarchies and the imposition of a stratified society on a former clan organization. This clan organization, be it remembered, still persists in great vigor. But all these civilizations, the West and East African and the Nilotic, have been in contact, direct or indirect, with the Arab-speaking world for about a thousand years, not to speak of the contacts they may have had with the various Mediterranean civilizations which preceded.

If it is difficult, therefore, to think of all but a few native African literatures as truly representative of aboriginal civilizations, that feeling is enhanced many times when we approach the literatures of Polynesia.[83] Polynesian society was based on the strictest of caste systems, a caste system which permitted a leisured and special class of literary artists to develop. Their compositions reflect this society and its ideals. They have all the defects such caste literatures so frequently develop, ornateness, elaboration for its own sake, oversophistication, and preciousness in the worst sense of the term. Their merits, however, are of a high order. In variety and richness of forms they are unsurpassed among preliterate peoples. In many ways Polynesian literature resembles the literature of the great He-ian period in Japanese history, A.D. 794-1159, except that it is probably richer. The latter civilization, too, was based on the most rigid of military caste systems.

There are stylistic peculiarities in Polynesian poetry and prose narratives which suggest, to me at least, that we are here in the presence of a body of literature which once may have been written and which then became secondarily oral. Were it not for

---

[82] What seems marginal, however, namely the non-official poetry, may really represent a much larger body of verse, for the tendency of investigators has naturally been to collect the "court" elegies and panegyrics.

[83] The literature on the subject is enormous and most of it is very good. Chadwick and Chadwick have summarized and discussed it with great discernment. Cf. *op. cit.*, vol. III, pp. 227-473.

the fairly clear-cut instance of what ancient India had succeeded in developing and elaborating long before it adopted writing, I feel the Polynesian record would be, not unjustifiably, suspect. This is, however, a large subject which cannot be dwelt upon here.

All in all, despite some pressure in the class and caste societies, pressure not remotely comparable, however, to what has existed in the great historic civilizations since 3000 B.C., authors were free to express what they wished. If any one generalization can be made for preliterate cultures it is this, that what one said was of comparatively little importance. What one did or refrained from doing, this it was that was dangerous.

Nor is it correct to think that rituals or magico-religious practices exercised a constraining and paralyzing influence upon the activities of an artist and that the texts connected with them were sacrosanct and fixed. Theories to that effect are indeed encountered in every preliterate community, but only where a highly organized and powerful priesthood exists has this native theory interfered, if it did then, with sacred prose texts being edited and changed or with variant versions arising. Since much of the energies of the most gifted artists has been expended on these sacred texts, it is small wonder that they are often among the finest works of aboriginal literature.

That literary craftsmen are to be found in preliterate societies the poems given in this essay attest. How these craftsmen work, how they find the necessary privacy, how, in oral composition, they select certain words and certain phrasings and reject others, this it is difficult to visualize. Yet we must assume that some of the best parts of the *Iliad* and of the hymns of the *Rig-veda* were thus composed.

Clearly the artist exists in aboriginal communities. Yet assuming that he has the chief characteristics of a poet, an amazing command of words and the knowledge of how properly to dispose them, and assuming, too, that as Richards says, he possesses the poet's "sense of how [words] modify one another, how their separate effects in the mind combine, how they fit into the whole response"; granted all this, it must still be proved that he lives in an environment which will permit him to function, in an environment where he will have an adequate audience.[84] In aboriginal societies, as we have already pointed out, the audience is of an unusual type. There the whole group is the audience, in fact, audience and chorus in one. There is no language barrier. Everyone in the tribe has a complete knowledge of his tongue, including most of its niceties. And all individuals have an equal command of the basic cultural background. This should lead to the production of an extensive literature and of excellent poetry and prose. And it does, to an amazing degree. But how many excellent poems, how many excellent prose narratives exist? This is the legitimate and important question that must now be asked.

It is not easy to answer this question because of the paucity of material from the majority of aboriginal tribes. Where precise and detailed records are available in Polynesia, in a few parts of Malaysia, Melanesia-Micronesia, and Africa, among the Eskimo, and among some of the North American Indian tribes; in all these areas the size and range of the literatures encountered is quite amazing. And these represent, after all, only the literatures of the last hundred years at best.

Whether it would be possible, however, to find in any of these tribes individual authors whose output is at all comparable to that of the major writers of our own civilizations, it is quite impossible to say. One suspects not, except possibly in Polynesia and in certain portions of Africa. Instead of a relatively few writers with an extensive output one finds many authors with a limited output.

The reason for this situation does not, however, lie so much in the absence of artists capable of great productivity as it does in the structure of aboriginal society and in the attitude of the community toward the artist and his works. Nowhere, not even in monarchical Africa and in the caste societies of Polynesia, would

[84] *Science and Poetry* (New York, 1926), p. 48.

an individual be permitted to devote any considerable amount of his time to literature. The community has other and, to their minds, better and more appropriate uses for his talents and his energies. Be it also remembered that value is attached to a given poem or prose narrative and not to the composer.

Such an attitude will unquestionably reduce the number of poems a person will produce. To what extent, however, it interferes with an author's craftsmanship is an open question. I strongly suspect that it must. However, it does not reduce the number of poems that will be composed in the community, for it does not interfere with the number of individuals composing them. The field is free and open to men and women, to old and young. Thus everything conspires to make for a fuller appreciation of the creations of the gifted poet and, most emphatically, for the production of better audiences. These conditions do not, however, make for better poetry, whether based on old or on new patterns.

And it is here that we arrive at what is perhaps the basic limitation which the structure of aboriginal societies imposes upon the development of literature: an artist is not permitted to expend any considerable portion of his energies on the perfection of his individual talents.

But if aboriginal peoples have fewer excellent poets than in our own civilizations, they have, per population, a far larger number of poems and, I suspect, a larger number of good ones.

What explanation are we to offer for this amazing literary productivity? The answer, for me at least, is clear. First, the presence of literary ability in all societies, and secondly, the existence in aboriginal civilizations of a societal structure which has not artificially interfered with literary expression, either by limiting it to a few selected talents or by confining audiences to a small fragment of the population.

2

Far Eastern Literature

Chinese Literature

SHAO CHANG LEE
MICHIGAN STATE COLLEGE

PROFESSOR SHAO CHANG LEE, *Head of the Department of Foreign Studies and Director of the International Center, Michigan State College, is one of the few reliable academic bridges between this country and the Orient. He was born in Canton, educated at several of the best Chinese and American universities, including Columbia and Yale, and has taught in universities around the globe, among them the University of California, the University of Hawaii, and Lingnan University, Canton. He has held high positions in the Institute of Pacific Relations, crossing the Pacific Ocean eighteen times in the course of dispatching his various responsibilities. He has delivered hundreds of public lectures in this country; he is the author of numerous articles and ten books on Chinese culture, history, and art, and the authority to whom many an editor of international works has turned with gratitude.*

Chinese Literature

CHINA has continuously produced great verse and prose since Confucius in 500 B.C. down to modern times, but Chinese literature was not known to the West until the middle of the seventeenth century, when the learned Jesuit Fathers, returning from their work of faith and labor of love in China, brought their translations of some of the Chinese classical works and published them. A sampling of Chinese classics thus appeared at a time when Europe was going through a period of tremendous intellectual as well as political ferment, the period which ushered in the Age of Enlightenment.

These early translations, although failing to produce the flavor of Chinese literature, succeeded in introducing some aspects of Chinese thought to the leaders of the Enlightenment. Books such as Prosper Intorcetta's *The Golden Mean* (*Chung Yung*), Ignatius da Costa's *Sapientia Sinica* (a study of *The Great Learning* or *Ta Hsueh*), and the first work on Confucius by Philippe Couplet aroused the active interest of a group of the "enlightened" thinkers in Chinese ethics and the Chinese way of life. For example, Leibnitz, after making a careful study of the translated Chinese texts, wrote the *Novissima Sinica* or *Latest News from China,* in which he made an appeal to the Protestants to join hands with the Catholics in establishing contacts with the East to effect an interchange of cultural elements. Voltaire, "the most famous leader of the Enlightenment to fall under the Chinese spell," after reading the French translation of *Chao Shih Ku Er* (*The Orphan of Chao*), wrote a play entitled *L'orpheline de la Chine* (*The Chinese Orphan*), in which he made Chinese civili-

47

zation triumphant over the warlike barbarism of Jenghis Khan.
Goethe, the great German poet, occupied himself in his old age
with the reading of translations from the Chinese. In 1827, after
reading the Chinese idyll *Hua Ch'ien Chi* (*Flower-paper Tale*),
he said to his friend and literary executor, Johann Peter Ecker-
mann:

> One hears all the time the goldfish splashing in the pools; the birds
> sing unceasingly in the branches; the day is always bright and sunny, the
> night always clear; the moon is often spoken of, but it makes no differ-
> ence to the landscape, its light is for them as bright as the day itself.

And further:

> I see more and more that poetry is a common possession of mankind
> . . . The expression "National Literature" does not mean much now, the
> age of World Literature is at hand, and everyone should endeavor to
> hasten its coming.[1]

Since the middle of the nineteenth century a number of Occidental scholars and linguists have endeavored to hasten the coming of the age of world literature by translating works from one
language to another; they included such pioneers as Stanislas A.
Julien (1799-1873), James Legge (1815-1897), and Herbert A.
Giles (1845-1935). Julien produced admirable French versions
of specimens of the Chinese drama and Chinese romances. Legge
gave the first English versions of the *Four Books* (*Sze Shu*) and
the *Five Classics* (*Wu Ching*), while Giles produced the first
History of Chinese Literature (1901).

From the appearance of Giles' work to the present day, Occidental and Oriental bilingual scholars interested in the promotion
of the study of world literature as a way to reach global understanding have produced a large number of excellent translations
of Chinese verse and prose, and some have written excellent
novels such as Pearl Buck's *The Good Earth* and Lau Shaw's *The
Rickshaw Boy*, works describing with stark realism the life of the
common people in North and Central China.

[1] Adolf Reichwein, *China and Europe: Intellectual and Artistic Contacts in
the Eighteenth Century* (New York, 1925), pp. 144-146.

Chinese literature is voluminous and many-sided It includes practically every form of writing. It has been estimated that in the seventeenth and even the eighteenth century there were written and printed in the Chinese language more books of history, religious, political and philosophical treatises, poems, plays, tales of marvels, together with beautiful examples of letter writing than in all other languages put together; and it has been pointed out that the choicest in Chinese literary composition is equal in quality to the world's best creative writing.[2]

CLASSICAL LITERATURE

It has been customary to divide the mass of Chinese literature according to its subject matter into four main sections: classical, historical, philosophical, and miscellaneous, which includes the collected works of the poets, essayists, and the like. Chinese literary works may be divided again into four categories as follows: (1) classical—works written in the classical style and universally recognized as manifesting a high standard of literature; (2) aristocratic—prose and poetry composed with high-flown diction and in the *p'ing-ti* or "parallel style"; (3) popular—songs, short stories, drama, and fiction written in the supple language of daily speech; (4) contemporary—works in a variety of forms recently composed. We shall consider the character of each, beginning with classical literature, which because of its wide influence in China, Korea, and Japan will be discussed at some length.

The term *classical* connotes Greece and Rome to an Occidental. The notion of antiquity applies to its use in China as well, but the word is by no means so restrictive as its western counterpart. In fact, the dignified and artificial language and style of Chinese classical writing has long been a Chinese literary standard, widely imitated and generally used by authors with any pre-

---

[2] Kenneth Scott Latourette, *The Chinese: Their History and Culture* (New York, 1934), vol. II, p. 296.

tense to serious purpose. Thus, for reasons of convenience, the classification which follows will be useful, but the reader should remember that the serene mood and elevated style of Chinese classics has always appeared prominently since the days of Confucius.

Classical literature is chiefly secular in character. It is philosophical and pedagogic and is composed with a terse, refined, dignified, and rhythmical language known as *Wen-yen* (which Christian missionary writers denominate *Wenli*). Its form is stately; its style concise and crisp; its spirit, liberal, tolerant, and kindly. Its value is ethical, for it aims to show man how to discipline himself and to live effectively at home and in society. It serves as a vehicle of moral truth. Its authors are high-minded literati, whose chief concerns are the advancement of the moral welfare of the people and the attainment of calmness, contentment, social harmony, and inward peace for the individual. In their daily living these men of letters seek intellectual achievement not material comfort, peace not power, beauty not efficiency. They respect nature and would never think of exploring its secrets for their own personal benefit or enjoyment. They take life as it is and endeavor to live it in accordance with the "Mandate of Heaven." The influence of their example and their writings upon the daily life of the Chinese people and on large numbers of Koreans, Annamese, and Japanese is tremendous.

Who are these literati? They are those who have produced such classical works as *The Four Books, The Five Classics, The Chuang Tse Book, The Elegy on Encountering Sorrows,* the *Historical Record,* and the T'ang-Sung poetry and prose. Let us examine these works.

The Four Books

The basics of classical literature in China and in the Far East are *The Four Books (Sze Shu)* and *The Five Classics (Wu Ching)*. Compiled as textbooks in the eleventh century A.D. by Neo-Confucian scholars, the *Four Books* are *The Confucian An-*

alects, *The Great Learning, The Golden Mean,* and *The Book of Mencius.*

(1) *The Confucian Analects* (*Lun Yu*) is a collection of the sayings of Confucius and his disciples and a record of incidents in the life of the sage and some of his beloved pupils. It deals primarily with the ideal of scholar-gentleman or *chün-tse.*

(2) *The Great Learning* (*Ta Hsueh*) is a book said to have been transmitted by the family of Confucius. It is a treatise on self-culture, based on knowledge as the means of reforming one's own person, family, society, and state. In it is found a passage, freely translated and quoted as follows:

> If there is sincerity in the heart,
> There will be beauty in the character.
> If there is beauty in the character,
> There will be harmony in the home.
> If there is harmony in the home,
> There will be order in the nation.
> When there is order in the nation,
> There will be peace in the world.

(3) *The Golden Mean* (*Chung Yung*) is a treatise on the conduct of life. It emphasizes the importance of pursuing the path of justice and sincerity by doing the right thing for its own sake. It points out the importance of being ever consistent and constant to the principle which governs the universe. A man is a scholar-gentleman, who endeavors to live his life so that automatically it exemplifies the universal moral order.

(4) *The Book of Mencius* (*Meng Tse Shu*) contains the writings of Mencius (*ca.* 372-289 B.C.), an ethical philosopher and a political scientist. As an ethical philosopher he believed in the innate goodness of human nature and in man's ability to achieve moral greatness. He maintained that the function of education is to give every individual the opportunity to develop fully the love of mercy, the sense of shame, the sense of courtesy and respect, and the sense of right and wrong. As a political scientist he contributed the ideas of equality and democracy to the development of Chinese political thinking. He pointed out that ordi-

nary people and the sages are of the same species; that all people can be as morally great as the philosopher-kings of antiquity; that in a state the people are more important than their rulers; and that people may rise in revolt against their ruler when his government has become oppressive. He developed his points by well-ordered arguments and apt illustrations.

The view of Mencius on human nature was challenged by the brilliant and learned scholar Hsun Ch'ing or Hsun Tse (*ca.* 298-238 B.C.), who said that human nature, when left to itself, tends to evil. He asserted that if a man appears to be good, it is due to his own effort and to good surroundings. The fact that a man is a willing slave to his animal passions and is ever striving to get all he can for himself without consideration for others shows that he has no innate goodness. But man can be transformed by the power of education (which includes music and rituals), and the influence of a good teacher and friend. Thus the fundamental question of the nature of human nature occupied two of the greatest minds China has produced and at a notably early date.

Hsun Ch'ing also pondered on other problems, such as the relationship between the individual and the state and the relative sphere of nature and man. His beautifully written and thought-provoking essays on these and other topics form a remarkable book that comes to us under his name, and is still widely read.[3]

The Five Classics

The Five Classics, compiled by Confucian scholars in 136 B.C., are *The Book of Songs, The Book of Historical Documents, The Book of Changes, The Record of Rites,* and *The Spring and Autumn Annals.*

(1) *The Book of Songs* (*Shih Ching*) is an anthology of ancient court songs, temple songs, and folk-songs. Tradition says that it was first compiled by Confucius, who selected 305 out of some 3,000 pieces current in his time. It is probably the most significant book of poetry of ancient China. Though its language

[3] Homer H. Dubs, *The Works of Hsun Tse* (London, 1928).

is archaic and difficult for the beginner, it is a fascinating book for poets, anthropologists, and historians. It introduces us to the ancient Chinese of the Yellow River Valley who, though they lived three to twenty-five thousand years ago, had the same aspirations, desires, and sentiments we have today. Here is the heart of China, the ancestral home and fountainhead of national culture. As we read, we see a succession of different scenes: pageants at the king's court and in the ancestral temples; farmers working their fields with simple, clumsy farm implements, and growing wheat, millet, hemp, melons, vegetables, mulberry trees, fruit trees, water lilies, and dye plants. We see farm women raising silkworms, chickens, pigs, ponies, and dogs. We see them occasionally bothered by rats, but frequently entertained by song sparrows. We see herdsmen tending sheep, potters turning their wheels, weavers making silk cloth, founders casting bronze vessels, and artisans fashioning household articles of wood and bamboo, and personal ornaments of gold, silver, and jade. We hear the temple bells and the singing of hymns, the words of endearment of the lovers in the grove, the cheers of merry-makers in the village, the murmur of a lonely wife in her chamber, the lament of homesick soldiers on the battlefield. We hear the lamentation of poor widows, motherless sons, and oppressed peasants. In a word, the *Shih Ching* presents to us not only an unsurpassed work of ancient Chinese metrical composition by unknown poets and bards, but also a panorama of the life of the people of ancient China.

Through his collection of ancient songs Confucius provided a strong stimulus to the creation and enjoyment of poetry. Through it, too, he revealed the power of poetry. Once he said to his disciples: "Poetry is able to stimulate the mind; to teach the art of sociability; to help a person to give his strongest feeling with restraint; to show man how to serve his father and sovereign; and to acquaint a person with the names of birds, animals and plants." Under his influence poetry has become the major literary achievement of the Chinese people, who find inward joy and spiritual happiness in a medium which celebrates the delights of nature and simple pleasures, and expresses the sentiments of domestic affection and the edification of cultivated friendship.

A song or poem in the *Shih Ching* usually consists of from three to eight stanzas. Each stanza has from three to twelve lines; and each line contains from three to seven characters or words. Most of the songs or poems, however, appear in quatrain form. Each line in the quatrain is composed of four characters. The second and fourth lines always rhyme. Sometimes the first, second, and fourth lines rhyme together. In general the last character of alternate lines are rhymed. The rhyme-characters often have a musical accent known as "even" tone. Rhythm and melody are brought out or accentuated by the proper pronunciation of the characters. Unfortunately both for Chinese literature and the occidental reader one can translate the substance—and possibly the form also—but not the manner and style of the original.[4]

(2) *The Book of Historical Documents* (*Shu Ching*) is said to contain Confucius' frequent themes of discourse with his students. In it are found the supposed speeches and declarations of the noted ancient rulers given on ceremonial or historical occasions, the counsels of the ministers at court, and accounts of various regions, expeditions, and wars. The speeches, declarations, and accounts reveal the style of ancient Chinese prose, which is marked by quaintness, terseness, and sincerity of expression. The ideas of benevolent government, of the voice of the people as the voice of the Supreme Being, and of the "Mandate of Heaven," are succinctly expressed. The book was lost in the third century B.C., but twenty-eight sections were reproduced from memory in the second century B.C. by an aged scholar named Fu Sheng. Later, sixteen more sections of the book were recovered from the site of the house of Confucius.[5]

---

[4] Possibly the best English version of the *Shih Ching* is *The Book of Songs*, trans. by Arthur Waley (Boston & New York, 1937).
[5] For a discussion of the book and a selected reading from James Legge's translation, see *The Wisdom of China and India*, Lin Yutang, ed. (New York, 1942), pp. 695-742.

The *Shu Ching* is a sort of a wisdom-book for the rulers and their ministers, but the wisdom is mainly of an earthly kind, which the pious souls of ancient days believed to be not infallible.

(3) The pious sought to acquire a higher wisdom by means of divination. The most important book for this purpose is the *Yi Ching,* commonly called *The Book of Changes,* which originally consisted of a set of sixty-four linear figures known as "hexagrams," with explanatory notes and expository comments.[6]

The explanatory notes, attributed to King Wen and the Duke of Chou of the twelfth century B.C., are composed in symbolic phraseology, which only mystics can understand. The expository comments, attributed to Confucius, are written in plainer language, and it is the comments which have changed the *Yi Ching* from a primitive book of divination into a work of ethical and philosophical importance. Here is a free rendering of the comment on the hexagram *Ch'ien.*

Great is Ch'ien, the original! All things owe to it their beginning. All things are under the general control of Heaven. By it the clouds move and rain is distributed, and all species and varieties of things appear in their developed forms.

Ch'ien is the Great Light that shines from beginning to end, bringing everything to fruition in due time . . . and in due time it will ride on the six dragons and rule over the heavens.

The way of Ch'ien is to change and transform so that everything may correct its nature and direct its destiny, that union may be preserved in great harmony and that all may be benefited and righted.

When Ch'ien, the head, appears high above all things, then all nations will enjoy peace.

[6] A "hexagram" is composed of any two of the eight "trigrams," each of which symbolizes some object. The eight trigrams and their symbolism are as follows:

| ☰ heaven. | ☷ earth. | ☳ thunder. | ☴ wind. |
| ☵ water. | ☲ fire. | ☶ mountain. | ☱ marsh. |

By placing, for example, the trigram symbolizing "heaven" on top of another we have the hexagram "Ch'ien" ䷀ to represent that which is perfect, all-pervading, benevolent, and pure.

Confucius is reported to have said:

If I had some more years to finish the study of *Yi* I might come to be without great faults.[7]

(4) Confucius also said: "Without a knowledge of the rules of propriety it is impossible to build character." *The Record of Rites (Li Chi)* is apparently compiled for the purpose of guiding youth. The book consists of a collection of treatises on the rules of propriety, ritual exercises, and education, but in it are found illuminating descriptions of ancient ceremonies, such as those relating to capping a youth upon his initiation to scholarhood, to competition in archery, and to marriage, burial of the dead, sacrifice in the ancestral temples, and social intercourse. In it are also found inspiring anecdotes about King Wen when he was a young prince and about Confucius as a teacher of men and as a mentor of his prince. It stresses the significance and beauty of proper performance of religious ceremonies and social conventions. The correct observance of form is believed to be the best expression of right motive and attitude, as well as the spirit of cordiality, sympathy, and respect for others. The most valuable section of the *Li Chi* to us today is the *Hsueh Chi (Record of Learning)*. Here we find a masterpiece of educational literature, which is astonishingly modern in thought and in tone.[8]

(5) Confucius compiled a brief chronological record of events that occurred in the "Middle Kingdom" (China) between 722 and 480 B.C., and named it *Chün Chiu (Spring and Autumn Annals)*. It contains the briefest possible notices of the births, marriages, wars, conferences, and deaths of the feudal princes, of the kingly acts of "the Son of Heaven," and of natural calamities and strange phenomena in nature. It could never have become a masterpiece of classical literature had it not been extended by

---

[7] Legge's unintelligible translation is the only English version of this book. See I King in *Sacred Books of the East,* Max Müller, ed. (London, 1899), vol. XVI. See also Richard Wilhelm, *The I Ching of Book of Changes,* trans. by Cary Barns (New York, 1950).

[8] See *Sacred Books of the East,* vol. XXVIII, the *Liki,* trans. by James Legge (London, 1899), Book XVIII, *Hsio Ki.*

Tso Chiu-ming, of the fourth and third century B.C., into a series of glowing narratives of events recorded by Confucius. The extended work is known as *Chün Chiu Tso Chuan*. Here we read exciting accounts of wars between the feudal states, of treaty-making conferences, and of weddings and other celebrations in the courts of the feudal princes. Scattered through the accounts are thought-provoking proverbs, maxims, and quotations from ancient unknown authors.

The Chuang Tse Book

The classics which we have examined thus far belong chiefly in the literature of ideas. There is another type, that of the imagination, which is well illustrated by the writings of Chuang Chou and Chü Yuan. Both have exerted tremendous influence upon later writers of prose and verse.

Chuang Chou was a contemporary of Tso Chiu-ming. He was an illuminating prose writer, and a "poet of freedom," who disliked the formalism of the privileged men and undertook to expose their hypocrisy. The *Chuang Tse Book* (otherwise known as *Nan Hua Ching*), which contains his writings and those of his admirers, shows him to have been a courageous thinker, who wrote boldly and logically and in scathing terms, laying bare man's weakness and discounting the civilization and the arts of the period. He used his literary and dialectic skill so effectively in flaying the worldly that the scholars of his day were quite unable to refute his sweeping criticisms. It is said that his ideas were like an overwhelming flood which spreads at its own will. But he was after all a gentle and kindly soul, who spoke in colorful anecdotes and simple parables with the aim of leading men to self-examination and to a quest for spiritual freedom and new life. He wrote—quite often in dialogue—to glorify the mysteries of Tao, which is thought to be the first cosmic principle, the highest creative force, the supreme intelligence and goodness, and the all-powerful, purposeful, unchanging, ever-existing "Mother of all things." As we read, we admire the originality of his thought, the richness and sweep of his imagination, his fine sense of humor, his underlying earnestness and devotion to truth, and his vigorous and charming style. Here is a sample of what he wrote in the lighter vein:

> Once upon a time I, Chuang Chou, dreamed that I was a butterfly fluttering here and there, contented with my lot. I was conscious only of following my fancies as a butterfly and was unconscious of myself as a human being. Suddenly I awoke and found I was Chuang Chou. Now I do not know whether I was then a man dreaming that I was a butterfly or whether I am now a butterfly dreaming that I am a human being.[9]

The Poetic Works of Chü Yuan

During the fourth and third centuries B.C. there appeared in the Yangtze River region a number of creative poets, who invented a new form of poetry and introduced into their lyrics a wealth of new material taken from the folklore and folk-songs of the inhabitants of the Yangtze Valley. The new form of poetry was then known as *fu,* which usually begins with a short preface introducing the reader to the poem. It differed from the songs and poems in the *Shih Ching,* which were composed in the Yellow River region, in three respects: (1) it was usually a long poem consisting of from two hundred to four hundred lines of unequal length or irregular meter; (2) it was highly allusive and allegorical; and (3) it was meant to be recited and not sung.

Among the creative lyric poets the best known is the beloved Chü Yuan (*ca.* 328-285 B.C.), whose soaring lyrics, like the poetic prose of Chuang Chou, still inspire the warmest enthusiasm among the elite of Chinese scholars after two thousand years. His famous *fu,* entitled *Li Sao (An Elegy on Encountering Sorrows),* and other metrical compositions such as *The Great Summons, The Nine Songs,* and *The Mountain Ghost* make very vivid to us the background of a great mind, whose highest aspiration was to build a stable basis for society founded on the spirit of moral obligation. His language is refined and elegant, especially in ex-

---

[9] Herbert A. Giles, *Chuang Tzu* (Shanghai, 1926), p. 32.

pressing sorrow. His style reveals him as a sensitive and generous poet, susceptible to every impulse of human emotion. The collected works of Chü Yuan and his school of classical poets are known as the *Elegies of Ch'u,* which serve as a model for later writers of *fu* to follow.[10]

Poetry and Prose of the T'ang Period

Since the time of Chü Yuan China has produced a legion of poets, but those whose works were accepted universally as providing a standard of excellence mostly belonged to the T'ang period (A.D. 618-906), a time of great political power for China, of general peace and material prosperity, of religious freedom and good will, and of inventions and discoveries. The great events, whether glad or sad, that occurred during this period brought forth great poets, kindled their imagination, and touched their heartstrings to immortal songs.

Before the T'ang era many outstanding poets such as Chi K'ang of the third century and T'ao Ch'ien of the fifth century appeared, mused, sang, and left to posterity their gems of verse. The poets of T'ang carefully studied these, seized all that was best in them, and then developed a new style of their own, composing and singing their songs of joy and sorrow, bringing into full play their spiritual energies, their inspired power of imagination, and unconsciously ushering in "the Golden Age of Chinese Poetry."

The rulers of the T'ang Dynasty were lovers of poetry and many of them were poets themselves. They encouraged verse writing as the highest form of literary art. Through the influence of Empress Wu (684-704), the composition of poems became a requisite in state examinations for literary degrees and governmental appointments, and accordingly, every scholar strove to be a poet.

[10] See Lim Boon Keng, *The Li Sao, An Elegy on Encountering Sorrows* (Shanghai, 1929); Arthur Waley, *170 Chinese Poems* (New York, 1922), pp. 39-44; *The Temple and Other Poems* (New York, 1950), pp. 12-29.

The poets of T'ang, like those who lived before and after, derived their views of life from three schools of thought. From Confucianism they learned the art of cultivating human relations, the importance of fulfilling one's duty well, and the joy of living in accordance with the rules of propriety and "the Mandate of Heaven." From Taoism they learned the love of nature, the art of living in the world, and the idea of immortality. From Buddhism, which was introduced from India and Central Asia, they acquired a new view of the cosmos, a sense of compassion, and a way of escape from this world of woe. What they learned they synthesized in their imagination, and produced poetry that is both glittering and soul-satisfying.

The T'ang poets use several forms, of which mention may be made of four, all regulated: (1) the five-word four-line form; (2) the five-word eight-line form; (3) the seven-word four-line form; and (4) the seven-word eight-line form. In these there are several interesting features, among which is the tonal arrangement of words in a poem. The words in one line are made to balance those in the next line in tones, of which there are four: namely, *p'ing* (even tone), *shang* (rising tone), *ch'u* (departing tone), and *ju* (entering tone). The last three are collectively known as *tse*. In a five-word four-line poem the arrangement of the tones usually appears as follows:

> Tse tse p'ing p'ing tse
> P'ing p'ing tse tse p'ing
> P'ing p'ing p'ing tse tse
> Tse tse tse p'ing p'ing.

Second, the last words of alternate lines are rhymed. In an eight-line poem the first line is rhymed, sometimes with the second, fourth, sixth and eighth lines. Third, the words of one line parallel as parts of speech those of the next line to form a couplet; thus noun with noun, verb with verb, adjective with adjective, and so forth. In the eight-line poems the first and last couplets may not have the nature of words paralleled. Fourth, words are seldom used twice in the same poem unless they are repeated for effect.

Constructing a poem in accordance with this elaborate technique clearly involves a good deal of artificiality. One sees it often in the verses made by poetasters. But no such defect can be found in the compositions of the great poets such as Li Po (701-762), Tu Fu (712-770) and Po Chu-I (772-846). These men of heaven-born genius, of broad learning and refined feeling, while restricting themselves religiously to the rigid rules of prosody, nevertheless pen their poems with ease and spontaneity.

Mention should be made of the "unregulated" form, which gives the poet much freedom in writing as many lines as he desires and in determining the number of words in each line. Then there is the unique five-word or seven-word four-line epigram, which differs from the "regulated" form of verse in that the train of thought is supposed not to stop with the last line.

Early in the eighteenth century *A Complete Collection* of T'ang Poems was published by order of Emperor K'ang Hsi (1662-1722). It contains some forty-eight thousand poems by twenty-two hundred major and minor T'ang poets. Several hundred pieces from this collection are now available in English translation.[11]

To a great extent the prose of the T'ang period shared the glory of the poetry. In earlier periods prose had been highly developed, as shown in the essays of such writers as Hsun Ch'ing and Chuang Chou, as well as in the writings of such historians as Ssu-ma Ch'ien (*ca.* 145-97 B.C.), the distinguished author of *Shih Chi* (*Historical Record*), and Lady Pan Chao (*ca.* A.D. 50-105?), the celebrated author of *Nu Chieh* (*Precepts for Women*),

---

[11] See Witter Bynner and Kiang Kang-hu, *The Jade Mountain, A Chinese Anthology: Being Three Hundred Poems of the T'ang Dynasty, 618-906* (New York, 1931); Shigeyoshi Obata, *The Works of Li Po, The Chinese Poet* (New York, 1922); Florence Ayscough, *Tu Fu, The Autobiography of a Chinese Poet* (Boston, New York, London, 1928); Arthur Waley, *The Life and Times of Po Chu-I* (New York, 1950).

who brought to completion the *Ch'ien Han Shu* (*History of the Former Han Dynasty*) by her brother Pan Ku. These historians used a style of writing which is stately but at the same time quite personal. They were humble and modest though their works were commanding and epoch-making. Ssu-ma Ch'ien said of his history: "My narrative consists of no more than a systematization of the material that has been handed down to us. There is no creation only a faithful representation." [12]

Inspired by the works of masters of prose such as those mentioned above, the leading poet-essayists of the T'ang era undertook to create a style of their own to write a prose which would be rich in intellectual content but simple in form and vigorous in spirit. There was, for instance, Han Yu (768-824), who wrote in defense of the doctrine of Confucius with the vigor of a propagandist; and Liu Tsung-yuan (773-819), who penned essays against excessive bureaucracy with the force of a satirist. Their style was simple, clear, lofty, robust, and at times fiery. Their essays, biographical sketches, ceremonial writings, and official memoranda became models for beginners in prose-writing, and their examples were followed by the renowned scholars of the Sung period (960-1279), called by Herbert A. Giles "the Elizabethan age of Chinese literature."

The Sung Period

During the Sung period the current method of block printing was improved by the invention of movable type; and, as a result, the annual output of books was greatly increased. Books were then, as they are now, the basis of Chinese cultural life. Books by the great Sung writers were written in a language that is direct, simple, heartfelt, and in a style that is lofty and grand. The style of such men as Ou-yang Hsiu (1007-1072) and Su Tung-po (1036-1101) in the words of Giles, and also in accordance with

[12] See Edouard Chavannes, *Les Memoires historiques de Se-ma Ts'ien* (Paris, 1895-1905), 5 vols.; Homer H. Dubs, *The History of the Former Han Dynasty by Pan Ku*, vol. I (Baltimore, 1938), II (Washington, D. C., 1945).

the previous standard of evaluation and literary criticism, is "massive and grand, without grammatical flaw, exquisitely cadenced, thrilling the reader with an inexpressible thrill. It is so lofty and beautiful that it resembles expression in music."

ARISTOCRATIC LITERATURE

Since the first century B.C. there has been in use a style of literary composition known as *p'ing-ti*, so called because sentences in the composition are constructed in pairs "like pairs of horses driven together." It is a subtle form of parallelism, which is marked by clever coupling of sentences, skillful balancing of word-sounds, and extravagant use of suggestive synonyms and classical allusions. A composition written in this style by a gifted writer is a pleasure to see and read, for the language employed is flowery and musical, appealing to the eye as well as to the ear. But the finished piece, though graceful, is without strength and intensity. To give some idea of what such a composition is like I shall attempt to reproduce a few paragraphs from the famous Nestorian Tablet, erected in A.D. 781 near Changan (now Sian, capital of Shensi province) in commemoration of the introduction and propagation of Nestorianism in China.

Thus it is said:

Everlasting and unchanging is His Truth;
He is the beginning of all beginnings and is without origin.
Extensive and fathomless is His Divinity;
He is the last of the lasts and is the most wonderful. . . .

He removed darkness and filled the void, and heaven and earth
    appeared;
He caused the sun and moon to revolve, and days and nights were
    created.
Skillfully He designed, fashioned, and completed all things;
Then He created the first man
Bestowing upon him the virtue of goodness and harmony,
And commanded him to have dominion over the sea of creation. . . .

Simple and innocent was the original nature of man,
Whose mind was open but not filled with haughtiness;

Whose heart was pure and all-embracing;
And who originally was without strange desires.
Not until Satan came and deluded him with false appearances
Was his pure spirit corrupted by fanciful things. . . .

One Person in Trinity, our Luminous Lord, the Messiah
Concealing His majesty, appeared in the world to associate Himself

Angels in heaven published the glad tidings
Of a virgin giving birth to the Holy One . . .
A bright star announced the blessed event;
Persians, seeing the glorious light, came to pay tribute.

Literary pieces composed in the *p'ing-ti* style may be called "aristocratic" literature, produced by sophisticated schoolmen and pedantic scholar-officials, whose aesthetic taste and linguistic craftsmanship are high, according to the old, aristocratic, literary standard. They write memorials, letters, and messages of greeting, praise, congratulations, and condolence in the most ornate language, embellishing them richly with metaphors and archaic expressions, which are usually devoid of ideas and unintelligible. These schoolmen and scholar-officials may be regarded as "literocrats," for they are primarily aristocrats in the literary world. The general pattern of their composition is characterized by intricate formality, economy of words, and looseness of expression. They aim to make the finished piece as beautiful as a piece of variegated embroidery on a rich background, or as exquisite as a delicate *lan* flower, the Chinese orchid. Poems or essays written in such a pattern can be appreciated only by those who understand the metaphors and classical allusions. In general it may be said that this "aristocratic" literature is artificial, effeminate, insincere and, above all, intellectually thin. It is regarded as a dead literature.

POPULAR LITERATURE

The kind of literature that the masses of the Chinese reading public turn to for relaxation and happy escape is popular or folk literature. Old folk-songs and folk-tales, old novels and plays such as *The Song of Lo Fu, The Ballad of Mulan,* the story of *The Monkey, The Romance of the Three Kingdoms,* the *Dream of the Red Chamber, All Men Are Brothers,* and *The West Chamber, A Melodrama* make up the body of this living literature. It is composed in *Paihua,* the supple language of daily speech or a mixture of *Paihua* with *Wenyen,* the standard language in which classical literature is written. Again one notes the enormous influence of classical style and the unwillingness of Chinese writers to abandon it entirely.

Old Novels and Plays

Fiction writing was started by interested scholars of the T'ang period (618-906), and was gradually developed on systematic lines in the succeeding periods. At first the fiction writers wrote solely for the entertainment of their intimate friends. They did not undertake to write stories of their own creation, but took the folk themes and so retouched them with the brush of intelligence and artistic genius that the tales were transformed into masterpieces of folk literature. But they did not claim any credit for what they had produced. They preferred to remain unknown and to live in blessed obscurity, for story writing was regarded by the conservative and classical minded scholar-officials as merely "little art unworthy to be placed in the Hall of Literature," and even the authors themselves sometimes disparaged story writing as nothing but "babbling nonsense."

In the course of time short stories were developed into full-length novels. According to their contents they may be classified into four general types:

(1) The historical novel, as represented by *The Romance of the Three Kingdoms* (*San Kuo Chi Yen-I,* English translation by C. H. Brewitt-Taylor, Shanghai, 1929).

(2) The religious and philosophical novel, as represented by *The Record of Western Travels* (*Hsi Yu Chi,* English version by Arthur Waley, under the title *Monkey, A Chinese Novel by Wu Cheng-en,* New York, 1943).

(3) The novel of social manners, as represented by *Shui Hu Chuan* (translated by Pearl Buck under the title *All Men Are Brothers*, New York, 1939), and *The Gold-Vase-Plum* (*Chin P'ing Mei*, translated by Clement Egerton as *The Golden Lotus*).

(4) Love romance, as represented by *The Dream of the Red Chamber* (*Hung Lou Meng*, translated and adapted by Chi-chen Wang, New York, 1929).

Space will not permit us to discuss in detail the character of these old novels which, generally speaking, are delightfully entertaining and stimulating. They are literary works with much humor and good-natured satire, common sense, and nonsense, but they are loose in plot and didactic in purpose. They thus suggest once more the enduring effects of Confucian classicism. They are written in simple, clear, and eloquent language, and they describe the chief characters and exciting incidents mostly in attractive verse form. Their pattern is that of a skillful professional story-teller, who begins each installment of his story with "It is said," then enters into the adventures of the characters in the story with brilliant feats of poetic imagination, ending his narration with such a sentence as this: "If you want to know what happens to So-and-so, please listen to what is told in the next installment."

The old-fashioned Chinese plays, which have been developed since the thirteenth century, may be classified into two types, northern and southern. The northern type deals chiefly with historical incidents and Buddhist and Taoist tales of marvels, while the southern type centers its interest in romance and domestic scenes. The best of them abound in lyric poetry, which, because it is less self-consciously formal, is thought by some to surpass the poetry of the T'ang era in beauty and power. According to Western standards, the plays, though high in aesthetic value, are far from being perfect, for they lack climax and other characteristics of the Shakespearean tradition. As in the old novels, the plots are weak and the purpose didactic. Samples of such plays in English translation may be found in L. C. Arlington's *The Chinese*

Drama (Shanghai, 1930), S. I. Hsiung's *Lady Precious Stream* (London, 1935), and H. H. Hart's *The West Chamber, A Medieval Drama* (Stanford University, 1939).

In the past, works of fiction and drama were not recognized by the conservative "literocrats" as legitimate classes of literature. With the downfall of the monarchy, the advent of the Chinese Republic in 1912, and the introduction of Western ideas this prejudice was removed. The literocrats, after the establishment of the new form of government, tried to modernize and democratize their thinking by a study of Western literature in Chinese translation.

CONTEMPORARY LITERATURE

Since the turn of the present century the Chinese reading public has demanded translations of Occidental writers along with the time-honored classical and popular works. Significant translations include Huxley's *Evolution and Ethics*, Spencer's *Study of Sociology*, John Stuart Mill's *Liberty*, Montesquieu's *L'Esprit des Lois*, Karl Marx's *Das Kapital*, M. Beer's *Social Struggles in Antiquity*, Nikolai Bukharin's *Sociology and the Materialistic View of History*, and works of fiction and drama by Pearl Buck, Anton Chekhov, Daniel Defoe, Charles Dickens, Alexandre Dumas, Anatole France, Johann Wolfgang von Goethe, Maxim Gorky, Henrik Ibsen, Eugene O'Neill, Erich Marie Remarque, Sir Walter Scott, William Shakespeare, George Bernard Shaw, Upton Sinclair, Count Leo Tolstoi, Ivan Turgenev, Oscar Wilde, and some noted contemporary Japanese writers. This flood of alien literature has given enormous impetus to the break with classicism and wider use of the vernacular as a writing medium. It would be difficult to exaggerate the impact of western literary techniques and themes upon Chinese writers since the beginning of the twentieth century.

The years between 1917 and 1949 were eventful and tragic years in the long history of China. During this time different groups of vigorous young writers, both men and women, rose to lead a new literary movement in their war-torn country. Their writings represented three distinct trends of current thought: namely, liberal, communistic, and nationalistic.

In its early stages the new literary movement was dominated by Hu Shih, the most important mind of the "Literary Revolution" of 1917, and his fellow liberal writers, who championed political democracy, individual liberty, and popular education. In writing they used freely the common idioms and Western terms, and also the Occidental points or marks in grammatical and rhetorical punctuation, an important innovation, when one considers the nature of the Chinese language. They would coin new words and expressions when the old ones failed to express their lines of "new thought." Their writings were usually brisk, witty, erudite, and earnest, but at times fiery and sharp. They advocated the study of world literature, modern science and social problems, and reconsideration of the rich literary heritage of their country. For the transmission of their "new thought" they made great use of periodicals, which offered readier access to masses of readers. Their writings, including essays, poems, short stories, and translations, held the attention of the reading public till about 1928, when they were almost completely overshadowed by the revolutionary literature of the leftist writers, whose political and social thinking had been shaped by the propaganda of Russian Communism.

The Chinese leftist writers started to produce what they called a "revolutionary proletarian literature." They published numerous translations of works by such Russian authors as Andreyev, Arashenko, Artzibashev, Brock, Bunin, Chekhov, Dostoevsky, Gogol, Gorky, Korolenko, Lupshkin, Ostrovsky, Pushkin, and Turgenev. Like the liberal writers, they made great use of newspapers and magazines of all sorts. In 1930 they formed the "China League of Left Writers" under the leadership of Lu Hsun (1881-1936), an intellectual and creative writer, whom they had won over to the "new revolutionary viewpoint." The influence of the leftist writers quickly penetrated into cultural circles. Alarmed by the popularity of their "dangerous" thoughts and ideas, the Kuomintang government under Chiang Kai-shek began to devise means to destroy them. From time to time some young writers and student editors mysteriously disappeared from their homes or schools, while the outstanding members of the League of Leftist Writers were secretly arrested, imprisoned, and some were either starved to death or executed.

During those chaotic revolutionary years a variety of literary "isms" such as romanticism, realism, impressionism, futurism, and decadent sensualism sprang up like mushrooms. The young writers who were guided by any one of these "isms" usually drifted to the position of sensualist or pessimist in the current of the unhealthy political and social atmosphere. Some, of course, became realists, in the best sense. Most of their books, together with such leftist periodicals as *The Sun Monthly* and the *Literature Monthly,* were banned by the Kuomintang government, which sponsored the production of the "Three Principles of the People Literature" to spread Dr. Sun Yat-sen's ideas of nationalism, political democracy, and the people's standard of living as interpreted by the orthodox writers of the Kuomintang party. Meanwhile the leftist writers began a "New Realism" movement to produce what they conceived to be the "real new literature" of China.

In July, 1937, the Japanese warlords launched a large scale attack on China. In common opposition to the ruthless aggressors, Mao Tse Tung, the leader of the Chinese Communists, and Chiang Kai-shek joined hands to present a united front, and both the leftist and liberal writers worked together to devote their combined efforts to the salvation of their country. By their songs, plays, short stories, long novels, and magazine articles they successfully reawakened the national consciousness of the masses of the people, increased popular fervor, and sustained a spirit of resistance to Japanese aggression.

It is not necessary to introduce here names of the many contemporary writers who have fought nobly with their pens and rendered signal service to the cause of their country. It is sufficient to say that because they had to work under tremendous handicaps and almost insurmountable difficulties, they have been unable to bring their literary productions to a high level. So far they have not yet given the world a picture of China's heroic struggle for freedom and independence in a notable novel of epic proportions. Perhaps in time they will have something worthwhile, something important and significant to contribute to the development of a new world literature.[13]

*   *   *

In closing may it be said that the four types of Chinese literature which we have briefly reviewed are somewhat like four of the several geographical features of the country. Classical literature is like the lofty mountains with ancient pine trees or cypress clinging on the rocks. Aristocratic literature is like the rolling hills with old bamboo groves, ancestral graves, and flower beds at their feet. Popular literature is like the delta plains dotted with paddy fields, vegetable gardens, fruit trees, and lotus ponds. Contemporary literature at present is like the muddy, choppy Yellow Sea, where clumsy Chinese junks and smart foreign ships ply between the ports of Shanghai and Tientsin, carrying not only rich cargoes but dynamic ideas which may stimulate those Chinese men and women who seek political and spiritual freedom to conquer the economic backwardness of their country and the illiteracy and ignorance of their people, and to create a new nation

[13] Among the contemporary works available in English are the following: *Living China: Modern Chinese Short Stories*, Edgar Snow, ed. (New York, 1936); T'ien Chun, *Village in August* (Cleveland and New York, 1943-44); Lao Shao (Lao Sheh), *Rickshaw Boy* (New York, 1945); *Ah Q and Others* (New York, 1943), and *Contemporary Chinese Stories* (New York, 1944); Fung Yu-lan, *The Spirit of Chinese Philosophy*, trans. E. R. Hughes (London, 1946), and *A Short History of Chinese Philosophy*, Derk Bodde, ed. (New York, 1948); Lin Yutang, *My Country and My People* (New York, 1935-38), *The Importance of Living* (New York, 1937), and *The Vigil of a Nation* (New York, 1944-45).

and a new literature. What the outcome will be, time alone can tell.

BIBLIOGRAPHY

GENERAL REFERENCE

GILES, Herbert A., *A History of Chinese Literature* (New York, 1924). Uncritical and out of date.

LITERARY FORMS AND STYLES

HIGHTOWER, James Robert, *Topics in Chinese Literature: Outlines and Bibliographies,* Yenching Institute Studies, vol. 3 (Cambridge, Mass., 1950). This reference will serve well as a guide to Chinese literary forms and styles for students interested in comparative literature. Among the topics discussed are The Classics, Early Expository Prose, Parallel Prose, Six Dynasties Literary Criticism, *Yueh-fu,* and Five-word Poetry, *Lu Shih,* The Ku-wen Movement, Fiction, and the Literary Revolution. The book describes and evaluates Chinese theories of literature and the Chinese attitude toward literary composition. Excellent bibliographies and index.

WYLIE, A., *Notes on Chinese Literature with Introductory Remarks on the Progressive Advancement of the Arts; and a List of Translations from the Chinese into Various European Languages* (London, 1923). A useful work.

TRANSLATION AND CRITICISM

PROSE

Good translations of Chinese essays, letters, memoranda, biographical sketches, etc. are found in the following:

CLARK, Cyril D. Le Gros, *Selections from the Works of Su Tungp'o* (London, 1931).

EDWARDS, Evangeline D., *Chinese Prose Literature of the T'ang Period,* A.D. 618-906 (London, 1937-38), 2 vols.

GILES, Herbert A., *Gems of Chinese Literature: Prose,* 2nd rev. ed. (London, 1923).

Shen, Fu, *Six Chapters of a Floating Life* (New York, 1932).

WYLIE, A., *op. cit.,* pp. 156, 161-169, 176-177, 184-190.

YUTANG, Lin, *The Wisdom of China and India* (New York, 1942).

POETRY

For good translations of Chinese poems, see:

ACTON, Harold, and HSIANG, Ch'en, *Modern Chinese Poetry* (London, 1936).

AYSCOUGH, Florence, *Travels of a Chinese Poet; Tu Fu, Guest of Rivers and Lakes* (London and New York, 1934).

———, and LOWELL, Amy, *Fir-Flower Tablets* (New York, 1930).

BYNNER, Witter, and KIANG, Kang-hu, *The Jade Mountain* (New York, 1929).

CANDLIN, Clara M., *The Herald Wind: Translations of Sung Dynasty Poems, Lyrics and Songs* (London, 1933).

CHRISTY, Arthur E., *Images in Jade* (New York, 1929).

KENG, Lim Boon, *The Li Sao, an Elegy on Encountering Sorrows by Chu Yuan* (Shanghai, 1929).

OBATA, S., *The Works of Li Po, the Chinese Poet* (New York, 1922).

PAYNE, Robert, ed. *The White Pony: an Anthology of Chinese Poetry from the Earliest Times to the Present Day, Newly Translated* (New York, 1947).

WALEY, Arthur, ed. *The Temple and Other Poems* (London, 1923).

———, *170 Chinese Poems*, 2nd ed. (New York, 1936).

———, *The Book of Songs* (London, 1937).

———, *The Life and Times of Po Chu-I* (New York, 1950).

The spirit of Chinese poetry has been interpreted by:

LUH, C. W., *On Chinese Poetry* (Peiping, 1935).

WU, John C., "The Four Seasons of T'ang Poetry," *T'ien Hsia Monthly*, vol. VI (1937), VII (1938), VIII (1939), IX (1939).

FICTION

Among the best translations of Chinese short stories and full-length novels are:

BUCK, Pearl, *All Men Are Brothers* (New York, 1939).

EGERTON, Clement, *The Golden Lotus: A Translation, from the Chinese Original of the Novel Chin P'ing Mei* (London, 1939), 4 vols.

GILES, Herbert A., *Strange Stories from a Chinese Studio* (New York, 1925).

CHUN, T'ien, *Village in August* (New York, 1942).

HOWELL, B. E., *The Inconstancy of Madame Chuang* (Shanghai, 1935).

HSUEH-CHIN, Tsao, and NGOH, Kao, *Dream of the Red Chamber*, trans. and adapted by Chi-Chen Wang (New York, 1929).

SHAW, Lau, *Rickshaw Boy*, trans. by Evan King (New York, 1945).

SNOW, Edgar, *Living China: Modern Chinese Short Stories* (New York, 1936).

WALEY, Arthur, *Monkey, by Wu Ch'eng-en* (New York, 1943).

WANG, Chi-Chen, ed. *Traditional Chinese Tales and Contemporary Chinese Stories* (New York, 1944), 2 vols.
———, *Ah Q and Others* (New York, 1943).
YUAN, Chia-Hua, and PAYNE, Robert, eds. *Contemporary Chinese Short Stories* (London, 1946).
For a critical study, see:
BUCK, Pearl, *The Chinese Novel* (New York, 1939).

DRAMA

Among the most popular plays available in English are:
Hsi Hsiang Chi, which has two versions: *The Romance of the Western Chamber*, trans. by S. I. Hsiung (New York, 1936); and *The West Chamber: A Medieval Drama*, trans. by Henry Hart (Stanford, Cal., 1936).
Lady Precious Stream, 2nd ed., trans. by S. I. Hsiung (London, 1935).
For synopses of some famous old plays see:
ARLINGTON, L. C., and ACTON, Harold, *Famous Chinese Plays* (Peiping, 1937).

Far Eastern Literature

Japanese Literature

YOUNGHILL KANG
NEW YORK UNIVERSITY

AND

JOHN W. MORRISON
UNIVERSITY OF NEVADA

PROFESSOR YOUNGHILL KANG *was born a Korean in the little village of Song-Dune-Chi in 1903, became a Japanese perforce at the age of seven when Japan annexed Korea, and an American as soon as he could after coming to this country eleven years later, one of the last immigrants prior to the ban upon Orientals. He thinks of himself as a writer who likes to do research and teach. He has just finished a period of research in Oriental literature, working as a fellow at Yale University, and for many years he has taught at New York University one of the few courses offered anywhere in Oriental and English-American literary relations. He first attracted wide attention in this country with an autobiographical novel set in his native country,* The Grass Roof *(1931), which was followed, after a Guggenheim Fellowship, by* East Goes West *(1937), a novel built upon the experience of Orientals in this country. He is the author, also, of many articles, of* The Happy Grove *(1933) and* Translations *(1929). "Kang is a born writer," Thomas Wolfe said of him; "everywhere he is free and vigorous; he has an original and poetic mind, and he loves life." He does. He also loves his friends and his family, with which he lives in Huntington, on Long Island.*

DR. JOHN W. MORRISON, *Assistant Professor of English at the University of Nevada, became interested in the Far East as an intelligence officer with the Marines during the recent war. Theoretically, his job on Okinawa was to interview Japanese prisoners, but he found he often had to capture the Japanese himself before he could interview them, a variation upon the difficulties of translation from which he considers he was fortunate to come back alive. He did come back to take a doctorate in Japanese culture at the University of Washington, and to work on a history of Japanese literature, now in press. His home is in Reno, Nevada.*

Japanese Literature[1]

JAPAN, a land unique in the world family, is perhaps also unique in being the victim of more mistaken notions abroad than any other. One reason for this general ignorance stems from the fact that her literature is almost entirely unknown outside her borders. Students of literature are vaguely aware of such productions as Nō plays and romances like the *Tale of Genji*. Japanese folk-tales occasionally find their way into anthologies, usually only because the compilers want them to provide a semblance of completeness. But in the main a large and important body of world literature is lost to most of us, or more accurately, remains undiscovered. Part of Japan's isolation arises from her own fault; the *Shogun* who ruled from 1603 until 1868 refused to have anything to do with foreigners, Asiatic as well as European. For the rest, Occidentals must bear the greater share of blame. Only within the last decade have Western nations taken more than the merest notice of Japan. Since 1941 she has forcibly obtained the attention of the West, and her position in this troubled world makes it likely that she will retain it. It is to be hoped that her extensive literature will win the attention it deserves, and that she can export some of her culture, as she has so wholeheartedly imported that of the West.

Scholars like George B. Sansom have shown that the Japanese have a compound origin, with elements drawn perhaps from Indonesia and the Philippines. The physical characteristics of the Japanese, however, are predominantly mongoloid, and the ear-

[1] Orientalists in the United States are busy people with many assignments, a fact which accounts for this collaboration. The original manuscript was written by Professor Kang, and the translations are his. Dr. Morrison added some material throughout, and is responsible for the account of post-feudal Japan, and for the bibliographical note.

liest weapons and primitive religion of Japan show striking re-
semblances to those of Northeastern Asia. The ancestors of the
modern Japanese most probably came from this region and supplanted the Caucasoid Ainu, the island aborigines. On the banks
of the Taedong River near the present Korean city, Pyungyang,
objects indicating technical and artistic skill have been excavated
from fourteen villages and 1,130 tombs. About the beginning of
the Christian Era, Korea was already contributing to the Han
culture of China. Remains found in Western Japan show many
similarities to the Taedong River objects of Korea. From this we
infer that there had already been Chinese and Korean influence
upon Japan by the first century A.D.

Japanese mythologies would seem to be based on Korean and
Chinese legends, in many cases being close copies. A great impetus to the art of writing was introduced into Japan about A.D.
405 when Wani came from Korea with the *Confucian Analects*
(*Lun Yu*), and the *One Thousand Characters* (*Ten Tsu Wen*),
the beginner's classics in China. It was said of the Korean scholar,
Wani, that there was no book which he could not thoroughly understand. Through him the Chinese written characters of the
time were imported, a step of great importance to the Japanese,
who as yet had no writing of their own. The Chinese ideograph
is a poor vehicle for expressing Japanese, owing to the fact that
the latter is both polysyllabic and highly inflected. In order to
write in their vernacular the Japanese developed *kana,* a system
of modified Chinese characters used phonetically, which enabled
them to render in writing their enormous battery of particles and
tense endings. But despite this cumbersome addition the ideograph remains the basis of Japanese writing.

Buddhism came from Korea in A.D. 552. As a result of the
Korean King's message to the Japanese Emperor Kimmei, holy
relics, Buddhist teachers, and priests were sent over from Korea
to Japan; and by the end of 624, there were 64 monasteries, 816
priests, monks, and 569 nuns. Soon the imperial household of
Japan was converted. The first Japanese Emperor to become a

Buddhist priest was Shōmu in A.D. 748. Buddhism stimulated the Japanese people emotionally and seemed more congenial to their racial temper than to that of the Chinese or the Koreans. When Buddhism first arrived, it came as an esoteric philosophy rather than a living faith, and was further transformed by many sects to suit the needs of every class. Taking roots in Japanese literature, it entrenched itself as a basis for all living and thought. The Jōdo (Pure Land) sect, started by Hōnen Shōnin in 1176, taught that a man's salvation did not depend upon his own strength but upon the grace of Amida. In other words the average citizen could not expect to be a saint and need not so aspire. Out of the Jōdo sect grew the Shin (True) sect, expounding those doctrines which relate to a man's duties as a model citizen. A model citizen is expected to marry, of course, and is permitted to eat meat and fish. This Shin sect was so far removed from the original Indian Buddhism with its denial of the world, that Shin priests married, enjoyed life as laymen did, and consumed meat and fish.

The Zen sect, although it originated in China (Ch'an), nurtured the ideal of Japanese nationalism. Zen taught the possession and the enhancement of intuitive powers to act on all occasions without hesitation. This became the religion of the Samurai, a warrior class supremely disciplined to self-sacrifice. By the end of the Heian period (A.D. 800-1200) the code of the Samurai had brought the spirit of loyalty and patriotism to a very high pitch. In the name of religion, the Samurai, in protest against national disgrace or personal injustice, committed harakiri. All members of the feudal family shared in this religion, which is still alive in national thought. Many will recollect the story of the young and pretty Japanese bride who killed herself so that her husband would fight all the better in China. Thus the code of the Samurai (Bushidō) eventually became the religion of the typical Japanese, who in pre-war Japan was ready to sacrifice everything, body and soul, for the Emperor.

The Nichiren sect, founded in 1258 by Nichiren Shōnin, (1222-1282), reformer and patriot, taught the unity of Buddhism and of patriotism. This identification of nationalism with religion was, and perhaps still is, the peculiar feature of the Japanese mind. Such is the fusion of all previous influences which had its culmination in the extraordinary national unity manifested by the Japanese in the recent war.

The passion for Buddhism found expression in literature. At times when Chinese classical learning languished, as during the Kamakura period (1186-1332), Buddhism was flourishing, and on the slopes of Hiyeisan alone, a mountain northeast of Kyoto, there were three thousand monasteries. Monks were culturally all-powerful, and their works became standard, deeply imbued as they were with Buddhistic imagination and indigenous sentiments. A certain small book called *Hōjōki* by Kamo Chōmei, A.D. 1212, suggests the spirit of Buddhist incubation. *Hōjōki* means *The Record of the Ten by Ten Foot Square* and refers to the author's own hut in the mountain hermitage whither he fled to avoid world calamities.

The Confucian doctrines of loyalty, filial piety, and ancestor worship were easily adapted to further Japanese nationalism, and were interpreted as devotion to the unbroken imperial dynasty. They thus attained an authority in Japan which they never enjoyed in China, where they were disturbed by the frequent changes of dynasties. Chu Hsi (Chusi, 1130-1200) gave Japan the orthodox Chinese interpretation of Confucianism, which amounts to a system of humanistic ethics, but this ultimately won no hold upon the Japanese, who have always been more interested in activity than in abstract speculation. As might be expected, Wang Yangming (Ō Yōmei, 1472-1529) appealed more to the Japanese. His was the doctrine of the sufficiency of self-knowledge and the unimportance of wide philosophical reflection. Moreover, Wang Yangming preached that all thought must be translated into daily conduct and activity; otherwise, learning is of no use. This preference for Wang Yangming resulted in men of action in Japan rather than thinkers and philosopher-dreamers. Ironically, this Japanese twist on Confucianism caused its decline and brought a restoration of Shintō, or the way of the gods, with Emperor worship.

Japanese art began by being closely imitative, so that style and method were as little changed as possible from the originals of Korea and China. Whenever possible, the art object or the book itself from abroad was brought in for admiration and imitation. An example of such importation is the Kudara Miroku, a graceful, pensive wooden figure with a sweet face and exquisite poise, from the Paikché Kingdom, Korea. There is also the portrait of Shōtoku with his sons, by a Korean artist of the seventh century A.D. But although the art impulse of Japan got its start from Korea with the introduction of alien Buddhism, by the ninth century native Japanese taste had realized itself and from that time has grown continually, alive, vividly decorative, charming with its own personality.

EARLY AND CLASSICAL LITERATURE

The earliest Japanese book is the *Kojiki* (*Records of Ancient Matters*) compiled by the imperial command in A.D. 712. *Kojiki* contains the legend of the creation of old Japan, the divine origin of the Japanese race, and the traditional and mythological history of Japan to A.D. 628. Although of little value historically, these myths and legends are useful to the student of folklore. *Nihongi* (*Chronicles of Japan*) was compiled in 720. Both books were done in Chinese under the supervision of Korean scholars. No doubt these chronicles, as well as the *Norito* (*Shintō Ritual*), another ancient book of Japan, had even so early a definite political aim, for a myth is often designed to furnish a noble family with a divine origin. At any rate the earliest Japanese books have little literary value.

By the time of the Nara period (710-794), Japanese literature began to take shape and schools for the study of Chinese classics and esthetics were established. Adaptation and imitation were presently to turn into creative originality, manifested largely by distinctive poetic forms. The two rather dull chronicles mentioned before contained 235 poems in the form of crude verse. But the first important Japanese anthology is *Manyōshiu* (*A Collection of Ten Thousand Leaves*). Its purpose was to make available all the *tanka* written up to the eighth century. The *tanka*, a form of verse writing practiced to the present day, is a short song, consisting of five lines, with thirty-one syllables in all, arranged five, seven, five, seven, seven, without rime or accent. Something like rime occurs in Japanese, although the users of the language are not conscious of it, since every Japanese word ends in a vowel or in the liquid consonant *n*. The *Manyōshiu* contains 4,173 short songs and 324 long songs, most of them written between 670 and 759, though a few may belong in the fourth or fifth century. Typical examples are:

> My feet are heavy
> From the dripping of the mountain.
> I wait for my sister,
> But arrive for just a wetting
> From the dripping of the mountain.

and:

> Upright the scimitar was
> Entering my body.
> I saw it in a dream.
> What could its meaning be?
> A sign: I shall meet my lord.

Or the following by Ōtomo No Tabito (665-731), whose son Yakamochi (d. 785), edited the anthology:

> Ikeru hito
> Tsuini mo shinuru
> Mono nareba
> Kono yo naru ma na
> Tanoshiku wo ara na

Which can be translated as:

> Must not death undo
> All that lives in the end:
> Which is verily true. So

> Take life while you have it,
> Live merrily here.

Another by the same author is:

> To sit with the long face
> That tries to look wise
> Is not congenial
> To good fellowship,
> So much as a loud drinking song.

The feel of these classical *tanka* is primitive yet formal. Japanese poets love the sharp swift stroke, but the gesture must be exquisitely appropriate.

> Oh, in Autumn wind
> Dawn's breath is chill!
> Oh, I would
> Extend my robe
> Over the hills of Sanu!
> —Akahito (*ca.* 720-750)

> I can hold her in eye,
> Whom I cannot hold in hand.
> As the cinnamon tree
> Living in the moon—to me—
> What's the good of her?
> —Prince Yuhara (seventh century)

> I could not weary
> Of sitting before you
> Ever, my sister.
> So I know not
> The phrase for farewell.
> —Abe no Mushimaro (*ca.* 730-770)

> Men have divided
> You and me, you and me.
> Oh, come, my lover.
> Even in a dream do not hark
> To man's officious word.
> —The Lady of Sakanoye (eighth century)

Another classical anthology is *Kokinshiu,* compiled in 905, containing 1,111 short songs and 5 long poems. These songs were placed under headings such as *"Seasons," "Greeting,"*

"*Joy*," "*Sorrow*," and "*Departure*." The form of the short songs is the same as in the *Manyōshiu*. The following by Saru Maru Taiu (*ca.* 800) is typical:

> Oku yama ni
> Momiji fumi wake
> Naku shika no
> Koe kiku toki zo
> Aki wa kanashiki

> In the mountains
> Sere leaves underfoot;
> Call of deer;
> Ah, ah, the season is
> Here of sad Autumn!

The Japanese poet loves to treat flowers, birds, moons, trees, all in a fingernail sketch. To him, a petal falling on air has an almost silent sound, and yet a sound. No clash, no thunder, just a faint breathing of decay and sensibility. The private lonely beauty writes its own music. *Kokinshiu* was compiled by Ki No Tsurayuki (883-946), who included many of his own poems.

The *Hyakunin-Isshu* (*Hundred Books by a Hundred Poets*) is the most popular anthology in Japan. Edited by the poet Sadaiye Fujiwara in 1235, it is arranged chronologically from about 670 to the date of compiling. The *Hyakunin-Isshu* repeats the conventional pattern of the earlier collections, and is the source of the poems on a deck of cards found throughout the homes in Japan and used for the well-known poetry game. Verses like the following are known to the very children in Japan, though the poems, and the symbols in them, like the cuckoo, may have various meanings and associations.

> Hototogisu
> Nakitsuru kata wo
> Nagamureba
> Tada ariake no
> Tsuki zo noko reru

> The cuckoo called.
> Long I examined the sky.

Nothing remained
But the moon
Paling to white.
    —Sanesada Fujiwara (*fl.* 1200)

Alas, alas, what
Is this breath
Of creatures endlessly adrift
I ask
With tears?
    —Do-in (tenth century)

At the moment I came forth
Along the shore of Tago
To behold Fuji's
Glistening white head, the
Snowflakes sifted down.
    —Akahito Yamabe (*ca.* 700)

The blossom fades.
I am in distress,
Grown old in the world.
Now comes the season
Of the long rains.
    —Komachi Ono (834-880)

Night-long I think of you.
Light has not come yet.
Even to the chinks
The bedroom
Is filled with gloom.
    —(tenth century, by the wife of Regent
    Kaiei; it is said that he came home late
    one night and had to wait before the
    guard let him in, and in sorrow she wrote
    this. She was also the mother of Michi-
    Tsuna, commander of the right imperial
    guard.)

Spring has gone,
Summer comes.
That eerie top of Mt. Ama-No-Kagu
Becomes the drying ground
Of dazzling raiment.
    —The Empress Jitō (reigned 690-696)

Drops from fitful showers
Are not yet dry on the

Tips of the Yew
When dewy mists rise:
An evening in Autumn.
—The Priest Jaku-ren (twelfth century)

The introduction to the anthology *Kokinshiu* written by Ki No Tsurayuki, is full of echoes from the *Preface* to the Chinese *Shih Ching*. Tsurayuki is better known for his *Tosa Nikki* (*Daily Record from Tosa*, 935) describing the voyage of the author back to the capital, Kyoto, at the end of his office as governor of Tosa in Shikoku.

The shortest form in conventional Japanese poetry is known as the *haiku*, three lines of seventeen syllables in all, five, seven, five. Like the *tanka*, it is without rime or meter, and is too stiff and too short to sing.

Furuike-ya
Kawazu tobikomu
Mizu no oto.

In the ancient pond
The frog leaps at the fly
With whir of waters.
—From Bashō Matsura (1644-1694)

GENRE OF THE MIDDLE PERIOD

From the tenth century on, the literature of *monogatari* (tales) grew in popularity. Some of the best known are *Taketori Monogatari* (*Tale of the Bamboo Cutter*); *Ise Monogatari, Utsubo Monogatari, Hamamatsu Chiunagon Monogatari, Ochikubo Monogatari*, all of which may be called romances. But the most famous of these romances is the *Genji Monogatari*. The hero, Genji, son of the Emperor by his concubine Kiritsubo, is a kind of Japanese Sir Lancelot. His fidelity is distributed among many ladies, including the Emperor's consort, Fujitsubo (Genji's stepmother) and his aunt by marriage, Princess Rokujo, his mistress from his seventeenth year onward. The latter's dark and neurotic harboring of jealousy, treated by the author as demoniac and compulsive, is one of the important binding threads of the plot. One of the ladies tenderly courted and loved by Genji is given the name of the author herself; she is the Lady Murasaki, adopted as a child by Genji, and perhaps his leading leading-lady, though debarred from being a full consort by her inferior birth. Murasaki herself is stainless and blameless of jealousy. From such a moral philosophy as the author's, and from such a fertile imagination, which has created more than eight hundred bewildering relationships for Prince Genji, it is hardly to be expected that the genteel monogamous Victorian Westerner should make much reason. Suffice it that to the tenth-century Japanese aristocrat the morality of Genji was highly decorous and according to the code. The thread of the story is often tenuous, the narrative diffuse, and the whole effect so disjointed as to suggest that the author suffered from too much imagination. However, it is undoubtedly one of the great art-works of Japan. One merit of the author Murasaki Shikibu (d. 992), is that she wrote in the pure Japanese of her day, while the great scholars of the time were still writing with pride in Chinese.

At the other extreme from the romantic Murasaki is another woman writer, Sei Shōnagon. While the former was describing her vision of that utopian world, the Heian Court (800-1100), the latter was producing there her *Makura No Shoshi* (*Pillow Book*), reminiscences in a notebook kept under her pillow, which offer an extraordinary insight into the author and a realistic notion of Japanese court life. There is keen penetration in Sei's observation of life, delicate beauty in her mode of expression, and her sense of humor is tinted with a slight cynicism. The book is composed of a series of topics such as "Things that certainly would not come," "Inappropriate things," "The things that make a bad impression," and "Amusing things." It covers a span of ten years, the period of the author's service to the Princess Sadako, entered upon when the Princess was fifteen, and the author twenty-four, and terminated when the Princess died in childbirth at twenty-five.

The *Tsure-Dzure-Gusa* is a collection of sketches, anecdotes and essays by Kenkō-Bōshi (*ca.* 1283-1350). Like Chuang Tzu, who influenced him, Kenkō-Bōshi was a contradictory personality. He was a Buddhist monk but a shrewd cynic as well. He was a believer in all and a believer in nothing. Every Buddhist sect claimed him, yet he belonged to none. "He who spends his life to get name and fame and gain is a fool" is a saying of Kenkō-Bōshi.

In the fifteenth century a new form of poetic art arose known as Nō, the lyrical drama, the most important and distinctive Japanese contribution to literature. The term Nō probably originated in Buddhism, referring to unity of mind between actors, chorus, musicians, and audience. Closely associated at first with religious dances of a pantomimic nature called *Kagura*, in connec-tion with Shintō ceremonies, Nō soon became a form of entertainment for the aristocratic and warrior classes of feudal Japan. Thus these plays were essentially court theatre-pieces, deeply permeated by religious feeling and folkways. They have that artless simplicity and stylization which all sacred and semi-sacred art expression of the Orient shows, but which is also their great limitation. A certain rigidity, a certain lack of humanism, kept these plays from developing into a great art form or from achieving the depth and plasticity which characterized the early dramas of ancient Greece, which in some ways they resembled. The Greeks were concerned with reality, and with the destiny that shapes men's lives. The audience of the Nō plays in Japan, being the hierarchy of Japanese nobility, were opposed to a reality which they regarded as vulgar, and demanded only refined entertainment and distraction.

The Nō plays are composed partly in verse and partly in prose, with many borrowings from the Buddhistic bible, from Chinese writers, and from Japanese songs. At the time of their origin in the middle of the fourteenth century, the prose parts were sung or recited, the poems were sung, and the chorus chanted in unison. Plagiarism went unrecognized. Seami Motokiyo (1363-

1444) and his famous father Kawanami Kiyotsugu (1333-1384) brought this form of drama to its most classical expression under the patronage of the Shōgun Yoshimitsu, leaving us also a record of his dramaturgical ideas.

Stylized as the Nō play is, it possesses qualities which are unique and curious. The characters are mere shadows pantomiming the original personages whose experiences they portray. They wear masks, neutral and expressionless. It is not by facial expression that the actors convey feelings, but by gestures and poses. As far as possible, the suggestive essence of an experience was sought by photographic realism. Yet a Japanese audience can see the most delicate shades of feeling in these painted wooden masks. The Nō plays are implicit with a delicate, flower-like music, and more is communicated than is written in them. Striking is their architectural balance and subtlety. The arrangement of a Nō is almost ritualistically prescribed: introduction, development, climax. Mood sequences dominate, achieved by couplets, chants, songs, dances, recitations. All have Buddhistic allusion. For instance, among the three hundred Nō plays extant, there is not one in which the priest does not appear with his power of prayer to suggest Nirvana.

The first popular theatre or *Kabuki Shibai* was originated by a woman, O Kuni, famous as a beautiful dancer. It is said she was originally a priestess in Kidzuki Temple, but that she eloped with a man, Nagoya Sanzaburō. In Kyoto dancing girls gathered for performances on the banks of the river Kamo. The name of O Kuni is always remembered in the study of *Kabuki* and its art of song and dance. Her love affairs and her popular folk-songs are fascinating legends.

Later her troop of dancing girls went to Osaka and formed the *Takemono Za*, a theatre made famous by the writer Chikamatsu Monzaemon. Between 1685 and 1724, when he died, he wrote fifty-one plays, the most celebrated being *Kokusenya Kassen* (*The Battles of Cozinga*), 1715, which concerns a famous pirate born of a Chinese father and a Japanese mother, who played his part in the wars during the last days of the Ming Dynasty in China.

As noted, the aristocrats have monopolized the classic drama. They now looked down on the popular drama as the entertainment of the common people. Self-expression from these millions of common people is crystallized best in the folk-songs or *Minyō*. Writers of *tanka* and *haiku*, trained never to display vulgar emotion and given to rarefied playing with words, often became the slaves of their own conventional forms. But the folk-songs were spontaneous, dealing not with literature but with life, and were handed down orally. To this day these songs are heard along the streets of Tokyo, in factories, on farms, in cheap cafes all over Japan. Here is one of the Japanese street songs:

> *He sings:* I'd like a branch
> of your fair flowers
> as a patriotic souvenir.

> *She sings:* My will to give is great,
> is greater than
> a mountain, mountain,
> But the flowers have not bloomed,
> so I cannot give.
> Come again, again.
> I will give you the first branch
> when my flowers open.

Folk-songs are sung usually with the *samisen*, a sort of guitar with three strings. Often the singer substitutes names and places extemporaneously, using the same music. Some of the songs are written on paper and sold on the streets. The following are some of the best examples of *Minyō*, all being handed down probably from the Yedo period (1603-1868):

> Nomi-yare uta-yare
> Sake ni yo wa yamiyo
> Ima wa nakaba no
> Hana-sakari

> The world before is dark,
> So let us drink, so let us drink

Here within the perfect instant
Of the blooming flower.

I am the pine of the shore.
Little ripples along the beach
Wake me
When I doze.

Will he come, oh, will he come?
I go to look at the shore.
Not a sound along the shore,
Only wind in the pine.

The dream I saw long ago
Comes back to me;
I think of a bygone time
And of its dream.

Now the flower blooms
Unthinking:
Even of its coming fall
Unmindful.

Wandering through a pine wood
Parted from my lord:
And the pine dews weep
Such tears!

How poignant, the moonlit night!
I think of him;
My pangs are written in tears
Across my face.

In the water I hear
The song of frogs bubble up;
Then I remember
Events long passed by.

The farther I go in this
Suffering body, I regret its
Former states that once
Seemed hateful.

RECENT LITERATURE

We have seen that feudal Japan, that is to say, Japan until
1859, developed her literature as a synthesis of Chinese and

Korean borrowings, together with a vigorous native tradition. Occidentals have commonly and rather snobbishly supposed that the much-advertised talent of the Japanese for borrowing is an implied discredit to their originality. This notion seems superficial, particularly when one remembers that no Western culture is an isolated phenomenon. What proportion of our literature would remain if we removed the influences of Christianity and the Classics? For a Japanese to borrow from Korean and Chinese is as natural as for an Occidental to borrow from Homer and the Bible. Similar purposes, moral as well as esthetic, were in the minds of Eastern and Western writers; and the impact upon their readers was the same. Students of Oriental literature always feel keenly the necessity of pointing out to Western readers that the complex interrelationships of culture which produce a great literature are as evident in Japanese as they are in, say, French or German. Occidentals who fail to realize this do so because of Asia's social isolation, and because of the mountainous barriers imposed by her languages. In the midst of contemporary events we are unable to assess the tragic consequences of our easy assumption that Orientals are a sort of chaotic subspecies of mankind. *Homo occidentalis* may still have time to extend his cultural horizons; the Japanese, for example, are willing to concede the superiority of his plumbing.

With the critical caution just suggested it is perhaps safe to proceed to the present state of Japanese letters. While the nation was absorbing wholesale the technology of the West, she was by no means unaffected (although often understandably bewildered) by the incoming culture. Soon after the opening of Japan, booksellers were carrying dozens of translations from the literatures of the West. A generation later saw thousands of Japanese, educated abroad but concerned with things at home, who dedicated themselves to the task of making the best of Western literature available to their countrymen. A list of good translations in Japanese would be impressive, but a mere catalogue; the fact is that nothing of any consequence in Western literature has been ignored by the diligent translators. For most books a Japanese has a choice of several renderings.

Feudal Japan ceased to exist politically in 1868. Largely because of this coincidence in time, Japanese writers turned to Western models and discovered that fiction was dominated by French naturalism. Despite protestations to the contrary, it did not take them long to discover that naturalism is one part experimental technique and nine parts social indictment. The medium was of course highly appropriate to the intellectuals of a nation just emerging from feudal institutions. But unleavened naturalism was no more self-sustaining in Japan than elsewhere, and was soon superseded by other movements. The important trend to note here is that the development parallels the West exactly, except in point of time. While European societies moved from feudalism to renaissance, to liberal capitalistic democracy, to socialism and Marxism, to whatever we have now, over some five hundred years, all these changes swept over Japan within a lifetime. A Japanese schoolboy might indite a dainty haiku poem to commemorate the accession of Emperor Meiji, only to discover himself to be a Zolaist in his thirties, a Christian socialist in his forties, and still something else in his fifties. That kind of flexibility is too much to expect of any but the most extraordinary mind, and the sharp transitions in Japan were always difficult and very often unsuccessful.

When the full force of naturalism began to abate, other movements came to the fore. However, it was not a matter of old literary gods giving way to the new; rather it was Kinoshita the naturalist becoming Kinoshita the socialist, of Nagai the naturalist becoming Nagai the esthete, of Shimazaki the naturalist becoming Shimazaki the writer of wistful memoirs. These and others like them found naturalism sterile, while still in the midst of their creative careers. The next step varied with the individual; some, like Hardy, reversed the usual order and became poets after having already achieved fame as novelists. Some returned to a kind of neo-romanticism as a reaction to the more sordid aspects of natu-

ralism. Still others became stylists and esthetes. Decadent manifestations such as bitter nihilism, the doctrine of sweet futility,
and a unique variety of Dadaism found their spokesmen. Finally,
by the twenties, Marxism had won over a large number of writers,
particularly among the younger people.

Japanese proletarian writers deserve much consideration in the
history of modern letters. They worked under tremendous handicaps, often being forced to write in jail, and with little assurance
of any audience beyond the reach of their pamphlets and occasional magazines. Their work, although polemic as always, was
nevertheless the major literary contribution of the period from
1923 until about 1930. The conservative writers tended to become
lost in the glorious past, or merely to whine; the literary left
banged away with vigor and enthusiasm, winning many admirers
because of its sheer exuberance. Like their predecessors they
kept foreign ideas before their countrymen by translations and
commentaries. Post-revolutionary Russian novels are perhaps more
accessible in Japan than in any other country outside Russia. The
fate of the leftist literary front was inevitable, of course. Japan's
continental adventure, beginning with what they still call the
"Manchurian incident" in 1931, saw to that. A few of the writers
escaped prison or death, but little has been heard from any of
them since. In fact not much of any artistic consequence has
come out of Japan since 1931.

Whether Japanese letters will come to life again under a
military occupation we cannot know, although we may doubt it.
At any rate, no student of culture will hesitate to predict that
the time will one day come when the enormous and excellent
production of the past ninety years of Modern Japan will be
repeated. The synthesis of the alien West with their own culture
was not achieved in full by 1931, to be sure, but one marvels that
it was so nearly accomplished. Large areas of contact with the
West have produced disaster in Japan, but her experience with
Occidental literature has been a happy one. The Japanese have
learned to discriminate between what is good and bad for them

in alien cultures; we may hope that they will profit by their hard-won wisdom. If they do we shall have a rich contribution to world literature.

BIBLIOGRAPHY

BIBLIOGRAPHY

CHAMBERLAIN, Basil Hall, *Things Japanese,* 5th ed. (London, 1905).
KOKUSAI Bunka Shinkokai, ed., *Catalogue of the K.B.S. Library: a Classified List of Works in Western Languages Relating to Japan in the Library of the Kokusai Bunka Shinkokai* (Tokyo, 1937).
NACHOD, Oskar, *Bibliography of the Japanese Empire, 1906-1926* (London, 1928), 2 vols.
——, *Bibliographie von Japan, 1927-1929* (Leipzig, 1931).
——, *Bibliographie von Japan, 1930-1932* (Leipzig, 1935).
WENCKSTERN, Friedrich von, *A Bibliography of the Japanese Empire,* vol. 1 (Leiden, 1895), vol. 2 (Tokyo, 1907).

LITERARY HISTORY AND CRITICISM

ASTON, W. G., *A History of Japanese Literature,* 2nd ed. (London, 1907).
DENING, Walter, "Japanese Modern Literature," *Transactions of the Asiatic Society of Japan,* vol. XLI, no. 1, pp. 1-186.
FENELLOSA, Ernest, and POUND, Ezra, *'Noh' or Accomplishment. a study of the Classical Stage of Japan* (London, 1916).
FLORENZ, Karl, *Geschichte der Japanischen Literatur.* In *Die Literaturen des Ostens,* vol. X (Leipzig, 1909).
HEARN, Lafcadio, *Complete Lectures on Poets,* Tanabe, Ochiai, and Nishizaki, eds. (Tokyo, 1934).
——, *Japanese Fairy Tales* (New York, 1918).
HENDERSON, Harold Gould, *The Bamboo Broom: an Introduction to Japanese Haiku* (Kobe, 1933).
KOKUSAI Bunka Shinkokai, ed., *Introduction to Contemporary Japanese Literature* (Tokyo, 1939).
MORRISON, John W., *A Study of Modern Japanese Literature with a Translation of Arishima Takeo's Descendants of Cain* (diss., University of Washington, 1948).

TRANSLATION

AKUTAGAWA, Ryunosuke, *Tales Grotesque and Curious,* trans. by Glenn W. Shaw (Tokyo, 1930).

DICKINS, Frederick V., *Chiushingura; or, the Loyal League: a Japanese Romance*, 3rd ed., trans. by Frederick V. Dickins (Tokyo, 1892).

IWASAKI, Yozan T., and HUGHES, Glenn, ed. *New Plays from Japan* (London, 1930).

——, *Three Modern Japanese Plays* (Cincinnati, 1923).

JIPPENSHA, Ikku, *Hizakurige*, trans. by Thomas Satchell (Kobe, 1929).

KIKUCHI, Kan, *Tojuro's Love and Four Other Plays*, trans. by Glenn W. Shaw, 4th ed. (Tokyo, 1925).

——, *Victory or Defeat (Sho Hai)*, trans. by Nishi Kiichi (Tokyo, Kairyudo; 1934).

KOBAYASHI, Takiji, and others, *The Cannery Boat and Other Japanese Short Stories* (New York, 1933).

MacCAULEY, Clay and DICKINS, Frederick, *Hyaku-Nin-Isshu or Single Songs of a Hundred Poets* (Tokyo, 1934).

MIYAMORI, Asataro, *An Anthology of Haiku, Ancient and Modern* (Tokyo, 1932).

——, *Masterpieces of Chikamatsu, the Japanese Shakespeare* (London, 1926).

MATSUHARA, Iwao, *Minyo: Folk Songs of Japan* (Tokyo, 1927).

NATSUME, Soseki, *Botchan (Master Darling)*, trans. by Yasotaro Mori, 10th ed. (Tokyo, 1922).

SADLER, A. L., *The Ten Foot Square Hut and Tales of the Heike* (Sydney, 1928).

WALEY, Arthur, The No Plays of Japan (London, 1921).

——, *The Tale of Genji* (Boston, 1936), 2 vols.

YAMAMOTO, Yuzo, *Three Plays*, trans. by Glenn W. Shaw (Tokyo, 1935).

3
Indian Literature

PHILO BUCK
UNIVERSITY OF WISCONSIN

PROFESSOR PHILO M. BUCK, JR., *long critic and teacher of world literature at the University of Wisconsin, never lost his early interest in India. Born of missionary parents, he attended Philander Smith Institute, Mussoorie, India, 1889-1893. He studied also in various American institutions, including Harvard (M.A., 1900), and taught in others—he was dean of the College of Arts and Science at the University of Nebraska—but he returned frequently to Europe and the Orient to lecture at the University of Bombay and in other Indian universities. He is perhaps best known in this country for two volumes of extremely sensitive and appreciative criticism,* The Golden Thread *(1931), which deals with various early literatures and key literary figures, and* The World's Great Age *(1936) which treats more recent writers. Other interests are suggested by titles such as the following:* Anthology of World Literature *(third revision now in press),* Literary Criticism—A Study of Value in Literature *(1929), and* Directions in Contemporary Literature *(1941). Professor Buck died December 9, 1950, while this volume was in press. Proof was read by Mrs. Buck.*

Indian Literature

A JOURNEY across India, from Cape Comorin in the South to Simla, the summer capital, in the North is as varied in scenery as a trip across the United States. It is no short journey, for the distance as the crow flies is about eighteen hundred miles. There would be first the strip of level sea coast, wide on the East, but narrow on the West, bordered by low ranges of hills, the Ghats. Beyond would be the table land of southern and central India, the Deccan, crossed by the Vindhya Mountains and the Nilgerry Hills, all covered once by heavy forest, in places semi-arid and even today only sparsely settled. Beyond are the alluvial valleys, broad and irrigated, of the Ganges and Jumna Rivers and their tributaries, all bounded on the north by the high ramp of the Himalayas, the loftiest mountain ranges in the world.

A similar trip from Karachi on the west coast through Sind and Rajputana, the Punjab, United Provinces and Bengal, to the frontiers of Bengal and Assam would be equally varied: the arid desert of the Indus valley, the irrigated land of the five rivers, the Punjab, the dense forests and foothills of the Himalayas in Assam. The distance, too, of such a journey as the crow flies would be again about eighteen hundred miles. India, the subcontinent, this huge peninsula, cut off from the rest of Asia by the bulwark of the Himalayas, is as varied in geography and almost as varied in climate as the continent of Europe.

It was a challenge to the imagination of its earliest visitors that history records. The silent and never-ending line of snow-clad peaks; the rich agricultural plains with their never-failing rivers, above all Mother Ganges. The almost impenetrable forests and jungle, the reaches of desert, the rough cirque that encloses the Deccan, the variations of climate, the clock-like regularity of the monsoons; all this mixture of the benign and savage could and did tinge deeply the poetry of the visitors who came into India for the first time out of the monotony that was Central Asia. It is no wonder that these invading tribes entered India with a song. Nor does the Indian imagination, from the day of these first visitors to Tagore of our day, ever for a moment forget its heritage of mountains, forest, and river. No people in the world in its literature is more nature-conscious.

Who were these first Indian visitors that made themselves at home through the centuries, spreading their descendants and their culture over the whole of this subcontinent? And what did they find when they came? Who were their predecessors?

That India had possessed, at least in places, a history and a civilization which long antedated the coming of our first historical Indians we know only vaguely. The newcomers called them Dravidians, and in their myths and poetry left slanderous references to their absence of culture. Nor can we answer, except with the vaguest of guesses, who were these Dravidians. But within our own century, almost by accident, the ancient city of Mohenjodaro and others like it have been uncovered in the Indus valley, perhaps as old as Babylon and with a civilization quite as advanced and strangely similar. These ancients even left us inscriptions, but alas as yet no Rosetta stone that will interpret them to us. It seems unlikely that our invaders from Central Asia ever met these people, for there is nothing in their poetry or prose or in their folklore or mythology that hints at their meeting. These cities are one chapter of the world's history for which we have the illustrations without one word of text. They remind us of the story of Crete and the city of Knossos. Only the Greeks and Homer had heard of Knossos, and they wove its wonders into a potent myth.

Who were these historical newcomers? They called themselves Aryans and felt a becoming pride in their lighter complexions. They brought with them a language, already calling itself sacred, the Sanscrit. From their language we can guess, and probably correctly, that they belonged to the peoples of Europe, for Sanscrit is closely allied to more than one European language beside early Greek. From their name, which seems connected with an Indo-European word for plow, we can guess, this time perhaps with some peril, that they were already an agricultural people, different in this respect from the nomads of Central Asia from where they broke into India.

They came through the passes of the Hindu Kush mountains, that Alexander the Great and later Kipling made famous, passes that every subsequent invader of India before the British has used. For these passes were India's one vulnerable spot in the land frontier defenses. It is generally accepted today that the invaders who began the long series of their slow conquest somewhere before the year 1500 B.C. were a succession of feudal families, or clans, or tribes, of the same people, perhaps even then speaking different dialects but bound together by a common religious liturgy in the classical and sacred Sanscrit. They were an aristocratic society, feudal in character, with the privileged orders and the underprivileged. And they spread their rule first over the land of the Five Rivers, the Punjab.

THE VEDIC PERIOD

The Aryans entered India with a song. For they brought with them and composed during the first centuries of their conquest the most sacred, most orthodox, most celebrated, and often most interesting of all Sanscrit poetry, the *Vedas*. The Vedas are as important a part of Sanscrit literature today, as on the day when they served as a ritual and an exercise of the imagination for their earliest singers.

They are sacred poems, in the main, chanted in celebration of the gods. There are few signs, yet, that the worship was largely centered in shrines and temples. We can fancy that in their beginnings they were a communal liturgy participated in by the people, held in the precincts of some nobleman's headquarters, and chanted by the priests, the Brahmins. These persons were already being consolidated into a special and most favored caste, like the priestly descendants of Aaron who gained a unique position in Hebrew society. They and the nobility, the princes and warriors, became the two elect and favored castes, and coöperated to give direction to this early feudal and aggressive life.

The gods celebrated are curiously no more than a myth and a tradition in the Indian life of the past thousand and more years. The favorite was Indra, the god of the sky, and he has the largest single number of hymns addressed to him. These lines which must be very early, in the earliest of the Vedas, will give an idea of his power and favor:

> I will proclaim the manly deeds of Indra,
> The first that he performed, the lightning-wielder.
> He slew the serpent, then discharged the waters,
> And cleft the caverns of the lofty mountains.
>
> He slew the serpent lying on the mountain:
> For him the whizzing bolt has Tvaṣṭar fashioned.
> Like lowing cows, with rapid current flowing,
> The waters to the ocean down have glided.
>
> Impetuous like a bull he chose the Soma,
> And drank in threefold vessels of its juices.
> The bounteous god grasped lightning for his missile;
> He struck down dead that first-born of the serpents.
>
> . . . .
>
> He who just born as chief god full of spirit
> Went far beyond the other gods in wisdom:
> Before whose majesty and mighty manhood
> The two worlds trembled: he, O men, is Indra.
>
> Who made the widespread earth when quaking steadfast,
> Who set at rest the agitated mountains,
> Who measured out air's middle space more widely,
> Who gave the sky support: he, men, is Indra.[1]

Agni, the god of fire, of the hearth, and of sacrifice is another. His power, beneficent and sinister, is never long absent from

[1] This and the other Vedic Hymns are trans. by A. A. MacDonell, in *A Vedic Reader for Students* (1928); used with the kind permission of Oxford University Press.

this early period when the powers of nature are personified, as in Greece, in the popular deities. One can easily see the swinging censer and the burning sacrifice as the honor of this god is celebrated—the mystery of fire—in the following hymn.

> Agni I praise, the household priest,
> God, minister of sacrifice,
> Invoker, best bestowing wealth.
>
> Agni is worthy to be praised,
> By present as by seers of old:
> May he to us conduct the gods.
>
> Through Agni may we riches gain,
> And day by day prosperity
> Replete with fame and manly sons.
> . . . .
>
> Who, like the Maruts' roar, or like a dart discharged,
> Or like the heavenly bolt, can never be restrained:
> Agni, the god, with pointed fangs consumes and chews;
> He, as a warrior his foes, lays low the woods.

There are female deities as well. The most attractive is Usas, Vedic parallel to the Greek Aurora, Homer's rosy-fingered dawn, the beauty of the sky before sunrise. Even today it is not difficult to wax eloquent. Her beauty must have appealed to the Aryans long before they made their way into India from the uplands of Asia.

> She throws gay garments round her like a dancing girl;
> E'en as a cow her udder, she displays her breast.
> Creating light for all the world, Dawn has unbarred
> The gates of darkness as when cows break from their stall.
>
> Her radiant shimmer has appeared before us;
> It spreads, and drives away the swarthy monster.
> As one anoints the post at sacrifices
> The daughter of the sky extends her lustre.
>
> We have crossed to the farther shore of darkness:
> Dawn shining forth, her webs of light is weaving.
> She smiles for glory, radiant like a lover.
> To show good-will she, fair of face, has wakened.

> The radiant leader of rich gifts, the daughter
> Of Heaven by the Gotamas is lauded.
> Mete out to us, O Dawn, largesses: offspring,
> Brave men, conspicuous wealth in cows and horses.

These words would not be inappropriate for a pre-sunrise communal liturgy.

There are other, and lesser deities whose place in the early pantheon is made known to us by hymns in the early Vedas. Among them it is easy to make room for the Maruts, the gods of storm. In India the breaking of the monsoons is an annual event of the importance of life and death. After the long arid months while the earth lay parched under the blazing sun, the oncoming rain cloud on the horizon is awaited with anxious anticipation. Then follows the slowly advancing storm, the wind, the billowing clouds of dust, the black thunder heads, crowned with the rays of the reluctant sun. All this would mean much to the poetic imagination. And we have a poem, a hymn that even yet stirs us with its power.

> Whenever, bright ones, growing strong,
> You have decided on your course,
> The mountains bend and bow themselves.
>
> Loud roaring with the winds, the sons
> Of Prsni raise themselves aloft:
> They have milked out the swelling draught.
>
> The Maruts scatter mist abroad,
> They make the mountain ridges quake
> When with the winds they go their way.
>
> When mountains bow before your march,
> And rivers, too, before your rule,
> Before your mighty, roaring blast:
> . . . .
>
> They rise, of ruddy hue and bright,
> Upon their courses with a roar,
> Across the ridges of the sky.

This is mature poetry, and yet nature animate with divinity. It will establish a long tradition.

To an untrained mind no human experience is more mysterious than that of alcoholic intoxication. Obviously nothing other than some divine power within the drink—some *spiritus*—is responsible for the amazing mental and physical transformations. The early Indians brewed a beer of the juice of the *soma* plant. The drink was probably heady. Fortunately or unfortunately we have lost the plant and the art. Quite appropriately Soma became a powerful and necessary deity. He was not a god of revelry; nor like Dionysus or Bacchus a god of orgies and later of the drama. But his power was acknowledged, first for the exhilaration, then as a sacramental deity associated with the growing crops. If god can exhilarate man he may have the same miraculous effect upon the fields. There is more than a little conscious self-inquiry in this:

> I think to myself: I must get a cow; I must get a horse;
> > Have I been drinking Soma?
> The beverages carry me along like impetuous winds;
> > Have I been drinking Soma? . . .
> The five tribes seem to me as nothing;
> > Have I been drinking Soma?
> One half of me is greater than both worlds;
> > Have I been drinking Soma? . . .
> My greatness reaches beyond the heavens and this great earth;
> > Have I been drinking Soma?
> Shall I carry this earth hither or thither?
> > Have I been drinking Soma?
> Shall I shatter this earth here or there?
> > Have I been drinking Soma?
> I am most great: I reach up into the clouds.
> > Have I been drinking Soma?

Some of the hymns of the early Vedas give us pictures of the lives of these invaders of India. One of the commonest of their vices for many centuries to come is that of gambling, especially with the Vibhidaka tree nut, ancestor of modern dice. This vice will play a central rôle in the epic *Mahabharata* and in many of the dramas. Here, I think, is the earliest poem about this dangerous pastime in all literature, as good today as it was the day on which some Brahmin who had suddenly lost all possessions sang:

On high trees born and in a windy region
The danglers, rolling on the diceboard, cheer me.
Like Soma draught from Mujavant's great mountain,
The rousing nut Vibhidaka has pleased me.

She wrangles not with me nor is she angry:
To me and comrades she was ever kindly.
For dice that only luckless throws effected
I've driven away from home a wife devoted.

Her mother hates me, she herself rejects me:
For one in such distress there is no pity.
I find a gambling man is no more useful
Than is an aged horse that's in the market.

Others embrace the wife of him whose chattels
The eager dice have striven hard to capture;
And father, mother, brothers say about him:
"We know him not; lead him away a captive."
. . . .

Grieved is the gambler's wife by him abandoned,
Grieved, too, his mother as he aimless wanders.
Indebted, fearing, he desiring money
At night approaches other people's houses.
. . . .

Play not with dice, but cultivate thy tillage,
Enjoy thy riches, deeming them abundant.
There are thy cows, there is thy wife, O Gambler:
This counsel Savitar the noble gives me.

Toward the end of the Vedic period (*ca.* 600 B.C.) the Indian mind became more and more concerned with questions of philosophy and metaphysics. This must have been preceded by a gradual stabilizing of the political, social, and economic institutions. It was then that the old nature polytheism began to be replaced by a cosmic monism, or better, pantheism. This is foreshadowed by one of the most famous of all Vedic poems, the *Hymn of Creation*. There are others like it that celebrate the oneness of all nature. They seem to have been composed at a time when the whole known world was harassed by the same deep thoughts. It was not long after that Buddha was born; that Confucius and Lao Tse were thinking and writing in China, Zoroaster in Persia, the

Hebrew major prophets in the Near East, and the European imagination took fire and gave us the Seven Wise Men of Greece. It was an interesting epoch, one of the greatest in human history. Here is the poetic thought of this unknown Vedic philosopher:

> Non-being then existed not nor being:
> There was no air, nor sky that is beyond it.
> What was concealed? Wherein? In whose protection?
> And was there deep unfathomable water?
>
> Death then existed not nor life immortal;
> Of neither night nor day was any token.
> By its inherent force the One breathed windless:
> No other thing than that beyond existed.
>
> Darkness there was at first by darkness hidden;
> Without distinctive marks, this all was water.
> That which, becoming, by the void was covered,
> That One by force of heat came into being.
>
> Desire entered the One in the beginning:
> It was the earliest seed of thought, the product.
> The sages searching in their hearts with wisdom,
> Found out the bond of being in non-being.
>
> Their ray extended light across the darkness:
> But was the One above or was it under?
> Creative force was there, and fertile power:
> Below was energy, above was impulse.

The poems I have quoted all belong to the earliest of the Vedas, the *Rig*. It has 1,028 hymns in all, some later, arranged in ten books. There are three other Vedas, all later, and of much lower poetic value. They are the *Yajur-Veda,* a ceremonial or liturgical, sacrificial hymn book; the *Sama-Veda,* again a book of liturgies largely drawn from the *Rig;* and the *Atharva-Veda,* which though early, is made up of spells and incantations that testify to the popular superstitions and sorcery. It is the *Rig-Veda,* and especially the philosophic and nature poems, that are still potent for the imagination of India; and give the work its world place in early literature.

The later poems in the *Rig* show that by the end of the second millennium the caste system was definitely established and

Indian society crystallized into an hierarchy. There were four castes: the preëminent Brahmin; the aristocratic *Kshatriah,* or warrior; the *Waish,* or professional and tradesmen; and the *Çhudra* or menial. Each caste had its prescribed codes, duties, and taboos. Each was the result of birth. A philosophy later will explain the reason for this inequality. Already by this time it is probable that the Outcast, the untouchable, was segregated and made the object of social horror. It is safe to assume that untouchability at first was the lot of some of the more primitive of the victims of the Aryan invasion.

THE UPANISHADS AND THEIR INFLUENCE

The effect of the domination of the priestly caste was most notable in its effect upon Indian thought and literature. In one sense there was as a result no secular literature in the Sanscrit. The Brahmin took as his own the guardianship of the thought and imagination of Indian society. As priest and scholar he took all learning into his province, with the result that literature became an edifying means of shaping the imagination and life of all India. He became priest, teacher, councilor, and poet. He turned his active mind to philosophy, and the centuries before Buddha witnessed the triumph of philosophy. This is the age of the *Brahmanas* and most of the many *Upanishads.* The philosophy of these will be transmuted into literature. One can not know Sanscrit literature without seeing it through the spectacles of Sanscrit philosophy.

The *Brahmanas* are the priestly code of ancient Vedic India; they are hardly literature. They are very ancient; probably close to the tenth century B.C. The *Upanishads* are the philosophical and metaphysical speculations of scholarly Brahmins on the meaning and end of life, and came a few centuries later. Of these two collections, the first must have been of chief service in the centuries before Buddha, as they defined the religious liturgies and ceremonies and fixed the spiritual preëminence of the Brahmin caste. The Upanishads have in the later centuries and down to our own day given their authentic theme and color to Indian thought, and to the religious and philosophical tradition. Indeed their influence is as strong today as ever, and they have carried over into the tradition of Europe and America.

At the same time the secular life of the age was carefully defined by a series of books not much less sacred—the *Çastras*. These are divided into two groups—First are those that defined specifically the code of duties which each individual must abide by in order to gain merit—the *Dharma Çastras*. Second are those that deal with the art of governing, the science of politics, and the virtues which will make for the security and success of a kingdom —the *Artha Çastras*. To these there was even added a *Kama Çastra*, named after Kama, the god of love, which laid down with alarming and scientific detail the art of cultivating the pleasures of sexual love. These educators of the human race overlooked nothing.

But our concern here is only with the Upanishads and their connection with succeeding Sanscrit literature. The central theme in these philosophical, mystical, often poetic sayings of the wise ones may be summarized in almost one word, the Oneness of the All. The title, *Upanishad,* tells the story of how the books were composed. The syllables mean *sit under,* and a double inference can be drawn: under the trees, in conformity with the life of the ascetic who to gain wisdom has retired to the forest from the world of affairs, like the *Sunyassi* of today, to gain wisdom. Those who attained and became teachers of the true way were called *Rishis*. And hence the word *Upanishad* may also mean to *sit under* the teaching of the master.[2] One very important moral to be drawn from these books is the vanity of life and the pursuit of earthly desires.

Their influence today can best be seen in the large school

[2] Perhaps the best Western book to which these can be compared is the teachings of Stoic Epictetus, as they were recorded by the Roman Aurelian in the *Encheiridion.* The translations are used with the kind permission of The Macmillan Company.

which calls itself the Vedanta. To understand their main theme perhaps I can do no better than to quote passages from them that are used by Rabindranath Tagore in his *Sadhana*. They will give better than any words of comment the essential poetic pantheism that pervades their whole philosophy.

I bow to god over and over again who is in fire and in water, who permeates the whole world, who is in the annual crops as well as in the perennial trees.

The knowledge of this All Being brings the ecstasy of bliss:

Listen to me, ye sons of immortal spirit, ye who live in the heavenly abode, I have known the Supreme Person whose light shines forth from beyond darkness.

Such knowledge had the Rishis.

They who having attained the Supreme Soul (Self) in knowledge were filled with wisdom, and having found Him in union with the Soul were in perfect harmony with the inner self; they having realized Him in the heart were free from all selfish desires, and having experienced Him in all the activities of the world, had attained calmness. The *Rishis* were they who having reached the Supreme God from all sides had found abiding peace, and had become united with All, had entered into the life of the Universe.

Such persons followed the injunction:

Know thou the One, the Soul (or Self). It is the bridge leading to the immortal being (Nirvana).

And we have the prayer:

O thou Self-Revealing One, reveal Thyself in me.

It is just a step from these lines quoted by Tagore to the *Bhagavat Gita*, though the distance between the two poets, one ancient, the other contemporary, is two thousand years. What does this ancient poem describe as wisdom for life?

In influence at least and general acceptance, if not in poetic merit, the *Bhagavat Gita, The Lord's Hymn,* is one of the world's chief poems. We would not be far wrong if we called it the Indian *Gospel of Saint John.* It has been translated into all foreign languages and into English almost times without number. Its *slokas* (stanzas) are chanted by countless holy men and philosophers. It is the Indian epitome of religion and philosophy, the distilled essence of its Upanishad doctrine.

It is a portion of the long epic, the *Mahabharata,* and its background is tragically dramatic. Five princely brothers have been unjustly exiled from their kingdom by usurping cousins. During their lives as hermits in the forest they have acquired merit and many royal friends. Arjuna, their military leader, now has a little army arrayed for battle, and beside him is his charioteer, the God Krishna, an incarnation of Vishnu, here on earth to help in the execution of justice. As the prince stands now before his chariot surveying his army, he sees across the narrow no-man's land, the enemy—not enemy always but old-time friends. His heart falters and he turns to his companion:

As I look, O Krishna, upon these kinsfolk meeting for battle, my limbs fail and my face withers. Trembling comes upon my body, and upstanding of the hair;

Contrary are the omens that I behold, O Long-Haired One. I see no blessing from slaying of kinsfolk in strife;

I desire not victory, O Krishna, nor kingship, nor delights. What shall avail me kingship, O Lord of the Herds, or pleasures, or life?

They for whose sake I desired kingship, pleasures, and delights stand here in battle-array, offering up their lives and substance—

Teachers, fathers, sons, likewise grandsires, uncles, fathers-in-law, grandsons, brothers-in-law, kinsmen also.

These though they smite me I would not smite, O Madhu-Slayer, even for the sake of empire over the Three Worlds, much less for the sake of the earth.[3]

The issues of life and death are involved in the question and answer. What is life? What is death? What is reality? What is duty? How may we live the good life and discover peace? These are fundamental questions, and for more than two thousand years Indian thought had grappled with them. The answers of the god are of them all, a complete philosophy of life and conduct, and their meaning.

[3] This and the following extracts from the *Bhagavat Gita* are translations by Lionel D. Barnett, in The Temple Classics; used with the kind permission of J. M. Dent & Sons, Ltd.

What is life and what is death? To this the god's answer parallels the poetry of one of the Upanishads:

If the killer thinks that he kills,
if the killed thinks that he is killed,
They do not understand; for this one
does not kill, nor is that one killed.

—*Upanishad*

He who deems this to be a slayer,
and he who thinks this to be slain,
are alike without discernment; This
slays not, neither is it slain.

This never is born, and never dies,
nor may it after being come again
not to be; this unborn, everlasting,
abiding Ancient is not slain when
the body is slain.

—*Bhagavat Gita*

Life is an endless chain, *Kalpa,* birth and death, each a link joined to its predecessor and successor, birth and death, birth and death. Therefore the slayer slays not, nor is the slain slain. The soul abides, then passes to a new body. Therefore the soldier should not evade battle.

Thou hast grieved over them for whom grief is unmeet, though thou speakest words of understanding. The learned grieve not for them whose lives are fled nor for them whose lives are not fled.

Never have I been, never hast thou and never have these princes of men not been; and never shall time yet come when we shall not all be.

As the Body's Tenant goes through childhood and manhood and old age in his body, so does it pass to other bodies; the wise man is not confounded therein.

But with what motive should the soldier accept his duty? Accept it he must because it is his *dharma,* his code, to uphold righteousness and punish injustice. Therefore was he in *this* body born as a Kshatriya, a warrior. Should he fail in his duty he would gain demerit.

Looking likewise on thine own Law, thou shouldst not be dismayed; for to a knight there is no thing more blest than a lawful strife.

But if thou wilt not wage this lawful battle, then wilt thou fail thine own Law and thine honour, and get sin.

However in thus discharging his duty he must not be conscious of his self or his selfish interests, nor have any hope of renown or favor.

Holding in indifference alike pleasure and pain, gain and loss, conquest and defeat, so make thyself ready for the fight; thus shalt thou get no sin.

For it is as one acquires merit by acting according to one's *dharma,* that one assures oneself a quicker gaining of the ultimate good of all life. But by sin, by demerit, through violation of dharma, one is penalized by being in his next life born into a lower and less intelligent station in life, and thus the goal of life indefinitely postponed. This is the doctrine of works, of *Karma.*

As the god speaks, more and more he speaks in the person of Brahma, the spirit of the universe, the Soul, the Self, the All. And the ultimate of life is to acquire this wisdom and to find for oneself the ecstasy of forgetting all separateness and losing all sense of unique self-identity in the Allness of the One. This is *Nirvana.*

In this wise holding himself ever under the Rule, the strict-minded Man of the Rule comes to the peace that ends in extinction and that abides with Me.

For all consciousness of self-identity, all separateness, is illusion, is *Maya,* in this kaleidoscope of the chain of life and death. All time and change are the result of desire, of greed to exalt the selfish self. Once catch the vision, once gain true wisdom, and the fetters are broken, and the separate soul is lost like a drop in the infinite sea of ocean. This knowledge and this vision are *samedi,* the highest and eternal bliss. Then time and change lose all meaning, and the chain of Karma is broken—Nirvana.

There are two highways to this wisdom and bliss, one the longer by works, the other direct by discipline, *Yoga.* Only the elect, those with very rare aptitude, may take the road of painful discipline. For it means almost perfect suspension of all human activity. It means retirement from life and from all earthly attachments, as is the life of the Rishi, as is the life of the hermit who seeks out the solitude of some mountain peak or some great forest.

And there he dwells, after he has by Yoga destroyed all attachment of the body, lost all consciousness of separate existence, and become powerful in spirit. There he dwells in perfect communion with the infinite—Brahma. He has attained the goal.

As a lamp in a windless spot flickers not, such is the likeness that is told of the strict-minded Man of the Rule [Yoga] who labours upon the Rule of the Self.

The *Bhagavat Gita* specifies in some detail the path of this discipline—a path that will be described in much greater detail in philosophical and ethical books to follow. It will be alluded to and described in poetic literature, as in the epics and dramas. In our own times it will be described as an ideal in the poetry of Tagore. And Indian life and Indian thought, in many varied philosophies, will give preëminence to those who strive after the highest wisdom.

But in the hymn chanted by Lord Krishna, it is the longer way of works that wins the higher commendation. Because for the multitude, life, through Karma and Maya, must go on. Complete and universal wisdom is not possible yet with the mass of mankind, imperfect and saturated with Ignorance and Passion, the two qualities (*gunas*) that make for imperfection. These need a light and a guide. The great ones, like the Prince Arjuna, must live in accordance with their code, acquiring merit and understanding for themselves, and spreading the fruit of unselfish example for others.

These worlds would perish, if I should not do works; I should make confusion, and bring these beings to harm.

As do the unwise, attached to works, O thou of Bharata's race, so should the wise do, but without attachment, seeking to establish order in the World.

They thus assist others to gain understanding and merit, establish order, and thus in the fulness of time the world of Karma moves forward, slowly to the far off event—the final triumph of spirit. For works are not a defilement:

Works defile Me not; in Me is no longing for the fruit of works. He who recognises Me as such is not fettered by Works.

He who beholds in Work No-Work, and in No-Work Work, is the man of understanding among mortals; he is in the Rule, a doer of perfect work.

It is only as they are undertaken in a spirit of selfish emulation or for some selfish profit that they lead the soul astray. From this point of view one can call the *Bhagavat Gita* a compendium of practical wisdom. It would be interesting to put it beside the Sermon on the Mount.

It was also by a philosophy and metaphysics that India defined and defended the caste system. The Brahmin owes his preëminence, to be sure, to his birth, but his soul came from some now dead body, and had in its earlier incarnation acquired exceeding merit. The soul does not come from either father or mother. It is immortal. It is the drama of this soul; the story of the merit or demerit gained by its works during its varied pilgrimages, that is responsible for the soul's advent on a scene as Brahmin or as Untouchable. There is a celestial bookkeeping, with its entries in the black and the red, that assigns to each his successive rôles in this drama.

*   *   *

During the uncertain period in Indian history, after the beginning of the sixth century B.C., while the scholarly Brahmin was fastening the caste system on Indian society, and the religious ceremonial was becoming more and more a matter of esoteric form all under Brahmin control, the prince Sidharatha was born and died revered as Sakya-muni, Buddha, the sage of the Sakya clan, the Enlightened. He was a protest against both the caste system and the stiffening ceremonial of worship. In truth he left the world not a religion, as we currently use the word, but a philosophy, a sermon on the vanity of life, and an appeal for human brotherhood.

Buddhism covered India for a space more than a half millennium; one of the world's great emperors, Asoka, was a devout follower. It cultivated a literature, for a time, but in the current vernacular, not in the erudite Sanscrit. But most of this was irretrievably lost when the Brahmin rose again and made Buddhism a political and religious offense. Hinduism accepted much of the Buddhist way of life. The sanctity of life, human and animal, was accepted, which act banished forever, except for one Hindu sect, all animal sacrifice. Buddhism profoundly affected Indian art. It is a pity that for a literature of Buddhism we must look for Chinese translations of the original Indian Buddhist scriptures.

Another historical event that came perhaps two centuries later must be alluded to, the conquest of a portion of Northern India by a much more worldly conqueror, Alexander the Great. The Hellenic civilization for the first time came into direct contact with that of India, and the influence of each on the other was profound, but difficult to define. We can read the effect of Greek art on Indian. How far the influence of Greek troops of wandering actors, and of Greek reciters of Homer and other poets influenced the Indian drama and epic we can only speculate. They may only have stimulated Indian pride in its own epic and dramatic material. For it was during these centuries that the *Mahabharata* and the *Ramayana* were receiving their final form; and it was not long after that India had a full-blown drama.

THE EPIC

"As long as mountain ridges stand, and rivers flow upon the earth, so long shall Rama's epic tale renew for men its ancient worth." This prophecy, from the lines of the *Ramayana* is true literally and in the deepest sense. The poem survives on the lips and in the hearts of Hindu India. With almost equal truth the same can be said of the other great epic, the *Mahabharata*.[4] I suspect no epic poems in any literature have for so long had so

[4] The last *a* in both titles is not sounded, as in the names of the heroes, not heroines.

powerful a shaping and guiding power upon a people's imagination. As the *Iliad* gave its ideals to ancient classical Greece so these poems have, for over two thousand years, given their ideals to India. Like the *Iliad* again these have as their substance the religious and historical myth. Indeed one can say, without myth Indian literature would be poor indeed.[5]

It might be well here parenthetically to define what we mean by myth and the reason for its universal power. It can be called the conscious or even unconscious account of some significant events in a people's experience. It is distilled into a story and is accepted as history. So far as its people is concerned it is *universal* in its appeal and *exemplary* in its meaning. It is related to some great man of a people, a hero, a superman, a god, who through his act has changed or modified the course of civilization, or made himself dear to his people or an object of extreme pity. It excites the imagination and provokes the creative poet. It is not static like recorded history, but renews its meaning for each succeeding epoch. It is plastic, bringing to each a renewed emotional appeal. The world of literature would be infinitely poorer without the stimulus of myth to its imagination. The myths of the Indian epics have all these characteristics.

It is difficult to set dates to these two epics. There may well have been a thousand years of poetic activity before they took their present forms. It is generally conceded that we can think of them as being fixed about the beginning of the Christian era. Both are ascribed to mythical sages or *rishis*. Vyāsa was of so forbidding an aspect, due to his many austerities, that of two widowed queens, one in horror shut her eyes on beholding him, with the result that their child was born blind. The other went so pale with terror that their child was born white, the color of fear. To him is ascribed the *Mahabharata*. Valmiki of the Ramayana is a much more genial rishi, the man who raised affectionately and wisely the two sons of Rama and comforted the exiled widow

---

[5] As late a poet as Tagore has used Indian myth in his dramas. And the Indian cinema exploits the myths of both these poems.

Sita. His is a beautiful picture of a romantic poet. Homer would have been compensated for his loss of eyesight could he have seen the one, but he would have loved and marveled at the other.

The *Mahabharata* is a long poem. It has something like two hundred twenty thousand lines. All the epics of all other countries in the world would be lost in its continental expanse. Yet its plot is simple. The digressions give the poem its magnitude, and some of them like the so-called *Nala* episode or the tale of *Savitri* are as good as anything in Sanscrit poetry. We can compare this epic as a collection to the mass of poems embodying the myth of the Trojan War that was the inheritance of Homer. Homer had the Greek genius of form. The Sanscrit College of Poets that put together the *Mahabharata* could not find the heart to leave anything for another poem.

The main poem is exemplary in its action. On his death a king Pandu, of ancient Hastinapura, near modern Delhi, has left five boys all in their minority to his blind brother Dhritarāshtra as regent. Unfortunately the regent has one hundred sons of his own, of whom the oldest, Duryodhana, excites his brothers into acts of jealousy against their more favored five cousins. These are all distinguished by a variety of virtues: Yudhisthira, the wise; Bhima, the incomparable wielder of the mace; and Arjuna, the romantic bow man and strategist. The other two brothers we need not name.

The hundred cousins finally persuade their father to banish the five, and they go obediently into exile, living as hermits that they may acquire merit and wisdom. There they are visited by royal friends and wise men to be schooled against the day of justice. There they acquire a wife, the peerless Draupadi. She was Arjuna's prize, but on an injunction by his mother, she became the bride of all—an obvious reference to the early existence of polyandry in some parts of Vedic India. There, by their meritorious lives, they acquire the favor of the gods, and especially of Krishna, an *avatar*, incarnation of the great god Vishnu.

After a period of years they are ready for their vindication. An army of neighbor kings is collected, and marches to battle. It is at this critical point that the philosophical poem, the *Bhagavat Gita* is inserted. They are victorious in a battle of magnificent and supernatural proportions. When it comes to such stirring incidents the imagination of the Brahmin Sanscrit poet ordains itself free of all limits and imaginary lines. The same is true, perhaps even in a greater degree, of the *Ramayana*. The lawful claimants to the throne are established in justice. Peace is proclaimed. A great sacrifice is celebrated, the *aswamehda* with its long ritual. But the end is not yet. The tale must be exemplary. Since complete harmony can never be restored, an heir to the throne is chosen, and the five brothers, the loving wife and their faithful dog, who accompanied all their adventures, make their way to the Himalayas. And then one by one, afflicted by their weakness, they drop by the way, but at last find peace, when Yudhisthira is accepted by the god Indra on the highest peak and with his brothers is received into Indra's heaven.

There is little room for realism in a poem with this design. But it has many passages that are profoundly moving. One thinks of the best of the episodes. The Nala story is one of wifely devotion, as was that of Savitri. Both are told to the wife, Draupadi, to comfort her during the years of painful exile. Both are stories of perfect wifely love that is stronger than tragedy. Both make the heroes victims of a malicious fate. Nala, like Yudhisthira in the epic, is the victim of an unrighteous game of dice, and gambles away all his possessions, and in shame forsakes his wife. But her fortitude wins him. Savitri chooses a prince who, she learns, is doomed to live only a year. They retire to the forest to spend the year wisely. On the fatal day her devotion is such that she overcomes Yama, the god of death.

But it is the *Ramayana* that is a household word and the images of its deified chief characters are the pin-up girl and heroes of all India. There is not a festival without trained minstrels chanting and explaining its exemplary *slokas*. The remot-

est village hears its poetry and listens enthralled to its magic.
For centuries the folk drama, the *Ram Leila,* has been witnessed by villager and merchant. In dumb show, while a *guru*
recites the lines, the actors in gorgeous costumes take the parts
of demons, monkeys, and heroes and heroines that are characters
of the drama. A Hindi version in the thirteenth century by
Tulsi Das has brought the epic into the vernacular. The *Ramayana* is almost modest in its length, only about ninety thousand
lines in the best accepted version.[6] It no doubt has a historical
background and in its allegory of demons and monkeys, bears and
vultures, tells the story of the conquest of Southern India by
the advancing Aryans. Consciously it is even more exemplary
in its moral than its longer rival.

Rama is the eldest and most gifted son of the *raja* of Ajodya.
He is also like his two brothers an incarnation of the god Vishnu.
Only this time the god has given Rama half of his virtue; to
Ladshman, a third; and the remainder to the youngest, Bharata.
By his skill in a trial of arms Rama has won for his wife, Sita,
the princess without rival, also mysterious and divine in her
origin. He is ordained by his father to be Yusvaraja, the king's
heir, and preparations are being made for his final accession to
the throne.

At this point a younger queen reminds the old king of the two
boons he had long ago promised her. Now will he fulfill them.
They are first to banish Rama, and then to place her son, Bharata,
on the throne. The king is powerless to protest, for a royal promise
can never be broken. With all signs of mourning Rama is banished, and with him go Sita his loving wife and Lakshman his
loyal brother. Even Bharata when he hears of it is distressed,
refuses the throne, hastens after his brother and begs his return.
But a promise is a promise. The time of exile is fixed at ten
years, and Bharata returns to sit before the throne on a footstool.
Rama's shoe, as a symbol, guards the throne.

[*]There are many versions of varied length. This fact complicates a study
of the poem, but also testifies to its long popularity. See bibliography for
translations of the *Ramayana* and *Mahabharata* most easily available.

But all this was of the devising of the gods. For during the exile Rama and Lakshman, his brother, exact a huge vengeance upon the demons, Rakshashas, who had been disturbing holy hermits in all the India south of the Ganges. In their war upon them, the gods had needed human hands, for by their magic the demons had become almost omnipotent. Finally, word reaches Lanka, Ceylon, and the king of demons, Ravana. His sister, too, is curious about these two rash mortals, and what is worse, falls in love with Rama. Unfortunately she gets her nose cut off for her pains; and Ravana determines to put an end to this insolence.

The rest of the story is full of virtue and incredible adventure. Sita is abducted by the king of the demons; and Rama and Lakshman set out on their revenge. They get the aid of the monkeys and above all of Huniman, their redoubtable leader. (He now is a familiar god and almost as popular as Rama and Sita.) All set out on the huge expedition, and as huge are the exploits. Finally Sita is rescued. But her wifely devotion must first be tested before a reconciliation would be honorable. A funeral pyre is built and Sita is placed on it. But before she is touched by the flame, Agni, the god of fire, picks her up and restores her to her husband. Virtue is vindicated, and they return to Ajodya and Rama to the throne.

Here the poem should end. But the poet's imagination saw farther. Whispers are heard in the bazar of the seductive power of demons, and again there is doubt of Sita's steadfastness. This time a decree of banishment is pronounced against her, and she goes out to lonely exile. There she gives birth to Rama's twin sons, meets and is protected by the poet-sage Valmiki. By his art and from Sita he learns the story, composes the *Ramayana*, and teaches it to the two boys now growing to manhood. When hunting in the forest, after many years, Rama hears these boys chanting his exploits and the grace and steadfastness of their mother. He recognizes and acknowledges them and asks for their mother. But now she is unwilling to return. She stamps on the earth, and calls on her mother to receive her. The earth opens and she disappears.[7]

No Hindu family today but exalts the divine qualities of Rama and Sita. Their alliance is the symbol and example of every union of man and woman. Even the wedding ceremony of these lovers, described in an early book of the poem, is the orthodox wedding ceremony today. Rama is the virtuous prince, warrior, husband; Sita his perfect consort. They are ideals for perfect manhood and womanhood, and both are tried by fire.

DRAMA

India, early in our era, cultivated a drama. Whatever its origins, what we have today differs markedly from the drama of ancient Greece. Like the Greeks, it draws nearly all of its plots from the sacred myths, but it has lost any sign of a communal origin. It is exemplary entertainment for princes and courtiers, entertainment for special occasions, like a royal marriage. During the centuries of its development it acquired for its patron a god, and for its conduct as elaborate a textbook of rules and stage behavior as the human imagination can conceive.[8] Quite in accordance with the orthodox Indian philosophy, there is no tragedy. For tragedy, as the Greeks and Shakespeare knew it, would violate the law of *Karma*. We can easily class all the Sanscrit drama as romantic comedy.

It is only within relatively recent years that the Indian as well as the European world has become aware of the large number of plays that were written, nearly all during the compass of a few centuries. By the year 1000 it seems that the urge was over. But there are now catalogued something over five hundred plays, and doubtless there are more ancient palm leaf manuscripts yet to be discovered. Even an emperor, Harsha (eighth

[7] There is a shrine, near Cawnpore on the Ganges, which marks this spot.
[8] For example, kissing, scratching, or biting are not permitted.

century), did not feel it below his dignity to allow himself to be styled a poet-dramatist. And the court of the Gupta dynasty (fifth century) produced at least one poet, Kalidasa, who has been called the Indian Shakespeare.

We know little about the production of these plays. There were no theaters as Europe knew them. As they were usually court entertainment they were probably given in the palace court on an improvised stage, in front of the royal pavilion where the king and his family and ministers sat during all court ceremonies. The rest of the audience, as in the inn courtyards of pre-Shakespearean days, could group itself wherever it could see and hear. For stage scenery, I suspect the audience depended on its imagination and the descriptions supplied by the poet. For example, the stage direction, "Enter so and so seated upon a cloud," and the several scenes in the *Çakuntala* that represent characters borne in the air in a heavenly chariot leave something even to a robust imagination. Improvised stage settings, as potted plants and furniture, we can expect. There was probably no curtain.

The characters, by the rules, early became fixed to definable types. The romantic hero, too, must be a man without moral blemish, of noble rank in one of the highest castes; the heroine, too, must be of the same rank, worthy and an ideal for feminine edification. The familiar plot is the story of their finally achieved union, but with the added moral that one must love wisely and not too well. Human passion must be neither blind nor overwhelming. Both hero and heroine have their companions, persons of lesser rank but faithful ears to which they can confide and loyal lips that will give fitting advice. There is often a villain, whose character is equally downright and whose downfall could be greeted with appropriate jeers. There can be, and often is, a touch of the comic in the male "gentleman in waiting." He has been compared to the parasite of the later Greek comedy and may even be a debt that India owes to Greece. But his genuine loyalty, though sometimes stupid, can always be relied on.

There are curiously no rules about the number of acts, and they vary from four to eight or nine. The reason is fairly obvious. It was after the classical period of the Greek drama that critics fixed upon five as the legal number of acts. None of the Greek tragedians had known of it. The Chinese drama allows as many as the poet's imagination can use. For where there is no curtain and scenery is scanty, the number of times the stage is left empty can be left to the requirements of the plot. The modern cinema is an illustration of how swiftly scenes and acts can change without inconvenience to the imagination of the audience. The plays begin with an elaborate introduction or prologue, usually with an address to the audience, followed by a dialogue between stage manager, or poet, and some of the actors, when the merits of the dramatist or the play are discussed and the play introduced. The play closes with a brief epilogue, much in the manner of the final words of the chorus in Greek tragedy. It points the moral that adorns the play.

There is little room for realism in a drama thus drawn from epic and myth. And yet in nearly all of them there will be characters, not of the heroic type, drawn from humbler circumstances, who do give valuable glimpses of contemporary life on the commonplace level. These scenes are often the most precious to us of the play and the most convincing. But according to the rules such characters must never be vulgar. They show their common origin only by speaking prose in one of the less renowned Prakrit dialects. The exalted characters always employ poetry and in the sacred Sanscrit.

To have watched and understood a Sanscrit drama, prose and verse, one must have been an alert linguist. For there were levels in speech as strict as the levels in caste and society. In some plays, as for example in the *Çakuntala*, there are a half-dozen dialects spoken by the varied characters to indicate their rank.

There is one play, however, and one of the best, that has a realism that reminds one of the practice of the West. It is the *Mricchakatika* or *Little Clay Cart*, and the fact that an adaptation of it was successful in this country only a few years ago testifies to its universal interest. Any Western dramatist would have been proud to have been its author. Its date is probably before 400 B.C. It claims to have been written by a king Çudraka, whoever he might have been. A brief sketch of its plot is no substitute for the very real enjoyment the play itself offers.

The title of the play is taken from a child's toy common even today in India. It is a clay saucer covered with a tight membrane, like a drum, mounted on wheels. There is a ratchet on the axle which operates two sticks that as the toy is dragged by the child beat a tattoo on the drum. It is the little son of the hero who longs for a gold cart to replace the common little clay one, a longing the heroine fulfills. The title can thus be read allegorically.

The hero of the play is a righteous Brahmin, Charudatta, now reduced to poverty because of his utter generosity to all in want. He has lost in consequence all of his friends except Maietreya who is his confidant and constant companion. The heroine of the play is the wealthy courtesan, Vesantasena, who has fallen in love with the hero's noble character. One must recall that the term courtesan implies no reproach against her moral character. She is simply a "free" woman, the Greek *hetaira,* who has refused to surrender herself to the secluded life of domesticity, but prefers to manage her own estate and life. Charudatta, the hero, already has a wife, who hardly appears in the play, and a little son. But polygamy in the India of that epoch was common, and this wife offers nothing but encouragement to the complicated romance that is the play.

The plot is to effect a marriage between the worthy but poor Brahmin and the wealthy, sympathetic, and affectionate Vesantasena. One must remember that the poverty of a "twice born" and sacred Brahmin is often an asset rather than a social liability. There are numerous opportunities for her to show her affection. She rescues a gambler, who once had been in Charudatta's employ. Pursued in the street by a robber, she takes refuge in the hero's house and leaves her jewels there for safe keeping. Then a thief, in love with Vesantasena's maid, breaks into his house and steals the jewels. Charudatta is charged with the theft, his wife gives up her last possession, a pearl necklace, to redeem him. But to no avail, for a villainous prince of the royal house is in pursuit of the heroine, and sees the opportunity not only to discredit the Brahmin but to have him put to death.

The plot is too complicated for any short summary. After the innocent victim is being led forth to impalement, after the loyal courtesan is almost strangled by the villain, after the just claimant to the throne is put into prison, and after tyranny has all but succeeded, the knot is untied, virtue is rewarded, and the happy lovers are united. The play closes with the moral—"Fate plays with us like buckets at the well." The intimacy of the plot is made consistent with life by the rich vitality of all the characters. But most important is that we are not here in an ideal world of pure romance, but in a very real and convincing India, an India recognizable after more than fifteen centuries.

When Kalidasa's *Çakuntala* was first translated into English almost a century and a half ago, it took Europe by storm. The poet Goethe broke into a rapturous lyric, and modeled some of the introduction to his *Faust* on its manner. It was precisely of the stuff that romantic Europe and England and America found to their intense liking. The play since has never lost its popularity. In India for more than a thousand years, like Shakespeare's *As You Like It,* it has been a textbook. There is nothing quite like it in the world of dramatic literature.

It deserves its popularity. In the first place, like Shakespeare's plays, it is in the very best tradition of poetry. There is no better poetry in all Sanscrit literature. It is a pity that no translation can do it half justice. Again it is uniquely in the Indian tradition—there is no region, there has been no region, in which it conceivably could have been written. And it has created a final standard or model for all succeeding Indian poetry and drama. Tagore writing only yesterday could quite appropriately have been living and writing as a contemporary of the elder poet.

Though there are many stories told of this poet, all that can be said to be known about him is exactly nothing. He is as mysterious as Homer. All we dare say is that he probably lived about A.D. 400 and that his name is one of his own choosing, the slave of the well known goddess Kali. He wrote some admirable nature poems, and two other dramas, neither of them of the same vintage as his masterpiece. He is not a people's poet, like the unknown authors of the epics; for he wrote for the cultured court. But there is not a boy or girl who has had a smattering of Sanscrit who has not labored over the translation of the *Çakuntala* as Europe and America labored over Virgil. Few anonymous writers can rival his interest for scholars and poets.

The plot of the *Çakuntala* or *The Lost Ring*, is simple. Dushyanta, a king, is out hunting; discovers that he is near the retreat of a famous ascetic; and, as is fitting, calls. He meets not the holy man, but Çakuntala, his beautiful foster daughter. She is the daughter of a nymph. They promptly fall in love, as is also fitting. They marry, in the celestial manner, by an exchange of vows. Then he leaves her for his palace, with the promise that he will promptly return with a retinue and install her as queen. As pledge he gives her his ring. The bride is so absorbed in her newly found love that she incurs the curse of a neighbor holy man: Her husband will forget her; and his memory can be restored only by the sight of the ring.

This is precisely what happens. Weeks pass into months. She is about to become a mother, and it is quite unthinkable that a child be born away from its father's home. So she and a small retinue of disciples set forth for the court. On the way, while performing her ablutions, her ring falls from her finger and is lost in the river. The king angrily refuses to acknowledge her; who is she, this adventuress and her preposterous claim? As she turns away in despair, her mother comes through the air and carries her away to a hermitage in a distant and quite unknown region.

The king is troubled. The last portent has moved him, and his memory like a vibrant chord echoes he knows not to what forgotten incident. Some fishermen recover the ring in a fish's gullet, but still the restoration comes years after, and only with the aid of the god Indra. The king has first to become a divine agent, and to slay pestilent demons, using the weapons, the chariot, and the charioteer of the god. Finally, he comes to the distant region, meets his son, sees in him the signs of royal parentage, and in a scene of disciplined ecstasy is reunited with his wife. The boy becomes Bharata, the ancestor of the rival prince whose story is the plot of the *Mahabharata*. The moral of this beautiful romantic tale: one must learn to love wisely and not too well.

It is impossible to say why and when the Indian dramatic instinct began to fade. There are many guesses. The most likely involves the Mohammedan invasions, which began not far from the year 1000, and the influence of the Mohammedan courts where the drama was unknown. For with the passing of the drama also passed the creative urge in Sanscrit. The vernaculars then began to come into their own and Sanscrit ceased to be a spoken language, even among the courtly. The vicissitudes of invasion by a foreign religion and culture, the wars for survival, the transformations in the social life, like the sequestration of women, all these must have had a numbing effect on the poetic imagination. A different India was coming into being.

THE FABLE

In India, the beast fable made an early appearance. We do not have to look far for a reason. The doctrine of Karma binds into one life all living creatures, and it is only merit or demerit in previous lives that determines whether a soul shall be now in the body of a beast or in that of a human being. It could not have been long after Buddha's death that the beginnings were made of the collection of his so-called birth stories, the *Jatakas*. For according to their preface, because of his exceeding merit, a complete memory was restored to Buddha·of all of his previous lives.

And these, in the form of tales, he recited to his disciples. Many of them were just such animal fables.

The love of tales is as old as human nature. The employment of them in the way of moral instruction is also as old. But it seems again to have been India with its love of artifice and complexity that loved to thread them together; with one half-told leading to the next, and thus to a long series, before each in turn receives its conclusion. The affect is as bewilderingly satisfying as the pattern of a Cashmere shawl, or the game of parchisi or chess. We know the less complex imitations as the fashion passed westward, the *Arabian Nights,* which is Indian in origin, the *Decameron,* and the *Canterbury Tales.* Only India loved this manner of tale telling with animals as characters and a strong moral in verse as a coda.[9]

When did these originate? Certainly early, perhaps shortly after Vedic times. The best of them are in the *Panchatantra.* How popular it has been and still remains is testified to by the large number of its variations. Creatures of all kinds, fish, fowl, animal, insect, crowd its stories and rub shoulders with human beings. And the whole is filled with moralizing and commenting poetry, easy to memorize. Another equally popular and like it is the *Hitopodesa.* The second of these collections in a vernacular translation is a popular textbook today.

They were not meant as pure entertainment. Like all the classical literature of India they are exemplary in their moral teaching. The *Panchatantra* concerns the education of a prince who remained obstinately dull to all other intellectual or moral education. Literally, they mixed the useful with the sweet. And with their subtle humor, rich worldly wisdom, and at times genuine farce, they, even in a translation, are as illuminating as ever. They are the Sanscrit orthodox philosophy, reduced to words of one syllable, and sent abroad for the edification of prince and

---

[9] The manner of the arrangement reminds one of the little boxes one used to buy in Benares, box within box, each perfect and each a container for its successor.

peasant. There is nothing quite like them in world literature outside India. They have their imitators. As the Greek boys were taught Aesop and the Roman Phaedrus, the Indian committed to memory the fables of man and animals and tried to emulate their wisdom.

BIBLIOGRAPHY

BIBLIOGRAPHY

Aufrecht, Thomas, *Catalogus catalogorum: an Alphabetical Register of Sanskrit Works and Authors* (Leipzig, 1891-1903), 3 vols.
Cumming, J. G., *Bibliography Relating to India* (1900-1927) (London, 1927).

HISTORY

Dodwell, H. H., ed., *The Cambridge Shorter History of India* (Cambridge, Eng., 1934).
Smith, Vincent Arthur, *Oxford History of India* (Oxford, 1917).

ART AND PHILOSOPHY

Akhilananda, Swami A., *Hindu Psychology: Its Meaning for the West* (New York, 1946).
Zimmer, Heinrich Robert, *Myths and Symbols in Indian Art and Civilization* (New York, 1946).

HISTORY OF LITERATURE

Frazer, Robert Watson, *Literary History of India* (New York, 1907).
Gowen, Herbert Henry, *History of Indian Literature from Vedic Times to Present Day* (London, 1931).
Keith, Arthur Berriedale, *Classical Sanscrit Literature* (London, 1924).
———, *History of Sanscrit Literature* (Oxford, 1928).
———, *Sanscrit Drama* (Oxford, 1924).
Macdonell, Arthur Anthony, *History of Sanscrit Literature* (London, 1926).

TRANSLATION

A Little Clay Cart, trans. by Arthur W. Ryder, Harvard Oriental Series (Cambridge, Mass., 1924).

Bhagavat Gita, Everyman's Library (London and New York, often reprinted); another translation, Arthur W. Ryder (Chicago, 1927).

Katha Upanished, trans. by Max Müller in *Sacred Books of the East* (Oxford, 1910), vol. 1.

RYDER, Arthur W., Kalidasa, *Works* (New York, 1913).

Panchatantra, trans. by Arthur W. Ryder (Chicago, 1925).

The Mahabharata and the Ramayana, trans. by Rhomesh Chunder Dutt (London, 1910).

Rig Veda, trans. by Arthur Anthony Macdonell in *A Vedic Reader for Students* (Oxford, 1928).

4

Near Eastern Literature
The Koran

EDWIN E. CALVERLEY
HARTFORD SEMINARY FOUNDATION

PROFESSOR EDWIN E. CALVERLEY *of the Hartford Seminary Foundation has had a lifetime of association with the Middle East as missionary, teacher, and editor. He served as a missionary in Arabia and Iraq for twenty years, and recently spent a sabbatical year in the American University at Cairo as visiting professor. He has worked with the American Council of Learned Societies on its committees for Near Eastern Studies, and has taught Arabic at Columbia University summer schools. He is author of* The Arabian Readers (1920), Worship in Islam (1925), *and is now editor of* The Muslim World.

The Koran

THE first book to be written in Arabic was the Qur'an (Koran). It is still the most important literary product of Arabia. But the Qur'an is not the first work of Arabic literature, for oral composition was common in Arabia in preliterate times.

THE PAGAN PERIOD

There were indeed two products of literary activity in existence in Arabia before the Qur'an was produced. These two classes of literature consisted in poems and proverbs, at first recorded only in the memories of men. People that did not know how to write knew how to make poetry which their contemporaries and their descendants remembered. They knew how to express ideas in words that remained in the minds of those who heard.

People living in the land of Arabia before the advent of Islam were called by their Muslim (Moslem) successors, "the people of the Ignorance," or "The uncultured folk," as indeed they were, in some respects. But these untutored folk had a culture that found expression in carefully observed and highly honored codes of personal and tribal conduct, a civilization which followed a recognized pattern. There were in those days, as there are in the deserts today, many who were nature's cultured men and gentlemen, even though they could not write or even read, and they were not without literary expression.

The language used by these untutored, pre-Islamic, commonly called pagan Arabs was rich in its vocabulary. Its grammar and rhetoric were regular, revealing highly intellectual development, and it had rigid rules for its prosody.

While it is improbable that early Arabic was written down at

135

the time it was composed, still the circumstances of its publication, that is to say, its being given to the public, favored its survival. The primitive Arabs, like many communal peoples of today who are conscious of their excellence, had annual fairs where intertribal rivalries found expression in poetic contests. The poems that won favor were remembered and repeated and so saved for written record after the establishment of Islam.

The best introduction in English to the whole of this literature is R. A. Nicholson's *Literary History of the Arabs*.[1] The book contains numerous examples of this poetry, together with adequate information about those who produced it. More complete collections of the poems and additional accounts of the poets and their times are given in two splendid works which can be highly recommended to those who desire information in English about the early Arab civilization, presented by those who knew it best because they described their own way of life. These two books are *The Seven Golden Odes of Pagan Arabia, Known also as the Moallakat;*[2] and *An Introduction to Ancient Arabian Poetry,*[3] by Sir Charles Lyall.

Any lover of poetry will find these books fascinating, but the value of these sources for Western students of other cultures consists in the candid and faithful pictures the poems preserve of the life of an unlettered but highly intelligent people. The social anthropologist, the student of primitive religions and, indeed, of the Bible as literature, and others interested in the earliest literary product of various peoples, will all find new source material in these translations of pre-Islamic poetry.

Poets of other generations in France, Germany, England, and America have found inspiration and subject material for their messages to their own peoples in the free and fine life and thought of the Arabs. The early pagan poet Antar is the hero of a long Arabian romance recently published in America, *The Ro-*

[1] (Cambridge, Eng., 1930).
[2] Trans. by Lady Anne Blunt from the original Arabic; done in English verse by Wilfred Scawen Blunt (London, 1885).
[3] (London, 1885; reprinted 1927).

mance of Antar,[4] while Leigh Hunt's *Abou Ben Adhem* still commands a place in anthologies of English verse.

INFLUENCE AND INTERPRETATION

It was the Qur'an that preserved the poetry of pre-Islamic Arabia. Although the religion of Islam opposed and supplanted the previous pagan life of the Arabs, the language of the Qur'an was found to need the lexical and grammatical aid that the other literature of poetry and proverb provided. So, what had been only oral became written literature, because unusual and unknown Quranic words and forms could be interpreted by their occurrence in other contexts. One most curious and paradoxical consequence of the preservation of the early literature has been that, although Islam destroyed the religious attitude of ancient Arabia, all the Arabs, though they are convinced Muslims, look upon that pagan time as the Golden Age of Arabic poetry. The Qur'an changed the religious climate of early Arabia, but increased the appreciation of its literature.

There is a traditional saying ascribed to Muhammad that has become a proverb and as such is the first recorded in Maydâni's great collection. It says, There is a kind of eloquence that is magical. "Magical" is the only term that expresses adequately the impression made upon the Arabs by the recital of the Qur'an. To most Western ears and minds, most of the Qur'an is dull and deadly repetitious. There are short suras and passages from the longer chapters that, translated into any language, would tend to elevate the human spirit. But to those Muslims whose mother tongue is Arabic, these fine passages and all the rest of the Qur'an are magical. This magic is, to them, one evidence that the Qur'an is divine in its origin and authority.

Therefore, the first fact that needs to be known about Islamic literature, is that, to the Muslims, the Qur'an is divine in its origin and authority. To the Muslims, Allah Most High, not Mu-

[4] Eunice Tietjens, ed. (New York, 1929).

hammad, is the Author of the Qur'an. Muhammad was the means, the instrument, the channel of the revelation of the very words of Allah. That was Muhammad's own belief. That conviction is expressed in the form and style of address of most of the Qur'an. That conviction made the Qur'an, or, better, the religion of the Qur'an, authoritative in the life of the Muslims as individuals and in the history of the Islamic peoples. Religion therefore is the most important factor in the history of Islam. Any attempt to understand Muslim life and literature without some knowledge of the fundamental principles of Islam will undoubtedly be inadequate.

It is not difficult to grasp the basic principles of Islam. The short Muslim creed contains two sentences, both found in the Qur'an. The first states, "There is no god at all but Allah" (47:21) and the second, "Muhammad is the Apostle of Allah" (48:29).

The first statement is interpreted to mean that Allah is the only supreme, divine, eternal Being, the direct and immediate Author of all else that exists and all that occurs. The second statement says that Muhammad is Allah's Apostle to His creatures, to reveal to them all they need to believe about Allah and themselves and how to obey Allah and belong to the religion of Allah and the Community of Muhammad.

All the orthodox theology of Islam comes under the first word or phrase of the creed. There are doctrines and religious beliefs, widespread among Muslims, that have not been derived from the Qur'an, but these represent later additions and modifications of the religious ideas of Muhammad, or they are customs and practices that the followers of Muhammad retained or adopted as part of their religious life. The second sentence of the creed simply means that the more the follower of Islam practices what Muhammad said and did, the better a Muslim he is.

Just as it was the Qur'an that stimulated the collection and preservation of the extant oral literature of the pre-Islamic Arabs, so the Qur'an created the need for the systems of grammar and other literary sciences of rhetoric and lexicography as well as all the branches of Qur'an introduction.

Further, just as the Qur'an produced many branches of science new to the Arabs, so the traditions of Muhammad and his followers caused the production of a vast literature of biography and law. The religion based on these two sources created or influenced all the other sciences and interests of the Islamic peoples. For instance, the religious laws of inheritance sanctioned the study of mathematics. The direction and times of the prescribed performances of the worship justified the study of surveying and astronomy. The required pilgrimage to Mecca and the recommended conquest of the world produced books on geography, history, and the political and social sciences.

Islam as a religion determined not only the concerns of the Muslim; it also determined the subjects with which he was not to concern himself. Surgery was one of these, and to a less extent medicine in general, because they both tended to interfere with the ceremonial cleanliness required for acceptable worship. The Muslims who nevertheless practiced medicine were generally suspected of heresy, or at least the quality of their Islam was under suspicion.

The second fact that needs to be kept in mind to understand Muslim life and literature and to interpret current events in the Muslim world follows naturally from the above-mentioned fact that Muslims believe the Qur'an is divine in its authority. According to Islam, the divine origin of the Qur'an gives to the religion it teaches the direction of all the thinking and activity of the Muslim. There is no aspect of the Muslim's life that is outside the authority of his religion. Islam is all-inclusive. It aims to control the social, political, economic, and cultural departments of life as well as that which the modern West thinks of as the specifically religious.

It is not too much to say that the one word *religion* provides the master key for the interpretation of the past history and present life in the Muslim East.

The inclusion of civil and political interests and governmental and military activities within the scope of religious authority naturally has had the reciprocal result that public opinion and the power of the state serve and preserve the state religion. Just as the individual Muslim honors and obeys the laws of the Muslim state to which he belongs, so he adheres to the religion of his nation. For him to abandon the communal religion is to give up his nationality, and in some respects to become a traitor to his state.

The basic principle is that Islam exercises an inclusive and compelling control over the whole life of its adherents. Examples of this compulsion can be given for all the activities of life. Islam forbids the taking of bank interest, and so financial institutions have difficulties, or use subterfuges in handling the accounts of scrupulous Muslims.

Again, modern science and technology have been based upon the operation of the natural law of cause and effect. But Islam's theology makes Allah the immediate and exclusive cause of all that exists and occurs. He is the sufficient explanation of everything, so that exploration, experimentation, investigation, and the like are unnecessary activities. Why be curious about the why of things when one already knows they are so because Allah so willed? Why experiment when Allah has decreed whatever comes to pass? Why be concerned about what has been or will be in this world when one's great and all-consuming concern should be with the world to come?

It may be said that the theology of Islam removed the idea of natural law and secondary causes from the minds of Muslims and thereby prevented progress in modern scientific and technological discovery.

There are some fields of life with which Muslims have been concerned. These are those associated with the Islam's control of life. Islam proclaims itself as a world religion, the best and final world religion. Islam aims to win the world. All that tends to prove the worth of Islam—its Book, its language, its adherents, and its supremacy—has claimed and still claims the support of the Muslims.

It would be wrong to think that, to the Muslims, there is anything insincere in spirit or unworthy in motive in their desire for Islam to dominate the world. Their motivation is religious; their desire is to bring the whole world under obedience to the one true God, whose name is Allah. They want the world to have the blessings that Allah has provided through Muhammad, the Qur'an, and Islam. The labor of Muslims to glorify Islam, to prove its doctrines, to describe and praise its practices, to honor the Arabic language in all its uses, to increase the power and dominion of Islam—all this has found expression in the history and literature of Islam, and made them great.

*   *   *

Great have been the powers and the empires of the rulers of Islam. Great have been the works of the poets and authors of Islam. Proud and gratified the Muslims have the right to be, for the products of their religion and their culture are important for the Muslim world and for the whole world.

But there is one aspect of the whole content and attitude of Islam that is supreme in its importance for the whole world. Islam —that is, orthodox Islam, the Islam of all but a few of the Muslims of the world—unites the government under religion and sanctions the use of official political authority to compel private religious conformity. It is doubtful that such Islamic sanction constitutes a world peril at the present time. But that principle has operated in the past. It provides another important key to the understanding of Muslim history and for the interpretation of current events.

In conclusion, Muslim history and literature are clarified by the recognition of the pervasive and authoritative place of religion in the life and thought of the individuals and peoples of Islam.

Near Eastern Literature

Arabic Literature

EDWARD J. JURJI
PRINCETON THEOLOGICAL SEMINARY

Dr. Edward J. Jurji, *Associate Professor of Islamics and Comparative Religion at Princeton Theological Seminary, Lecturer in Semitic Languages at Princeton University, and sometime member of the Institute for Advanced Study, was born in Latakia, Syria, and comes to this country by way of the American University of Beirut and the Iraq Ministry of Education. He holds a Ph.D. degree from Princeton, and a B.D. from Princeton Theological Seminary. He is associate editor of* Muslim World Quarterly, *author of* Illumination in Islamic Mysticism (1938), *co-author of* Tarikh al-Arab (History of the Arabs) (1950), 2 vols., *editor and co-author,* Great Religions of the Modern World (1946), *and contributor to many critical and scholarly collections, including* Arab Heritage (1944), Saudi Arabia (1947), *and* History of Philosophical Systems (1950). *He writes with penetration and balance of a literature which is all but unknown in this country.*

Arabic Literature

WHETHER in the Near East, Moslem India, or elsewhere in the world-wide Mohammedan community, Islamic culture rests upon a common ground of religious and historic traditions. The first spark which provided ignition for this
cultural system was undoubtedly religious in origin and its fuller
development cannot be properly understood or interpreted apart
from its religious premises.

Be that as it may, the particular literature which best reveals
the essence of Islamic civilization was one whose Arab beginnings themselves sprang from both the allegiance of the believers
to the Koran and their reproduction in their daily lives of that
pre-Islamic spirit transmitted in poetry and prose.

Beyond the Koran and the other literary documents which
came into being, moreover, were other streams which fed the
ever-widening river of medieval Islam. These were streams flow-
ing out of Persia and Greece. From Greece came orderly thought,
philosophy, science, and psychological gifts. From Persia came
artistry, mystical strains, epic and dramatic themes which in due
course encouraged and enriched literary productivity. But the
central motifs of Islamic literature, in their lyrical, autobiographical, and dogmatic character, were fundamentally Arab in inspiration if not execution.

With this all-pervading Arab strain in mind, it is easy to see
that the literary theory behind the Islamic classics was something
more than such external features as the rules, meters, and terminology of prosody, presumably originated by al-Khalil ibn-
Ahmad (d. *ca.* 791). For the basic assumption of literary theory
among the Arabs—true Semites as they were—was inherent in the
belief that self-expression through words, spoken or written, was

the highest artistic form open to mankind. The art of speech as such was therefore conceived as the chief vehicle of culture and refinement, surpassing in value every conceivable achievement in the realm of music and sculpture which, with all their glories, must remain insufficient and vague when compared with the excellence and adequacy of verbal expression.

This glorification of verbal expression is a characteristic of Islamic civilization. It is the key to the literary genius of Islamic peoples. It is the most obvious element in the culture of the Arabs who in medieval times created, alongside the Greek Byzantine and the Latin Western worlds, a world of their own excelling the other two in vitality and intellectual attainment. Due consideration must therefore be given to the medieval roots of Islamic literature before the aspects of its decline and subsequent revival are taken up.

THE ROOTS ARE MEDIEVAL

For the Near East—the Arabic-speaking countries, Turkey, and Iran—as well as for Moslem India and other Islamic regions of the earth, the literary aspect of culture is embedded in medieval soil. And the medieval Islamic heritage was mainly produced through the medium of the Arabic tongue. This Arabic literature was rich and extensive. To the present day it shows a remarkable continuity. In poetry and prose, it is technical, specialized, and departmentalized. Science and philosophy, theology and history, geography, medicine, astronomy, mathematics, biography, philology, and jurisprudence, as well as rhetoric, romance, and poetics are among its features. Molded by the pre-Islamic and Koranic norms, it reflected the diverse cultures and environments which constituted the ethos of medieval Islam.

The genesis of Arabic literature is commonly traced to the Koran, wherein Mohammed (*ca.* 571-632) proclaimed his theistic faith. Preceding the rise of Islam, however, an important oral and written literature—known to us only in part—was represented by the sumptuous odes, oracles, and other compositions, which exercised a determining influence on the stylistic character of the Koran and the forms and techniques of subsequent writings. The next major stage was the urbanization (632-750) of the Arabs through contact, in the wake of their dramatic conquests, with the peoples of ancient culture in Syria-Palestine, Persia, and Egypt. This gave rise to the period of ingathering (750-833) culminating in the translation of foreign texts, particularly Greek. Thereafter, in the shadow of empire (833-1517), the body of Arabic literature was formed at such centers as Baghdad, Damascus, Cairo, and Cordova.

From these and other centers, the poets observed the unfolding drama of Arab history. Defined as "register of the Arabs" and recognized as "lawful magic," their art attained increasing popularity. The poetic forms of the Arabian Peninsula, immortalized in the unforgettable odes of the desert bards, were transformed under the impact of a new age which gave birth to novel ideas and manners. Yet, to the present day, nothing seems to stir an Arab audience like a well-spoken poem whose artistry reflects the agony and hope of the people.

An illustrious representative of the new poets was Bashshar ibn-Burd (d. 784) of Basra. Of Persian descent and stone-blind, he was tall and well built. His verse drew laughter and provoked a sensation, especially his love songs which were everywhere on the lips of lads and girls. Combining the charm, ingenuity, and originality which were then in great demand, he once referred to himself as one so worn out by love that a mere breath of air might fell him. Among the leading poets a furious search for metaphors and similes was the fashion, and the enlightened public engaged in a rush for hitherto unheard literary material and manners of expression. Elegance and tenderness were called upon to match the grand style and follies of the intellectual élite and privileged classes.

These trends, with their emphasis on rosy cheeks and cheeks pressed together, threatened the existence of the pre-Islamic bardic lay with its Platonic love, camel songs, the march of horses, desert austerity, and heroic encounters on the battlefield. Nevertheless, the new songs reproduced with more accuracy the soul and passion of a maturing society, alternating between the joyous moods and quiet sobriety of an urban culture.

Notes lofty and notes trivial appeared side by side in the classic poetry of the Arabs. In Baghdad, abu-Nuwas (*ca.* 750-*ca.* 810), also Persian in origin, successively won the admiration of two caliphs, Harun al-Rashid and his son al-Amin. His wine songs and pederastic odes breathed a seductive tenderness and were the embodiment of a brilliant though debauched mind. But the blue ribbon of medieval Arabic poetry belonged to al-Mutanabbi (915-65), of Iraqi birth and Syrian training. Of him a critic could sing:

> More merit can no man achieve
> Save that his faults are numbered.

He adhered to the desert tradition. While others sang of their experiences, he gave expression to universal themes. In its penchant for ornate imagery, lavish use of metaphor, and proud spirit, classical Arabic poetry produced no greater figure than al-Mutanabbi.

The story of prose is no less striking. Arabic prose was no more Arab than the Latin was Italian. With Greek and Persian as well as Arabic ingredients, it was a monument to a great culture rather than the projection of the Arab soul. To be sure, prose had been a virtue of the early Arabs, an art wherewith they claimed superiority over all other nations. The ideal picture of the orator, of equal prestige with the poet, was imperishable. But there was incorporated in the basic theory of prose a Persian motif which manifested itself in an esthetic turn of phrase, in rhetorical and epistolary style, and in the narrative texture of the *Arabian Nights* and the *Fables of Bidpai*. The Greek impulse was represented in the psychological, philosophical, and logical standards of Arabic prose as well as in a heightened concept of love.

Chief among the early prose writers was al-Jahiz (d. 868/9)

of Basra. His *Rhetoric* won him immortal fame by its originality, wit, satire, and learning. His style, a conscious art entirely his own, though at times chatty, was notable for its comparative freedom from pedantry, which until his time was still in the ascendancy. The celebrated historian al-Masudi (d. 943), who admired al-Jahiz for the perfect arrangement and solid structure of his words, wrote of him, "When he fears that the reader is weary, he instantly passes from the serious to the humorous, from sublime wisdom to elegant oddities."

But the old passion for rhymed prose and the ornate rhythm of words did not subside. It grew stronger with the years, reaching its climax in the embellished, elegant anecdotes of al-Hamadhani (969-1008) and al-Hariri (1054-1122). Known as *Maqamat* (Assemblies, Lectures), these anecdotes were miniature pieces of verbal art, belonging to the picaresque genre. They reflected the profound thought and great learning of an author who also was master of the language.

Al-Hamadhani thought little, however, of the style of al-Jahiz. He condemned its simplicity and found it too close to the speech of the common folk. In fact, though, Arabic prose throughout the medieval period fluctuated, with many variations and peculiarities, between two extremes—the dignity and simplicity of al-Jahiz and the embellished artistry of al-Hamadhani.

THE MODERN DAYBREAK

With the Mongol invasion of Western Asia, culminating in the sack of Baghdad (1258), desolation hung over the Near East. Despite their gradual impoverishment, however, the Arabs continued to cultivate the art of letters until the coming of the Ottoman Turks into Syria-Palestine and Egypt in 1517. The eclipse of literary activity soon followed in an epoch of barrenness which lasted nearly three hundred years (1517-1800).

A general apathy, rendered more conspicuous by the phenomenal strides of Europe in exploration and free inquiry, settled on the Arabic-speaking lands. But authorship was not altogether lost. The Algerian al-Maqqari (1591-1632), for instance, produced his *Gust of Fragrance,* a historic literary work, which is the principal authority for that cultural effervescence which Spain saw under the Arabs. Meanwhile, the expansion of Islam in Africa, Asia, Europe, and the islands of the seas brought new domains within the embrace of Arabic letters.

The Turks, in Asia Minor and Eastern Europe, at first showed more dependence on Persian than on Arabic models. During the fifteenth century, the only Arabic works written by Turks were on theological and scientific subjects. However, the incorporation of the Arabic-speaking lands into the Ottoman Empire in the early sixteenth century slightly increased the use of Arabic. The most imposing Arabic literary monument by a Turk is an elaborate bibliography of Arabic, Persian, and Turkish works compiled by Hajji Khalfa (d. 1658). The literary tradition of Ottoman Turkey, Islamic in spirit and dependent on Persian and Arabic models, is typified by Galib (1759-99), head of the mystical order of Whirling Dervishes, whose *Love and Beauty* is a long allegorical poem, of the Sufi genre, which may be regarded as the *Pilgrim's Progress* of Ottoman literature.

A literary daybreak marked the opening of the nineteenth century. Among its primary causes were the contagious ideals of the American and French Revolutions, the educational and cultural atmosphere created by the Christian missionary, the awakened interest in the medieval heritage, the Islamic theological reformation, and the smoldering embers of national consciousness. Overlapping and frequently interwoven, these factors were inevitably reflected in a body of writings which were the unmistakable evidence of a new orientation in the life and world outlook of Islamic and Near Eastern peoples.

The American and French revolutions, with their emphasis on the rights of man and the ideals of freedom reached the Near East, whether directly or indirectly, and roused the flagging spirit of a somnolent culture. With Napoleon's invasion of Egypt

(1798-1801), Western culture and a new desire for modernization began to seep in. The staff of scientists and artists accompanying Bonaparte into Egypt included a number of dramatists who set up a theater for army entertainment. Fifty years elapsed, however, before the first Arabic play, *The Miser,* a translation of Molière's *L'Avare,* was staged by the Lebanese Antun Naqqash (1817-55). Two years later his *Harun al-Rashid* was played.

The coming of the Christian missionary, Roman Catholic and Protestant, channeled the new democratic ideas in the Near East along educational, spiritual, and humanitarian lines. The Jesuits, whose connection with Syria-Lebanon dated back to 1625, had left the Levant after the suppression of their order in 1773. Not until 1831, when the American Presbyterians and Congregationalists began to arrive, did the Jesuits return. There were other orders including the Lazarists, Capuchins, and Carmalites. The spread of education and the revival of Arabic literature owed much to these two missionary communities, especially the Protestant.

Eli Smith (1801-57) issued a new Arabic translation of the Bible. Daniel Bliss (1823-1916) founded in 1866 the Syrian Protestant College, now the American University of Beirut. This largest overseas American university, together with its Jesuit sister, the St. Joseph University of Beirut (founded in 1875), exerted a decisive influence on the new literature.

Butrus al-Bustani (1819-83), to name only one product of this missionary activity, was a Lebanese of Maronite birth who, thanks to his contact with the American missionaries, achieved great recognition as a man of letters and as an educator. To his credit are a dictionary, several periodicals, an encyclopedia, and a school. From these pioneer beginnings, the leap to politics and national resurrection was natural.

It is a significant fact that the modern daybreak in literature should be marked by a resurgence of medieval studies and that the leading light should be Nasif al-Yaziji (1790-1862), a Lebanese Christian who had been touched by the spiritual enlightenment. Having heard the enchanting voices of medieval Arabic literature, al-Yaziji became its foremost herald among Moslems and Christians alike. From his puristic study of the Arabic classics he drew his unique linguistic erudition. His twelve-year service as secretary to the Amir Bashir, autocrat of Lebanon, won him prestige and self-reliance. His devotees in Beirut were held together by the single-eyed vision of literary revival as the safest way to national emancipation. Intended primarily for use in the schools of the American mission, his books on grammar, logic, rhetoric, and prosody became standard in the teaching of Arabic and made him an apostle of the literary awakening.

More resounding were the efforts of thoughtful Moslems to introduce a theological reformation. Jamal-al-Din al-Afghani (1839-97), and his disciple Mohammed Abdu (1849-1905), broke virgin soil. The former labored for the consolidation of the Moslem peoples. His was a gospel of pan-Islam under the Ottoman Caliphate. The latter achieved renown as the chief modern theologian of Islam. Born near Kabul in Afghanistan, al-Afghani came to Egypt where he set in motion a religious nationalism that paved the road to the Arabi Rebellion leading to British occupation in 1882. The son of an Egyptian peasant family, Abdu fought fearlessly for a modern system of thought which was to replace the archaic dogma of Islamic theology. His treatise *On the Unity of God* won him esteem as a formidable Moslem thinker whose aim was nothing less than the rehabilitation of Islam as a religion.

The challenge of Western ideals and ambitions did not fail to produce a response. Nor did the internal call for literary and religious revival go unheeded. But the transformation which was in the offing did not come about without the agony of conflict and revolt.

REVOLUTION, REFORM, AND DISPERSAL

Throughout the four centuries preceding World War I, Ottoman Turkey dominated the Near East. Constantinople was capital of a vast empire and religious seat of a caliphate that exercised paramount influence in the far-flung world of Islam. Despite waning international prestige, the Ottoman sultan retained wide powers over his subjects and co-religionists during the nineteenth and early twentieth century. On their part the vast majority of Near Eastern peoples, whether inspired by the bond of Islam, awakened by the challenge of freedom, or responding to Western influence, remained generally loyal to the Ottoman suzerain. The witness of their poets, writers, educators, and journalists bears out this verdict. Thus the Lebanese Christian, Farah Antun (1874-1922), founded in 1897 at Alexandria his journal *Ottoman Union* which advocated the need for a political organization of the Near East, even under Ottoman leadership, as an expression of indigenous solidarity and as a bulwark against Western designs.

Even in Egypt, where the ambition of Mohammed Ali and his heirs, particularly Ibrahim (1789-1848), hastened the day of withdrawal from the Ottoman fold, the bond of Islam prescribed loyalty to the Sublime Porte. Well might Egypt pursue the course of revival, but her literature lost little of the Ottoman spirit. The prose and poetry of such littérateurs as Abdullah Fikri (1834-90), Ali al-Laythi (*ca.* 1830-96), and Abdullah al-Nadim (1844-96) were saturated with adulation of the sultan-caliph. As titular head of the world's Moslem community, the Ottoman sovereign was also the object of panegyric outpouring in Syria, Lebanon, Iraq, and Arabia. Praise and eulogy were showered upon his henchmen, generals, and governors as custodians of military power and defenders of the Islamic realm.

Beneath this apparent harmony, however, were the growing pains of a younger Near East, the alarming clashes between an immature generation and their mighty though corrupt and senile elders. Tension was felt on the religious, social, and ideological fronts. There were those who saw no other solution than the use of force and open revolt. Within the Moslem majority, there were divisions separating the fanatical conservatives from the progressive liberals and the secularizing moderates, and there were

diverse racial antipathies, overshadowed by the ancient rift between Christians and Moslems, Arabs and Turks. Among the
educated few, the ideas of the French Revolution were gaining
steadily. Others followed Anglo-American thought: they extolled
the Industrial Revolution and the political theories of Thomas
Jefferson and Benjamin Franklin. Here and there among the intellectuals were echoes of Darwin, Jean Jacques Rousseau, and
Hegel.

These developments had their literary reverberations, notably
with Midhat Pasha (1822-84) during whose governorship in
Syria a vigorous literary movement arose, committed to the promotion of nationalist consciousness and resistance to the high-
handed rule of Constantinople. Fiery odes protesting tyranny
were posted on the doors of mosques and churches, and although
much of the new literary zeal was driven underground or into
exile during the reign of Sultan Abdul-Hamid (1876-1909), evidence of the power of solidarity continued to appear. The attitude of the Arab world at the time of the Boer War (1899-1902)
was crystallized in an ode by Khalil Matran (1872-   )—a creative poet of modern Arabic, Lebanese by birth, Egyptian by adoption—in favor of the South Africans. Even more significant was
the pro-Japanese literature evoked by the Russo-Japanese War
(1904-05), on the grounds that Japan was an Eastern power acting in self-defense against the encroachment of imperialist Russia.

From this confusion arose an all-inclusive nationalism, supported by the adherents of Ottoman citizenship and the defenders of Near Eastern solidarity. As a result, amid bloodshed and
social unrest, the long-awaited reforms in the Imperial adminis-
tration of the Ottoman state were proclaimed in 1908. Ostensibly, at least, this was a victory for the intellectuals and the enlightened statesmen, a victory which was embodied in the new
constitution.

What did this constitution promise? What did it mean? It
promised common citizenship throughout the empire. It meant
that regardless of race, creed, or national origin, all subjects of

the Sultan were to be recognized as free and equal before the law. It was the closest approach, ever visualized, to a common Near Eastern citizenship. It was an answer to the prayers of all who longed for political and civic solidarity in that part of the world.

Such was the promise of the constitution, but the literary works of the time soon began to betray signs of bitter disillusionment with the highly publicized document. Even in Turkey itself, the Young Turks who had been responsible for the recently introduced reforms proved quite as selfish as their corrupt predecessors, and quite as oblivious to the nation's welfare. They listened to the wooing of the Kaiser's Germany and lost little time in ranging themselves on the side of the Central Powers about to be interlocked with the Western Allies in World War I. Typical of these adverse critics was Wali-al-Din Yakan (1873-1921), who spoke for the rank and file of the liberals. Constantinople-born yet thoroughly Egyptianized, Yakan was a brilliant poet, and his verse pulsates with contempt for the Ottoman regime, even though his tender affection for his original Turkish homeland was irrepressible.

The defeat of Ottoman Turkey in World War I shattered all hope for Near Eastern solidarity. Out of the debris of the colossus, however, a new *modus vivendi* was achieved under which the Arab, Turk, Persian, and others learned to fend each for himself. Increasingly, the strategy of relations with the outside world consisted in resort to defense in depth and the tactics of dispersal.

The temper of the times, with its despair and its obstinate struggle for survival, was reproduced by Mustafa Lutfi al-Manfaluti (1876-1924). An Egyptian of Turkish-Arab descent, al-Manfaluti was a graduate of the Azhar school of Islamic theology. In addition to pan-Islamic zeal, nationalism, and Syrian literary influence, his prose wore a mantle of characteristic Egyptian wit and wisdom. His sermonic exhortations, collected under the title of *Speculations,* were a biting criticism of Islamic society as it existed in the Near East. They expressed the confused outlook of his generation. Occasionally, as in his other widely read work, *Tears*, he lapsed to a state of utter pessimism and melancholy not uncommon among his contemporaries.

THE FOURFOLD PATTERN

The loss of central caliphal authority deprived Islamic society in the wake of World War I of its last semblance of organic unity. Instead of a single Islamic world, there came into being a number of communities which in certain cases were as widely scattered as the Moslems of Sinkiang in China and those of the Cameroons in Africa. Arabic and Persian, if only because they are repositories of the most extensive literatures ever produced by Moslems, remained the two primary classical languages. Other areas came into prominence also as centers of intellectual life and literary vitality. Of these, especially Turkey and Pakistan attracted international attention. In the remaining portion of this essay, therefore, we may well consider the chief characteristics of Islamic literature in four key areas: Turkey, Iran, India, and the Arabic-speaking countries.

TURKEY'S REBIRTH

Turkey's reforms, and the Revolution to which they gave rise, stemmed from a principle which may be described as opportunism. Underlying the principle was an ideal which only the dreamer Mustafa Kemal, whom his compatriots later knew as Ataturk (d. 1938), had the power to fulfill. Successive generations of literati had contributed to the formation of the ideal; political reformers and their foes, the counter-reformers, had prepared the way; finally Mustafa Kemal, maker of modern Turkey, released the forces which made the dream come true. The result was a state established within the historic confines of Asia Minor and comprising the irreducible minimum of land which every Turk recognized as his homeland.

For the new state, the year 1922, when the Turks expelled the Greeks from Anatolia, and the year 1908, when the Young Turks wrung a Constitution from crafty Abdul-Hamid, had entirely different connotations. For the new Turks of the Republic, the only significance of the Young Turks was that their great rehearsal foreshadowed the events which took place under the leadership of Kemal. In the opinion of Ahmet Amin, the Young Turks' revolt offered the world an unexpected solution of the Near Eastern question. Therewith Turkey expressed her desire to become entirely Western in government, social life, and technical equipment. The principles of the French Revolution were introduced in the attempt to amalgamate the heterogeneous elements of the empire. The vision of the Young Turks was clear and forthright. But Turkey was not yet ready for release from the bondage of medievalism, reaction, and corruption.

That unfulfilled vision was nonetheless important in molding the nation's thought and forecasting the shape of things to come. The literary seeds of Turkey's modern nationalism were sown by Ziya Gokalp (1876-1924). He was the intellectual father of *devrim*, the stream of rejuvenation including both revolt and reform. No story of modern Turkey would be full, or biography of Ataturk complete, which left out the literary influence of Gokalp. A layman in an age of militarists, he became, nevertheless, his country's leading sociologist and the most penetrating interpreter of Turkism for his own people. Gokalp may well be remembered as the apostle of Turkey's new nationalist consciousness.

Gokalp conceived of Turkism as cultural rather than political. As the Prussians of his day regarded themselves as the élite of Germany, so he believed that the Turks in their own way were destined to triumph. Sometimes he drew this interpretation of Turkish history and culture in exaggerated lines. The de-Persianized and de-Arabized poetry which he turned out soon won him the reputation of a radical. Rejected by the metropolitan press, his writings began to appear in provincial papers. A profoundly religious man and a devout Moslem, he coveted nothing more, however, than the glory of Islam. To that end, he sought the reconciliation of religion with modern thought. His influence is detectable in the Constitution of 1924 wherein an article, since eliminated by amendment, proclaimed Islam the official religion of the Turkish state.

The official translation of the Koran from Arabic, language of revelation, into Turkish corresponded with the spirit of Gokalp. This act fitted into the general pattern which he mapped for his people. The innovation consisted less in the mere fact of translating the Koran into a foreign tongue—devout Moslems had undertaken to do the same thing before—and more in its authorized liturgical use in a language other than Arabic. This step, according to Halide Edib, distinguished authoress and feminist leader of modern Turkey, was in keeping with Gokalp's conviction that the progress, freedom, and democracy of the Western world were by-products of the Protestant Reformation. Neither Turkey nor any other Islamic country, he therefore maintained, could travel the road of progress and attain international stature without the advantage of a thoroughgoing religious reformation.

Other views and insights regarding the nature and destiny of the Turk competed with those of Gokalp. Felix Valye points out that in their political genius and aptitude for military science, the Turks are the most notable Islamic people. They were the first nation in Asia to assimilate Western culture. What he had in mind apparently might have been the military missions and legal advisers which Turkey had already received from Europe long before the opening of Japan by Commodore Matthew Calbraith Perry (1853).

On the literary level, the writings of Gokalp and his school were calculated to deepen Turkey's consciousness of her singular position in the Islamic world. This in a sense was a check on her keen eagerness for reform and revolution. Leadership in the Islamic world, let it be remembered, implied that Turkey must follow the impulse to restore the original teachings of Mohammed.

On the other hand, the more spontaneous demands of nationalism threatened to leap into flame. This in turn tended to neutralize the purely Islamic spirit. In the end, the architects of modern Turkey made their choice. They chose to be men of action, only moderately concerned with matters of ethics and theology. Questions of theory, together with the norms of sociology and religion, were sidetracked.

Less unfavorable was the response to that other thesis propounded by Gokalp and his associates on the subject of women's equality with men. The literary minds of the period supported the legend that the Turks were descendants of a virgin. Gokalp associated himself with those who held that the original thearchy of the Turks included a form of worship wherein women participated. In order to substantiate the antiquity of this parity between the sexes, the ancient edicts of an otherwise forgotten king and queen were unearthed. The subsequent deterioration of woman's position in society was blamed on Persian and Byzantine mores and customs. The man Gokalp did in Turkey what Qasim Amin (1865-1908) had done in Egypt to initiate the feminist movement.

The story of Turkey's rebirth may be closed on the note of the literary productivity which the name of Mustafa Kemal inspired. Varied and multicolored, this output enshrined the complicated strife and remarkable accomplishments of modern Turkey. Its central theme—derived from the name of the founder—was Kemalism. This is the core of modern Turkish life, the soul of the literary renaissance. It is at once a program of action and a way of life. As a program it proclaims itself republican, nationalist, *étatist, laïque,* and reformist. As a way of life it is dedicated to Westernization in the firm conviction that shorn of its medieval heritage Islam can achieve contemporary greatness.

IRAN MAKES A FRESH START

When Riza Shah Pehlevi was summoned by the National Assembly of Iran to take the oath which enabled him in April, 1926, to ascend the Peacock Throne, a new constitutional state, with an ancient and glorious heritage, made a fresh start. Though the Western world only gradually learnt to substitute the name Iran for Persia, the cultural and artistic fame of the country were beyond dispute. If the Arabs are rightly reckoned as the creators of religious thought in the Islamic world, and the Turks as the militarists and lawgivers, then the Iranians are truly the artists and men of letters.

Nor is the splendid accomplishment of Iran limited to the realm of art. Imperial pomp and religious intuition combine to heighten the ancient importance of the land. Three leading dynasties, the Achaemenid, Arsacid, and Sassanid, successively occupied the throne of Iran. Founded by Cyrus (559-29 B.C.), the Achaemenid Empire lasted until the overthrow of Darius III in 330 B.C. by Alexander the Great. Following an interval, came the Parthians who achieved independence in 250 B.C. in their native province of Parthia, and beginning under Arsaces (*ca.* 248 B.C.), founder of their empire, governed Iran until A.D. 226. They were followed by the Sassanids whose dominion collapsed in 641 under the military blows of the Arabs.

The religion of ancient Iran is enshrined in the *Avesta,* a work which, like the *Rig-Veda* of India and the Greek Homeric literature, depicts a naturalistic polytheism. At the head of the pantheon stood Ahura Mazda. Among the chief deities were Mithra, god of light, and the goddess of fertility, Ardvisura Anahita, "the great stream, the unblemished one." Zoroaster, sometime in the seventh or sixth century B.C., preached a new gospel, the general nature of which is manifest in that part of the *Avesta,* the *Gathas* (hymns), which is ascribed to him.

The *Gathas* magnify Ahura Mazda. He stands at the top of a high ethical system illustrated in the life of Zoroaster and his fight against evil. Though this belief found no lasting universality, the voice which the Iranians thus heard was clearer than any other in the natural faiths of antiquity. Alone among the sacred writings of the time, the *Gathas* are comparable to the prophetic literature of ancient Israel. They disclose the living picture of a prophet, his environment, and the opposition that he endured. In all his career, we find Zoroaster ever pressing for a choice, a decision between good and evil. The *Gathas* may be said to define religion as dynamic action against fearful odds in obedience to a high purpose and faith in the living Lord.

With the Islamic conquest (641), the ancient culture of Iran suffered eclipse. Arabic became the language of learning and piety. Until the last half-century, most religious books in Iran continued to be written in Arabic. But the artistic and intellectual genius of Iran did not altogether vanish. The sons of Iran are to be recognized among the foremost makers of medieval Arab civilization. Since they composed their writings in Arabic, they are commonly regarded as Arabs. In poetry, abu-Nuwas (*ca.* 750-*ca.* 810), in philosophy, Avicenna (980-1037), and in theology, al-Ghazzali (1058-1111), and a host of other Iranians, were giants of the spirit and intellect who made possible the rich medieval literature of the Arabs.

In a little more than two centuries, the Persian language itself began to experience revival. Spoken by the adherents of the new Islamic faith and written through the medium of the Arabic alphabet, it was reborn with amazing vitality. Its literature gained momentum in direct proportion to the decline of Arab dominion. This trend dated from the Samanid dynasty (A.D. 874-999), which despite nominal allegiance to the Abbasid caliphs of Baghdad asserted its virtual autonomy. Omar Khayyam (*ca.* 1050-1123)—freethinker, mathematician, and astronomer—symbolized the mystic, life-loving, and agnostic aspects of Persian culture.

The rising literary tide was expressed in poetry. The growth of this department of letters was phenomenal. Among the masters of prosody, six names deserve mention: the greatest writer of poetic romances was Nizami (1140-1203); of Sufi verse, Rumi (1207-73); of love poetry, Sadi (1184-1291); of lyric poetry, Hafiz (1320-89) and Jami (1414-92). The national heroic poem of

Iran, the *Shahnama* (*Book of Kings*), in sixty thousand couplets, was finished by Firdawsi (935-1025) when he was about eighty years of age. A full account of the legendary and historical rulers to the Arab conquest, it is one of the masterpieces of Near Eastern literature. Belonging to the Islamic period of Iranian history, it is nonetheless fervent in its Iranian patriotism. Vigorous and spirited in the movement of battle scenes, the work is embellished with the ornaments of poetry and fable. It breathes the undying spirit of a great people with whom the gifted poet had fully identified himself.

The literary soul of Iran in its ancient and medieval manifestations may be studied, then, in two foremost creations, the *Avesta* and the *Shahnama*. There are a host of other expressions of the Iranian spirit but none as powerful in impact or as noble in structure. The schismatic character of Shiite Islam, of which Iran is the historic sponsor, was in no small part due to this feeling which Iranians had for their distinctive rôle in history.

Despite the turmoil of two world wars, the aspirations of Iran for international recognition remains unchanged. While no direct assault was made on Islam, religion in general was circumscribed, although not to the extent that it was in Turkey. Keeping pace with the national effort toward reform was a revival in the field of letters. Here the effervescence of the twentieth century consisted largely in poetry, the writing of history, and the publication of the classics in new editions. Much as in Egypt and the other Arabic-speaking countries, few novels were written and activity in the field was largely confined to the translating of Western works, mostly French.

Iran's fresh start, which owes much to the ingenuity and initiative of Riza Shah (abdicated on September 16, 1941), followed the Turkish pattern in its intention to purify the language from foreign, especially Arabic, words—about seventy per cent of the known vocabulary. An Iranian academy, called into being in March, 1935, sought to prepare a modern dictionary. Three years later, it put out its first, rather slim, volume. No attempt was made to eradicate all foreign words but the trend in that direction was unmistakable. In popular speech, however, the old forms are likely to remain for a long time to come.

RECONSTITUTION OF INDIAN ISLAM

The emergence of Pakistan as a sovereign state in the summer of 1947 added a new link to the chain of nations constituting the Islamic world. The decision of the British Government to lay down their imperial responsibility in the Indian subcontinent led to the partition of India and to the reconstitution of Indian Islam as a political state, and to the corresponding enlargement of the sphere of political ascendancy exercised by Moslems in the modern world. Apart from the purely political and nationalist activity which preceded the event of Pakistan's birth, a considerable degree of cultural and literary leavening had taken place.

This cultural and literary leavening sharpened the differences between Hindu and Moslem. To the latter, it emphasized that he was the descendant of the Arab, Persian, and Turk conquerors, or the progeny of those native Indians who had accepted the conqueror's faith. It showed that the religious roots of Islam were in the Arabian Peninsula and akin to the Monotheistic faiths of the ancient Near East, whereas Hinduism was born in the land of rivers and forests out of the wedlock of Indo-European and Dravidian life and thought. The fact was, moreover, emphasized that the Hindus worshiped many gods, Moslems only one. While Hinduism observed a rigid caste system, Islam proclaimed the inherent equality and brotherhood of all believers.

The literary works of Indian Moslems stressed, furthermore, the point that Hindu culture stemmed from the Sanscrit classics and Vedic wisdom whereas Islamic culture was mediated through Arabic and Persian, with the unchallenged primacy of Arabic as the language of the Koran. Nor could Moslems any longer forget that the daily speech of their Hindu neighbors was Hindi, whereas the vernacular of Moslems was Urdu, a variant of Hindustani. In contrast to the metaphysical, other-worldly and pessimistic overtones of Hindu society, was the pragmatic, this-worldly, articulate, and theistic faith of the Islamic community.

The first Moslem conquerors of India were led in A.D. 711 by the Umayyad general, Mohammed ibn-Qasim. The Islamization of the country, however, did not mature till after the tenth century when a Turkish warrior, Mohammed of Ghaznah (999-1030) captured Lahore. Various rulers, known collectively as the Sultans of Delhi (1206-1526), laid the foundation of that Islamic authority in India which attained its height under the Mongol Dynasty (1525-1857).

Mohammed ibn-Qasim and his successors attempted the conquest of India from southern Persia and Baluchistan. Their conquests followed the northern land route into the country. Antedating the military phase, however, were Arab traders who, traveling by sea, came into contact with the people of Travancore, a state on the Malabar coast in southern India. It is therefore true that, whereas Islam penetrated India from the north by force of arms, its earliest reported converts were made in the south. This peaceful penetration of the south is evidenced by the conversion to Islam of such important figures as the last of the Cheramon Perumal sovereigns of Malabar, who allegedly left his kingdom on a pilgrimage to Mecca.

The Hindu thinker Shankara (*ca.* A.D. 800), last and greatest of the scholastic commentators, formulated the Vedanta philosophy along highly idealistic lines. His birthplace, Kaldi, belonged to a small principality in the Deccan whose king had accepted Islam. Already a living force in India, Islam presumably left an impression on Shankara. His passionate insistence upon non-duality (*advaita*) and the unity of Brahma reveals a secret source of affinity with the Islamic religious ferment.

In the Vaishnava poetry of Bengal (fourteenth-sixteenth century), the fusion of Hindu and Islamic motifs was apparent. This poetry was produced by the devotees of Vishnu, preserver god who comprised, with Brahma (creator) and Shiva (destroyer), the Hindu mythological triad. In songs and lyrics, this poetry bridged the esthetic gap between the passive Hindu philosophy of illusion and the Islamic affirmations which, though centered in this world, allowed both for empirical and transcendental considerations. On the artistic level at least, the Vaishnava poetry of Bengal was a resolution of the Hindu-Islamic conflict. Love was not merely a physical or mental state. Nor was it a mere expression of *maya* philosophy. The beloved became a lover in keeping with the activated, personalized, and dynamic Islamic emphasis, and the quest of the human soul for satisfaction was given greater rein. As a counter influence, a Vishnuite revivalist who gave a new turn to the Hindu faith, Chaitanya of Bengal (1486-1533), was by no means free from Islamic concepts.

Upon Hindi, the real Hindustani dialect spoken as a kind of lingua franca by some 170 million Indians, the Islamic assault left an indelible mark, notably through the literary activity of such synthesists as Ramananda, Kabir, and Nanak. A Vishnuite of Benares, Ramananda, in the fifteenth century, emphasized that salvation comes through divine grace. Among his greatest disciples was the foremost Hindi poet and preacher, Kabir (1488-1512), whose kindly theism burst forth in poems since incorporated in the sacred scriptures of Sikhism. Nanak (1469-1539), founder of Sikhism, was a second-caste Hindu of the Punjab, who under the influence of Islam preached one god for Hindus and Moslems alike. Although all the Sikh *gurus* used Hindi, Sikhism itself being the greatest contribution to Indian religion and society ever made through the Hindi language, yet Nanak used mainly Punjabi in his *Granth,* sacred text of the Sikhs.

Urdu, the characteristic vernacular of Indian Moslems is, nonetheless, a variant of Hindustani. Written in the Arabic alphabet with certain modifications, it is the most commonly used and understood language of modern India. The first Persian Moslem of India to employ Arabic script in the writing of Hindustani, and thereby to lay the foundation of Urdu literature, was Amir Khusru (1255-1325). Thereafter, a literary development, not unlike the literature of the Turks, Persians, and Arabs, began to appear in Urdu.

With the Indian Mutiny of 1857, modern Urdu literature actually began. Since then it has ceased to be a mere handmaiden of Persian. As the Moslems of India advanced, Urdu, their daily speech, acquired increasing importance. The Aligarh Movement, led by Sir Ahmad Khan (d. 1898), which started a university and a potent cultural stream, combined religious education with modern scientific knowledge. Sir Mohammed Iqbal (d. 1938), attained international fame as a thinker, poet, and writer. His *Reconstruction of Religious Thought in Islam* (1934), first published in Urdu, gave a new importance to this language.

Of the three sectarian developments in modern Islam, Bahaism, Wahhabism, and Ahmadiya, the last was founded by Mirza Ghulam Ahmad. Starting in the Punjabi village of Qadian in 1879, he pressed his personal claims as Mahdi, Messiah, and avatar of Krishna. He united in himself what Islamic theology had ever put asunder. In line with his self-proclamation as the likeness of Jesus, Mirza Ghulam proceeded to expound the doctrine of *jihad,* not as a holy war against non-Moslems but as a striving after righteousness. Subsequent to his passing in 1908, his followers formed two branches of the faith, one at Qadian, the other at Lahore. Taken together, these are regarded as the most aggressive and missionary-minded sect of contemporary Islam. They sponsor an international network of zealots whose literary activity extends far beyond the confines of Asia into the lands of Africa, Europe, and the Americas. As controversialists and apologists these preachers of Islamic renewal seek to impress their message upon the cultured classes and to counteract the application of rationalist and agnostic theories to Islamic doctrine.

THE ARAB WORLD

Arabic literature, through the vicissitudes of two world wars and their aftermath of political, economic, and social storm, registered the emotion, determination, and reasoned faith of a nation struggling to find itself. In Egypt and Lebanon, as well as in Syria and Iraq, new visions captivated the human heart. With all their shortcomings, the theatricals of Ahmad Shawqi (1868-1932) marked a turning point. Of Turkish descent though a second generation Egyptian, Shawqi produced prose which served as a vehicle for a number of theatricals which were the brilliant achievement of a pioneer. He combined the traditional dignity of Arabic expression with the novelty and refinement of French.

The literary spirit was symbolic of the national saga of kindred peoples, all claiming some sort of relation to the main Arab stock, who walked the road leading from bondage to freedom and from conflicting purposes to the final goal of integration. Shawqi's literary career throws the spirit of Arab lands into bold relief. He used meter and rhyme as means to an end. He further perfected the art of dialogue and introduced the use of the vocative and the rhetorical apostrophe. As a prose writer he broke virgin soil in *Princess of Andalusia*. Here he abandoned the archaic pattern of exaggeration, tossed away pretentious verbiage and empty embellishment, taking the direct course of a modern writer.

While Iraq, Syria, Lebanon, Egypt, and Palestine fought the mandatory system and the foreign occupation bequeathed by World War I, their bards and writers rendered an invaluable contribution. They helped awaken a broad world outlook with national and international implications. The ideals of emancipated men, the perplexities of a changing social order, the torch-bearing task of an exploring mind, the longing of the soul in its mystical endeavors, the materialistic goals disguised in the garb of piety and meekness—these, though not yet fully mature objectives were already discernible in the works of writers and poets. At long last, Arabic literature was breaking from its moorings and forging ahead toward the modern world.

The growth of regionalism was evident in this era. The regional literary development owed its inception in modern times to two political and historic events of the latter nineteenth century: 1) in 1860, in Lebanon, civil war between the Druzes and the Maronites disturbed the status quo in Moslem-Christian relations; it led to the secession of Lebanon from the Ottoman Empire under an internationally guaranteed autonomy, and the new national consciousness encouraged Lebanese poets and writers to enshrine the literary productions of the age in new patterns of style; 2) in 1882, the British occupied Egypt; thereafter, Egyptian literature took up the cudgels against foreign domination, giving birth to a national literary technique and temper that in due course swept through the other parts of the Arabic-speaking world.

In the wake of World War I, then, new states covetous of their right to sovereignty, and militant in their opposition to any political organization save that of home rule, came into vogue throughout the Arab East. Having shaken off the yoke which gave Great Britain jurisdiction over her, Iraq in 1932 became a member of the League of Nations. Egypt followed in 1936. Since World War II, these states, together with Saudi Arabia, Syria, Lebanon, and Yemen, have joined the United Nations.

Whereas a literary sectionalism was promoted by these regional attainments of independence, the Arab peoples did not altogether lose their desire for the larger linguistic and cultural community. Since 1914, creative writing proceeded in several ways; while preserving in each instance the local, regional color, it generally, at its best level, reached a widespread, Arab-world audience. Particularly through the novel and the theater, with Egypt dominant in both, a literary monophysitism was engendered. The integrating principle had a host of literary champions. Of these, a chief figure was Yaqub Sarruf (1852-1927). Born in Lebanon and educated at what is now the American University of Beirut, Sarruf settled in Cairo, where in 1876 he founded his scientific-literary journal, *al-Muktataf* (Cullings). His writings proved the adequacy of Arabic for the translation of modern scientific ideas. His lucid yet pure and sturdy prose, an elegant vehicle of literary concepts, cut across regional and sectarian frontiers.

Regionalism and federation, these are the two socio-political motifs which inspired much of Arabic literature about the middle of the twentieth century. On March 22, 1945, the League of Arab states—Egypt, Iraq, Lebanon, Saudi Arabia, Syria, Transjordan, and Yemen—signed a pact. This brought to fulfillment the endeavors of those Arab patriots and leaders who had created the Arab League in October, 1944. With due regard to the internal structure of each state, the pact in Article Two set forth its purpose to promote coöperation among the several member states in their economic, social, political, and cultural programs. Under the Arab League, Moslem Arabs demonstrated their ability to create, together with their Christian countrymen, a secular, political front.

A new political philosophy was born, ready to accept both the establishment of sovereign Arab states and the jurisdiction of the League. Charles Malik (1906-   ), Lebanese philosopher and diplomat, enunciated in his *Addresses* (1946) faith in a Lebanon that was free and independent yet fully in communion with the Arab League. Costi Zurayk (1908-   ), like Malik on the faculty of the American University of Beirut and one-time envoy of Syria in Washington, D. C., offered in *National Consciousness* (1940) a critique of the Arab heritage in terms of its meaning and validity for all Arabs regardless of lesser regional loyalties and difference in racial and religious background.

Nor did such liberal concepts stop even at the door of Cairo's Azhar Mosque, Islam's Oxford and the world's oldest university, whose delegate led the procession at Harvard's tercentenary in 1938. Mohammed al-Maraghi, rector of al-Azhar, introduced in the summer of 1929 reforms aimed at the rationalization of the Mohammedan faith and the liberalization of Islamic law, custom, and theology. These moves evoked a heated debate in the Arabic press and drew the fire of Islamic fundamentalists throughout the world. Although meager and inadequate, these reforms were a remarkable event in contemporary Islamic thought, surpassing in their long-range importance the much-heralded Kemalist religious innovations. The introduction of modern sciences, languages, and skills, contemplated in the Maraghi reforms, promised to emancipate Islamic theology from the shackles of medievalism. Interpretation of the Koran was thus encouraged without violence to reason and tested knowledge. To the extent that these reforms were a product of Islamic realism, they assumed importance as a fountainhead of Arab revival and literary strength.

BIBLIOGRAPHY

GENERAL BACKGROUND

ADAMS, Charles C., *Islam and Modernism in Egypt* (London, 1933).
Valuable analysis.
CHEW, Samuel C., *The Crescent and the Rose* (New York, 1937).
Treats relations of Islam and England during the Renaissance.
DUNBAR, George, *A History of India*, 2nd ed. (London, 1943), 2 vols.
HOUTSMA, M. Th., *et al.*, ed., *Encyclopedia of Islam* (London, 1913-34; Supplement, 1938).
Indispensable reference on Islamic culture and civilization.
VON GRUNEBAUM, Gustave E., *Medieval Islam* (Chicago, 1946).

LITERARY HISTORY AND CRITICISM

BROCKELMANN, Carl, *Geschichte der Arabischen Litteratur* (Berlin, 1898-1902; Supplement, Leyden, 1937-1942).
Arab authors and works generally.
BROWNE, E. G., *A Literary History of Persia* (New York, 1902-24), 4 vols.
A standard English work.
———, *The Press and Poetry of Modern Persia* (London, 1914).
GIBB, H. A. R., *Modern Trends in Islam* (Chicago, 1947).
The spirit of Islamic literature generally.
———, "Studies in Contemporary Arabic Literature," School of Oriental Studies, Bulletins 2-7 (London, 1928-1935).
A first-hand account.
GIBB, E. G. W., *A History of Ottoman Poetry* (London, 1900-1909), 6 vols.
Period preceding Kemalist Turkey.
HUART, Clement Imbault, *Littérature Arabe* (Paris, 1902), English trans-

lation by Mary Loyd, *A History of Arabic Literature* (New York, 1903).
Uncritical in parts and somewhat dated.

ISHAQUE, M., *Modern Persian Poetry* (Calcutta, 1943).

KAMPFFMEYER, George, ed., *Die Welt des Islam,* vol. V-XVI, (Berlin, 1918-1932); Kampffmeyer and Jaschke, eds., vols. XVII-XXII (Berlin, 1935-1940).
Gives valuable biographical materials.

MEZ, Adam, *The Renaissance of Islam* (London, 1937).
An analysis.

NICHOLSON, R. A., *A Literary History of the Arabs* (London, 1930).
Standard in the field.

RAMSAY, Allan, and ADLER, Cyrus, *Told in the Coffee House* (New York, 1898).
On Turkish literature.

SHAIKH, Chand Husain, "Urdu Literature," *Encyclopedia of Literature,* Joseph T. Shipley, ed. (New York, 1946), pp. 567-71.
Literature of Pakistan.

SMITH, Byron, *Islam in English Literature* (Beirut, 1939).
Develops little-known phases of the subject.

STOREY, C. A., *Persian Literature: A Bio-Bibliographical Survey* (London, 1927-36), 2 vols.
Literature of Iran.

WILSON, Epiphanius, ed., *World's Greatest Classics, Turkish Literature* (New York, 1901).

STUDIES OF CULTURAL AND POLITICAL SIGNIFICANCE

AMBEDKAR, Bhimrao, Ramji, *Pakistan: The Partition of India* (Bombay, 1946).

ANTONIUS, George, *The Arab Awakening* (Philadelphia, 1939).
In a nationalist but sober vein.

DURRANI, F. K. K., *The Meaning of Pakistan* (Lahore, 1946).

EDIB, Halide, *Turkey Faces West* (New Haven, 1930).

ELLWELL-SUTTON, L. P., *Modern Iran* (London, 1941).
A contemporary report.

HITTI, Philip K., *History of the Arabs,* 4th ed. (London, 1948).
Political and cultural significance of the Arab empires.

KABIR, Humayun, "Influence of Islamic Culture on Indian Life," American Academy of Political and Social Science Annals, vol. CCXXXIII (1944), pp. 22-29.

MARTINOVITCH, Nicholas N., *The Turkish Theater* (New York, 1933).
Background materials.

TOYNBEE, Arnold J., *Turkey: A Past and A Future* (New York, 1917).

WEBSTER, Donald Everet, *The Turkey of Ataturk* (Philadelphia, 1939).
Turkey's rebirth down to the eve of World War II.

5

Hebrew Literature:

An Evaluation

EISIG SILBERSCHLAG
HEBREW TEACHERS COLLEGE

DR. EISIG SILBERSCHLAG, *Dean of the Hebrew Teachers College, Roxbury, Massachusetts, is peculiarly qualified to relate Hebrew literature to other literatures of the world. He was professor of Hebrew literature before he became dean, and a contributor to learned and literary periodicals. His doctoral dissertation at the University of Vienna concerned English-Russian relations during the period of Catherine II, and was written in German. He is a translator of Aristophanes from Greek into Hebrew, and has been editor of* Poet Lore *(1939), and of* Hatekufah. *He is a poet in his own right, and the author of* Revolt and Revival in Poetry *(1938), written in Hebrew. As a matter of course he has traveled extensively in Europe and the Orient.*

Hebrew Literature: An Evaluation

BORN in the mists of tribal history more than three thousand years ago, Hebrew literature belongs to the oldest living literatures of the world. As an uninterrupted and—in the domain of lyrical poetry, legal utterance, and prophetic harangue—unexcelled record of achievement, it wanders with its people to the four corners of the globe, influences alien peoples and is, in turn, influenced by them. This multiplicity of spiritual and intellectual interests is balanced by a unity of ideas which stems from the twin foundations of Hebrew literature, the Bible and the Talmud, and never ceases to exercise its directive force. Even the progressive deterioration of the traditional form of Jewish life from the close of the eighteenth century onward has not been wholly able to impair the traditional content of Jewish thought—ethical monotheism, which, translated into modern terms, means conduct commensurate with the dignity of a human being and responsibility to a transcendent, higher-than-human Being.

The Bible and the Talmud

Centuries of biased criticism impressed the deep cleavage between the Bible and the Talmud on civilized humanity. While the former earned hyperboles of commendation, the latter received superlatives of condemnation; while the former came to be regarded as the noblest monument of ancient literature, which culminated in the New Testament and in a new religion, the latter was viewed as an exemplar of petrified legalism, which led to the decadence of the Jewish people and its religion. Yet the Bible and the Talmud exhibit striking similarities: they are, first of all, not books but literatures. The Bible (from the Greek *biblion*, diminutive of *biblos*, book) is a collection of thirty-nine books which are chiefly dedicated to the ancient history of the Jews, to their laws and to their social aspirations. At the same time individual books are not merely histories, legal codes or lyrical anthologies; they are often histories *and* codes *and* poetic collections. Similarly the Talmud (from the Hebrew *lamad*, learn, study) is a collection of numerous treatises which are chiefly dedicated to the laws and legends of the Jews. But the individual treatises are not merely codes or collections of legends. They are often legal polylogues *and* collections of legends teeming with sundry bits of extraneous knowledge.

The same alleged formlessness dominates the Bible and the Talmud. But it is formlessness necessitated by the passionate expression of deeply felt insights. While the Hellenic love of form degenerated into effete estheticism, the Hebraic love of justice, with the progressive loss of its initial impetus, led to the endless minutiae of talmudic law. And then, this alleged formlessness may be an invention of Western criticism. Though patristic references to hexameters and pentameters in the Bible were later followed by scholarly treatises which insisted and still insist on laborious quests for non-existent meters, no demonstrable similarity to Greek prosody could be discovered either in prophetic or in psalmodic literature. Nevertheless there is form in the predominantly poetic books of the Bible—simple form with endless variations, first noticed by medieval Jewish commentators of the Bible, thoroughly investigated in the eighteenth century by Robert Lowth and happily named by him *parallelismus membrorum*. It is a peculiarly Eastern form of poetry. Cherished by the Canaanite peoples and perfected by the Hebrews, it relies on symmetry of "members," syntactic units of verse rather than on symmetry of feet.

> What is man, that Thou art mindful of him?
> And the son of man, that Thou thinkest of him?

The parallelism of thought, still discernible in translation, is matched by the parallelism of the four Hebrew words in each line. And perfect symmetry of form and content is, no doubt, the cherished ideal of ancient Hebrew poets. Not only do the psalmists, the prophets, the authors of Proverbs and Job, Song of Songs, Lamentations and Ecclesiastes use parallelisms but even the prose portions of the Old Testament often approximate a parallelistic lilt.

To the Western reader the Talmud represents a hodge-podge of legal casuistries, nonsensical and penetrating observations, graceful and innocuous legends. Yet it, too, has its form: precise terminology and strict logic—though not patterned after Aristotle. Finally the Bible and the Talmud share this characteristic: both are literatures fashioned roughly over a period of a thousand years by numerous, mostly anonymous authors. While the former, coinciding with the growth of its people, is essentially poetic, the latter, paralleling the mature age of its people, is predominantly prosaic. Jewish tradition never lost sight of the unity of the Bible and the Talmud. Both were Torah, Teaching or Law. The Bible was Written Torah, the Talmud Oral Torah. In the wider sense of the word, the latter was regarded as an extensive commentary on the former. And though it was finally committed to writing, it retained its discoursive characteristic. Discussion was its hallmark, dogma its horror.

Up to the eighteenth century, which marks the end of the Jewish Middle Ages and the end of religious hegemony in Jewish life, Torah and the acquisition of its legal and non-legal wisdom was the paramount interest of the people. Originally a term applied to the Pentateuch, it gradually embraced all genres of religious literature and molded an entire people in its image. The dichotomy of religious and secular life which was to plague modern nations and modern literatures did not disturb the intellectual placidity of the Jewish Middle Ages. Life was religious in its trivial and majestic aspects. Even occasional outbursts of heresy were motivated by religious zeal and by dedication to religious literature.

This mass absorption in the Torah is a unique phenomenon

in the cultural history of the world and it can only be explained as a substitution on a gigantic scale: political activity was transmuted into educational and cultural activity. Even at the end of the nineteenth century a talented young author, Mordecai Zev Feierberg, was able to write: "Three thousand years ago God committed his Torah to us and made us soldiers. We are the army of godliness and saintliness in the world. . . . These are the words of the covenant and the oath which we swore to our commander: 'Thou hast avouched the Lord to be thy God . . . and the Lord hath avouched thee to be His own treasure.'" The well-known adage "Israel and the Torah and the Holy One Blessed Be He are one" was no mere phrase: It was a reality. This identification of Israel and the Torah led to a degree of literacy which had no parallel either in ancient or in medieval times. At the time when Theodoric the Ostrogoth forbade elementary education because "those who were made to fear the rod of the schoolmaster would never have the courage to face swords and lances with bravery," almost all Jews knew how to read and write, and many knew sections of the Bible and the Talmud either by heart or almost by heart. The ancient biblical precept, "This book of the law shall not depart out of thy mouth, but thou shalt meditate therein day and night," and the rabbinic precept to read the prescribed weekly portion of the Pentateuch twice in the original and once in the Aramaic translation of Aquilas created a people with firm cultural ties, with an overdeveloped memory and with subtle brain power. Yet their intellectual prowess was to become another weapon in the arsenal of anti-semitism.

Segregated as they were for centuries from their Christian and, to a lesser extent, Moslem neighbors by ghetto walls, the Jews erected their own cultural walls. They led their anomalous existence till these double fortifications were shattered by the impact of emancipation. The new adjustments which were made and the new values which were created are part and parcel of modern Hebrew literature. But that transformation began with an enthusiastic endorsement of the style and the content of the Bible.

THE BIBLICAL PERIOD

Mountains of hypotheses surround the Bible. Some of them are based on textual emendations, some on archaeological discoveries, some on the ingenuities of a priori or a posteriori reasoning, some on a combination of several or all methods of approach. The first recorded conjectures on the biblical texts in the first translation of the Bible in any language, the Greek Septuagint version of the third century B.C., were followed by interpretations of Jewish, Christian, and Moslem scholars. Unfortunately the immense labors of Jewish exegetes from pre-Talmudic times to the twentieth century have not been sufficiently utilized by non-Jewish biblical scholars. Had they been properly studied, they would have contributed to a finer and fuller understanding of the biblical text, for they were composed by men who were taught the Hebrew language since early childhood and who were steeped in the subtleties of oral interpretation.

Before the great archaeological discoveries at Ras Shamra[1] and Lachish[2] in the last two decades it was fashionable to emphasize the derivative character of the Bible. The narratives of Sumer and Akkad, the myths of Egypt and Assyria, the laws of the Babylonians and the Hittites, were eagerly studied and plagiarisms in the Bible eagerly noted. As the new texts accumulated, as old texts were interpreted with greater precision, as the artistic remains of the Jews and their neighbors were uncovered, it became clear that, though the ancient Hebrews were attracted to the cultures of their eastern neighbors, they created a cultural realm of their own, superior to that of their neighbors. When the

[1] Hundreds of clay tablets and clay fragments from the fourteenth century B.C. were excavated by C. F. A. Schaeffer at Ugarit (Ras Shamra in Northern Syria) between 1929 and 1939. They have preserved fragmentary liturgies and rituals as well as portions of mythological epics in cuneiform alphabet and in a Canaanite dialect.

[2] Letters dating from 589 B.C. were discovered between 1935 and 1938 in the town of Lachish, a few miles north of Jerusalem. They furnish invaluable philological and historical data for the final years of the Kingdom of Judah.

political independence of Judah was destroyed by the Chaldeans in 586 B.C., the literary and plastic arts of that tiny kingdom attained the level which even Greece had not reached at the time, and its highly developed music was in demand from Egypt to Babylonia. Perhaps the greatness of the achievement of ancient Israel is to be sought in its felicitous absorption of neighboring cultures. The Sumerian paradise myth of Enki and Ninhursag antedates the biblical story of paradise, and the Code of Hammurabi is older than the Mosaic code. The Egyptian proverbs of Amenemope resemble the biblical Proverbs, and the love songs of the Chester Beatty papyri parallel the Song of Songs. But the biblical story of Paradise, with its psychological and philosophical overtones, is a masterpiece of simplicity and grandeur; the Mosaic code is superior in ethical content to its Babylonian prototype. As for the book of Proverbs, it is a model of home-spun wisdom. And the Song of Songs is a record of young passion—a hybrid of voluptuousness and chastity—which has drawn perennial admiration from countless generations. In the dawn of their nationhood, perhaps in the fourteenth century B.C., the Jews outdistanced their Canaanite neighbors. It was then that they commenced to transmute myth into history, polytheism into monotheism, licentiousness into ethics.

Unlike the Semitic narratives of Ras Shamra and the Greek epics, the *Iliad* and the *Odyssey,* the Hebrew account of a nation, from freedom through slavery to liberation and conquest, as recorded in the Hexateuch (the Pentateuch and Joshua), and continued in Judges, Samuel, Kings and Chronicles, is history. The literary and artistic skill of the Greek writers may have been greater than that of their Hebrew colleagues. But the Greek theme was inferior to the Hebrew theme. The wrath of Achilles and the wanderings of the wily Odysseus, aided and abetted by spiteful deities, dwindle in importance when they are juxtaposed with the noble design of an omniscient and omnipotent God who inspires a small people with a passion for justice. The climax of the *Iliad* and the *Odyssey*—the sack of Troy and the slaughter of the suitors of Penelope—is overshadowed by the culmination of the biblical narrative in the theophany of Sinai and the revelation of the Ten Commandments, which were to serve as a basis of righteous living to Jews and Gentiles and, which, with the concept of a day of rest for freeman and slave and animal, were to initiate a new era in the social and economic development of mankind.

That theophany was to be of transcendent value to the Jewish people and to its literature. The prophetic books of the Bible— the most original contributions of the Jews to world literature— are merely elaborations of and variations on the Sinaitic theme. And even the historical books are suffused with its spirit. It is no accident that the Bible begins with history—Genesis—and ends with history—Chronicles. For Judaism is a historical religion: Jewish rites and festivals, rituals and ceremonies, laws and customs, ideas and ideals, whatever their origin, have received historic interpretations. Thus, to quote one example out of many, the Sabbath, originally a Babylonian nature festival paralleling the four quarters of the lunar month, came to be known as the day of rest of the Almighty after the six days of creation—a symbol of the beginning of history and an example to be imitated by man.

But ancient Hebrew historiography is not the documentary and scientific historiography of our times. It is a union of legend and fact, imagination and naive speculation. What happens has been decreed by a superior power. Yet fatalism is not the hallmark of the biblical historians. If acts are divinely ordained, they are also freely chosen. This paradox, implicit in the Bible and classically explicit in the apophthegm "All is foreseen, but freedom of choice is given" (Pirke Abot[3]), was to harass Jewish philosophers in the Middle Ages. And religious thinkers, whatever their creed, still wrestle with the unconquerable paradox.

The greater part of the Bible, then, from Genesis to Kings, and

---

[3] Commonly called *Sayings of the Fathers*, 3:16 (trans. by Danby), 3:19 (trans. by Herford).

sections of the Hagiographa is history. If an entire book of the Torah, Leviticus, and sections of Exodus, Numeri, and Deuteronomy deal with laws, these, too, are a part of history. Differentiation between literary genres belongs to later ages. In ancient literatures all genres are one. The historical narrative of the Bible, interrupted by the legal narrative, is resumed with a sudden discontinuity which characterizes the modern literary techniques of a Joyce or a Stein or an Eliot. Editorial changes and emendations may have corrupted the original text of the Bible. Yet it was not written to conform to the theories of Wellhausen on the multiple sources of Hebrew literature but rather to express the ancient awe and wonder of mankind. That is why the same formula "and God said" serves as a legal preamble and an historical introduction. And the same terseness of style characterizes the legal and historical portions of the Bible. The former have been a living influence in Anglo-Saxon law, in Puritan England and America. The latter have won the admiration of the greatest literary masters of modern times, Goethe, Tolstoy, and Thomas Mann.

While history is written in rhythmic prose, prophecy is expressed in the parallelistic form of poetry. It is this latter genre which distinguishes ancient Hebrew literature from other literatures. The Greeks had their *mantis,* their soothsayer, but only the Hebrews had their *nabi,* "one who is called" and transformed in an unaccountable way by visionary tensions. Already Philo noted that "No pronouncement of a prophet is ever his own; he is an interpreter prompted by Another in all his utterances, when not knowing what he does he is filled with inspiration, as the reason withdraws and surrenders the citadel of the soul to a new visitor and tenant, the Divine Spirit . . ." The prophet is a poet, a social reformer, and a statesman, but like genius, he eludes definition. When he appears on the scene of history, the political independence of his people is seriously threatened. Under the shadow of national doom he produces poetry which reflects the tragic present and foreshadows an ideal future. He is the eternal faultfinder, but he is also the architect of a society founded on uncompromising justice. In the intensity of his message there is no room for elegance or triteness of expression. Lyric brevity invests his passionate utterances with inexpressible dignity and power.

Prophecy—a remarkable phenomenon in world history—lasted more than three hundred years, from the middle of the ninth to the end of the sixth century. From its first appearance in Amos, who addresses himself to Aram and Phoenicia, Edom and Ammon, it transcends the boundaries of a single state and takes a bold leap into universalism. If the Jew is chastised more than his neighbor, it is because he is assumed to possess the superior knowledge of right and wrong and the superior duties toward his fellow men:

> You only have I known of all the families of the earth;
> Therefore I will visit upon you all your iniquities. (3:2)

Already this ancestral prophet, with his passion for justice, created a distich, unforgettable in its simple majesty:

> Let justice well up as waters,
> And righteousness as a mighty stream. (5:24)

The future generations of prophets seized upon this idea of justice as the uniting bond and basis of humanity. What they added to his message was an idyllic counterbalance of a future golden age to his sombre evaluation of the present.

The master visionary of the utopian world state was Isaiah. In classic lines which have not lost an iota of their freshness since they were first pronounced more than two thousand six hundred years ago, he evoked a future of peace and love and tender compassion:

> And they shall beat their swords into plowshares,
> And their spears into pruning hooks;
> Nation shall not lift up sword against nation,
> Neither shall they learn war any more . . .
> And the wolf shall dwell with the lamb,
> And the leopard shall lie down with the kid;
> And the calf and the young lion and the fatling together;
> And a little child shall lead them. (2:4; 11:6)

Other prophets elaborated upon this theme, none excelled him.

The striking impact of Hebrew prophecy is felt in its intensity of expression backed by intensity of experience. If conflict is conducive to tension, then a partial explanation of the prophetic phenomenon is to be sought in the perpetual assault of the prophets on surrounding cultures and on their ominous attraction to the Jews. The debilitating influence of Canaanite lewdness and levity they opposed with their vigorous ethos and earnestness. They were anti-Canaanite, anti-Assyrian, anti-Chaldean, just as their lesser successors, the scribes and the sages, became anti-Hellenic and anti-Roman. If they advanced the maligned ideal of a chosen people, they did not endow it with the attributes of national pride and ruthlessness which characterized a similar ideal of the Greeks and later European nations. Superiority was not a path leading to subjection and enslavement but to service. The *Ebed Adonai,* the Servant of God, whether he be an individual or a symbol of a nation, serves by his superior ethos. It took a later prophet, Deutero-Isaiah to create that ideal. But it was implicit in earlier prophets. The suffering genius of Jeremiah might have served as a prototype.

The three hundred years of Hebrew prophecy have an amazing thematic unity: a passionate summons to Israel to serve by example and precept as a precursor of a society based on peace and justice and kindness. What the prophets lacked by the very virtue of their passionate temperaments, was philosophic reflection and speculation. Since they influenced every genre of Hebrew literature, this deficiency became apparent in the entire Bible. Job and Ecclesiastes fall below the systematic philosophies of Plato, not to speak of Aristotle. But the dramatic tension of the former and the intellectual tension of the latter are rarely matched even in Greek philosophic literature of the fifth and fourth century. And mankind adopted Job as its symbol of incomprehensible suffering and Ecclesiastes as the epitome of vanity of all human endeavor.

Both Job and Ecclesiastes belong to the last part of the Bible, the miscellaneous Hagiographa where some of the finest poetry of world literature is to be found: the hundred and fifty hallowed poems known as the Psalms, the love poems known as the Song of Songs, the Lamentations. They are the final and incontroverti-ble demonstration of Israel's lyric depth and ardor.

The Bible is the fortune and misfortune of Hebrew literature. It is its fortune because it set a high standard of excellence to future generations. It is its misfortune because it robbed these generations of literary initiative and did not permit any devia-tion from or abrogation of its hallowed precepts. Hence the more or less derivative character of Hebrew literature from the post-biblical era down to the present time. The qualities of the parent reappear in the offspring to a disconcerting degree. Bold depar-tures from the biblical text are neither approved nor desired. The commentary on the Bible in its literary, allegorical, homiletical, and mystic form became the beloved vehicle of composition for centuries and centuries to come.

But the salutary influence of the Bible on other literatures is a fact too well known to need elaboration or substantiation. In the Latin translation, the so-called Vulgate version, the Bible be-came the most potent source of the Christian Middle Ages. Eccle-siology and theology, vernacular tales and folk-songs (*cantilenae vulgares*), recited by minstrels and bards and jongleurs, the en-tire fabric of life and thought was colored by the Vulgate. In the English version the Bible molded the English language and pene-trated English life as no other book has done. In the German version of Martin Luther it fathered modern German literature and in the many obscure dialects which held its contents in trans-lation, it became the civilizing agent par excellence.

The intelligent layman still considers the Bible as almost the sole literary representative of the Jews. Beyond the Bible he is apt to think of a vague period of many centuries where a sin-gle figure of importance, Moses Maimonides, via quotations by Thomas Aquinas, stands out in his memory. And beyond Mai-monides he sees an absolute literary vacuum. There is a twofold reason for this ignorance: the separatist existence of the Jews and the paucity of good translations from Hebrew classics. The ignorance persists in spite of the upsurge and popularity of Zionism, which is to a large extent the product of Hebrew literature—the liturgy and the laws and the philosophic discourses which emphasized the ultimate return to Zion and the reinstatement of Hebrew as the national language of the Jews.

THE POST-BIBLICAL PERIOD

The immediate post-biblical period is merely an extension of the biblical period. In spite of the sharp inner cleavages, engendred first by the Hellenic and later by the Latin civilization between 300 B.C. and A.D. 200, Hebrew literature withstood the glitter of foreign blandishments. The rush of Greek and Latin words and phrases into the vernacular Aramaic—a close kin of Hebrew—which was spoken by the Jews of that time, and the affectation of Western mannerisms by the upper strata of Jewish society did not change the character and direction of Jewish literature. On the contrary: a certain conservatism seems to be prevalent in the initial post-biblical era.

Many apocryphal and apocalyptic books patterned themselves after biblical prototypes. Ecclesiasticus reads like a new and enlarged edition of Proverbs, the Psalms of Solomon bear close resemblance to Psalms, and First Maccabees is composed in the classic style of Kings. Yet the apocryphal and apocalyptical books brook no comparison with the Bible. They belong to a literature of epigones, they are the feeble imitations of robust exemplars. Where the Bible is simple and direct, they are tortuous and allegorical and obscure. The path to their understanding is blocked by a jungle of visions.

In this period powerful Jewish centers developed outside Palestine, notably in Alexandria where the Jews advanced the institutions and ideals and ways of life which, with various adaptations, were to follow them into all the lands of their dispersion. The most obvious problem then and in later times was to find a mean between the environmental and the traditional culture. Such a mean was sought in Alexandria by Philo, in Babylonia by Saadia, in Germany by Mendelssöhn. But assimilation and conversion were ever-present realities of the diaspora. In Alexandria the Jews spoke and wrote and even prayed in Greek. And there, for the first time in their history, they entered a new field of intellectual endeavor, philosophy. The epoch-making researches of Professor Harry Austryn Wolfson revealed that Philo, who was regarded as an eclectic at best, created a philosophy which dominated the Jewish, Christian, and Moslem philosophies for seventeen centuries. Its newness consisted in a radical departure from pagan philosophy, in a belief in the superiority of revelation as contained in Scripture to the superiority of reason as contained in philosophic literature. That was Philo's gift to posterity. For his own time he resolved the sharp conflict between Judaism and Hellenism which, originally a conflict of religions and cultures, was still a hotly debated problem of philosophical criticism in the days of Matthew Arnold.

The contribution of Philo to the Hellenistic literature of the Jews was preceded and made possible by three centuries of Jewish thinking and writing in Greek. The Greek translation of the Bible, the so-called Septuagint, is the very cornerstone of that literature. Though its origins are lost in a mist of legends, its text was so highly esteemed that the translators were regarded by Philo himself as "possessed and under inspiration" and an annual festival was held on the island of Pharos off Alexandria "to pay reverence to the spot on which the translation first shed its light." While it benefited Jews who no longer understood the original, it also served to impress the Gentiles. Thus the Septuagint may be regarded as a work of apologetics, perhaps the first and noblest work of Jewish apologetics. This branch of literature, which flourishes to this very day, is in its lowest form propaganda, in its highest form, as in the Cuzari of Judah Halevi, the expression of the innermost spirit of a nation.

Perhaps it is no exaggeration to say that an apologetic note characterizes all Jewish writings in languages not their own. It is certainly true of Jewish literature in the Greek language from the Septuagint to Philo and to Josephus Flavius whose voluminous histories of the Jews are implicitly apologetic, while his *Contra Apionem*, a diatribe against an Egyptian Jew-baiter, is an explicit defense of his people.

The most powerful branch of Hebrew literature in the first centuries of the Christian era, Halakah (from the Hebrew *halak*, go, a principle to follow, a rule to go by), grew in the various centers of Jewish learning: first in Jerusalem; and, after its fall in A.D. 70, in Jamnia; then in the cities of Galilee; and finally, from the third century on, in numerous academies of Babylonia. When Justinian closed the schools of Athens in A.D. 529 and extinguished the light of Greek speculation, the Hebrew academies were to flourish for centuries to come. In them masses of oral traditions, customs, folklore, as well as new interpretations of the old laws were ordered, systematized, discussed, and finally collected in the Palestinian and Babylonian Talmud. The latter work, with its six large Orders and subdivisions into sixty-three tractates, was subjected to intense study and played a normative rôle in the lives of the Jews to the end of the eighteenth century. It was an encyclopedia of unwieldy dimensions, which in sheer bulk was a frightening monument of human intelligence and diligence. And it was the great hoard of national heritage.

For the sake of convenience the Talmud is designated as a collection of law and legend. But just as the Hebrew term *Halakah* is more than law so the Hebrew *Haggadah* (from *higgid*, tell) is more than legend. Professor Louis Ginzberg, the authoritative compiler of "The Legends of the Jews," justly remarks that it can be explained by a circumlocution, but cannot be translated. For it embraces folklore, theology, ethics, history, poetry, science, almost any extra-legal or non-legal material. And it is the peculiar creation of the common people and the refined imagination of the sages. Like Halakah, it uses the biblical verse as a point of departure. And like Halakah, it is essentially an investigative and, at times, farfetched interpretation of a biblical text. But unlike Halakah, it ranges over the human and superhuman realm with evocative boldness. Whether it uses the form of fable or parable, epigram or apophthegm, homily or diatribe, it retains a didactic character: it imparts instruction with subtlety and without apparent effort. That it is a cherished brand of Hebrew literature is attested by the numerous extra-talmudic collections of haggadic material which were edited in Palestine and elsewhere until the very end of the Middle Ages. The medieval commentators of the Bible, the early mystics, even the church fathers preserved Jewish legends which, for some reason or another, failed to appear in the Talmud. In them the heroes of the Bible reached the stature which the heroes of Greek mythology attained in the world of Homer, Hesiod, and the great tragic authors of Greece. For the Haggadah transformed the historical and semi-historical personalities of the Bible into prototypes of justice and mercy. And it interpreted the fate of Israel as a revelation of divine grace and grandeur.

Even when the Talmud reached its final version, the Babylonian academies were busily engaged in its preservation. Scholars committed entire tractates to memory and gave their legal acumen staggering opportunities of achievement. By constant reference to its laws and legends and even its *obiter dicta*, they succeeded in investing the Talmud with a sanctity that once was the exclusive prerogative of the Bible and in imposing their authority on both the oriental and the incipient occidental centers of Jewry. To the eager questions of near and distant communities, less learned in matters of Jewish observance, they sent their responsa, and thus inaugurated a new branch of literature which is invaluable for its historic material and which still fulfills a function of importance in the religious life of the Jews.

But Law and Legend, Halakah and Haggadah, remained the classical manifestations of Judaism. While the former led to the intellectual love of God, to borrow a phrase from Spinoza, the latter was conducive to the knowledge of God through experience, to use a phrase of Thomas Aquinas. Both sought to guide humanity beyond the realm of humanity and into the sphere of the divine.

THE MIDDLE AGES

When, after its glamorous conquests in the seventh and eighth centuries, Islam became the foremost world power, the Jews were forced to adopt new techniques for survival. Not only did they assist the Arabs in reaching a high level in science and literature, and in ushering in an Eastern Renaissance in the early middle ages, but they patterned their own intellectual movements after Arab models. Jewish heterodoxy, which preached revolt against the tyranny of talmudic law and a return to the literal interpretation of the Bible, was paralleled by an insistence of Moslem sectarians on a literal interpretation of the Koran. Since it needed clever attorneys for the defense, it engendered a vast literature of theological import. In the welter of religious conflicts medieval Moslem, Jewish, and Christian philosophy received a vigorous impetus. Insistence on the literal interpretation of the Bible led to its renewed study and gave birth to the new disciplines of Hebrew grammar and lexicography. Most important of all, Arab love for poetic composition spurred the Jews to renewed poetic output. But by the eleventh century, the oriental period of Jewish history was drawing to an end. The second great period, the occidental, which was to continue to the twentieth century, was slowly evolving in Spain, Italy, France, and Germany. This shift to Europe entailed again adaptation to foreign cultures and, incidentally, created an almost insurmountable difficulty for the literary historian of Hebrew literature. For over and above his equipment in Hebrew and Aramaic and a few other ancient languages, he had to master the languages, histories, and mores of many European countries.

During that period the greatest cultural advances were made in the realm of poetry, philosophy, science, and law. They partly coincided with the Arabic advances in these fields and partly developed toward the end of the Middle Ages when Arab sources of creative activity were almost dried up.

Biblical poetry had known only one form—parallelism. Under the impact of Arabic literature latent and new poetic devices came to the fore: rhyme and a cumbersome metric which were to shackle Hebrew poetry throughout the Middle Ages except in countries like France and Germany where Arabic influence was either insignificant or non-existent, and in Italy where, under the influence of the *dolce stil nuovo,* new European forms like the sonnet and a new tone of laxity were introduced into Hebrew poetry. The greater poets, Gabirol and Halevi, rebelled against the tyranny of Arabic versification. The former used an untrammeled though rhymed form for his chief philosophical poem *Royal Crown,* which, in its flaming devotion to God, anticipates the poetry of Rilke's *Book of Hours,* the chief religious cycle of poems in the twentieth century, while the latter complains that "Jews long for a prosody in imitation of other peoples, in order to force the Hebrew language into their metres." But most poets were powerless against the prevailing passion for lingual arabesques. They sought euphony at the expense of content, artificial neologisms at the expense of simple diction. The result was a superficial glitter instead of an inner glow, an enrichment of vocabulary instead of an enrichment of life, bookish obscurity instead of immediacy of feeling. For medieval Hebrew poetry was chiefly a poetry of conceits, a poetry of *pièces d'occasion* on an enormous scale.

The Arabs succeeded in imposing an oriental tyranny on form and content. Pages upon pages of medieval poetry were filled with variations on the theme of wine, war, nature, sensual love, and friendship in the form of eulogies and encomiums. The greater poets showed originality even in the conventionalized patterns of poetry. A Moses ibn Ezra could produce poems of spring which still delight with their freshness, and poems on death which have a Villonesque touch of poignancy.

> Where are the graves of men who died
> In our fair world in days of old?
> Grave hewn on grave, and corpse on corpse
> Laid to enduring rest.
> They dwell in holes, the common chalks
> And the rare carnelians.

Halevi wrote immortal sea poetry and Abraham ibn Ezra, made famous by Robert Browning's poem, composed humorous verse which was and still is a rarity in Hebrew literature. But they were the exceptions. The so-called secular poetry of the Jews, produced by thousands of poetasters, was chiefly an exercise in the art of versification. In time everything was subjected to rhyme: games, grammar, history, science. Even the greatest medieval poets did not disdain to misuse their lyric talents for moot themes.

But the sacred poetry which was partly incorporated in the liturgy for recitation on holidays showed an intensity of feeling beneath the thick crust of Arab ornamentation. The humiliations of the diaspora and the longing for redemption inspired even minor poets and, *mirabile dictu,* initiated an epic trend in Hebrew poetry. Historical episodes and half-legendary personalities were utilized with the same predilection that medieval French poets showed for their national heroes in their *chansons de geste* and the *romans d'aventure.*

Like the non-Hebrew poet who lived on literary patronage down to the eighteenth century, the Hebrew poet in Spain and even in Italy lived off the bounty of the Maecenas who was rewarded by him with expected flattery. It was a precarious existence at best, or the life of a pauper at worst. Even with an intelligent patron, the dependent bard was subjected to an inordinate amount of humiliation. Poets like Abraham ibn Ezra or Judah al-Harizi were saved by a sense of humor or by perpetual peregrinations from country to country, ready to sell their poetic wares for a pittance or to pour their wrath for a denial of a pittance. Poets in the Christian Middle Ages met with a similar, if not worse, fate. As a class they were eyed with suspicion and placed at the bottom of society. The Church legislated against them in a vain endeavor to curtail their influence and in a mistaken belief that their influence was of a pornographic nature. Fortunately both commoner and knight enjoyed them, patronized them and assured their immortality by constant references to their carefree verse.

Philosophers fared better than poets. After the conquests of the Arabs and their subsequent contacts with the cultured East and West, philosophy emerged again from its recondite position in Europe. Though translations, or rather paraphrases, of Plato and Aristotle created a ferment of heterodoxy, philosophy remained a true *ancilla theologiae,* a servant of the faith on a rationalist basis, for seventeen centuries. More than a harmonization of Greek wisdom and Hebrew ethics, it was a welding of rationalist principles and emotional predilections. It began with belief, not with doubt, in revelation which found expression in Scripture. This was the first source of human wisdom. The second source embracing "truths discovered by reason" was Greek philosophical literature. But God, who was considered to be the father of the truths of revelation and the truths of reason, could not permit any real conflict between them. The apparent conflicts which had to be resolved formed the main task of so-called medieval philosophy. "The existence of God, the unity of God, creation of the world, divine providence, and the divine origin of rules for human conduct"—these, according to Professor Wolfson, were five problems endlessly discussed, endlessly substantiated by Jewish as well as Christian and Moslem philosophies. The compendia on logic which were composed in that period served merely to facilitate the rational substantiation of these five problems. All the classics of Jewish philosophy, from Saadia's *Beliefs and Opinions* to the Maimonidean *Guide of the Per-*

plexed, exhibit a marked similarity in content. An exception to the rule is the somewhat original form of dialogue between the Khazar king in search of the true faith and the Hebrew scholar in Judah Halevi's *Cuzari,* which can only be compared with the poetic flights of Platonic dialogues. But the *Guide of the Perplexed* achieved greater popularity than the *Cuzari.* Immediately translated into Hebrew and Latin, it was quoted and interpreted by Albertus Magnus, Thomas Aquinas, and Abu Bekr al-Tabrizi in the thirteenth century. For it was the most incisive exposition and critique of philosophy in the Middle Ages.

It was also Maimonides who made the greatest advances in the development of Jewish codes. Preceded by a galaxy of commentators on the Talmud and authors of responsa, he utilized their insights and composed a comprehensive, systematic, and lucid code of laws in the Hebrew language. No later code, not even the authoritative *Shulhan Aruk* of Caro, which has served as the legal guide of European Jewry to the present day, exceeded the Maimonidean code in clarity of exposition, in beauty of style, and in the succinctness of its decisions. With the Mishnah and the commentaries of Rashi on the Bible, it forms a trio of neo-Hebraic prose classics. And like the Roman code which was admired by generations of non-legal minds, or the Napoleonic code which inspired Stendhal's prose, the Maimonidean code served as an example of Hebrew style to generations of writers and as a guide of conduct to countless Jews in the West and in the East, especially in Yemen, where is was preferred to the study of the Talmud itself. The hope of Maimonides, that his code might become the authoritative book of Jewry, was partially fulfilled.

The conspicuous characteristic of the great exemplars of Spanish Jewry is the breadth of their intellectual interests. Only in the Italian Renaissance does one encounter men who, like Gabirol and Halevi, combined intensity of poetic insight with philosophical acumen or who, like Abraham ibn Ezra, made contributions to poetry, philosophy, and science. Their passion for welding on a grand scale the various branches of knowledge into a coherent system of thought was balanced by the efforts of Franco-German Jews who had a passion for analytical dissection of texts, shunned philosophy and, with few notable exceptions, eschewed poetry in the grand manner. But they were excellent commentators on the Bible and the Talmud—from Gershom of Mayence who is responsible for the legal sanction of monogamy among Western Jews to Rashi who was the commentator *par excellence* and who is still considered a valuable guide to the Bible and Talmud. While the polyhistors are characteristic of Spanish Jewry, the *Tosafists*, writers of addenda on the Talmud, are the peculiar products of Franco-German Jewry. Between the twelfth and the fourteenth centuries they composed their commentaries and supercommentaries on the Talmud and made themselves so indispensable to its understanding that no serious study of its text can be undertaken without their aid.

Throughout the centuries, from post-biblical to modern times, an esoteric stream of mysticism mingles with the broad river of law, poetry, philosophy, and science. It can be neither overlooked nor neglected in a critical account of Hebrew literature, since three thousand published and more than three thousand unpublished mystical texts have been established on good authority. In common with the Christian and Moslem mystic, the Jewish mystic aspires to union with God. For monotheistic religion, in creating a bipolar world of God and the universe, impels him to re-establish the old unity which was the possession of man in his mythical childhood, when the world was with him, in him and around him. Yet the mystic does not revert to primitivism, but strives for an intuitive experience on the plane of a new religious consciousness. Unlike Christian mysticism, which revolves to a great extent around the person of the Savior, or Moslem sufism, which revolves to a certain extent around the personality of Mohammed, Jewish mysticism concentrates on the Creator and on creation. But it uses some of the means of all mystics: ecstaticism and asceticism, contemplation and even magic.

Jewish mystics are rarely given to autobiographical accounts of their illumination. Moreover, there are no Elizabeths of Schoenau and no Theresas of Jesus among the Jews. Jewish mysticism is a masculine discipline where every law becomes a mystery, every commandment a cosmic event, every Jew a partner of God in the process of creation. Similarly, every legend, being close to the popular myth, is an incentive to a bold leap into the celestial spheres, and every prayer a preparation for a celestial journey, a hymn recited by angels or a dialogue between God and man.

All forms of Hebrew literature were intended for mass consumption, but philosophy and mysticism were the exclusive prerogative of a spiritual elite. While the former discipline never relinquished its inaccessability, the latter succeeded in permeating larger segments of the Jewish population and in leading them on an adventurous tour of redemption, which in the seventeenth century ended in disappointment and disillusion; and in the eighteenth century created a pietist movement, Hasidism, which for sheer religious exuberance had few counterparts in the modern world.

In no other book did Jewish mysticism reach as classical an expression as in the *Zohar* (Splendor). Composed by Moses de Leon in thirteenth-century Spain, it became in the course of two hundred years a cherished work of such humanists as Pico della Mirandola, and achieved the sanctity which is commonly associated with the Bible and the Talmud. Formally a mystic commentary on the Pentateuch, the Song of Songs, and Ruth, it is, in the words of Professor Gershom G. Scholem, almost a "mystical novel" teeming with discourses, monologues and dialogues, long and short stories strung indiscriminately together on scriptural texts. It is also a hoard of ancient traditions of cosmogony, Philonic ideas, and gnostic musings on man in the universe. Above all, it is the vademecum of mystics throughout the world.

THE MODERN PERIOD

The expulsion of the Jews from Spain in 1492 had disastrous consequences on Hebrew literature. No other literary center of the Jews ever rivaled the Iberian center in range of achievement. It is true that, in the development of Jewish law, the Jews of Poland had no negligible influence in the sixteenth and seventeenth centuries. It is also true that, together with the Jews of Russia, they were the bulwark of modern Hebrew literature. But no man of stature, comparable to Maimonides, arose in Eastern Europe. In Spain Hebrew literature achieved its last classical expression. Between the expulsion and the reëstablishment of the Jewish state in Palestine it continued on an unsteady course in other countries of Europe and in America.

There is a popular theory, adopted by standard textbooks on Hebrew literature, that modern Hebrew literature begins in the eighteenth century—either with Moses Hayyim Luzzatto or with Moses Mendelssohn. In reality no definitive beginning can be assigned to so complex a thing as modern Hebrew literature. If increased secularization and Westernization are taken as its sole criteria, then it may be said to begin in various countries at various times. In Italy it can be traced to the sixteenth, in Holland to the seventeenth, in Germany to the eighteenth, while in Poland and Russia it had its belated inception in the nineteenth century.

Modern Hebrew literature exhibits three main trends which are easily discernible and distinguishable from each other: pre-enlightenment, enlightenment, and nationalism. The pre-enlightenment period extends roughly from the Renaissance to the eighteenth century. Though its most important ancestor and antecedent, Immanuel of Rome, showed as intense an interest in erotic themes as did Dante, his more famous contemporary, he could not help being merely a theoretical Don Juan. For sexual morality, protected by the rigid standards of the community, showed no public lapses among the Jews of the Middle Ages as, for example, under

William IX of Aquitaine-Poitou (1087-1127), who founded a nunnery with prostitutes as members and with a courtesan as Mother Superior. It was Immanuel of Rome who introduced the sonnet into Hebrew literature when it was still unknown in France, Germany, and England. Altogether European metric, paralleling Arabic metric and later superseding it, found a way into Hebrew literature through the mediacy of its Italian poets. The future will decide whether it will shackle Hebrew poetry, as did Arabic metric in medieval times, or prove to be a boon. Already some poets who use it to the exclusion of any other metric call for a return to biblical parallelism, and the ultra-moderns take refuge in blank or free verse *à la* Walt Whitman or Arno Holz.

While Immanuel of Rome introduced new forms and audacious themes into Hebrew poetry, Jewish historians in the period of the Renaissance like Azariah de Rossi sounded a new note of critical approach to the hallowed texts of the Bible and the Talmud. On the basis of his enormous erudition, which included a thorough acquaintanceship with Jewish sources and patristic literature, Azariah de Rossi admitted somewhat cautiously that one may differ from the rabbis and that the Talmud is subject to error. This was an extraordinary act of boldness when one considers that more than a century later even the French Encyclopedists trod warily on religious ground. Indeed scientific historiography may be said to have begun with Azariah de Rossi rather than with Jost or Graetz, who wrote their massive histories of the Jews in the nineteenth century. It is probable that he would have met with the fate of Spinoza, had not Caro, the great author of the authoritative code of Jewish laws in the sixteenth century, died before he had time to issue the ban.

But perhaps the most important development of modern Hebrew literature was in the domain of Hebrew drama. It was in Italy that the first Hebrew comedy, written by Leone de Sommi, inaugurated a vast dramatic literature which was almost nonexistent in previous centuries. Unlike the church in the Middle Ages which fostered miracle and mystery plays, the synagogue did not develop or encourage plays until the very end of the Middle Ages. In the period of the Renaissance the Jewish playwright, like his Italian confrère, had to seek the favors of a Maecenas in order to advance his literary fortunes. It was at the court of Don Cesare Gonzaga that Leone de Sommi composed various comedies in Italian but his *Comedy on Marriage* is the first original Hebrew play. As in the Italian comedy of the sixteenth century and in the French comedy of the seventeenth century, types rather than individuals dominate the action: the disappointed lover, the loyal and disloyal servant, the *nouveau riche* who vaunts his ignorance and betrays his humble origins in speech and gesture. Love is, of course, the central theme, but complicated obstacles impede its progress to a victorious finale.

Though Leone de Sommi's comedy may have been produced in Italy, no Hebrew theatre existed there or anywhere. Acting companies were organized in the twentieth century and the first Hebrew theatre was built in Palestine. Nevertheless, plays continued to be written and even produced before the establishment of a Hebrew theatre. At the time when Puritan England shut the doors of its theatres, Moses Zacuto wrote two plays, one of which, resembling a mystery play in verse, was sung by a musical group in Ferrara. As late as the middle of the eighteenth century a biblical play was produced in the ghetto of Rome. But performances of Hebrew plays were the exception rather than the rule. Most plays, though intended for the stage, languished in private and public libraries.

Against this rich background of playwriting and playproducing Moses Hayyim Luzzatto can be evaluated in proper perspective. He is neither the father of modern Hebrew drama nor the father of modern Hebrew literature. More known and more famous than his predecessors whose reputation was localized and whose plays rarely reached the printing press, he exercised an enormous influence on Hebrew literature in Russia and Poland. His purity of style, modeled on the Bible, dominated poetic drama, epic poetry, and even prose to the very threshold of the twentieth century.

If the Hebrew language became a mosaic of biblical verses, a pseudo-classic monstrosity, a cult of a precious elite, he is partly to blame. He was also a fatal influence in the choice of allegory as a vehicle of drama. Popularized in world literature by Philo, it was a cherished vehicle of expression in the Middle Ages, reaching its peak in the thirteenth century in the well-known *Roman de la Rose* of Guillaume de Lorris and Jean de Meun which inspired Chaucer. With its didacticism and moralization, allegory was peculiarly well suited to the medieval man, but unfortunate as a mirror to the life of modern man.

From this point of view the style of Luzzatto must be seen as a retarding rather than elevating influence. The naive, black-and-white characterization of his dramatis personae had an equally unfortunate influence. But in his fine sensitivity to pastoral simplicity and to the call of the hill and the forest, the field and the glade, he initiated that return to nature which Rousseau made fashionable in the literatures of Western Europe. With the critical minds in the period of pre-enlightenment, he shared an impatience with Judaism in its petrified form. But unlike them he became a devotee of esoteric doctrines and exposed himself to attacks of Jewish authorities who, disillusioned with the dangerous adventures of Sabbatai Zevi and his followers, frowned on mystic manifestations among Jews.

The period of enlightenment lasting roughly from the middle of the eighteenth to the close of the nineteenth century parallels the inception of a new age in Jewish history. The American and French Revolutions put an end to the Jewish Middle Ages which, in Eastern Europe, did not terminate before the Russian Revolution in 1917. The most remarkable characteristic of Hebrew literature in that period was a pronounced tone of inferiority. Curiously the great persecutions in the Middle Ages did not rob the Jews of the conviction of superiority to their neighbors, but confirmed them in it. But when the disabilities and discriminations gradually disappeared from the statute books of Europe, and a freer access to its economic and social life was granted to all strata of society, the Jews were ill-prepared for the change and dazzled by the opportunity. A wave of assimilation and conversion swept over Western Jewry, which was the first to be emancipated from the restrictions of ghetto life. Neither the reform movement, which abrogated the separatist laws of the Jews and attenuated their religion with uncritical importations and imitations, nor the so-called *Wissenschaft des Judentums*, which was a cold, scientific evaluation of the classic culture of the Jews, stemmed the tide. In the hundred years of its existence reform was a comfortable refuge of the well-to-do but a poor vehicle of vital values. And though the *Wissenschaft des Judentums* made impressive contributions to Jewish historiography, Semitic philology, and scientific exegesis, it was apologetic in tone and it operated in the disastrous belief that Judaism was a dead culture which, like the Latin and Greek cultures, was ready for the dissecting knife of the savant but incapable of further development.

The reform movement and the scientific evaluation of Judaism were balanced by a vigorous conservatism which emphasized literal interpretation of the Talmud instead of casuistry, and by a pietism which swept the Jewish masses of Eastern Europe and overwhelmed them with an almost mystic passion for their ancient customs. The conservative trend expressed itself in an intensified study of the Talmud. Fostered by the saintly and erudite Elijah of Wilna, the nestor of talmudic criticism, it achieved previously unknown finesse in conjectural emendations and critical evaluations of rabbinic texts. But the conservative trend, untouched by ideas of enlightenment and fed by the cold resources of the intellect, was powerless to stem the movement of Hasidism, which, originated by the simple and deeply mystical Israel Baal Shem Tob, swept the most powerful center of Jewry of that time, the countries of Eastern Europe, and overwhelmed them with religious vitality. The song, the dance, the parable, the communal and almost sacramental meal—these were the means of persuasion which the founder and his successors used in developing Hasidism. No great works of learning, but great stories and great sayings, and above all, saintly personalities emerged from the movement. In the end, conservatism degenerated into rigidity and Hasidism into superstitious obscurantism. The enlightened writers, distressed by an all-pervasive feeling of inferiority, stooped to imitation of European models of literature on the one hand, and to half-hearted criticism of Jewish religion on the other. A great variety of mediocre translations from European languages inundated the Hebrew book market. The fine art of adapting and surpassing neighboring cultures, which characterized biblical and medieval Jewry, was a forgotten art. Only toward the nineteenth century, with the inception of a new era of nationalism, did Hebrew literature show a certain independence of European models. But for a hundred and fifty years the influence of German models was preëminent. Schiller was the idol of Jewish enlightenment, Lessing via Mendelssohn the arbiter of literary taste.

Since Hebrew literature in the era of enlightenment was a literature of imitation, no literary genre showed robust vitality. Even such an important novel of that period as *The Love of Zion*, mother of all Hebrew novels, can be read with difficulty today. Though it valiantly strives to reconstruct an important era of Jewish history, the age of Isaiah and Hezekiah, it sins with an excessively complicated plot and an excessively simple characterization and style *à la* Luzzatto. In non-historical novels Hebrew writers strove to teach the lessons of enlightenment, to fight for the ideal of secular education and to denounce the conservative leaders of Jewry rather than to create living characters and give esthetic pleasure. The true novel came into its own toward the end of the nineteenth century when such masters of realism as Mendele Moker Sefarim began to dominate the literary scene.

What is true of the novel in the era of enlightenment is also true of philosophy. With the single exception of Krochmal's *Guide to the Perplexed of Our Time*, philosophical works were either popularizations of, or commentaries on medieval texts. Rarely did they venture into unexplored fields of epistemology, rarely did they inspire a generation with a comprehensive view of life. Not until the dawn of the twentieth century, when Ahad Haam succeeded in imposing a set of values on an entire generation did philosophic writing show signs of maturity. The father of Hebrew enlightenment, Moses Mendelssohn, had a philosophic mind, but he occupies a prominent place in German rather than Hebrew philosophic literature. His incidental Hebrew writings served as a directive rather than as a source of inspiration. His translations of biblical books into German in Hebrew characters enabled Jews to study a foreign European language, and his commentary reënforced an interest in the Bible, which had already been emphasized by Moses Hayyim Luzzatto in Italy. If all writers of the enlightenment modeled their styles on the Bible —N. H. Wessely, creator of the epic poem, the *Mosiad;* Shalom Cohen, the creator of the *Davidiad,* an epic work on King David; and J. L. Gordon, the most powerful poet of the enlightenment— they partly owe their excessive archaism to Moses Mendelssohn and partly to Moses Hayyim Luzzatto. Not only was epic, lyric, and dramatic poetry biblical in theme and style, but also criticism focused its attention on the Bible. Thus Solomon Lewison, spurred by the spirit of the age, wrote what was perhaps the first esthetic appraisal of the Bible in the Hebrew language, and gave the first free adaptation of a Shakespearean fragment in biblical style.

Mendelssohn also fathered periodical literature in Hebrew. Inspired by the *Tatler* and the *Spectator,* he created with the help of a few friends a Hebrew periodical which was the center of literary activity for several decades. And yet, such was the inexorable logic of history, Mendelssohn, who observed all the minutiae of Jewish law, defended them against detracting zealots, and made a special plea for Jewish religion in his philosophical work *Jerusalem,* unconsciously encouraged assimilation and conversion. His direct and indirect efforts in behalf of emancipation

contributed to the promulgation of the famous Edict of Toleration in 1782, and his ardent belief in secular education as a
short-cut to full emancipation resulted in the establishment of
schools with a preponderant emphasis on non-Jewish disciplines.
Both emancipation and secular education acted as powerful cen-
trifugal rather than centripetal tendencies in Judaism. Mendelssohn's friends and even his own descendants were ready to
embrace Christianity under certain conditions and disappear as
a separate cultural entity.

When the brief burst of creative effort in the German center
terminated with assimilation and conversion, reform and the
scientific efforts of Jewish scholars—poor substitutes for the living
wells of literature—assumed the character of a religious and intellectual coterie. The center of Hebrew literature shifted to the
Austro-Hungarian empire, especially to Galicia, where the undisturbed medieval calm was only slightly ruffled by the Edict of
Toleration and the movement of enlightenment. The first torch-
bearer of the movement in Galicia and in neighboring Poland,
Mendel Levin of Satanov, knew Mendelssohn personally and
heeded his sage advice. He popularized scientific books and
published a paraphrase of Benjamin Franklin's *Poor Richard's
Almanack*. As the protégé of the Polish prince Czartoryski, he
was immune to attacks from his co-religionists, though he advocated the establishment of Jewish schools with secular curricula.

What the German center of Hebrew literature lacked, and the
Austro-Hungarian center possessed in abundance, was a sense
of humor. Writers attacked the shady sides of Hasidism—the
greed, the fanaticism, the luxurious mode of life—the lay and
the clerical professions, the physicians, the cantors, the butchers,
and the rabbis. Pretense, sham, cant, hypocrisy were castigated
mercilessly. Poetry had none of the heavy, epic gait which characterized the Hebrew writers of Germany: it was simple, naive,
almost a folk-song.

When enlightenment came to Russia it did not mature before
the middle of the nineteenth century. In Russia it achieved

its summit and slowly transformed itself into a truly national literature. It is not an exaggeration to say that the Jews of Poland and Russia built modern Hebrew literature which, in turn, inspired the masses and their leaders to build the state of Israel. American capital would have been of no avail without the efforts of the Jewish pioneers of Poland who forsook schools and professions, sometimes out of idealism and sometimes out of economic necessity and often out of a combination of these motives, and built a homeland in the desert.

The father of Russian enlightenment, Isaac Ber Levinsohn, who was more practical than Mendelssohn, emphasized the need for agricultural labor among the Jews and buttressed his arguments with rabbinic quotations. It was he who may be regarded as the father of the pioneering movement which eventually resulted in considerable restratification of Jews and in the establishment of communal and privately owned farms in Palestine. And it was he who inspired even poets with a greater regard for practical needs. He continued the trend of popularization of foreign masterpieces and useful works on history and natural sciences. But he was rent by a dichotomy which is characteristic of the movement of enlightenment in Russia: the allure of the trans-Judaic in the present and the nostalgia for the pulsating Jewish life in the past.

NATIONALISM AND ZIONISM

The movement of enlightenment ended in a complete breakdown. The acquisition of statehood by the various Balkan states and the mass pogroms in Russia in 1881 paved the way for an intense brand of nationalism among Jews. In the years which elapsed between these pogroms and the Russian Revolution of 1917 a remarkable literature was born. If the drama and the novel showed no unusual vigor, the short story and the poem achieved remarkable finesse and subtlety. Whatever is creative and buoyant in Jewish life at the present time is, in some measure, a direct emanation from Hebrew literature. Even the various forms of Zionism, political, orthodox, and labor Zionism, were advocated by Hebrew writers before the Zionist movement spread among the masses. The entire Hebrew literature of that period was dominated by the ideological outlook of Ahad Haam. Steeped in the Talmud and the medieval codices and considered a rabbinical authority before his twentieth year, he managed, nevertheless, to preserve a refreshing originality of thought and a lucid style. So scrupulously did he avoid the worn phrases and the profuse citations which most of his contemporaries used for padding their writings that he achieved an almost occidental rhythm in his prose. Throughout his creative period, which terminated in the second decade of this century, he never swerved from the ideas which he propounded at the outset of his literary career and from the form of the essay which proved to be his only mode of expression. It is a small circle of ideas but, as Romain Rolland justly remarks, art moves in a narrow circle of ideas. However, the force of personality which the artist succeeds in imposing upon the world remains active beyond his lifetime. Ahad Haam had that force. He was one of the most harmonious personalities in modern Hebrew literature, at peace with himself though often, being uncompromising and unyielding, at war with the world. His theoretical abilities were so well blended with practical acumen that his activities appeared to him and to others as natural corollaries of his writings.

Ahad Haam maintains that the mosaic code has one purpose only: the welfare of the nation in a land of its own. With the first destruction of the Temple and the loss of political independence the philosophy of individual welfare prevailed in Jewish life and, being well suited to the exigencies of a scattered people, worked for the disintegration of national feeling and, consequently, of national responsibility. The first task, therefore, that devolves upon the modern Jew is the education of the heart, a task which has often been overlooked by critics who depicted him as a cool and detached writer. Yet his belief in the potency of national feeling amounted to a mystical creed. He even asserted that Western Jews who have become assimilated with an amazing rapidity, remained Jews only because a spark of national feeling was still alive in them.

> Every true Jew, be he orthodox or liberal, feels in the depths of his heart that there is something apart in the spirit of our people . . . He who still has that feeling will remain within the fold of Judaism. This national feeling permeates even such men as Maimonides to an extent that it conquers their logic.

That he harped on the revival of the heart was more than a need of his heart: It was mature wisdom. He aimed at a national movement, and national movements live on the heart rather than on the brain. Yet political Zionism which purported to be a national movement incurred, from its very inception, the enmity of Ahad Haam. He was too much a realist to relish Herzl's diplomatic activities which were to pave the way for the acquisition of Palestine from the Turkish government. This, to him, was a strange phantasy conceived in the brain of a Jew whose nationalist fervor grew out of an assimilationist background. That is why Ahad Haam acted as a constant corrective to Herzl. With a knowledge of Jewish affairs which has lost nothing of its timelessness and without a trace of bitterness he complains: "Almost all of our great men . . . are spiritually removed from Judaism, and have no true conception of its nature and its value."

Herzl advocated a panacea for the ills of the Jews, and Ahad Haam emphasized the urgency of the ills of Judaism. This divergence of ideas was conditioned, to a certain extent, by temperamental differences. Ahad Haam was slow and careful in his judgments; Herzl impatient and flashy in his actions. Perhaps the former had, to use a mystical notion of Thomas Mann, a physiological foreboding of a long life. At any rate, he did not see the immediate necessity for an independent state. Even a good-sized settlement of Jews in Palestine, growing gradually, could, in his judgment, achieve a lasting significance and become in the course of time the center of the nation wherein its spirit will find pure expression and develop in all its aspects up to the highest degree of perfection of which it is capable. Then from this center the spirit of Judaism will go forth to the great circumference, to all the communities of the diaspora, and will breathe new life into them and preserve their unity.

Spirit, spirit before all—this, to paraphrase Verlaine, was the principal thesis of the father of spiritual Zionism. He acknowledged the indubitable fact that in the past only those were considered Jews who adhered to the tenets of the Jewish religion. But, as a result of the emancipatory trends, there emerged a new type of Jew, unobserving yet national. Ahad Haam gave him a *raison d'être* because he postulated a nationalism limited to ethical duties. He distinguished between ethical principles which are common to all civilized nations and form an international code, and ethical principles which are typical of a single nation and may be termed national ethics. The latter is, in his opinion, the national asset par excellence and mirrors the peculiar spirit of the nation. His revaluation of the national life and letters of the Jews gave a powerful impetus to modern Hebrew literature. The controversies which many of his articles aroused in current periodicals were, of course, of a passing nature. Much more important were those lasting stimuli which went out of his work to his generation. It is not an exaggeration to say that there was hardly a contemporary writer who was not drawn as friend or foe to the magic circle of his ideas. The novel, the essay, and the poetry of the time bore the imprint of his personality. Even his opponents benefited by his lucid thinking.

Bialik, the poetic counterpart of Ahad Haam, was the singer of the spirit of Judaism. His phenomenal reputation in modern Hebrew poetry, paralleled in contemporary British and American poetry only by that of T. S. Eliot, is perhaps to be attributed to the felicitous blend of personal and national elements which has characterized Hebrew poetry since the days of the Psalms. Not only did he mirror the misfortunes of the Jews in his alternately gentle and irate verse, but he sought to strengthen their inner

resources. Even in an hour of tragedy, in the aftermath of the
Kishenev pogrom of 1903, he castigated his people rather than
the perpetrators of the criminal attack:

> Avaunt ye, beggars, to the charnel-house!
> The bones of your fathers disinter!
> Cram them within your knapsacks, bear
> Them on your shoulders, and go forth
> To do your business with these precious wares
> At all the country fairs!
> Stop on the highway, near some populous city,
> Your customer, and spread on your filthy rags
> Those martyred bones that issue from your bags,
> And sing, with raucous voice, your pauper's ditty!
> So will you conjure up the pity of the stranger
> And so his sympathy implore.
> For you are now as you have been of yore
> And as you stretched your hand
> So will you stretch it,
> And as you have been wretched
> So are you wretched! [*]

With his nostalgic songs of the past and his lyrical longing for a
nationalist future, Bialik marks the end of a literary road. It was
Tschernichowsky, his brilliant and less famous contemporary,
who discovered a new "realm of being" in the beginnings of the
Jewish nation and reinforced modern Judaism with the hoary,
half-mythical past. He did not hesitate to identify himself with
the worshippers of Tammuz—Adonis, and the Semitic Venus,
Astarte. He was even moved to compose psychological and liturgical sonnets to the sun, which, in their perfection of form and of
pagan homage to the forces of nature, have no equal in Hebrew literature. A few other poets—Shneour, Cohen, Fichman,
Schimonowitz—created a veritable renascence of poetry at a time
when, paradoxically, the reading of poetry outside schools and
universities became an almost obsolete discipline.

At the end of the First World War, Russia was supplanted by
a major center of literature in Palestine and by a minor center in
the United States. Fiction which was confined to the sentimental-

[*] Trans. by A. M. Klein.

ized historical novel and the ghetto life in the little town has gradually widened its horizons both in and outside Palestine. In the United States it drew the metropolis into its orbit and the numberless varieties of types and individuals which make up the metropolis. But the language of the Hebrew writer was the learned language of the scholar or the elegant language of the bookish dilettante. Thus an inevitable romanticism accompanied Hebrew literature in the United States where lyric poetry reached maturity in the books of Silkiner, Ginzburg, Bavli, Halkin, Regelson, Efros, Lisitzky, Feinstein, and Preil. Dramatic composition attained unusual tensions of mystic finesse in the plays of Harry Sackler; the critical essay probed into literary phenomena in the works of Epstein, Ribalow, and Ovsay, and present-day psychological and educational trends found a keen exponent in the books of Touroff.

In Palestine the preoccupation with the natives—Jew and Arab —and especially with the landscape has become a dominant theme. Severed from his country for centuries, the returning Jew became intoxicated and obsessed with the beauty of the Palestinian scene and with the passion for agricultural labor in Palestinian fields. The Palestinian writer reflected that intoxication and obsession. The reclamation of the land, the joy and excitement in the new homeland, the adaptation of the Jews to productive labor, coming fast on the heels of the unproductive life in the ghetto, rushed like a fresh wind into his work. He even reached out to the forgotten Jewries of the Orient and their quaint customs and mannerisms which were not greatly affected by the Palestinian habitat. Poetry was also fired with the theme of imminent redemption and with the ardor of pioneers who settled with a new hope and an old despair in Palestine. They were depicted as the heroes of a nation fighting for its existence on the old, historic soil, or as Messiahs in the disguise of farmers. Though Massada[4] became the ominous symbol of modern Pales-

---

[4] A Palestinian fortress which heroically resisted the Romans after the fall of Jerusalem in A.D. 70. On the eve of its capture, the defending garrison decided on self-extermination rather than on submission to the foe.

tine, the hope that the heroism of the modern pioneers will avert the fate of old Massada from the new Palestine, was kept alive by such poets as Isaac Lamdan:

> The dance of Massada is aflame
> And aflare.
> Clear the way, o destiny,
> Beware!
>
> The fire of our feet will burn the stones,
> As it must.
> The rocks will fall with a heavy fall
> And turn to dust.

In the remote past the Jews produced the Bible, which, along with Greek literature, Roman institutions, and Arabic science became one of the four pillars of the West, the mother of the civilized world. The new state of Israel was nourished by the dream of a new culture, which was first traced by the anonymous bards of Palestine in the second millennium B.C. It will justify itself when it converts that dream into a reality and becomes the center of a new humanism.

BIBLIOGRAPHY

GENERAL BACKGROUND

ABRAHAMS, Israel, *Jewish Life in the Middle Ages* (Philadelphia, Jewish Publication Society, 1920).
An account of Jewish life and letters in the Middle Ages. Based on source material.

ALBRIGHT, William Foxwell, *From the Stone Age to Christianity* (Baltimore, 1940).
Presentation and evaluation of the Jewish religion to the time of Christ.

BARON, Salo Wittmayer, *A Social and Religious History of the Jews* (New York, 1937), 3 vols.
A scholarly and critical appraisal of "the interrelation of social and religious forces" in Jewish history.

212   *The World Through Literature*

MOORE, George Foote, *Judaism in the First Centuries of the Christian Era* (Cambridge, 1927-1940), 3 vols.
Scientific coverage of the literary, religious, and social background of Christianity.
RUPPIN, Arthur, *The Jews in the Modern World* (London, 1934).
Pioneer work in Jewish sociology.

PHILOSOPHY AND MYSTICISM

HUSIK, Isaac, *A History of Mediaeval Jewish Philosophy* (New York, 1930). A concise history of the religious philosophy of the Jews in the Middle Ages.
SCHOLEM, Gershom G., *Major Trends in Jewish Mysticism* (New York, 1946).
A historical and critical evaluation of Jewish mysticism from its beginnings to the present time.
WOLFSON, Harry A., *Philo* (Cambridge, 1947), 2 vols.
Second book of a projected series of monumental studies on the structure and growth of philosophical systems from Plato to Spinoza.

LITERARY HISTORY AND CRITICISM

KLAUSNER, Joseph, *A Short History of Modern Hebrew Literature* (London, 1932).
A brief sketch of Hebrew literature in the last two hundred years.
PFEIFFER, Robert H., *Introduction to the Old Testament* (New York, 1941).
An appraisal of Biblical literature in the light of the present state of higher criticism.
STRACK, Hermann L., *Introduction to the Talmud and Midrash* (Philadelphia, Jewish Publication Society, 1931).
"Objective and scientific information concerning the whole of the Talmud."
TORREY, Charles C., *The Apocryphal Literature* (New Haven, 1945).
"A concise handbook treating of the Jewish post-canonical literature."
WAXMAN, Meyer, *A History of Jewish Literature* (New York, 1933-1947), 4 vols.
An account of Jewish literature from post-biblical times to the present.

6

Greek and Latin:
The Philosophic Tradition
in Literature

ALLEN R. BENHAM
UNIVERSITY OF WASHINGTON

PROFESSOR ALLEN R. BENHAM, *long a member of the strong department of English at the University of Washington, is best known for his studies of the literature of his native tongue—among his books is the widely admired* English Literature from Widsith to the Death of Chaucer *(1916). But he began his academic career as a student of the classics, and he has never lost this interest. He has just finished a translation of the fifth-century* De nuptiis Philologiae et Mercurii, *a volume which is supposed to have grafted the seven liberal arts on the whole of Western European education. He began his research at the University of Minnesota and took his doctorate at Yale. He has been visiting professor at New York University, the A. E. F. University at Beaune, France, and elsewhere. He is now emeritus, but lives in Seattle, Washington, within reach of the university library.*

Greek and Latin: The Philosophic Tradition in Literature[1]

THE Greeks broached at least five problems which are still live problems in the philosophy of literature. These are as follows:

(1) The problem of the "poetic temperament," which has two phases as discussed by the Greeks—*Inspiration* and *Imitation*. This is a psychological problem.

(2) The problem of the relation between poetry and reality. This is a metaphysical problem.

(3) The problem of the responsibility of the poet. This opens the whole question of the relations between art and morals and between art and society. Propaganda in art is also involved.

(4) The problems of the various types or forms (genres) of poetry, *e.g.*, epic, comedy, dithyramb, lyric, tragedy, and the various sorts of oratory.

(5) The problem of the proper language for artistic uses. This is a linguistic question.[2]

[1] "Philosophic tradition" is, I admit a rather awkward term; but "criticism" frequently used as a synonym for it (*e.g.* in many anthologies) is, I think, inaccurate. "Criticism" means to me "judgments of value" and their expression. I am here dealing with the grounds for judgments of value. "Interpretation" is also frequently confused with "criticism" but I think the two can be easily distinguished. It is quite proper in preparing to express a judgment of value to indicate what it is that you are evaluating. This latter process is "interpretation" not "criticism." The Greeks had no general word for literature. They discussed poetry and rhetoric.

[2] It may seem strange that I do not include here some problem that might be described as specifically esthetic. On this point see F. W. Chambers, *Cycles of Taste* (Cambridge, Mass., 1928). The Greek word ποιήτης translated literally by many English writers of the fifteenth, sixteenth, and seventeenth centuries as *Maker*, is derived from the verb ποιέω, "to make" or "to create." Other terms relevant to this discussion are *genius, original, creative.* The native Latin word for poet, *vates,* means *seer, diviner,* or *prophet.* Poets have long been known as

215

I shall discuss these problems in the above order. The object
of this exposition will be to set forth the views of Greek and
Roman writers, as I understand them, on these subjects. The first
three problems have an obvious connection; the last two may
be regarded as independent questions, though some writers have
integrated them quite closely with the first three.

THE PROBLEM OF THE POETIC TEMPERAMENT

Homer, Hesiod, Pindar and many other Greek poets[3] regularly
appeal to the Muses for inspiration. Since this practice has been
imitated by many other later poets in many literatures, we are
prone to pass this over as a purely conventional literary device.
But we forget that among the earlier Greeks this probably expressed a real belief that divine inspiration was a necessity to the
poet.

Most of these Greek invocations of the Muses are general and
brief. In at least one instance Homer, however, where he is dealing with what we might think of as statistics, is more specific and
we may reasonably think of him as definitely inaugurating the
Western tradition of the poet as inspired. This specific case is
the prologue to the catalogue of the ships in the second book of
the *Iliad*.

It is well known that Homer was regarded by the Greeks as

---

dreamers or visionaries. See Rosamund E. M. Harding, *An Anatomy of
Inspiration*, 3rd edition, revised and enlarged (Cambridge, Eng., 1948). Miss
Harding's references in her text and items in her extensive bibliography are
primarily concerned with artists and scientists from the seventeenth, eighteenth,
and nineteenth centuries A.D.

[3] Appeals to the Muses for "inspiration" are missing in the Greek dramatists.
This is because neither in prologue nor in epilogue nor in any other place did
the Greek dramatist speak in his own person. This is one of the faults that
Plato finds with him. If we can infer, however, from the titles of several Greek
comedies, problems in literary criticism and in the philosophy of literature were
frequently treated in Greek comedy. Thus, we have the following titles for
Greek comedies now lost: *Poetry, The Poet, The Muses, The Harp-Players,
Sappho* (the Greek poet?), *Tritagonistes* (the name for the third actor in a
play), *Herakles the Stage Manager, The Rehearsal, Phil-Euripides, The Archi-
locuses*.

much more than a poet; the *Iliad,* it has frequently been said, had a position among the Greeks similar to that of the Bible among Jews and Christians. He was a wise man, a teacher of multiform doctrine, a great educational instrument. His position was unchallenged until the rise of Greek philosophy in the sixth century B.C. Then began what Plato, in *The Republic,* calls "the ancient quarrel of poetry and philosophy." Probably here Plato has in mind remarks of Xenophanes, Heraclitus, and Democritus on the poets as boastful rivals of the philosophers as purveyors of sound knowledge and wisdom.

Plato himself taking up "the ancient quarrel" on the side of the philosophers[4] devotes the whole or large parts of five dialogues[5] to an analysis and exposition of the poet's claim to divine inspiration and what the admission of that claim does to the poet himself. The net result of Plato's account is that the poet should be described as an inspired madman; that he knows nothing of what he is saying and, therefore, should have no credit for it.[6]

Aristotle makes very little use of the theory of inspiration in the poet's make-up. In Chapter XVII of *The Poetics,* where Aristotle is giving some practical advice to writers devising their plots

[4] But see F. J. E. Woodbridge, *Son of Apollo: Themes of Plato* (New York. 1929). Professor Woodbridge holds that Plato was not a systematic philosopher but a poet. It is suggestive that of all philosophers, perhaps, Plato is the one who has appealed most widely to poets.

[5] *Ion, Meno, Symposium, Phaedrus, Phaedo.*

[6] *Ion* is the dialogue in which Plato presents his attack on poets as inspired in its most elementary and vivid form, especially in the analogy of the magnet and its attractive power. Ion was a professional reciter of Homer and asserts that he is a specialist on Homer and that Homer is a source for sound knowledge and wisdom of all sorts. Ion does not stand up very well to his cross examination by Socrates and is compelled to make several damaging admissions. Socrates professes admiration for Ion, and says that he hopes some time to hear Ion declaim. Ion gives Socrates several opportunities to hear him declaim, but it is noteworthy that Socrates accepts none of them.

In the magnet analogy referred to above, Socrates compares the Muse or God who inspires the poet to the magnet; the poet to the primary iron filings attached by the magnet; and the declaimer like Ion, to the secondary iron filings attached by the primary ones. So Ion is two removes from the original inspiration. It should be added that in the *Phaedrus* and *Phaedo* the poet's inspiration brings him into the realm of theology and immortality.

and selecting their diction, he says, "poetic art is the affair of the gifted man rather than the madman," though in his *Rhetoric* (III, 7) he remarks that "poetry is a thing inspired by the god." [7] It rather looks as if Aristotle thought that on the whole the poet is obviously inspired but that he saw no reason for setting this inspiration as a debit against the poet.[8]

Horace in his *Art of Poetry* assumes that inspiration or genius is necessary to the poet. But he at once indicates that inspiration is not emphasized, for he cautions the prospective poet not to get beyond his depth, and holds that hard work, study, and constant polishing are necessary to bring the poet's art to perfection.[9] Quintillian takes it for granted that the literary artist has some kind of initial impulse to composition which might be described as inspiration. Longinus holds that the best and surest basis for an elevated style is an elevated personality, but his remarks are rather general and vague. The neo-Platonists, starting perhaps from Plato's *Phaedo,* expound a mystical doctrine of inspiration which brings the artist nearer to God than did Plato.

We have, then, on the subject of artistic inspiration, Plato's elaborate account which on the whole concludes that the inspired artist is dangerous because he is irresponsible and unconscious of reality. As against this, we have the views of Aristotle, Longinus, Horace, Quintillian, and the neo-Platonists, who apparently assume that the artist is inspired but see no particular danger in it.

[7] I am adopting here the readings of Professor A. H. Gilbert in his *Literary Criticism: Plato to Dryden* (New York, 1940), pp. 94-117.

[8] In Book XXX of the *Aristotelian Problemata* published in vol. VII of the *Oxford Aristotle,* Aristotle gives a physiological explanation of the peculiar temperament of poets *and* philosophers. He says they are atrabilious. This theory is analogous to the "humors" theory current in medieval medicine and in sixteenth- and seventeenth-century psychology; cf. the humor theory in the comedies of Ben Jonson.

There has been some difference of opinion as to whether the *Aristotelian Problemata* are genuine works of Aristotle, but Cicero in the *Tusculan Disputations* says that these statements about the melancholy of both philosophers and poets are genuine Aristotle.

[9] Compare the words of Ben Jonson on the relation between a poet's nature and his art in his lines in Shakespeare.

The neo-Platonists in fact asserted that inspiration is an asset rather than a liability.

The second item in the artistic temperament to be discussed by the ancient philosophers of literature is imitation. This is prominent in the *Republic* of Plato and from one point of view seems inconsistent with Plato's theory of artistic inspiration, for if the artist is an imitator he must be alert to what he is imitating and cannot be so unconscious as Plato maintains.

Plato's theory of artistic "imitation" is linked closely with his notorious "ideas." Ideas in the mind of God are to Plato the ultimate realities. Thus, in the famous illustration of the bed: the "real bed" is the idea of the bed in the mind of God; the cabinetmaker who produces an object known as a bed (because of its resemblance to the archetypal bed in the mind of God) is closer to reality than that painter or poet who paints or describes an object called a bed (again because of its resemblance to the archetypal bed) which is twice removed from ultimate reality (as Ion the declaimer of Homer is likewise twice removed from ultimate reality).

Hence, says Plato, people who depend upon poets or other artists for their knowledge of reality are really putting their trust in second-hand dealers. This is very bad for the state because citizens by all means should be in close touch with ultimate reality and should not be content with imitation. Hence, poets are excluded from Plato's ideal state. Since poets do not, by reason, get into touch with ultimate reality they are reduced to dealing with the senses, the imagination, and the feelings, the play of which in the state is dangerous.

Plato's theory of imitation, as I see it, conceives of imitation as the imitation of a product, a theory which would eventuate into something like the modern theory of literary realism. It is difficult, however, to conceive of Plato's going this far; for there was no writing in Greek literature that would correspond to the modern realistic novel until very late in Greek history.

Aristotle too would put imitation down as one of the aspects of the artistic temperament. But Aristotle accepts imitation; he does not deprecate it as Plato does. Imitation to Aristotle, however, is a different thing from Plato's imitation. Just as Plato's theory is involved in his theory of ideas, so Aristotle's is to be regarded as a part of his whole system of philosophy.

Aristotle should probably be classed as a biologist. At any rate, his philosophy is closely bound up with his studies in biology. In his scientific writings Aristotle shows a teleological trend; that is, to him nature as a whole, which he calls φύσις, and nature in detail, works toward a purpose. Nothing happens in nature without some purpose as its goal. And so, when Aristotle describes the artist as imitating nature, he at least partly means that the artist also is purposeful. This would certainly imply that the artist is not the unconscious dreamer of Plato's theory. In fact, Aristotle gives us in solution the most abstract definition of art that we have. Art to Aristotle is the adaptation of means to ends. Anyone who adapts means to ends is an artist. If the ends are what we call immediately practical, we term the resultant arts, the useful arts; if the ends are not so immediately practical, the fine arts are the results. The artist is thus a person who knows very clearly what he is trying to do and equally well how to arrive at his goal. The Aristotelian artist is, therefore, quite different from the Platonic artist.

Aristotle goes on to further dissent from Plato. "Yes," says Aristotle, "the artist does play on the senses, the feelings and the imagination, but this on the whole is a good thing for the individual and for society. For in this way, human tendencies which might become dangerous if inhibited or suppressed, have a healthy outlet." The best known expression of Aristotle's position on this point is found in his famous definition of tragedy in which the play offers a catharsis for pity and fear.

With Horace starts a new concept of imitation, found also in Quintillian and Longinus, the basis for the later neo-classic view of imitation. In this concept imitation becomes the copying of other writers.

Among the Greek and Roman writers, heretofore, we have three notions of imitation expressed. To Plato, imitation is of objects; is static and deprecated. To Aristotle, imitation is of processes; is dynamic and is welcomed. To Horace, imitation is of other writers and is urged.[10] And now we pass to the second problem.

THE RELATION OF POETRY TO REALITY

It was, however, the Platonic and later the Horatian view of imitation that prevailed in later times rather than the Aristotelian. In the Platonic view, poetry has very little relation to ultimate reality and is, therefore, bad. Plato in referring to the ancient quarrel between the poets and the philosophers of course recommends the latter rather than the former as guides to the knowledge of ultimate reality. When this injunction is brought under analysis it must mean that Plato recommends his own views as a guide to knowledge of ultimate reality. For a survey of Greek philosophy before and after Plato shows us a history of vast dissent rather than agreement on the epistemological and metaphysical questions involved.

Greek philosophy before Socrates raised one general metaphysical and one general epistemological problem. The first is, what is reality; and the second, how do we know reality?

To the first question the Ionian thinkers, Thales, Amaximines and Heraclitus in the sixth century B.C. on the West Coast of Asia Minor offered answers. They were trying to nullify the conclusions of the current cosmogonies and mythologies and doubtless started from the findings of the senses to contend that water, mist, or fire was the ultimate reality. But even that early there

---

[10] See the paper of Richard McKeon, "Literary Criticism and the Concept of Imitation in Antiquity," *Modern Philology*, vol. XXXIV (1936), pp. 1-35.

were thinkers, who, using an acute and theoretical logic, determined that the contentions of their contemporaries were too crass and that ultimate reality is either indeterminate or is mind. The latter is a view that very likely influenced the Platonic Socrates.

There were also philosophers who, speculating on the vast panorama of existence, held that ultimate reality, whatever its character in detail might be, was changeless. And they were opposed by others who contended that constant change is the outstanding quality of ultimate reality.[11]

The early atomists, however, to close the cycle of metaphysical speculation, put forth the view that matter, though revealed to the senses in various concrete wholes, is really made up of numbers of small bodies called atoms,[12] imperceptible to the senses, which combine and separate mostly by chance. They add that nature, φύσις, as a whole is also made up of atoms; so that their view of reality might be described as a "supersensible materialism."

In *The Clouds* Aristophanes shows us Socrates in a basket in the air discussing in mystifying language questions allegedly philosophic. This is not the ordinary view of Socrates, who, if the portrait by Plato is checked with that presented by the more prosaic Xenophon, came very much down to earth and was deeply interested in "practical" matters.

Growing from the Socratic root were several philosophic plants. There were differences between Plato, Aristotle, the Cynics, and the Sceptics which persisted late into classical times. Cicero's philosophical dialogues are valuable in presenting these varying views.

We see, thus, that Plato's injunction to go to the philosophers rather than to the poets for our knowledge of reality might lead to vast confusion. The philosophers, all supposedly following

[11] Compare the views of Bergson. Pythagoras and his followers, who according to tradition considered number the ultimate reality, should also be considered.

[12] The word *atom*, coming from a Greek word meaning *to cut* and the negative prefix *a*, means "something that cannot be cut up." In these days of atomic fission, our philosophers and scientists should really get a new word for their new views.

reason rather than sense, feeling, or imagination, did not agree among themselves in their answers to the question, what is reality?

In regard to our second question, how do we know reality, the Greek thinkers seem mainly to be interested in discussing how valid general statements can be made. This is involved in the many samples we find of the "Socratic method" in Plato's *Dialogues*. This method consisted in inducing some one of Socrates' hearers to make some general statement which Socrates took apart by the use of concrete examples and showed to be invalid. The positive result of this method would be to show that some form of induction would be necessary to the formulation of a valid general statement. Aristotle adopted this method for example in his *Poetics* and his *Politics*. Plato and especially the neo-Platonists seem to have taken refuge in some form of intuitive conviction.

The negative result of the Socratic method is an agnostic attitude seen in the Cynics and Sceptics. And in the mind of the accusers who brought Socrates to trial this negative result loomed so large that one of the charges, according to Plato, against Socrates was "that he made the worse appear the better reason." According to this point of view, Socrates was always tearing down traditional views and never providing satisfactory, understandable substitutes for them.

Perhaps the suggestion I made earlier in this discussion has now become clear. In urging men to go to the philosophers for their knowledge of reality, I contended that Plato must mean, "Come to me or to Socrates as represented by me." For, as we have seen, in "the shifting borderland between literature and philosophy," the philosophers were no more agreed than the poets were varied in the representation of reality. So we come to our third problem.[18]

[18] For a lengthy discussion of art and reality see F. O. Nolte, *Art and Reality* (Lancaster, Pa., 1942), and John Hospers, *Meaning and Truth in the Arts* (Chapel Hill, N. C., 1946). Mr. Allen Tate expresses the view that poetry presents an independent view of reality, at least equally valid with that presented by science or philosophy.

Bernard De Voto's *Literary Fallacy,* in its indictment of recent American novels for claiming to represent the United States of 1920-1940 and saying nothing about several important aspects of contemporary American life, also rests implicitly on the theory that art to be valid should represent reality.

THE RESPONSIBILITY OF THE ARTIST

As a consequence of the situation set forth in the discussion of the second general problem, we get to the following question: if the artist does not represent reality (and there are many apologists for poets and other artists who contend that they make no claim to represent reality and so should not be brought to book on the charge that they do make such a claim and fail to make good on it[14]) what is his responsibility to society? This question might also be asked, as we have seen, about the philosophers. But there seem to be two assumptions here that have an important bearing on the answer. The first is that the poets are more read and better known than the philosophers; and the second, that poems, plays and other types of literature are more influential than the findings of science and philosophy. Of course, the qualms involved in the influence of a product presenting imaginative and emotional views of reality are not, strictly speaking, esthetic qualms. They are moral and religious. This problem involves the whole question of the relations of art to morality and to religious belief, and since it is the recent view that morality is a social product, the whole subject of art as related to society is relevant now. The question of propaganda[15] in art is also involved here.

The subject of the social relations of art and the judgment of artistic values on social grounds is generally assumed to be a very modern development. But when we look into the history of literature we find that this subject is not so new as some have supposed.

[14] See Allan H. Gilbert's paper "Did Plato Banish the Poets or the Critics?" *Studies in Philology,* vol. XXXVI (1939), pp. 1-19.

[15] From my own point of view, *words,* the medium in literary art, whether spoken or written, are the villains in this case. Words are sounds that have meanings. Meanings are of two sorts, denotative and connotative. It is in the realm of connotation that the difficulties chiefly occur. "Pure" literary art would be possible only if words had no meanings, especially no varying connotations. This is a question of semantics.

The findings of Aristophanes against Socrates and Euripides really belong in this field. And the question raised by Longinus in the latter part of his treatise on *Elevation of Style* as to why there are no great writers in his time is also relevant. Longinus suggests that perhaps the reason for the dearth of great writers is that the social environment is not favorable.

The writer, however, who goes into this subject on the greatest scale is Plato.[16] In *The Republic,* one of the greatest or perhaps the greatest of his dialogues, the subject for discussion is the nature of justice in the individual and in the state.

The Republic opens in a charmingly casual fashion. Socrates and several of his friends had been spectators at a religious festival and they repair to the house of Polemarchus at the Piraeus, the port of Athens. After some miscellaneous conversation the question of the nature of justice arises. Various members of the party offer definitions, the flaws in which are pointed out by Socrates.

The latter after some urging says that in his opinion justice is finding one's place and keeping it. This, he adds, will be more easily seen if the discussion is carried on not on the level of the individual but on the level of the state. His definition, he avers, is just as true in the individual as in the state; but whereas in the individual the legend is written in small letters, in the state it is written in capital letters.

But in the state, he continues, there must be set up some sort of machinery in order to diagnose the various levels in the citizenry. This machinery is the educational system through which all the citizens must pass. The materials to be used in this system, the means by which the caliber of the people is to be discovered, are physical training, music, mathematics, and philosophy. Music in this list is not music in the narrow sense, vocal or instrumental music, but consists of music in the ordinary meaning of that word and literature, or as Socrates expresses it, poetry.

Now poetry had long been an educational instrument among

[16] The most thorough-going discussion of this subject is Werner Jaeger, *Paideia* (New York, 1939-1945), 3 vols.

the Greeks. Homer, as I have stated before, was almost a Bible among them. But Homer and the other poets will not do in Plato's ideal state. The traditional poets are imitators; Plato's ideal citizens must get down or rather up to reality. Homer and the other poets, again, play upon the feelings, the imagination, and the senses. This again will never do. Plato's citizens must be instructed to use their reason. So the poets are excluded from *The Republic*.[17] A new literature must be written which will expound in the plainest and most direct form the doctrines which will best form the characters of the prospective citizens. Besides, only that music which induces civic virtue can be tolerated.

Once the musical material is selected, the educational system may start working. All the pupils start at the bottom and are given severe periodic examinations. Those who pass their tests go on to further study. Those who fail, it is assumed, have found their level and should be content to stay there. Early in the course, those who fail become laborers, then soldiers. Those who have the physical stamina, and the intellectual caliber to persist are the candidates for governors of the state and they are given training in philosophy which, again, I assume must be Plato's philosophy.

Plato's *Republic* is, like most of the utopias, a totalitarian state which has a perfect right to dictate what the citizens shall read, what music they shall hear, what plays they shall see, and what religious beliefs they shall hold.[18]

---

[17] Allan H. Gilbert, *op. cit.*

[18] One of Plato's indictments against Homer and the other poets is that they tell lies about the gods. The common drama is to Plato suspect because actors in plays take on other characters than their own. It is interesting that our word *hypocrite* is a word derived from the Greek word for an actor in a play.

Aristotle in his *Politics* takes exception to Plato's conclusions in *The Republic* along two lines. One of these is to the whole plan of totalitarian training, the value of which Aristotle says Plato does not prove. The second is a very shrewd point. "Plato," says Aristotle, "puts his ablest pupils through a strenuous and long regimen in order to find their level. The less able pupils who fall by the way are expected to find their level with less training and be content in it. Does not this imply that the allegedly less able pupils are really more able than their supposedly more fortunate colleagues!"

Aristotle goes on in *The Politics* to outline a utopia which he arrives at by an inductive examination of real and ideal states.

Now transferring his conclusions on the state to the individual level, Plato holds that obviously the reason is the noblest of the human faculties and the just person is the one who is governed by reason, which should dominate the other faculties. Plato thus shows that he feels very keenly the importance of the artist's responsibility to society and has outlined what he considers a foolproof scheme for insuring society against subversive acts.[19]

Horace, in his *Epistle to the Pisos,* better known as *The Art of Poetry,* is the progenitor of later neo-classic theories of literature. In this work of Horace there are two passages relevant to our present topic.

In a passage beginning with line 309 of his *Epistle,* Horace writes (I paraphrase his lines) that knowledge is the basis of good writing and that this knowledge can best be got from the *Dialogues* of Plato.[20] Here the poet will find set forth the just dues of country, friends, relatives, and public officials. Equipped with such reading and with acquaintance with the active life of the world the poet can not go wrong and is bound to rouse the interest of his readers or hearers. These remarks certainly imply that it behooves the poet to be very careful to stay in the beaten paths of tradition. Horace says, to be sure, that this is the way for the poet to be certain of an appreciative audience. He does not catalogue any penalties for the writer who does not like his advice, nor does he specifically assign to the writer any particular responsibility in this matter. But some ideas on the responsibility of the

---

[19] Aristotle does not go to Plato's length in discussing this question. In his *Rhetoric,* however, there are some statements which imply his beliefs. Aristophanes in his various comedies also has hints as to his views, though he might use the alibi that the views expressed are those of his characters.

Mr. F. W. Chambers in his *Cycles of Taste* cited above has collected the scattered critical remarks of Greek and Roman writers on poetry, painting, and sculpture. These remarks award merit on civic or moral grounds.

In *The Laws* Plato outlines another ideal state not so good, he admits, as the one set forth in *The Republic.* In *The Laws* Plato is not so dictatorial nor so puritanical as in *The Republic.* But he maintains his general view of state control of culture.

[20] Horace, it appears from this reference, differs from Aristophanes in his view of the upshot of the teaching of Socrates.

writer to his public seem to me to be floating around in the neighborhood here. Horace was of the Emperor Augustus's courtly company, and the Augustan regime was much concerned with literary support. We must inevitably think of the fate of Ovid in this connection.

In a later passage in *The Epistle,* beginning line 333, there are some better known remarks of Horace. *The Epistle* is so casual, in appearance at least, that I am not sure whether the ideas set forth in the earlier lines just paraphrased and discussed are carried over here, but perhaps they are. In this later passage (again I paraphrase) Horace writes that poets wish to benefit their readers or to delight them or to set forth ideas that are both pleasant and suitable for life. This is the shortest path to the mind of the reader—delightfully to teach him. Even the wildest flights of the imagination should seem to be true. Old people will condemn that which fails in useful truth and dry commonplaces will not appeal to young readers.

In those lines Horace does not say just what lessons the poet shall delightfully teach. But again there is some connection with our present topic suggested.

Plato, then, shows himself very sensitive to the problem of the relations between art and society. He is very outspoken in his contention that society has a right to control the arts. Horace is very adept in urging the poet to play safe.[21] We have come to our fourth topic which takes us into a new field, apparently not very closely connected with the fields already entered. As I have before remarked, however, some thinkers closely integrate their concepts of the types of literature with our other problems.[22]

[21] Compare the writings of the new humanists in this connection and the lecture by F. Brunetiere, *Art and Morality* trans. by Arthur Beatty (New York, 1899).

[22] Ferdinand Brunetière is one of these. He makes one's attitude toward the types of literature a moral question. Thus, if epic is a higher literary type than lyric or satire, you are guilty, according to Brunetiere, of moral delinquency if you spend your time on lyric when you should be reading epic.

THE VARIOUS TYPES OF LITERATURE

There is a wealth of material in Greek and Roman writers on this subject.[23]

Literature is a Latin word; the Greeks apparently had no corresponding word. They talked about *poetry* and *rhetoric*. The Greeks also lacked a consistently general term for prose; sometimes they used *logos* for this, and what they had to say about it they said for the most part in works on rhetoric. Here *oratory* was the one subject always presented. There are some passages on *history*, but these do not always consider historiography. *Philosophy* was also recognized as a legitimate field for artistic writing; but except for hints in treatises on logic, there is little attention paid by classical writers to the question on how philosophy should be written.

Coming now to the literary kinds in their narrowest guise,[24] we find many vague and naive ideas before Plato. These Plato brought "into speculative focus." [25] As we have already seen, Plato has a low view of literary art in general. It stimulates the senses, imagination, and feelings. But he does recognize, with some contempt, four principal types of literary form: lyric poetry,

[23] The most thorough-going treatment that I know of this subject is James J. Donohue, *The Theory of Literary Kinds: Ancient Classical Literature* (Dubuque, Ia., 1943) which lists the following major or minor contributors to the classical fund of this discussion: Aristotle, Aristophanes, Cicero, *The Coislinian Treatise,* Dio Chrysostom, Demetrius, Diomedes, Dionysius, Horace, Isocrates, Longinus, Lucian, Petronius, Philostratus, Pindar, Plato, Plutarch, Polybius, Quintillian, Servius, Sidonius, Strabo, Suetonius, Tacitus, and Varro. He does not consider the late neo-Platonists.

Dr. Donohue starts his discussion with an account of the classical views of the relationship of spoken to written communication, follows this with an exposition of classical comments on the differences between prose and verse, shows that Greeks and Romans distinguished between *artistic* and *practical* communication in language, and concludes by setting forth the classical definitions of the literary kinds in the narrowest sense of the term; *e.g.,* epic, lyric, drama. I shall lean heavily on Dr. Donohue, though I shall confine myself to his last section.

In this treatise, Dr. Donohue makes side glances at other topics in my discussion, *e.g.,* inspiration, imitation, and literary diction.

[24] See the preceding note.

[25] These are Dr. Donohue's words; see p. 53 of his treatise.

narrative poetry, drama, and oratory. By giving all these the proper concept they can be useful in his ideal state.

Plato thinks of *lyric* and *non-lyric* as the basic divisions of literature and further separates non-lyric into verse and prose. Among the kinds of the non-lyric is narrative poetry. Poetry to Plato has an affiliation with music and this is probably what made lyric to him a prime form of poetry.

Lyric had several divisions among the Greeks. Some of these divisions were made on the basis of content; some, on the basis of verse-form. Of the latter the best marked was iambic which included lampoon. Melic poetry—the dithyramb and the ode—has obvious connections with music, vocal and instrumental. Elegiac poetry, written in the limping couplet, was, to start with, a funeral lamentation, but it came to be used for all kinds of content; and out of it came forms like the epigram.

Narrative poetry in which the poet might speak in his own person or in the persons of characters is, of course, seen in the *Iliad* in its highest form, the epic.

Drama is to Plato a hybrid form, originating in lyric dithyramb but coming in Aeschylus, Sophocles, and Euripides to include narrative sections also. This comes under Plato's ban because the dramatist is masquerading in various ways and thus imitating various other persons. And imitation to Plato was bad, as we have seen.

Aristotle wrote two works, *The Poetics* and *The Rhetoric*, which are apropos here. At the outset of the former Aristotle starts out bravely with the statement that he proposes to deal with the various kinds of poetry and the capacities of each. But he does not make good this promise. Tragedy is the only form which he treats at any length. Sixteen of the twenty-six chapters of *The Poetics* are concerned partly or wholly with the drama. In one of these Aristotle outlines the origin of the drama. In chapters five and twenty-six, comedy[26] is touched on. The chief point that

[26] In his *Rhetoric* Aristotle discusses the various devices at the command of the orator. Among these is the possibility of ridiculing his opponent. Here Aristotle takes the opportunity to expound his views of the ludicrous, and says that comedy is one species of the ludicrous.

Aristotle makes here is that comedy and tragedy differ in that the former presents men as worse than they are; in the latter, as better than they are. The rest of his discussion of drama is concerned with tragedy in itself or as compared with epic. There is mention but no discussion of the lyric.

In his inductive review of tragedy Aristotle outlines its evolution, lists various narrative devices, sets forth the prime requisites for an eligible tragic hero and gives us his famous definition. The most important feature of tragedy is the plot, or as it is called in some translations of *The Poetics,* "the fable." This I take it differs from "the story" in that plot is the pattern or arrangement in which the story is set up. The story should be "of a certain magnitude" and as it is arranged in the plot should have unity. This unity, later called "unity of action" is the only one of the later well-known "dramatic unities" to which Aristotle pays much attention. He does remark, to be sure, that the Greek dramatists tried to get their action "within the revolution of the sun"; that is that they endeavored, to limit their action to twenty-four hours. But he does not say that they always succeeded nor does he say that all prospective dramatists should follow their examples. Unity in drama and epic is to Aristotle not merely logical. Not the life story of the hero but only those events which are integral to the plot are to be found in the best examples of epic and tragedy. In the latter, since the story was already known to the audience the Greek writers did not devote much time to dramatic exposition.[27]

In fact, notwithstanding its later history, *The Poetics* is not primarily a book of rules. It is an analytic descriptive account of how one should recognize a tragedy if he saw one. In chapter seventeen, to be sure, Aristotle gives some brief advice to writers,

[27] On this point see the fragment of Antiphanes quoted in J. D. Denniston, *Greek Literary Criticism* (New York, 1924), one of the volumes in *The Library of Greek Thought.* Antiphanes remarks that it is much easier in Athens to write tragedy than comedy. For the writer of comedy has to make up his story as well as arrange his plot; whereas the writer of tragedy has merely to arrange his plot.

but this is confined to urging them to make an outline of their prospective work and this bears out what was said earlier in this essay in Aristotle's view of the author as purposeful.

What Aristotle says about epic is to be found in chapters five, twenty-four, and twenty-six. In the first of these he remarks that epic agrees with[28] tragedy in treating serious actions in metrical form, but differs in that it uses a single meter and is much longer than tragedy. Epic and tragedy should be judged, he holds, on the same basis; hence one who knows what is excellent in tragedy can recognize the same excellence in epic. For all the matter in epic is found in tragedy, not vice-versa. In chapter twenty-six, he writes that tragedy has been thought a lower form of poetry than epic because tragedy, through scenery, actors, and gestures, can appeal to the vulgar crowd. This leads him to the defense of tragedy in chapter twenty-seven, in which he concludes that tragedy is superior to epic because it uses music and spectacle, and because it is more concentrated than epic. It appears that Aristotle personally preferred tragedy to epic and is anxious to defend himself.

We shall not have space to go into Aristotle's *Rhetoric* in detail. Suffice it to say that he gives much space to the psychology of communication; for *rhetoric* to the Greeks and Romans meant *oratory*. Further it is in him we find the beginnings of the later divisions of the various kinds of speeches which are discussed at such length by later writers.

Horace did not classify himself as a poet,[29] though perhaps he would not have liked to hear anyone else say so. His *Art of Poetry* appears to me to be a somewhat indirect way of advising people not to write poetry. It seems to me rather amusing that this work has come to be regarded as a manual for poets. Horace is known as one of the neatest and sanest of lyric poets and the most urbane of satirists, but in *The Art of Poetry* he says very little about the

[28] A recent translation of *The Poetics* which reports Aristotle as saying here "Epic follows tragedy" is ambiguous.

[29] This attitude on Horace's part toward his own works is probably due to the fact that he, taking to heart his own advice to prospective poets, did not aspire to write an epic or a tragedy. He advises poets to be fully aware of their own abilities, and avoid subjects and forms beyond their powers.

lyric and nothing about satire. In fact he gives his attention to the drama. Some have thought that the reason for this is that the Pisos to whom Horace was writing were ambitious to write tragedy.

In his account of tragedy Horace adds a few details to Aristotle's exposition. Thus, Horace says that tragedy should not go beyond five acts. He probably got this idea from the Alexandrian critics with whose work he was familiar, though just where he got it we do not know. Greek tragedies are not divided into acts, and the first tragedies to be written with this idea in mind are probably those ascribed to Seneca. It is true that the comedies of Plautus and Terence are divided into acts and scenes, but the earliest manuscripts of Plautus and Terence belong to the fourth century of the Christian era, and modern editors agree that these act and scene divisions in Plautus and Terence are editorial.

Again, Horace in his discussion of tragedy proscribes violence on the stage. He says the eye gives us more convincing evidence than the ear and that he would not believe in the reality of death if we saw it on the stage. Therefore, violent scenes should be reported, not acted on the stage. Here, of course, Horace is correctly summarizing the practice of Greek tragedy, and his dictum was very potent, especially in classic French tragedy.

Horace makes up for his omission of any discussion of satire in *The Art of Poetry* by numerous remarks on the subject in his *Conversation Pieces* (*Sermones*) which is the name Horace gives to his *Satires*. He connects satire with the old Greek comedy, a view which most modern students of Horace think wrong.[30] He began his studies in satire with judgments on his predecessor in Latin satire, Lucillius, who, Horace thought, was too violent in his attacks and crude in his style. The satirist, to Horace, should avoid political invective and playfully attack human "follies not crimes" as Ben Jonson later says with reference to comedy.[31]

[30] Quintillian is nearer right in his judgment that "satire is wholly ours," *i.e.* Roman.
[31] Quintillian holds many of the same views of the kinds of poetry as Horace. But in Quintillian these views are only incidental since his main interest is in prose.

Coming now to Latin prose, we find that Cicero and Quintillian deal most extensively with this subject, though they are mainly concerned with only one form of prose, namely, oratory. Here, we find the various kinds and styles of oratory explained and practical advice given to students and practitioners of oratory set forth. In Cicero's time oratory was still an art influential in public life, while in that of Quintillian it was mainly an exercise in the schools, so there is a good deal of difference in the connotations of their respective pieces of advice.

All the kinds of oratory—judicial, epideictic, and legislative—use historical evidence and illustration; hence, Cicero especially has a good deal to say of historiography. He regarded it as a serious matter, for he holds the historian should be frank and truthful. He thought that history was an ethical teacher, and provided material useful for instructing men in public life. Some of Cicero's views in history and historiography are found in his dialogues on oratory; some, in his dialogue *On the Laws;* and some in his philosophical dialogues, especially *On Purposes (De Finibus).*[32]

We have not been able to include every writer and to go with detail into every point in one discussion of this topic. But we have made it clear that the subject of the literary types was of interest to the literary theorists of Greece and Rome. And so we pass to our last topic.

THE PROPER LANGUAGE FOR LITERATURE

The common Homeric phrase "winged words" testifies to the ancient belief in the power of the spoken or written word. And the distinction made in ancient times between practical and artistic communication implies that the ancients thought that the vocabulary of artistic communication differed from that of prac-

---

[32] The most exhaustive recent book on the subjects of this paper in Latin literature is J. F. D'Alton, *Roman Literary Theory and Criticism* (New York, 1931).

tical communication, and ancient writers do not leave us merely an implication here.

Thus, Aristotle in his definition of tragedy includes among the features of tragedy "language embellished with each kind of artistic ornament." [33] He follows this up later with two brief but meaty chapters on poetic language. The first of these is concerned with grammar and need not detain us here. The second opens with a statement in which Aristotle shows that he is using the same principle of "the golden mean," which he employs in his *Ethics* and his *Politics*. "The perfection of style," he says, "is to be clear without being common-place." The easiest way to be clear is to be colloquial; but this is to run the risk of being common-place. On the other hand the other extreme is to be found in the writer who uses exotic words only. He runs the risk of obscurity through his use of unusual words. These are strange or rare words, combined words, words borrowed from foreign languages or from dialects other than that normally used by the writer, compound words, synonyms, and metaphors, the term Aristotle uses for figures of speech in general. The writer who judiciously combines ordinary language with these extraordinary locutions will be in the way of achieving a distinguished style.[34]

Horace, who by dint of hard work attained the "curiosa felicitas" [35] of his style, gives much attention to poetic language in

[33] This is S. H. Butcher's translation. I prefer this to A. H. Gilbert's "language made sweet." I do not like the connotations of "made sweet." And by the way I do not find that the Greeks made any clear distinctions between "denotation" and "connotation." Aristophanes in *The Frogs* pokes some fun at Aeschylus for his ponderous style; and at Euripides, for the meanness of his. But Aristotle in the *Poetics* commends Euripides for using an unusual word for *eating*, whereas Aeschylus uses an ordinary one.

[34] Aristotle is discussing here the proper language of tragedy; but I think we may safely assume that he would think in the same terms of comedy, epic, and lyric. He says that in poetry very often it is necessary for the poet to argue or explain, and then the poet is edging into the field of oratory. The language proper for oratory he discusses in his *Rhetoric*.

[35] This phrase was applied to Horace by Petronius. The phrase is a stroke of genius, very hard to translate; "careful happiness" is a literal translation. It means that Horace worked hard in his style and attained the result of having come on excellence by chance.

The Art of Poetry.[36] In his *Satires* and *Epistles* Horace has many remarks on the infelicities and crudities of the earlier Latin poets on whose work he had been brought up. His acquaintance with the Greek poets had shown him how to remedy these defects. His study of the critics from Aristotle down to his own time had led him to reflect on the theory and practice of poetry. These studies and his practical experience as a poet find their consummation in *The Art of Poetry.* He carries on from Aristotle and makes some of the latter's data more explicit. Thus, he recommends that in coining new words the Latin writing should draw on Greek especially.[37] He has an interesting passage in which he compares the changing vocabulary of a language to the leaves of a tree, and points out that usage is the final arbiter and sets the rule and plan used in language. He has much to say about decorum in language; that is, to the suitability of the language to the particular situation in a given poem or other literary work.[38]

The most elaborate discussion of the proper language for literature is to be found in the work ascribed to Longinus and usually entitled *On the Sublime.* This title is misleading, for in the work you find little discussion of the nature of the sublime. Longinus's basic assumption is that literary style should rise above the ordinary level. Hence the titles *On Elevation of Style,* given by Professor T. G. Tucker in his translation of the essay, or *On Literary Excellence,* given by Professor A. H. Gilbert, are superior to the traditional *On the Sublime.*

Longinus does not limit himself as Aristotle does when the

[36] There is much material on poetic language in such Greek writers as Dionysius of Halicarnassus, Demetrius, and Plutarch. Lucian ridicules the self-consciousness of some writers over their style.

[37] Just as later the Renaissance theorists urged modern vernacular writers to draw from Greek and Latin sources.

[38] Cicero does somewhat the same kind of thing for prose. *Decorum* is a term that is applied to many things in classical theories of literature. Thus it means consistency in characterization, no mixture of comedy and tragedy. See the many references to *decorum* in J. F. D'Alton, *Roman Literary Theory and Criticism* (London, 1931). Quintillian follows up the trail of Cicero and is particularly interesting in his advice that the orator read the poets in order to increase his vocabulary and add brilliance to his style.

latter says that a good style is a medium between the clear and the ordinary. Longinus is mainly interested in pointing out the dangers which beset the path of the writer who strives for an elevated style. He touches on but dismisses the contention that literary excellence comes by nature, not by art. Training is necessary for the good writer, and he can avoid the dangers mentioned above if they are pointed out to him. These dangers all arise from the search for novelty, and the results of this search may be bombast, puerility, ill-timed pathos, and frigidity.

A literary classic is one that has kept its appeal to men in all ages. And the basis of this appeal is fivefold: great ideas, vigorous and inspired emotion, figurative language that is appropriate, language otherwise notable, and fitting and dignified composition.[39] It is obvious that the third and fourth of these are relevant to the discussion here.

The figure-making power is a basic poetic power and is justified by strong and inspired emotion. Longinus discusses and illustrates the rhetorical question, asyndeton, hyperbaton, polyptoles, grammatical novelties, apostrophe, periphrasis, metaphor, simile, and hyperbole. In most cases good and bad samples of the figure under discussion are adduced.[40]

"Now since the thought and the diction of a literary composition are mutually dependent," remarks Longinus in a generalizing but not a concluding statement, "let us see if there is something still to be said on diction. It would be superfluous to explain to those who already know it that the choice of noble and grandly appropriate words is wonderfully effective in moving and influencing the reader, and that all orators and historians set the attainment of this as their chief object. For this in itself gives at one time grandeur, beauty, antique richness, weight, energy, strength, and a sort of polish like that on the most beautiful statues; it endows the facts with a speaking sound as it were. "Truly

[39] In his discussion of these topics Longinus uses many specific illustrations from Greek literature, and is the first Greek or Latin "critic" to refer to Hebrew literature. The order of this discussion often appears illogical in Longinus.

[40] Longinus holds that the great are superior to the faultless.

beautiful words are the very light of thought. Yet majesty in diction is not always to be desired: to array petty affairs in noble and stately words would be to put a great tragic mask on a puny child." [41]

It is thus quite clear that on the five topics discussed in this essay, the Greeks and Romans had many things to say, many things that are repeated in the works of succeeding philosophers of literature. And that these topics are still live topics is clearly evident in any recent bibliography of the subject.

BIBLIOGRAPHY [1]

BIBLIOGRAPHY

Bibliotheca philologica classica, 1874-1932 (Leipzig, 1875-1934), 59 vols. This is the standard.

Carey, M., ed., *The Oxford Classical Dictionary*, 6th ed. (Oxford, 1949). See also the three appendices for an excellent brief bibliography.

Foster, Finley Melville Kendall, *English Translations from Greek: a Bibliographical Survey*, Columbia University Studies in English (New York, 1918).

Peck, Harry Thurston, ed., *Harper's Dictionary of Classical Antiquities* (New York, 1897).

Sandys, John Edwyn, *A Companion to Latin Studies* (Cambridge, Eng., 1910).
A good supplement with the Oxford Classical Dictionary.

HISTORY OF LITERATURE

Hamilton, Edith, *The Greek Way* (New York, 1930).
——, *The Roman Way* (New York, 1936).
Both of these references offer stimulating interpretations.

Wendell, Barrett, *Traditions of European Literature from Homer to Dante* (New York, 1920), 2 vols.
Has the advantage of including writing outside the classical stream.

[41] I am quoting the translation by Professor Allan H. Gilbert in his *Literary Criticism: Plato to Dryden* (New York, 1940).

[1] Critical and expository matter elucidating the literature of Greece and Rome is so extensive that no brief statement can be more than suggestive.

7

Italian Literature

GIUSEPPE PREZZOLINI

COLUMBIA UNIVERSITY

Professor Giuseppe Prezzolini *is an international figure, not only because he was born in Perugia and was for twenty years professor of Italian literature at Columbia University, but because for almost a half century books and articles have been pouring from his pen, in both English and Italian, and many are translated into French, German, and Spanish. With Papini he founded* Leonardo *in 1903; he published in 1950* America in pantofole. *In the years between he wrote many books, critical, historical, social, biographical, bibliographical, political, educational. His* Repertorio bibliografico della storia e della critica della letteratura italiana, 1902-1942 *is standard; best known in this country are* The Legacy of Italy *(1948), and* Rome *(1949). He was head of the Information and Literature Section of the Intellectual Cooperation Division of the League of Nations; New York City knows him as director of the Casa Italiana (1930-40). He is now emeritus, but not the less prolific for that.*

Italian Literature

CHARACTERISTICS

I FIND the most striking characteristic of this literature to be its universality: that is, its prodigality of authors who more than in other literature have attracted the attention and interest of people of all lands and of other literary, civil, and religious traditions. St. Francis, Dante, Galilei, Manzoni, Leopardi—there is a veritable roster of literary geniuses of all centuries who belong not solely to Italy but one might say to the whole world, and who have elicited not only translations but also critical and historical works by scholars of other languages, of other cultures, and of other religions.

This position of eminence among the literatures of Europe vanished when romanticism introduced a new concept of art not founded on "models," and several countries, like Germany, Russia, the Scandinavian countries, which previously from a literary point of view were minor or non-existent, produced great writers of European importance. And it might be added that this universal characteristic of Italian literature was even further damaged by the unification of Italy (1861). Carducci, the greatest poet of the unification period, did not possess this same capacity of attracting readers from other countries, and if D'Annunzio won this universal appeal it was only insofar as he reflected foreign trends.

I would say that Italians, in unifying Italy, deprived cultured Europeans of their second fatherland; Italy became a little competitor among other nations, and no longer the dream nation of those who already had their own country.

In addition to the appeal to readers, there was also a universality of interest in the authors; indeed, in few civilizations are found so many writers as in Italian literature with such varied interests. An Alberti, a Da Vinci are famous for having been artists, thinkers and scientists, but cannot the same be said—though not in equal measure—of Michelangelo (poet, sculptor, painter, and architect), of Galilei (writer, scientist, musician, and literary critic), of Machiavelli (political philosopher, dramatist, and philologist) and of many others who were versatile even to the surfeit of this virtue, dilettantism?

A second characteristic of Italian literature is its basis in the classical world in general, but with greater emphasis on the Roman rather than on the Greek ideal, whereas French humanism and particularly German romanticism stemmed from Athens rather than from Rome. The most famous authors of Italian literature were educated in the Latin tradition (with the exception of artists like Leonardo, Cellini, and Michelangelo) and when they were not actually university graduates or priests, they had a classical education. But there were few Greek scholars. We must wait for Poliziano (1454-1494) before coming to an Italian author who was well versed in Greek. Metastasio knew Greek well, but his was a caricature of the Greek spirit. Dante and Petrarch, Boccaccio, Ariosto, Tasso, Machiavelli, and Manzoni were not exposed to Greek influence. Galilei showed evidence of it not only in his thought but perhaps also in his style. But it is only at the onset of the nineteenth century, with Foscolo and preeminently with Leopardi, that the Greek spirit is manifest.

We may also say that Italian authors come from the cultured classes. Their writings suggest the scholar's library rather than the open market places, with the exception of one writer who is, however, primarily an artist—Cellini.

It is also well known that the chivalric ideal, as soon as it had crossed the Alps from France, became in Italy the object of a parody (Pulci, *Il Morgante maggiore*); or of nostalgic sentiment (Boiardo, *L'Orlando innamorato*); or of an artistic transformation into a fantastic world (Ariosto, *L'Orlando furioso*), leaving its realistic traces only in the literature of the people of ports and mountains who were the last to become enthusiastic over the exploits of Orlando. Italian authors were merchants, clergymen, scholars, artists, thinkers, lovers, and in their thought and expression more or less remote from military life and martial enthusiasm; they thus reflected the state of mind of a country which did not create a warlike civilization. Even with Machiavelli, military life is a technique, not an ethic.

The classical and Roman continuity in Italy is in part tied in with what German historians called "Romgedanke," on which they have written many provocative works. In a certain sense Italian classicism is different from that of other countries, inasmuch as it grew in expectation of a renewed Italy, or of a renewed world with Rome as the center. The illusion of being the inheritors of, or the successors to Rome, and of being able to renew its grandeur, inspired in a literary way the Italian cultured classes, from Petrarch to Mazzini, from Machiavelli to Alfieri. Whether that has been a blessing or a curse to the nation we will not say; but certainly it has always played a large rôle in Italian literature, even at times when it was a cause of bombast and hyperbole, as in Filicaia and in the early Leopardi.

Of course there have been several investigations on the permanence of the national idea in Italian literature. Italians have had but a literary ideal of national unity; the political will emerged only in the nineteenth century and solely among the rich and cultured classes, and not even there unanimously. For centuries Venice and Florence, Milan and Naples, Rome and Turin have followed their own policies, each city jealous of the other; but in speaking and writing there was, more or less, an agreement. Italy was not only a geographical expression, as Metternich put it; it was fundamentally a literary expression.[1]

The Catholic religious life has left a profound imprint in the literary structure that is sustained by the two columns of Dante

[1] Edmund G. Gardner, *The National Idea in Italian Literature* (Manchester, 1921).

and Manzoni—a visible influence even when it manifests itself
in negative forms of reaction, whether naturalistic, as in Boccaccio, or anticlerical as in Carducci. Save for Ariosto, whose
fantasy seems to elude even Catholicism, it looms for all as an
engrossing problem—of conscience for Petrarch, of competition
for Mazzini, of philosophy for Leopardi; it torments Tasso, limits
Vico, agonizes Michelangelo, irritates Machiavelli, and provides
virtually all authors with familiar images, expressions, artistic
tricks, starting-off points for thought. It is impossible to understand nine-tenths of Italian literature without the knowledge,
not only of the doctrine but of the life of Catholicism.

On the other hand, it is evident that some trends of the Reformation are visible in Italian literature; even where the Reformation would be less expected as in Machiavelli, and certainly in
Michelangelo, in Sarpi, in De Sanctis, not actually to mention
the few but important Italian Protestants like Socini and Ochino,
who brought their most audacious sects outside of Italy with
them, where they had significant developments.

As in every literature of the world, love is a principal subject
in the Italian. In every century, in every period, almost in every
writer, love appears. It is not true, as has been said, that the image
of the angelic lady, or Mary, is the ideal of Italian literature.
That would be correct for Dante's Beatrice, but not for Laura,
who, although in the imagination of Petrarch is more alive when
she is dead, is always flesh; it is not correct for Ariosto's Angelica,
who is a coquette, nor for Boccaccio's Fiammetta or Pampinea,
both of whom are fully satisfied with earthly love, not even for
Manzoni's Lucia, who has the premonitions of a pure and simple Christian soul, but not the aureole of sanctity; and not for
Leopardi's Silvia, who possesses a sort of pre-Christian Greek
purity.

There are loves in quantity, and loves of every quality. To the
common taste of many sanctimonious Anglo-Saxons it seems that
Italian literature is lewd and obscene. This would be true if one
were to separate certain pages of realism from the context of the

work in which they belong. The most daring scenes of Boccaccio, for example, have not an obscene meaning, but are only details of a work praising the intelligence of man and regarding with an amused smile the work of Fortune in the world; sometimes this realism, obscene in appearance, is in reality a caricature, and therefore could even be interpreted as essentially ethical. For school work, however, it is evident that several passages or cantos of Italian writers, even of modern authors, cannot be read and commented upon in class; but this does not reflect upon the writer so much as upon the maturity of the students.

A permanent and fundamental characteristic of Italian literary art has been its ability from the beginning to combine creation with thought; poetry with esthetics, even with rhetoric as in the *Convito* of Dante. None is so intimately diffused like the Italian with the discussion of the problem of language, which goes from Dante to Carducci and Croce, proceeding through Machiavelli and Manzoni.

No other literature has produced such a vast number of books of literary rules which were transmitted to other people and accepted by others of different intellectual aristocratic tastes. The literary artistic disputes and controversies, which occur only in a society where the value of art and of its importance for human perfection is felt, are always frequent in Italy.

For centuries, therefore, Italian literature has been considered the most refined, smooth, and perfected of all the classical models, due to the very deliberateness with which these ideals seem to have been cultivated; and one might say that up to the epoch of romanticism, through the time the classic ideal was supreme in the world of European letters, even works that now seem to us bereft of originality—labored products of indifferent talent but in possession of a most studied technique—were admired and imitated outside of Italy. Hence, up to the eighteenth century Italian literature in Europe held an eminent position, close to the model literatures of the Romans and the Greeks; and even in the centuries of its decadence (in the seventeenth and eighteenth centuries) it was considered the third classical literature, a knowledge of which was essential to a cultured person. Perhaps for that reason, Italian literature was branded as false, pompous, artificial, and rhetorical, the changed view starting with the famous French polemic of Dominique Bouhours and continuing to the German romantics.

There was no lack of Italians who subscribed to this view, from Giuseppe Baretti in the eighteenth century to Ruggiero Bonghi and even to Enrico Thovez in the nineteenth, who charged Italian poetry with a lack of originality and lyricism, excepting only the works of Dante and Leopardi.

Another characteristic of Italian literature seems to me to be its close connection from the beginnings, but particularly during the Renaissance, with the fine arts. No other European literature before the nineteenth century has such a large number of artist-writers as the Italian. Prominent in this category are Leonardo, Michelangelo, and Vasari; but Ghiberti already marks with Giotto this alliance in the fourteenth century, which will continue in all centuries (Salvator Rosa in the seventeenth), and has recently been seen in the group of painter-sculptor-art critics which flourished in the period of Italian impressionism (the Macchiaioli) and of futurism (Soffici, Carrà, Boccioni).

The relations, in various limited periods, between Italian literature and music must not be overlooked. A great part of the lyricism of the origins was assuredly written to be accompanied by song, and at times by dancing. The religious canticles of St. Francis—one of the first documents of vernacular poetry—like those of Fra Jacopone were actually sung, and Dante makes mention in the *Purgatorio* of one of his songs being set to music by Casella; and thus were sung many now famous poems celebrating love, like that of Lorenzo il Magnifico and of Poliziano, without mentioning the *Canti carnascialeschi* (whose music was often identical with that of the *Laudi spirituali*) and many poetic *intermedi* of the sixteenth-century comedies. Also the chivalric poems of popular character (probably not *Orlando Furioso* of

Ariosto but the *Morgante* of Pulci, for example) were sung in the streets and squares of the city. In the seventeenth and eighteenth centuries Italian poetry combines with music in the madrigal and in numberless ariettas which are musically conceived; standing out above them all is Metastasio, in whose dramas one cannot distinguish where the poetry ends and the music begins. But this tendency had already begun with the pastoral drama of Tasso and Guarini, a large part of which, even though not expressly written for music, was to be recited in singing tones and continued with melodrama (1601). Further apart were the two arts in the Romantic and veristic period except for the unfortunate and, at times, ridiculous opera librettos. At the end of the eighteenth century, however, the collaboration of Lorenzo da Ponte and Metastasio with Mozart, and of Renato de' Calzabigi with Gluck brought good results. Both German masters took the words from the Italian, as did Beethoven for his *Fidelio* and Händel for his *Ariodante*. The Italian language and literature apparently seemed to them to be the most adaptable for music.

It is difficult to make previsions in a field such as that of letters, but considering tendencies which have developed in Europe after romanticism, one is tempted to consider Italian literature as a dead literature which will be studied in the future in the same way as the Greek and Latin literatures, rather than as a living literature. Verism and decadentism, even though they had illustrious contributors from the Italian—such as Verga and D'Annunzio—seem but slightly favorable to the tradition of idealism and order of the Italian genius, the universal contribution given by Italy recently being in the field of philosophy (Croce) and in that of criticism (De Sanctis and his followers) rather than in that of literary creation (in spite of Pirandello). Moreover, the political and military defeats of Italy in its last period cause one to foresee a period of indifference on the part of the world public, which could only be overcome by the emergence of a personality of great stature.

ASSUMING ITALY'S LITERATURE IS ALL A RENAISSANCE:
A LIST OF FIFTY IMPORTANT AUTHORS

Generally all histories of Italian literature follow its division in three periods: Middle Ages, Renaissance and Modern times, corresponding to the three periods of European history. But, as can easily be seen, the historians, after having made these divisions, are obliged to do their best in order to patch them up, recognizing that the authors do not always fit into the three categories. It is better to recognize that such distinctions are not much of an aid in understanding Italian literature. What we can see is that in the peninsula between the eleventh and thirteenth centuries there is a strong vitality manifested through deep movements which present economical, artistic, political, social, religious aspects; and that at the same time some powerful literary figures come to the fore of the stage—Dante, Petrarch, Boccaccio —who establish a sort of cultural tradition, having used the language of the uncultivated people of Tuscany (*vulgare*) instead of Latin, for some of their works, which were much more alive, and earned more popularity than those written in Latin. This tradition is, in a certain sense, still operating.

The distinctions of the Middle Ages and the Renaissance are so elastic, the Renaissance being so deeply rooted in the Middle Ages, that now many historians say that during the Middle Ages there were several Renaissances, and that many great representative men of the Renaissance continue having Middle Age characteristics. It would be better to say that with the eleventh to the thirteenth centuries there is a new history in Italy and we may call it a Renaissance, if we put more emphasis on *naissance,* than on *re.* That is, we may consider as the most important fact the appearance of a new people with political and artistic manifestations like the *Comune,* and later the *Signoria* (the paintings of Cimabue and Giotto, the poems of the *Dolce Stil Nuovo,* etc.).

In this sense Italian literature is simply a Renaissance literature, and I do not see why the author of the *Canto* on Brunetto Latini and on Ulysses ought not to be considered a Renaissance author; not to mention Petrarch and Boccaccio, who, among other characteristics, were conscious of belonging to this new epoch.

For centuries Italian people have shown a continued interest and an ever fresh ability in literature and in the fine arts: it is a commonplace, but I cannot alter it, to say that Italy is the country of arts. There are moments in which the heart of Italy seems to send great streams of blood through its veins, and through the world in general; and there are moments of weaker force. But certainly it never ceased, not even in the centuries of political and military decadence, the seventeenth and eighteenth centuries, because then it was manifested in music. Not only are there thinkers, poets, and musicians throughout the life of the Italian people, but there is a general popular interest in art; more, I think, than there has ever been in any other European country, except in Athens.

This is all we can reasonably say. It is impossible, although it has been attempted, to fix a main feature of this literature. All these constructions seem to fall to pieces as soon as we examine even superficially two or three authors of a period, even the beautiful and tempting one, borrowed by De Sanctis from the dialectic of Hegel, with its three moments: affirmation of a world where form and content are balanced, in the fourteenth century; negation in the sixteenth where this world loses the content for the love of form; and synthesis in the nineteenth, where it regains the balance.

Certainly the fourteenth and the sixteenth centuries appear to have more vitality, the most famous authors, the creation of vogues that penetrate the cultured world; but there is not a line along which you can see them march toward a fixed goal. And the fifteenth century, with its pause of erudition and eloquence, like the seventeenth, with its pause of lightness and segregation of thought, do not give any clue to the following resurrections—

and besides there are always such formidable exceptions, like Galileo in the seventeenth or Leonardo in the fifteenth centuries! Certain of these centuries, however artificially divided, became in the past the object of idealization for those who tried to find the peak or the golden period of Italian literature; and Italy had literary schools for which the first centuries did not exist, because they were rough and ignorant, and others in which everything that was written by the most inconspicuous friar of the thirteenth century was considered as worthy of the jeweler's scale; for others the sixteenth century was a peak.

Like centuries, writers also became models, but not only for Italy. Petrarch in poetry, Boccaccio in prose were for centuries "the masters," and Italian literature is full of authors who were trying to imitate them and, sometimes, notwithstanding this purpose, succeeded in writing good works. It is remarkable that the gentleness and sweetness of Petrarch and the magniloquence of Boccaccio excited more enthusiasm and called forth more imitators than the realism of Dante or the sinew of Machiavelli. The cult of Dante and recognition of him as the "master" is relatively recent; that is, it came with romanticism and the nineteenth century. Also, Manzoni's historical novels had more followers than Leopardi's lyricism, at least immediately. Every great writer created some frames of mind and style, in which other inferior writers found it easy to entrust their feelings and thoughts, and hence several historians speak of "schools," which is a crutch to memory and hinders the penetration of each author. It is, however, very useful for classroom purposes.

A general design of Italian literature would be entirely useless here, as there are several in the better encyclopedias. A list of the most famous authors, with some remarks on each of them, will be more practical. Of course there is always the element of personality in every choice. But I imagine that nine out of ten contemporary critics of Italian literature would agree that the following list would be a good one for a foreign student: Dante Alighieri, Petrarch, Giovanni Boccaccio, the authors of the *Fio-*

retti, Santa Caterina da Siena, Leon B. Alberti, Lorenzo il Magnifico, Angiolo Poliziano, Luigi Pulci, Leonardo da Vinci, Matteo Maria Boiardo, Nicolò Machiavelli, Francesco Guicciardini, Ludovico Ariosto, Michelangelo Buonarroti, Baldessar Castiglione, Benvenuto Cellini, Giovanni Della Casa, Pietro Aretino, Torquato Tasso, Giordano Bruno, Tommaso Campanella, Traiano Boccalini, Galileo Galilei, Francesco Redi, Pietro Metastasio, Giambattista Vico, Giuseppe Parini, Vittorio Alfieri, Carlo Goldoni, Carlo Gozzi, Giuseppe Baretti, Gaspare Gozzi, Vincenzo Monti, Ugo Foscolo, Vincenzo Cuoco, Giacomo Leopardi, Alessandro Manzoni, Giuseppe Mazzini, Giuseppe Giusti, Giosue Carducci, Francesco De Sanctis, Giovanni Pascoli, Antonio Fogazzaro, Giovanni Verga, Gabriele D'Annunzio, Giovanni Papini, Benedetto Croce, Luigi Pirandello. Limited to about fifty names, this list is open to additions, but I do not believe it could be subjected to corrections. Personally, I would prefer one a little different: but these are "recognized" values, many of them important for their European reputation and influence.

Of course for each author there is generally only one work that counts; the others acquire a meaning and present an interest only because of the major one. Very few would spend time reading the *Convito* of Dante, were there not to be found in it (so, at least, many *dantisti* believe) the secret of some passages in the *Divine Comedy.* The light comes from the highest, not from the lowest. And sometimes the minor works are to be considered only as preparation or grades to the major one, even when they are profoundly dissimilar in form; the *Inni Sacri* of Manzoni are a bud of the flower called *Promessi Sposi.*

Many Italian works have lived after the death of the author, showing the difference between the work that lives on in humanity, and the actual person that lives in an individual. Indeed we may say that some of these works began to live only after the physical death of their authors. Historians of literature call this second life the "fortune" of the author, a term not altogether exact, inasmuch as it seems to indicate an arbitrary fact. Literary reputation is, instead, interwoven with the profound streams of life and it is not dependent upon casual vogue, but upon interests and thoughts of men. There is no real "fortune" of Machiavelli, whose principal books were published after his death. You need only look at the works of Friederick Meinecke[2] to see that Machiavelli keeps reappearing on the stage at every turn; in reality the story of the science of politics almost coincides with the history of Machiavelli's thought.

But several other Italian writers have had an interesting story after death: Dante, for example, whose fortune in Italy and outside of Italy has been the subject of many studies. In Italy the point of view of national feeling, of the Italian character, and of the appreciation of poetry predominates; outside of Italy the name of Dante, always more or less in good repute, became famous only with the romantic era and, together with Shakespeare, constituted the two "aspirations" of the romantic soul, for Germany as well as for France.[3]

Petrarch was imitated a century after his death in France and two centuries later in England; the imitation took the form of a school of social refinement and of psychological culture more than an art.[4] Boccaccio and the Italian short story writers and the jocular collections of puns and witticisms of the Renaissance were copied, imitated, interwoven into material taken from the life of France, England, Spain, Germany. They furnished many plots and jests for the playwrights of the English Renaissance and for Shakespeare himself.[5] The spirit of Boccaccio became lost outside of Italy except in France, and in Italy itself only certain exterior movements and cadences of his sentences remained for centuries as a model. Silence cloaked certain great Italian writers for centuries when they suddenly reappeared, evoked by great

---

[2] *Geschichte der Staatsraison* (München, 1924) and *Die Entstehung des Historismus* (Berlin, 1936).

[3] A. Farinelli, *Dante in Spagna, Francia, Inghilterra, Germania* (Turin, 1922).

[4] A. Meozzi, *Il petrarchismo europeo* (Pisa, 1934).

[5] P. Rebora, *L'Italia nel drama inglese* (Milan, 1925).

events or by the spell of great minds: Cellini was "discovered" by Goethe and became for many a symbol of the strong Italian man of the Renaissance; Leonardo da Vinci's writings remained practically buried until the second half of the nineteenth century.

Castiglione's *Cortegiano*, on the other hand, enjoyed an almost immediate European success, and was instrumental in the formation of the aristocratic behavior in Spain, France, and England; always, of course, with national deviations or transformations— the English "gentleman" had a tendency to be a "leader" in the community, and the French "gentil'homme" an inclination toward success in a salon. The fortune of this book declined after the French Revolution, when diplomacy in business suits replaced the aristocracy in culottes; but then it became a source of historic interest and a document of the Renaissance. That, in minor proportions, is the case of the *Galateo* by Giovanni della Casa, a favorite book of manners up to the nineteenth century. It still makes delightful reading because of its wit and its picture of customs.

Tasso himself was as popular in Europe as his poem, and formed the "legend" of the unhappy genius, oppressed by the ignorant ruler and snubbed by the indifferent lady, which even inspired Goethe.[6]

Around Galileo the conflict between science and religion, free thought and social order was reopened several times after his trial; new accusations and new defenses having been brought out on both sides down to our own times.

Even the aristocratic Ariosto, who seems so remote from human conflicts, has passed through periods of ebb and flow in his European reputation.

Leopardi in foreign countries is somewhat different from Leopardi at home. Foreigners saw him especially as the expounder of pessimism; Italians saw the patriot in him and, in recent years, have considered him rather as an idealist, devoted to such lofty

---

[6] Alberto Castelli, *La Gerusalemme liberata nella Inghilterra di Shakespeare* (Milan, 1936).

thoughts that nothing on the earth could satisfy him except the love of a few pure souls, and have viewed him even as an incurable optimist and a Christian.

Less important figures than these also present interesting adventures, such as the incredible fortune of Carlo Gozzi's *Useless memoirs* written to pay off a grudge, and his fantastic dramas, written to prove a point, found among the German romanticists,[7] or as Traiano Boccalini's *Ragguagli di Parnaso* (Parnassus News Reportage), directed against the Spaniards' rule over the Italian peninsula, but much translated and imitated in Spain itself.[8]

I could enlarge on other similar cases; let us say that for great writers their real life begins when they die. When present interests cease to exist, their spirit, free of every casual accident and expressed in their thoughts and in the characters they have created, develops itself in the life of humanity. The Manzoni who suffered from agoraphobia is dead; his body is dissolved in the earth; but Don Abbondio and l'Innominato, Lucia and Perpetua still live among us, posing their problems, suggesting new answers, mixed with our feelings of the present day; and his radically Christian position is always present in our discussions, even if we do not mention his name.

On this note I will close these suggestions that I wanted to give to an imaginary student devoid of a knowledge of the history of Italian literature and desirous of undertaking its study in relation with other world literatures. An examination of cultural relations, furthermore, will make use of non-literary sources. For example, the plastic arts, music, sciences, the history of religions, geography, and so on offer many suggestions of connections with Italian literature.

[7] Rusack, Hedwig, *Gozzi in Germany* (New York, 1930).
[8] Robert H. Williams, *Boccalini in Spain* (Menasha, Wis., 1946).

BIBLIOGRAPHY [1]

BIBLIOGRAPHY

Betz, L. P., *La littérature comparée* (Strasbourg, 1900) ch. VI; 2nd ed., with additions of Fernand Baldensperger (1904).

Prezzolini, G., *Repertorio bibliografico della storia e della critica della letteratura italiana dal 1902 al 1932* (Rome, 1938); from 1932 to 1942 (New York, 1946-1947).

Societa Filologica Romana, *Un cinquantennio di studi sulla letteratura italiana 1886-1936, saggi dedicati a Vittorio Rossi* (Florence, 1937), 2 vols.

The second volume contains reviews of Italian publications concerning various European literatures.

LITERARY HISTORY AND CRITICISM
In Italian Language

Borgese, Giuseppe A., *Storia della critica romantica in Italia* (Milan, 1920).

De Sanctis, Francesco, *Storia della letteratura italiana* (Naples 1871). A religious history of the Italian people; the affirmation of an esthetic which fuses matter and form; a cultured contribution to the formation of the new Italy; and a series of critical pages altogether a masterpiece. His ideas have been rendered into philosophical form by Croce, in his *Estetica*.

Foscolo, Niccolo Ugo, *Edizione nazionale delle opere*, vol. 7, 8 (Florence, 1933). With his work, literary history with esthetic criticism was first introduced to Italian literature.

Medici, Lorenzo de, *Opere*, Attilio Simoni, ed. (Bari, 1913-1914), 2 vols.

The introductory letter to his *Canzoniere* is considered the first literary sketch of a history of Italian literature.

Rossi, V., *Storia della letteratura italiana* (Milan, 1903-1904), 3 vols. Reprinted many times with changes and additions. Factual with a tincture of ideas.

———, *Storia dei generi letterari italiani* (Milan, 1902), 16 vols.

———, *Storia letteraria scritta da una società di professori* (1st ed., Milan, 1913; 2nd ed., 1930-1940), both 9 vols.

---

[1] With a view to maintaining a modicum of consistency throughout the book the editors have altered the style and reduced the content of Professor Prezzolini's original bibliography.

In the edition of 1930-40, *Trecento* by Sapegno and *Quattrocento* by Rossi are the best; *Seicento* by Belloni and *Settecento* by Natali are both good; *Ottocento* by Mazzoni is a large basketful of information and nothing more; *Cinquencento* by Toffanin is confused; *Origini* by Novati and Monteverdi, and *Duegento* by Bertoni are interesting. The too-recent material of *Novecento* by Galletti seems not well enough digested.

ZONTA, G., *Storia della letteratura italiana* (Turin, 1928-1930). Illustrated.

The following works, part history and part anthology, are perhaps better than the actual literary histories. They offer glimpses of the original writers and are accompanied by explanatory notes.

CARLI, Plinio, and SAINATI, Augusto, *Scrittori italiani* (Florence, 1930-1935), 6 vols.

CASINI, Tommaso, *Manuale di letteratura* (Florence, 1886-1887), 3 vols.

D'ANCONA, Alessandro, and BACCI, Orazio, *Manuale della litteratura italiana* (Florence, 1925-1929), 6 vols.

LIPPARINI, Giuseppe, *Le pagine della letteratura italiana* (Milan, 1928), 18 vols.

PREZZOLINI, Giuseppe, *I Maggiori* (Florence, 1929), 6 vols.

MALAGOLI, G., *Crestomazia per secoli della litteratura italiana* (Florence, 1921-1926), 4 vols.

TORRACA, Francesco, *Manuale della letteratura italiana* (Florence, 1920), 3 vols.

In Other Languages

BELCIUGATEANU, Anita, *Curs de istorie e literaturii italiene* (Bucharest, 1923).

DE SANCTIS, Francesco, *History of Italian Literature,* trans. by Joan Redfern (New York, 1931). Excellent translation.

FLETCHER, Jefferson B., *Literature of the Italian Renaissance* (New York, 1915).

GARDNER, E. G., *Italian Literature* (London, 1928).

HAUVETTE, H., *Littérature italienne* (Paris, 1906; rev. and enl. 1932).

MAZVIDAL, Aurelio Boza, *Historia de la literatura italiana* (Havana, 1946).

MODULISKIJ, S. S., *Italijanskaja literatura* (Moscow, 1931).

PREZZOLINI, G., "Modern Literary Criticism in Italy," *Columbia Dictionary of Modern European Literature,* Horatio Smith, ed. (New York, 1947).

SCHISHMANOV, Iv. D., *Litteratura Istoria na Vzlasgdianeto V Italia* (Sofia, 1934).

SPINGARN, Joel Elias, *A History of Literary Criticism in the Renaissance* (New York, 1908). On the poetics of the period.

VOSSLER, Karl, *Italienische Literaturgeschichte* (Göschen, 1900).

WIESE, B., and PERCOPO, E., *Geschichte der italienischen Literatur mit Ausbildungen* (Italian translation, Turin, 1904). Illustrated.

Relations with England

CUNLIFFE, John William, *Influence of Seneca on Elizabethan Tragedy* (New York, 1907).

EINSTEIN, Lewis, *Italian Renaissance in England*, Columbia Univ. St. in Engl. and Comp. Lit. (New York, 1902).

JEFFREY, V. M., "Italian and English Pastoral Drama of the Renaissance," *Mod. Lang. Rev.*, vol. XIX (1924), pp. 56-62, 175-87, 435-44.

LEE, Sir Sidney Lazarus, *Shakespeare and the Italian Renaissance*, British Academy, The Annual Shakespeare Lecture (London, 1915).

LEE, Vernon, *Renaissance Fancies and Studies* (London, 1909).

PRAZ, Mario, *Machiavelli and the Elizabethans*, British Academy Annual Italian Lecture (London, 1928).

SCOTT, Mary Augusta, *Elizabethan Translations from the Italian* (Cambridge, Mass., 1916).

HISTORY

SALVATORELLI, Luigi, *Concise History of Italy*, trans. by Bernard Miall (Oxford, 1940).

SEDGWICK, Henry Dwight, Jr., *Short History of Italy* (New York, 1905).

TREVELYAN, Janet Penrose, *Wandering Englishmen in Italy*, British Academy Annual Italian Lecture (London, 1930). Short general history.

GENERAL BACKGROUND

ANDREWS, Charles McLean, *Reformation Historically Considered*: Syllabus, Am. Soc. for the Extension of Univ. Teaching (*ca.* 1912).

BALZANI, Ugo, *Italy* (New York, 1883). Covers the origins and the Middle Ages.

CHURCH, Frederic Cross, *Italian Reformers, 1534-1564* (New York, 1932).

COTTERILL, Henry Bernard, *Medieval Italy During a Thousand Years* (305-1313) (New York, 1915).

CROCE, Benedetto, *History of Italy 1871-1929*, trans. by Cecelia M. Ady (Oxford, 1929).

EMERTON, Ephraim, *Humanism and Tyranny*: Studies in Italian Trecento (Boston, 1925).

FERGUSON, Wallace K., "Humanist Views of the Renaissance," *Am. Hist. Rev.*, vol. XXXXV (1939), pp. 1-28.

HARE, Christopher, *Courts and Camps of the Italian Renaissance* (New York, 1908).

――, *Life and Letters of the Italian Renaissance* (New York, 1915).

KING, Bolton, and O'KEY, Thomas, *Italy Today* (London, 1909; New York, 1913).

LEA, K. M., *Italian Popular Comedy* (London, 1934).

MAZZINI, Joseph, *Essays*, Bolton King, ed., Thomas O'Key, trans. (London, 1894).

ROEDER, Ralph, *Man of the Renaissance:* Four Lawgivers: Savonarola, Machiavelli, Castiglione, Aretino (New York, 1933).

SMITH, Winifred, *Commedia dell' arte:* A Study in Italian Popular Comedy (New York, 1912).

ƆYMONDS, John Addington, *Renaissance in Italy* (New York, 1935).

THOMPSON, James Westfall, et al., *Civilization of the Renaissance* (Chicago, 1929).

VILLARI, Pasquale, *Two First Centuries of Florentine History,* trans. by Linda Villari (New York, 1912).

ANTHOLOGY

DE BOSIS, Lauro, *The Golden Book of Italian Poetry* (London, 1932).

DE LUCCHI, Lorna, *An Anthology of Italian Poems* (New York, 1924).

PETTOELLO, Decio, *Great Italian Short Stories* (London, 1930).

Italian Short Stories from the Thirteenth to the Twentieth Century, Everyman's Library (New York, 1932).

LINGUISTIC STUDY

GRANDGENT, Charles Hall, *From Latin to Italian:* an Historical Outline (Boston, 1927).

HALL, Robert Anderson, Jr., "Linguistic Theory in the Italian Renaissance," *Language,* vol. XII (1936), pp. 96-107.

PEI, Mario Andrew, *Italian Language* (New York, 1941).

"Significance of the Italian Questione della Lingua," *Studies in Philology,* vol. XXXIX (1942), pp. 1-10.

SELECTED STUDIES

BELL, Mary I. M., *Short History of the Papacy* (New York, 1921).

CARLYLE, Sir Robert Warrand, and CARLYLE, Alexander James, *History of Medieval Political Theory in the West,* vol. 6, *Political Theory from 1300-1600* (Edinburgh, 1936).

CARTWRIGHT, Julia (Ady, Mrs. Henry), *Italian Gardens of the Renaissance* (New York, 1914).

DENT, Joseph Edward, *Music of the Renaissance in Italy,* British Academy Annual Italian Lecture (London, 1933).

GRAF, Herbert, *Opera and Its Future in America* (New York, 1941).

HAYWARD, Fernand, *History of the Popes,* trans. from French by the monks of St. Augustine's Abbey (Ramsgate, 1931).

NICHOLS, Rose Standish, *Italian Pleasure Gardens* (New York, 1928).

PASTOR, Ludwig, *History of the Popes from the Close of the Middle Ages,* trans. by I. Antrobus (St. Louis, 1891-1941), 10 vols.

RUBSAMEN, Howard, *Literary Sources of Secular Music in Italy* (ca. 1500) (Berkeley, Calif., 1943).

VENTURI, Adolfo, *Short History of Italian Art,* trans. by Edward Hutton (New York, 1926).

VENTURI, Lionello, *History of Art Criticism,* trans. by Charles Marriott (New York, 1936).

WEINSTOCK, Herbert, and BROCKWAY, Wallace, *Opera, a History of Its Creation and Performance* (New York, 1941).

WHITE, Lynn Townsend, *Latin Monasticism in Norman Sicily,* Medieval Academy, pub. no. 31, monograph no. 13 (1938).

WOODWARD, William Harrison, *Vittorino da Feltre and Other Humanist Educators* (Cambridge, Eng., 1897).

8

French Literature

H. R. HUSE
University of North Carolina

Dr. H. R. Huse—*the doctorate is from the University of Chicago by way of the University of Dijon, France— is professor of Romance languages at that excellent southern university, the University of North Carolina. Under pressure he has admitted that he "tried, like Ulysses, but without great success, to learn something about the world and about men." He may have been thinking, when he made the statement, that before he settled down to an academic and literary life he worked his way around the world, being successively, then and afterward, journalist, teacher in the Philippines, salesman in Australia, seaman, dock worker in London, lecturer for Burton Holmes, interpreter for Sarah Bernhardt's company, second lieutenant in the United States Infantry, and assistant to the United States Trade Commissioner in Athens and Constantinople. He has written, besides articles and textbooks,* The Psychology of Foreign Language Study, Reading and Speaking Foreign Languages, *and that ever-entertaining* The Illiteracy of the Literate.

French Literature[1]

[1] The author wishes to acknowledge his indebtedness to a number of manuals of French literature, notably those of Lanson, Des Granges, Latham, Lévêque, Mornet, Nitze and Dargan, and to the authors included in *Histoire de la littérature française*, L. Petit de Julleville, ed.

THE MIDDLE AGES

AT VARIOUS times French culture has dominated the Western world. The first of these periods, the twelfth and thirteenth centuries, marks also the beginnings of French literature. Before then almost nothing of literary importance existed in the Old French which had gradually developed out of spoken Latin.

In France, as in other countries, literature begins with an epic, the *Song of Roland*. It is the first and greatest of a series of *chansons de geste* (songs of deeds) which celebrate an historical event or a hero. These were composed originally in unrhymed verse by *trouvères*, and were recited, sometimes to a musical accompaniment, by *jongleurs* or minstrels.

The subject of the *Chanson de Roland* is not a vulgar victory, as one might expect, but rather a defeat—the destruction of the rear guard of Charlemagne's army in a pass of the Pyrenees. The hero, Roland, exhausted from slaying vast numbers of pagans, left almost alone, decides to call for help, and blows his horn so hard that his temples burst. In one derivative account the blast is said to have split the horn. Many of the happenings are equally fantastic, although there is a slight historical basis for the poem.

The language in which the *Chanson de Roland* is written is immature, incapable of expressing delicate or abstract concepts. There are few images, no thoughts on the great problems of human destiny, and little gracefulness of expression. And yet the work is powerful through its evocation of the Christian and chivalric virtues. To express the feelings of heroes whose uncomplicated business is only to fight and to die, brief words, a few prayers, certain touching gestures are enough. And the characters live: they are individualized, have minds and hearts. There is some description, much reverence for the Emperor with his white and "flowering" beard, and above all a love for *la douce France* which gives nobility and feeling to the lines.

Many of the *chansons de geste* were translated into other languages and became known from Iceland to the Levant. It is said that chapbooks based on them were still thumbed by peasants in out-of-the-way villages in the nineteenth century.

Unfortunately, the *chansons de geste* suffered from their success. To satisfy the appetite for them they were lengthened, changed, reworked. New *trouvères* rehandled the old material until, by the fifteenth century, they came to be expanded into diffuse and extravagant romances of adventure. The spirit and aspiration that gave them their original grandeur were lost.

After the earliest of the *chansons de geste* a notable cultural change occurred. Manners became softened, woman rose in the social scale, and Christianity became refined and mystical in character. The troubadours of Provence, in southern France, had developed a form of courtly love in which the lady is exalted and worshipped almost as a goddess by her humble lover. This Provençal influence reached the North and filled French literature for centuries. Traces of it survived down to the tragedies of the seventeenth century, and the triangular love pattern (love for a married woman), made almost obligatory by the social conditions in Provence, became a literary convention that survives today in almost all French novels.

This change is apparent in a rich narrative literature which also contributed greatly during the Middle Ages to French literary preëminence. The touching story of Troilus and Cressida, treated later by Boccaccio, Chaucer, and Shakespeare, appeared in the Old French *Romance of Troy*.

In the stories grouped under the "Breton cycle," courtly love was fused with Celtic legends to produce "romances" which have enchanted generations of readers in many countries. The Breton romances include, among other items, the work of Marie de France, the story of Tristan, and the legends of King Arthur and the Round Table.

Almost nothing is known about Marie de France except that she came from the continent and lived in England. She wrote little poems called "lays," delicate, frail accounts of lovers in an enchanted world where miracles are the only law. In *Tristan and Iseult* (by Béroul and Thomas) as in the lays, the love is not entirely courtly, but rather Celtic, a love that can give all joy, but which consumes and leads to death.

The Arthurian romances were written by literary men and, unlike the *chansons de geste,* were intended to be read, not just recited. Here, too, we have a world of magic, full of dwarfs, giants, unicorns, enchanted forests and castles, and an Orient that never was.

The most famous writer of romances of adventure was Chrétien de Troyes. In long poems written, for the most part, without great art or poetic feeling, he traced the ideal type of the amorous knight devoted to his lady.

A work similar in some respects to the Arthurian romances and yet unique is the charming *chantefable, Aucassin et Nicolette,* in prose, but with interpolated bits of verse, a masterpiece of French medieval literature.

Besides epic and narrative poetry, some lyric forms were cultivated in the twelfth and thirteenth centuries. One of the most interesting of these is the *aube* which tells of the parting of lovers at dawn, a reflection of which occurs in Shakespeare's *Romeo and Juliet.* The theme of the *pastourelle,* the meeting of a knight and a shepherdess also appears, travestied, in *As You Like It.*

In addition to the works already mentioned which were aristocratic in inspiration and character, a realistic, satirical, licentious, and bourgeois literature flourished with extraordinary vitality. The *fabliaux,* of which about 150 are extant, are little stories in verse similar to the more risqué ones in the *Canterbury Tales,* and form a pendant to the aristocratic literature.

The *Romance of Renard,* begun somewhat earlier, resembles the fabliaux in spirit. It is a collection of disconnected stories in verse about Renard the fox, Isengrin the wolf, Chantecler the cock, and other such worthies, the sources of which go back in some cases to antiquity. It is a parody of human society, a mockery of the most venerable institutions and people. The dominating idea would seem to be the glorification of slyness, a vice that becomes obligatory in a world where might makes right. The literary value of most of the branches of this work is slight, but one, the "Judgment of Renard," is a devastating travesty of the feudal system, a masterpiece which became a model for various Flemish and German versions. In the apparent apotheosis of the fox, the mind triumphs over force: this sly creature represents the People getting revenge on the feudal lords.

The most influential French work of the Middle Ages was the *Romance of the Rose.* The first part, left unfinished, is an elaborate allegory, intended as a guide to courtly love. The author, Guillaume de Lorris, inspired by classic influences, notably Ovid, shows his love for nature and beauty, and anticipates, in that sense, the poets of the Renaissance.

The second part was composed by Jean de Meung some forty years later. It is scientific, positivistic, and prosaic in tone, a kind of compendium of knowledge. The author discusses such problems as the inequality of wealth, the basis of royal power, the origin of the state and of private property, even such modern questions as that of dual personalities. He does not believe in ghosts, is not afraid of meteors, thinks that nobility is not dependent upon birth, and is free from theology. He has been called the Voltaire of the Middle Ages, and is one of the first of a long line of positivistic French thinkers.

The *Romance of the Rose* circulated from one end of Europe to the other, and for a long time made allegory obligatory. Dante felt its influence, and Chaucer developed his verse style by translating part of it.

Besides the *Romance of the Rose,* a considerable didactic literature flourished in Latin and some works in the vernacular, notably bestiaries (about animals), lapidaries (on precious stones), encyclopedias, and summaries of knowledge of various sorts.

Two historians merit an important place in the history of literature. Villehardouin, in describing the Fourth Crusade, writes in a simple, bare, vigorous style, admirably suited to the military actions he describes. Joinville, the biographer of St. Louis, is an incomparable narrator: he had imagination, sympathy, candor, and reveals in his writing the great charm that was in himself.

The prestige of France in the thirteenth century was enormous. The University of Paris, the leading institution of learning in Christendom, attracted students from all of Europe. The Crusades had expanded French imagination and brought contact with other civilizations, notably the Arabic. And yet the old sources of inspiration in Honor and Faith were still intact. Gothic architecture, which is really French architecture of the Middle Ages, spread over Europe. The cathedrals of Upsala, Canterbury, Milan, Burgos, Lemberg, and Cologne are all in the French style. And something like the smile a French sculptor had dared to put on the face of an angel spread from France over the Western world.

The success of French literature was universal. In Germany, Hartmann von Aue, Wolfram von Eschenbach, and Gottfried von Strasburg all adapted French works. Dante and the Italians generally were familiar with this literature. Even as late as Ariosto and Cervantes, the popularity of Old French literature still endured.

The fourteenth and fifteenth centuries, however, in contrast with the twelfth and thirteenth, are a period of decay, an epoch of painful transition to a new social order. During this time the Hundred Years War, accompanied by plagues and disasters, ravaged France until grass grew in the streets of Paris, and wolves howled outside. The dazzling folly of the knights in the battles of Crécy and Agincourt revealed the bankruptcy of the nobility. The Church likewise was weakened by the scandalous luxury of the cardinals and archbishops, and by the great schism and quarrels of the antipopes.

The literature reflects the spirit of the times. Writers, uninspired, make poetry an exercise requiring ingenuity above all, so that rhetoric and poetry become synonymous terms. The Middle French period produced, however, two notable poets, two great historians, and a voluminous dramatic literature.

Charles d'Orléans and Villon, the most admired, although not the most characteristic poets of the age, stand at the extreme ends of the social scale. The first was the father of a king, the second a vagabond, thief, and manslayer. The one continues the line of aristocratic, courtly *trouvères,* the other the realistic and bourgeois tradition.

The poems of Charles d'Orléans are, for the most part, dainty trifles written to amuse himself, to forget, to express during his captivity in England a vague homesickness for *la douce France.* In them he tells of love affairs that existed only in his imagination. He has charm and style, shading, delicacy—qualities eminently French. Because of the reticence his high rank imposed, his poems were not published by his royal heirs until the eighteenth century.

Villon's title to fame is a thin volume containing mock legacies in verse interspersed with poems in fixed forms, *ballades* and *rondeaux* principally. The tone varies constantly, passing sometimes in a line from the gay to the thoughtful, from the licentious to the sad. His ideal is not spiritual, but materialistic: from the poverty in which he lived he could appreciate the comforts taken for granted by most of us. He is the poet of remorse; of the transience of life; of Death, which was always close to him and about which, unlike so many who have written on that dark theme, he really knew something. With him the lyric is not just an exercise or an amusement, but a medium to express personal emotion; and in this sense he is the first of modern French poets.

Of the historians, Froissart was a delighted spectator of the follies of his time. He visited Scotland and Italy, saw Robert Bruce, Chaucer, and Petrarch. He wrote chronicles in the spirit of a belated troubadour, curiously pleased with his age and with the external trappings of the chivalry whose decline and end he could not see. He is a reporter rather than an historian, but vivid, picturesque, and inspired. Commines, on the other hand, is essentially intellectual. He wished to understand events and to explain them with clarity. He showed an objectivity and lack of moral inhibitions that make him a French counterpart of Machiavelli.

During the fourteenth and fifteenth centuries, miracle and mystery plays became a dominant literary form. One of the mysteries lasted forty days and required five hundred characters. The actors usually took their rôles gravely: a priest almost died while hanging realistically on the cross. But in spite of all this seriousness, fervor, and popularity, the literary value of these plays is slight.

The real dramatic masterpiece of the age is a farce, *Maître Pathelin,* the humor of which is still fresh today.

THE RENAISSANCE

In the fourteenth and fifteenth centuries, while France was languishing, Italy was developing one of the most brilliant civilizations the world has known. There, one could find palaces, beautiful gardens, paintings, sculptures, libraries, schools. And in the framework of a fascinating physical environment, Italian authors developed the concept of the perfect man of society, a complete man, skilled, intelligent, refined, capable of appreciating the joyous festival that life could offer. An esthetic feeling dominated: in almost every activity there was a sense of form, of beauty, that was new in the world.

The Renaissance is essentially an Italian movement. French

knowledge of it came through the accident of several foreign wars. In 1494 Charles VIII invaded Italy, to be followed shortly after by Louis XII and then by Francis I. The "barbarians" (as the Italians called all foreigners) coming out of their drab, medieval castles and villages, were dazzled by the new world they saw. When they recrossed the Alps they took pictures, statues, books, ideas, artists, teachers, engineers, scientists, architects with them; they took as their baggage the Renaissance, a new age.

The effects were soon obvious everywhere, in court life, in the new châteaux, in the joyous optimism of the age. The guides are no longer the Christian moralists, but rather Cicero, Seneca, Lucretius, and Plutarch. The essentially popular literature of the Middle Ages was replaced with learned, consciously artistic works intended for an intellectual elite. This change, however, did not occur all at once. In the early writers, Marot and Rabelais, the influence of both ages is apparent.

Marot had deep roots in the past. He edited the *Romance of the Rose* and the works of Villon, and wrote poems in the Middle French forms. But he composed eclogues and sonnets, also, and was familiar with the works of Boccaccio, Petrarch, Catullus, Virgil, and Ovid. He felt the moderation and elegance of the new age. As a court poet, he wrote without lofty inspiration or deep meaning, but with a gracefulness and wit that have endeared him to all subsequent generations of Frenchmen.

On the surface, the monstrous, diffuse, obscene, grotesque works of Rabelais have all the characteristics of the medieval tradition. In him there is no platonism and little consciously artistic intent. Yet he is the apostle of the epicureanism of the new age. His dominant theme is an affirmation of the goodness of life in all its aspects and functions. He opposes repressions and distortions of human nature, ascetic disciplines, mortifications, fasting, claustrations, and so on, which are, he says, inventions of the Devil.

He conceived the *Abbey of Thélème,* the antithesis of a monastery of the Middle Ages. Here the only rule was *Fay ce que voul-*

dras (do as you please). In the Spring of the French Renaissance, this exaggerated confidence in human nature was still possible.

The epicureanism of Rabelais is presented in works of extraordinary literary power. His vocabulary is the most extensive in French literature: his interest in words is similar to that of our modern James Joyce. As a creator of characters, few writers can equal him. Panurge, Pantagruel, Friar John, Gargantua are not only types, but individuals, alive, and functioning physically and mentally. The author's narrative skill is equal to his character portrayal. Apart from the incredible grossness, unnecessary even in that lush age, the writings of Rabelais are among the most humorous ever written. Among his English followers are Jonathan Swift and Sterne.

Ronsard was the leader of a school of poets called the *Pléiade*. He cultivated various classic forms, but succeeded mainly in his sonnets and Anacreontic odes. Whenever spontaneous, not displaying his erudition or trying to soar too high, he was a charming poet. He helped to form the French literary language, to reveal the resources of French versification, and to prepare for the masterpieces of the next century.

His fame suffered from the strangest of vicissitudes. In his day, it was boundless. All Europe admired him; Queen Elizabeth and Mary Stuart sent him presents. Then, after his death, he fell into utter oblivion until rehabilitated by the romanticists of the nineteenth century.

Du Bellay, a member of Ronsard's group, felt less the joy of living, the pagan, sensuous beauty of things, but was more thoughtful, and has, for various reasons, appealed particularly to English readers. With him the sonnet becomes a medium for expressing satire, personal emotion, description, and elegiac moods as well as love. He is one of the French masters of this poetic form.

Two Huguenot poets, Du Bartas and D'Aubigné, have remained outside of the current of French taste. The *Semaine* of Du Bartas, an account of the Creation, was translated into numerous languages, and was a source of inspiration for Milton, Jeremy Taylor, Tom Moore, and Byron. Goethe regarded Du Bartas as a great neglected French poet. D'Aubigné wrote the *Tragiques,* in which he attacks the Catholics in a style of epic grandeur. His works were published when the mood that had inspired them had passed.

In the last part of the century, the religious wars came as a penalty for the former hope, exuberance, and individualism; and the pagan, artistic movement was withered by a blast from the North. This disillusionment is represented best by Montaigne. From his study in the tower of his castle, he contemplated the world, witnessing the common but sad spectacle of men killing and getting killed for words, for emotive terms, that none really understood.

Montaigne studied man in himself and in those around him and throughout the ages. He found that the truths of one period are denied in the next, the convictions and moralities of one place unheard of in another. He brings together a mass of these contradictions and presents an encyclopedia of human error. Even conscience, so proud and sure of itself, is, he shows, an eternal dupe.

The purpose of this deflation was to destroy the fierce convictions for which men kill and get killed. Montaigne's scepticism is not absolute, since there is no absolute scepticism or absolute anything, but the query *Que sais-je?* (what do I know?) always rises to his lips. Although he depends on reason as a better guide than authority or imagination or emotion, he has no naïve faith in it, as did the rationalists of the eighteenth century: he knows about *its* errors, too. The burden of his work was to recommend tolerance in an age that was fiercely intolerant.

Montaigne's *Essays* are written in a familiar style without consistent plan or order. Some chapters have one page, others fifty. Sometimes the author digresses to the point of forgetting the subject he started with. But this very naturalness conceals a great and not wholly unconscious art, and has a peculiar charm.

The *Essays* of Montaigne have appealed to generation after generation of men in all countries. In English, the Florio (1603) and Cotton (*ca.* 1670) translations have been reprinted frequently, to mention only two of the translators. Nearly every thinker since his day has been influenced by him. Shakespeare and Bacon are notable debtors, and he was the favorite author of Emerson, who never fails to pay tribute to him.

THE CLASSICAL PERIOD

During the first part of the seventeenth century, French literature underwent various influences. By 1660, however, the classic viewpoint was definitively established and dominated in France and to a large extent throughout Europe down to the nineteenth century.

The principles of classicism were derived mainly from the Ancients. Struck by the incontestable superiority of Greek and Latin authors, critics studied their works to find out what qualities might account for their greatness. Certain rules, they thought, could be derived which govern successful literary activity, and by the application of these rules, modern authors might attain or approach the excellence of the Ancients.

The fundamental principle, they found, was that of Reason. In comparison with the lives of the saints and the romances of chivalry, ancient works seemed rational, sensible, plausible, without exaggeration or distortion of reality. These rational qualities explain the universal appeal of ancient works, since reason, unlike the imagination and the emotions, is essentially the same in all men at all times. Classicism identified, therefore, Truth (the object of Reason) with Beauty (the object of Art), and maintained with Boileau that "nothing is beautiful except the true, the true alone is likable."

Reason demands verisimilitude (probability), the general, the abstract, the universal rather than what is individual and accidental. Extraordinary events and characters, local color, peculiarities of manner and of dress, are without significance and, therefore, relatively, without interest.

Classicism demands naturalness, also. Affectation, exhibitionism, verbal cleverness, pedantry, preciosity, posturing—all are frowned upon; likewise emotion, fancy, imagination, rhapsodic or lyric utterance, hyperbole, and conceits. The style of the classicists is precise, plain, sober, lucid: they have no knowledge of such things as "the light that never was on land or sea."

The characteristics of French classicism were determined in part by the public to which it appealed. Aristocratic society demanded a literature which would reflect formal qualities, intelligence, moderation, restraint—a literature, in short, that would exemplify the social graces.

The classic formula was too narrow. It hardly allowed for lyric poetry or for history which deals with particular events and persons. But French classical literature explored what is universal in man's mind as few literatures ever have, and created a language admired above others for subtlety and precision.

Of the influences which helped to establish the classic ideal, some were institutions, such as the Hôtel de Rambouillet and the French Academy, and some were individuals, notably Malherbe and Descartes.

At the residence of the Marquise de Rambouillet, men of letters joined certain members of the nobility in forming an elegant and polished society. Conversation became an art: the guests vied with each other in speaking with distinction. As intelligent and cultivated people, they were interested primarily in man and in the workings of man's mind. A few of the members and especially imitators of the group developed affectations in speech, an absurd preciosity which Molière and Boileau later were obliged to attack. But an interest in psychological analysis and in precise and elegant diction remained.

The French Academy was founded by Richelieu to control, as

far as possible, the language and literature. Its influence, naturally, was conservative, hostile to popular trends, to emotion and to unrestraint. It helped to intellectualize French, and to eliminate concrete, picturesque, emotive, and fanciful terms.

Malherbe, besides composing a slender volume of verse noted for nothing except excellence in form, was a reformer and legislator in matters of language and poetic style. He pruned the French language ruthlessly, cutting out all the additions of the *Pléiade* that had not been assimilated into usage. His reforms aimed at order, clarity, common sense, self-criticism, and, above all, careful workmanship. He understood that poetry is an art, and that art, almost by definition, is not improvised.

Descartes belongs to philosophy rather than to literature, but expresses the common spirit of his age. In his treatise on the passions, he conceives of Reason, the Emotions, and the Will as separate entities or powers. The turbulent emotions, like an unruly legislature, must be under control of the dictator, Reason; and the Will (a kind of sergeant-at-arms) is to carry out the executive's decrees. This psychology, which occasions a smile nowadays, characterized also the proud dramatic work of Corneille.

Descartes' *Discourse on Method,* a far more important work, marks the beginning of the triumph of rationalism over authority and revelation. In its emphasis on reason, it conforms also to the spirit of classic literature, and by making common sense the supreme judge, it gave the layman a justification for opinions on religious, political, and artistic matters. Cartesianism led ultimately to the destructive philosophy of the eighteenth century.

Of the literary forms in the classic period, tragedy was by far the most important. After much experimentation, Corneille's *Cid* finally established the characteristics of this type of play. Classic tragedies are in five acts, in verse; the characters are legendary or historical, and of exalted rank; the tone is unified; the language constantly elevated, and the so-called Aristotelian unities of Time, Place, and Action are observed. A more important characteristic is the psychological action: the main happenings are in the minds and hearts of the characters, whose inner conflicts determine the plot.

Corneille's exalted conception of man induced him to complicate the intrigues of his later plays in order to provide obstacles for the hero's will to overcome, and he tended to portray supermen. But in his early masterpieces, the characters seem real enough and are touching, especially to those who tend to idealize man. The phrase "beautiful as the Cid," became proverbial.

Later in the century Racine continues the type of tragedy developed by Corneille, but changes the spirit of it. Here there is greater simplicity, greater naturalness, greater verisimilitude. The subjects treated are essentially commonplace events, like the crimes of passion that reach our police courts, but elevated, enlarged, made great and tragic by the rank and glamor of the historical characters involved, and by a style which is a language the gods themselves might speak. Here romanesque, melodramatic elements are almost entirely excluded. The tragedy is exclusively psychological. And in the struggles that go on within the characters, the emotions triumph, not the will. In this respect Racine seems to our generation more realistic than Corneille, whose strong men are harder for us to recognize. But although Racine's characters are dominated by their emotions, they are beautifully intelligent: they know what they should do, yet in them, as in all of us, there are forces that the mind and will cannot control. A determinism weighs upon them—like heredity, or the Fate of the Greeks—and they work out their sad or happy destinies knowingly and with the tragic inevitability and persistence that we can observe in real life.

In Racine's style there is a simplicity that comes close to prose, a naturalness that does not seem at first sight like art, precision, exactness, condensation. But this apparently simple style is as learned and complex as the art of the Parthenon, and has the same almost absolute perfection. The models for his characters are the great ladies and men of the brilliant society of his day, but magnified without distortion, idealized by a great artist. The superiority they show by their words and manners bestows on them an importance ordinary people cannot have, and their place in history or legend gives at least the illusion of probability to that superiority. In Racine we find the culmination of the classic genius.

Molière who has no close rival in comedy, unless Aristophanes, wrote farces, ballets, comedy-ballets, comedies of character, and comedies of intrigue, some in prose and some in verse, some conforming to the unities and some violating them all. In the space of thirteen or fourteen years he wrote about thirty plays, many of them masterpieces of world literature.

Molière had observed life closely, and all kinds of people appear in his work—bourgeois, nobles, peasants, doctors, lawyers, misers, social climbers, hypocrites, snobs, *précieux*, illiterate peasants, and even respectable people. The main characters are individualized and yet they represent types also, and have universality and significance.

Although Molière never disdains popular devices to make people laugh, in his great comedies the plots are of slight importance. He takes his stories wherever he can find them, and uses them as a framework on which to display his characters. He does not depend, either, on wit or verbal cleverness. And he keeps in close contact with reality: the truth is as necessary to him as to Descartes or Racine.

The philosophy of Molière is not formal or profound. He believes, like other epicureans, in the goodness of nature, and he combats with all his ridicule whatever tends to violate or deform nature. The characters he seems to admire are frequently young people, simple, natural, and undeformed. He exalts the polite, social graces—sympathy, benevolence, tolerance—rather than the heroic or austere virtues. His moral doctrine does not rise high, but it has a wide and useful application.

Molière's style shows occasional negligence due to speed of composition, but on the whole he writes a peculiarly effective language for the stage. His peasants, his bourgeois, his doctors, speak the true language of their class and of their rôles.

The history of the fable as an art form begins and ends, one may say, with La Fontaine. His fables are the most popular poems in the French language, loved by both young and old. They are stories, dialogues, comic anecdotes, little tragedies, idylls, elegies, satires, farces, burlesques, lyric poems, didactic pieces, and so on. The tone changes as capriciously as the character of the events, now solemn, now farcical. There is even *sensibilité* and confidences on death, friendship, love, solitude, and nature.

La Fontaine paints animals and country scenes with skillful sympathy. His dramatic sense is especially notable: each fable is a little play with a climax and end, in which each character speaks in his rôle. The vocabulary of La Fontaine is rich precisely in the colorful terms classicism tended to eliminate, and in versification also, he does not follow the rules. In many respects he would seem to be the antithesis of the classicists. Yet he belongs in their company. His animals are disguises for various types of persons—kings, bourgeois, peasants, priests, the stupid and the wise, the brave and the cowardly. Like Molière, he extols sympathy, prudence, and classic common sense. Above all he ridicules affectation; and for naturalness he himself stands as a supreme example.

Among the prose writers of the century, La Rochefoucauld ranks as the world's most famous writer of maxims. This literary form grew out of salon life, where analysis of motives and character became an elegant diversion. The dominant attitude of La Rochefoucauld toward man is expressed in the aphorism: "Virtues are lost in self-interest as rivers are lost in the sea." All human actions are related to the primary drive of the ego for its own selfish satisfactions. Our modern psychological understanding has done little to weaken the observations of this author whose work, by common consent, is one of the most penetrating, hard-headed, and realistic ever written.

Two works of Pascal count in the history of literature, the *Provincial Letters*, written to defend the Jansenists in their dispute with the Jesuits, and the *Pensées*, thoughts in fragmentary form intended to constitute an apology for the Christian religion.

In the *Pensées*, Pascal shows man's insignificance and the vanity of this Cartesian rationalism which is an enemy of the Faith and which led the following century into so many illusions. Pascal's prose often has a poetic quality.

Bossuet's works include sermons and especially funeral orations which match by the pomp of their eloquence the glamor of the princely subjects who occasioned them and the magnificence of the ceremonies. In his *Discourse on Universal History*, Bossuet outlines the events of the world from the beginning down to Charlemagne, showing how divine Providence determines the course of human events. It is one of the first attempts at "philosophical history," that is, history that explains as well as narrates.

Boileau was the leading literary critic and satirist of the classical period. His *Art Poétique* is a succinct exposition of the ideas of the great classic writers: he represents here, in a formal way, the genius of his century, its bourgeois spirit, common sense, and realism. With an almost infallible judgment, moreover, he chose for praise precisely those men, his contemporaries, the value of whose works posterity has confirmed.

Toward the end of the seventeenth century a new generation began to criticize, not man within the social framework, but the social order itself, and to show other tendencies of the following age. La Bruyère, in his *Characters*, transforms the psychological realism of the past into a materialistic, external realism. He is especially expert in noting the signs through which feelings are shown—glances, tics, gait, gestures, and so on. His style, moreover, with its short sentences, suggests that of the eighteenth century.

Fénelon, a great churchman like Bossuet, shows a sensitiveness and humanitarian spirit suggestive also of the following century.

His *Télémaque,* an indirect criticism of the policies of Louis XIV, is written with a simple, almost feminine charm, and served for many decades as a favorite text for foreigners learning French.

Two women writers in this century of extraordinary talent are notable. Mme. de Sévigné ranks with Cicero and Voltaire among the greatest letter writers of all literature. Her missives reflect the events of her time and contain personal criticism, reflections, reminiscences, and gossip. They are the history of a curiously interesting personality and the chronicles of a curiously superior society.

In the *Princess of Clèves,* Mme. de la Fayette transferred to the novel the classic feeling for truth, precision, restraint, and for psychological analysis.

*   *   *

The classic devotion to rationalism and truth, which would normally have led to a scientific rather than an artistic literature, was combined in the seventeenth century with study and imitation of the Ancients, a practice which preserved a sense of form. Almost all the masterpieces of the period were written by a small group of men devoted to antiquity. But toward the end of the century, the *Quarrel of the Ancients and the Moderns* (the *Battle of the Books*) occurred, which weakened the classic tradition. With the elimination of the cult for antiquity, rationalistic tendencies had no artistic corrective, and literature as an art progressively declined.

The eighteenth century, although part of the classic period, is different in spirit from the seventeenth. It is destructive, anti-Christian, interested not in the analysis of man's character and feelings, but in his ideas and social order. Literature, in a sense, ceases to be an art and becomes a weapon.

Many causes produced this change. The Church was weakened by theological disputes, abuses of power, and by the luxury and nepotism of the higher clergy. The monarchy likewise was undermined by wars and economic distress, by the luxury of the court, and by a privileged, parasitical nobility.

The first part of the century, from the death of Louis XIV to about 1750 is moderate in its criticism of the social order; from 1750 to 1789 the revolutionary forces enter into line and are almost unopposed. Most of the architects of the Revolution died before the violent phase of it had begun. Their work seemed completed; they thought that since man is rational and had been shown the road to happiness and virtue, a Utopia was at hand. The Age of Reasoning ends in an idyllic atmosphere, symbolized by Marie Antoinette and the Petit Trianon.

Of the literary forms, classic tragedy continued to dominate, but produced no works comparable with those of the past. Voltaire tried to invigorate the form by introducing picturesque elements, stage setting, costuming, Shakespearean innovations—even a ghost—but to little avail. He lacked the imagination and psychological penetration necessary for so difficult a form of art. Although his failure was not apparent to himself or to his contemporaries who thought his *Zaïre* and *Mérope* equal to the *Cid,* he started on the path which led ultimately to the bourgeois drama, to melodrama, and to the romantic tragedy.

The comedy of the eighteenth century is superior to the tragedy. In *Turcaret,* Lesage presents a monstrous picture of a financier, subordinating all else to the portrayal of this hateful character.

Marivaux introduces into comedy an element of fancy and of beauty. In a kind of fairyland, characters like those painted by Watteau move and speak their elegant language. As in the tragedies of Racine, love is the matter involved, and the most delicate shades of this feeling are portrayed with poetic insight. But the love here is not tragic; it does not devastate and kill; it is rather a simple, natural, nascent love, concerned only with the acceptance of a proposal. Here, too, as in Racine, the happenings, often minute, are in the minds and hearts of the characters.

The bourgeois drama, of which Diderot became the theorist, represents a fusion of tragedy and comedy. Instead of the heroic actions of exalted characters, we have now the intimate life of ordinary people treated seriously, the secrets of private existences. The serious tone represents the growing influence of the bourgeois: it is tearful, sentimental, like the English pathetic comedy, and leads ultimately to much of the drama of the nineteenth century. The masterpiece of the new form is Sedaine's *Le philosophe sans le savoir,* a work that is an omen.

At the end of the century, Beaumarchais, using the almost forgotten framework of the farce, founds a new type of comedy. The stock characters reappear, but transformed into brilliant talkers, brilliant thinkers, and brilliant rascals. The dialogue is a display of verbal pyrotechnics. In the *Mariage de Figaro* the barber hero becomes the mouthpiece of the revolutionary spirit: it is this sad rogue who demands the four (or more) freedoms and who arouses the most generous and humanitarian illusions. In this play the old social order becomes the victim of a universal mockery.

Of the strictly literary forms, only the novel made notable progress. Lesage in *Gil Blas* excels, not in psychological realism, but in painting the appearances of men and of life. In contrast to the romances of adventure and the précieux novels, the spirit of this work is earthly, materialistic, without illusions.

Marivaux also paints manners, but with much psychological analysis and some pathos. The heroine of the *Life of Marianne* is probably the most minutely analyzed girl in all literature. She tells all she feels in all the situations she is in and what she would have felt in all those she was not in.

The masterpiece of the novel, however, is *Manon Lescaut,* an episode in a larger work, written in a moment of unconscious art by the Abbé Prévost. Here we meet with true romantic love, the dominating, fatal, inescapable passion felt later by Werther, Saint Preux, and René. In the story of this beautiful "Virginie mal tournée" about whom the nervous, vital, and frustrated abbé dreamed restlessly, there is the kind of innocence we find in children and in animals, and an infinite charm.

The "philosophers" took up the novel as a medium for propaganda. The uncontested masterpiece of this type of fiction is Voltaire's *Candide,* a miracle of rapid narration, witty, clear, licentious, thoughtful, urbane, significant, useful; but without kindness, love, or beauty.

Science enters literature most notably in Buffon's *Natural History.* Here, even humble creatures, the rabbit or the donkey are treated with scientific devotion to fact, but in the grand, literary manner, in a style more suitable for the phœnix or the hippogriffe. Buffon chose this means to give dignity to science, and he succeeded, apparently, in his attempt.

Three works of Montesquieu count in the history of literature. The *Persian Letters* offer a witty and amusing criticism of French society—a preliminary skirmish before the main battle. Montesquieu's work on Roman history inaugurates, one may say, rational, if not scientific, history. In his *Esprit des Lois* he becomes one of the founders of sociology as well as of political science. This work influenced the framers of many democratic constitutions, including our own.

The philosophic movement centered in the Encyclopedia, the burden of which fell principally upon Diderot. Besides giving the usual information, this publication had a reforming purpose. It heralded the new rationalism, using it to refute conventional and orthodox viewpoints. Diderot's own writings suffer from improvisation and lack of restraint. But he had one of the boldest and most fruitful minds of his age, and the further advantage of a large fund of positive knowledge.

Voltaire's work and actions fill the century. His fifty large volumes contain nearly everything—poetry, epistles, satires, an epic, a mock epic, history, tragedies, comedies, even a drama. Whenever he adopts a familiar tone, as in his occasional verse, letters, and incidental works of criticism and of malice, he attains a kind of lucid perfection, a gracefulness and urbanity that have seldom been equaled.

As an historian, he wrote admirably about Charles XII of Sweden, and gave an almost definitive picture of the age of Louis XIV. He was careful and critical in his documentation and was one of the first to consider the development of civilization more important than the personal life of kings. Of his critical works, the best known are the *English Letters,* and the *Philosophical Dictionary,* which served as a catechism for the philosophic party. Through these and similar works, Voltaire became a power, a creator of public opinion, a man feared by governments and kings. The dissolvent he used was disrespect for authority and tradition, and an appeal to the common sense of his readers. But not all of his work was negative: he fought hard for tolerance, for liberty of thought and of speech.

As a writer of correspondence, Voltaire ranks with Cicero and Mme. de Sévigné. The tone of his letters varies with each person he addresses. For richness of ideas, malice, wit, politeness, urbanity—the most notable qualities of his age and country—nothing can surpass the extensive correspondence of this versatile writer.

With Rousseau comes romanticism both in feeling and in ideas. By origin and education, this author does not belong to the highly intellectual, aristocratic society of his age: he felt this, and made a virtue of the maladjustment.

Many tendencies in literature are contemporaneous with Rousseau—sentimentality, lyricism, nature description, exaltation of rustic and simple life, melancholy, the superior claims of the heart over the head. His influence is everywhere. As Goethe said, "with Voltaire a world ends, with Rousseau a new world begins." He formulated the faiths of the democratic crowds.

In the *Nouvelle Héloïse,* a novel which took Europe by storm, he taught what a jaded generation was anxious to believe—the beautiful or tragic quality of domestic love—and he gave to his hero's association with the technically virtuous Julie a glamor usually associated only with illicit adventures. He inaugurated nature description also, which became an almost necessary accompaniment of prose fiction for a hundred years.

In *Emile,* Rousseau expounds his ideas on education. Here we hear of the rights of instinct and of Nature. This work converted fashionable ladies to the practice of nursing their own children, and even at the opera some took pride in exhibiting Nature in themselves and in their voracious babes.

The *Social Contract* was based on neither investigation nor experiment and illustrates some of the dangers of Cartesian rationalism. It became the Bible of the Revolutionaries, and inspired the Declaration of the Rights of Man. Rousseau's sentimental republicanism, his protest in the name of the common man, made of him the revolutionary *par excellence,* and he still fulfills, to some extent, that rôle. In his favor one must note that he saw how the State alone can weaken the forces in society that oppress the individual.

The *Confessions* of Rousseau inaugurate personal literature. Here and in the *Rêveries d'un promeneur solitaire* he is a great literary artist. His musical prose, his descriptions of rustic, simple life come in this age of dry reason like a breath of fresh mountain air.

Bernardin de Saint-Pierre followed Rousseau like the unintelligent pupil of not too sound a master. And, like Rousseau, he was a literary artist. He introduced exoticism, and for years his idyllic *Paul and Virginia* delighted those with tender minds and hearts.

Lyric poetry, although much cultivated, did not prosper in the Age of Reason. Still, at the end of the century, a great poet arose, André Chénier, who felt the very spirit of ancient art. Although claimed by the romantics, he seems rather to be the ancestor of their repudiators, the Parnassian poets of the nineteenth century.

French influence throughout the continent was never as absolute as in the eighteenth century. Frederick the Great of Prussia became French in language and in the character of his intelligence; Catherine of Russia, likewise, felt French influence strongly, and Christine of Sweden took refuge in France. French actors, tutors, artists, tailors were everywhere. In Russia, French influence lasted down to the Communist revolution.

But at the very height of this triumph, new and strange tendencies appeared. The senses awaken; there are vast, unrequited desires. Perhaps the most brilliant, the most intelligent society that has ever existed ended in vague longings, in *ennui*, in romantic melancholy. The world of the philosophes died of dryness, of atrophy of the heart, and classic literature died with it.

THE NINETEENTH AND TWENTIETH CENTURIES

The French Revolution changed the social and political order and, following it, an artistic revolution gave rise to a new literature. Authors were obliged to address a different and growing mass of readers, and the old standards could not be maintained. Although various publics existed throughout the nineteenth and early twentieth centuries, the vulgarization of the aristocracy proceeded more rapidly than the rise in cultural level of the enlarged and dominant bourgeois class.

The press, taking the place of the old guides in the *salons* and elsewhere, tended to establish new prestige values. To some extent journalism supplanted literature, so that many never learned how to read anything except ephemeral work, written rapidly and intended to be perused without effort and at high speed. As the century advanced, writing for a mass market became for some a lucrative trade. Many authors refused to corrupt their standards, but the pressure to do so was constant and great, and in the inherently popular literary forms, the drama and novel, many compromises were made.

Fortunately, in France, the traditions of the past were not completely obliterated; cultivated readers survived, and great works could still be addressed to them. On the whole, until the *débâcle* brought on by the war of 1914, the gains were probably greater than the losses. Although the proportion of serious and intelligent readers decreased, the actual number of them probably grew.

The immediate effect of the French Revolution on literature was a sudden vulgarization, noticeable especially in the drama. Then, under the Empire, literature fell under a control which delayed the romantic revolution until 1815. The romantic period extends roughly from that date until 1850, when realism prevails which, in turn, gave rise to naturalism after 1870. In poetry the Parnassian movement coincides roughly with realism and symbolism with naturalism. These changes in artistic climate correspond closely with certain political events, the Restoration in 1815, the revolution of 1848, and the Franco-Prussian war of 1870.

In spite of these different movements, a few characteristics are constant in the literature of the entire period. A feeling for external nature; sympathy or indulgence for religion; and an interest in science, in local color, and in social problems run through the whole age.

The first movement, romanticism, represents a violent reaction against nearly all the classicists stood for. Imagination takes the place of reason. There is a return to Christian and nationalistic subjects, to individualism and to artistic freedom. The dominant literary influences are no longer the works of the ancients, but such northern writers as Ossian, Young, Gray, Goethe, Scott, Byron, Schiller, and Schlegel.

In France itself, among the immediate personal influences, were Chateaubriand and Mme. de Staël.

To the Rousseauistic sensitiveness, subjectivism, and exaltation of the ego, Chateaubriand added a Christian element. In his *Genius of Christianity,* he awakened a latent religiosity, rehabilitated the Middle Ages, and extolled Gothic art and national history, which became sources of lyric inspiration. In *Atala* and *René* he presents the very type of the romantic hero, proud, melancholy, dark, fatalistic, who will be duplicated many times in the works of Lamartine, Vigny, Hugo, and others.

Chateaubriand is hardly more convincing as a realist than Bernardin de Saint-Pierre, but he has an overwhelming sense of harmony and of color. He has been classed the creator of "poetic prose." As a painter of natural scenes he surpasses Rousseau and becomes a model for later French writers.

Unlike Chateaubriand, Mme. de Staël was not primarily an artist. She furnished the new movement with ideas, theories, and critical viewpoints, and showed the relativity of artistic merit. Her *Corinne* is the first cosmopolitan novel in France and, incidentally, one of the first to present the feminist viewpoint. Above all, Mme. de Staël made known the literatures of northern Europe.

Romanticism succeeded mainly in those forms which classicism tended to neglect: namely, lyric poetry, the personal novel, and evocative history.

In poetry, the *Meditations* of Lamartine were welcomed with delirious enthusiasm. A new spirit pervades them, spiritual, emotional, elegiac: in fluid and harmonious verses they recall forgotten things—God, immortality, and Providence—and express a new tenderness.

Alfred de Vigny is considered the most philosophic of the French romantic poets: he thinks, or seems to think, deeply. For him men are indifferent or hostile; Nature is cold, uncaring. Ultimately he embraces a tender stoicism. In a form of his own, the *poème*, Vigny excels in painting vast panoramas, majestic and austere.

Alfred de Musset has a less prophetic and apocalyptic manner, but, in his serious work, seems superior to other romantics in intelligence and psychological understanding. His *Nights* which relate the delusions of romantic love (with George Sand) suggest Dante for condensation and evocative power. In his plays a kind of poetic beauty returns to dramatic literature.

The leader of the romantic school was Victor Hugo. He had industry, fecundity, pride, and the talent for imposing on his contemporaries. He progressed with the century from a common devotion to monarchy to a lyrical republicanism, so that his death in 1885 was the occasion for such honors as kings had seldom received.

Hugo's principal poetic works are his *Châtiments, Contemplations,* and *Légende des siècles.* He is praised for epic qualities, color, relief, and for a prodigious series of images. He makes frequent use of words which occasion stock responses: God, Oblivion (*le Néant*), Humanity, Vice, Misery, Progress, Duty. He seems to live familiarly with these entities, and has an incomparable air of grandeur and nobility. As a technician of verse he stands first in all of French literature.

Hugo's dramas have literary and lyric qualities without technical or dramatic skill. His plots are usually melodramatic: they require secret doors, disguises, stupendous recognitions, and other similar devices. The characters are likely to be walking antitheses, showing the greatest virtues in the most unexpected places. Hugo's preface to his play, *Cromwell,* is the manifesto of the Romantic school, and the presentation of his *Hernani* marked the triumph of the new ideas.

The historical novel, popularized by Scott, was also cultivated notably by Victor Hugo. His *Notre Dame de Paris* is diffuse, replete with dissertations and digressions, episodes and fantastic scenes. Another novel, *Les Misérables,* enjoys popularity among young readers, but reveals little understanding of man or of the world in which he lives.

In drama the romantics denounced generally almost all that the classicists required—the unities, the separation of tragedy and comedy, the noble and elegant style. Only verse was retained now and then to give an artistic character to what otherwise might have differed little from melodrama.

Dumas, in *Henri III et sa Cour,* introduced local color, and in *Antony* he puts on the stage a Byronic hero, exalted, mystic, rebellious. His dramas differ from those of Hugo in showing technical skill without much literary talent.

The romanticists succeeded better in the novel than in the

drama. Stendhal, early in the century, wrote *The Red and the Black* and *The Chartreuse of Parma* in a bare, cold style, addressed to "the happy few." He expected to be appreciated about 1880 and was; and the cult for him has continued.

Various inspirations characterized the novels of George Sand—idealistic, ultra-romantic, socialistic. Her most admired works are lyric in quality and treat in an idyllic manner the rustic life of her province.

The prolific genius of Alexandre Dumas also took hold of the novel, and in some 257 volumes carried it right out of the domain of literature and of art.

Mérimée, whose works include *Colomba* and *Carmen,* treats the novel and short story as art forms. He aims at precision and objectivity, and his style is as remarkable for condensation as that of most romantics for diffuseness. His place in the novel is that of a transitional figure between romanticism and realism.

Balzac is commonly considered the leading novelist of world literature. In his vast picture of French society, *The Human Comedy,* characters of all social classes, professions, and trades move in and out. An inadequate style, an inability to picture delicate manners, and improbabilities, find compensation in the author's prodigious imagination. Balzac is unequaled in presenting the lower middle classes. His descriptions of places are meticulous, minute, and help to characterize people. With him we pass from romanticism to realism, since, although both elements are present in his work, the part that has shown greater durability is almost devoid of a romantic character.

Théophile Gautier was by temperament a painter who had strayed into literature. The objectivity and precision customary in the pictorial arts alienated him progressively from romanticism until he became a connecting link with a later naturalistic or objective school of poets. It was he who affirmed the doctrine of art for art's sake, eliminating ethical and philosophic ends. His *Émaux and Camées,* as well as some novels, have a classic objectivity and are, in fact, like cameos in their workmanship and appeal to the eyes.

After the reaction against romanticism around 1850, the dominant spirit is that of realism, which later becomes intensified as naturalism. The subjectivity and exhibitionism of the romantics were replaced by objectivity and impersonality as dominant aspirations. To a considerable extent this realism represents a return to the classic spirit, although the human nature of the classicists now becomes nature as a whole, external as well as internal. The new realism, moreover, is scientific rather than esthetic, and tends to be amoral and without dogmas.

The new tendencies in poetry were represented most clearly by the Parnassian School, of which Leconte de Lisle and Hérédia were the masters. In their violent reaction against romanticism they made a cult of a serene objectivity and impassiveness and produced work of a rare perfection that appeals powerfully to an artistic elite.

Baudelaire, a transitional poet, marks the change from the hard, classic perfection of the Parnassians to the insinuating, fluid manner of the symbolists. He reveals his feelings through impersonal or symbolic forms. He broke away, moreover, from the conventional subjects of poetry to include crude and brutal scenes of daily life. A new accent pervades his work, a kind of agony due to an epicurean sensuality joined with a Christian sense of sin. He is a powerful but unequal artist whose work has enjoyed an increasing vogue.

Verlaine, in verses that are music, evokes the fugitive states of his moods. He invented a new poetic phrase, flexible, even incorrect, but suited perfectly to express vague longings, nostalgia, half-lights, sadness, and regret for a wasted youth.

Mallarmé endeavored to present, not feelings, like Verlaine, but ideas. He transforms poetry into an incantation which has a peculiar fascination for those who can penetrate his difficult, hermetic lines, and who can perceive the gentle and exquisite soul behind them. The brief *Afternoon of a Faun* is the best-known poem of this esoteric writer in whom (together with Huysmans and a few others) the conscious esthetic movement that began in the Renaissance perhaps culminates.

The symbolist movement reached its height in the last decade of the nineteenth century. Of the poets who have carried on this tradition into the twentieth century or who have sought individual paths, the best known are Moréas, Henri de Régnier, Verhaeren, Francis Jammes, Apollinaire, and Valéry.

Modern literary criticism has been cultivated most notably by the French. Among the principal exponents of that art are Sainte-Beuve, the leading literary critic in modern times, Taine, and Ernest Renan.

After 1850, realistic and naturalistic works replaced the romantic drama, which died almost suddenly as if from high blood pressure. Augier showed on the stage the rôle of money in society. Although his plays are not notable for philosophic depth or poetic imagination, they serve as studies of manners. Dumas, *fils,* also interested in social problems, uses the theater to preach the integrity of the family, a matter which, with him, was an obsession.

The naturalistic drama proposed to show on the stage a *tranche de vie* (a cross-section of life). Becque was a leader in this sociological and scientific effort. Later Brieux, following Ibsen's example, used the theater for presenting and solving social problems.

With Maeterlinck, symbolism comes to the stage. His childlike characters struggle in a world of mysterious and nefarious powers.

Other dramatic works are those of Rostand, who represents a romantic regression, the ideological drama of François de Curel and the psychological studies of Porto-Riche. Among still other late or contemporary dramatists are Lenormand, Raynal, Bernard, Sacha Guitry, and Denis Amiel.

In the field of prose fiction, Flaubert had both romantic and realistic tendencies, and he alternated between the two manners. He spent six years writing *Madame Bovary* and four years on *Salammbô*; but *Madame Bovary* ranks as the masterpiece of the novel in the nineteenth century. For accurate observation, psychological perspicacity, beauty of structure and of style, it stands alone.

Émile Zola exemplifies the extreme naturalistic theories. He wished to apply the experimental method to the novel, imagining somehow that his characters could be guinea pigs in a laboratory, and he analyses minutely the influence on them of heredity and environment. Like others of the group, he chooses the less pleasant aspects of life. He excels in describing crowds: his style appears to most critics as undistinguished, his psychology elementary.

The Goncourt brothers wrote both historical studies and novels in a consciously artistic style that has been called "impressionistic."

Maupassant, the master of the short story, also belonged to the realistic or naturalistic movement as shown by the scientific detachment with which he wrote.

In the period that extends from the last years of the nineteenth century to the first World War, the principal novelists were Loti, a word-painter, Bourget, and Anatole France. The latter shows in his early work a gentle, epicurean wisdom, and an indulgent and kindly scepticism. Later he protested against the current politico-economic system, "the reign of money." His exquisite culture shows itself in his naturalness, clarity, and in the music of his prose style.

After the first World War, Proust became the leading French novelist. In the *Remembrance of Things Past*, he gives a picture of the rich Parisian society in which he lived. Like Freud, he is interested in the unconscious, and seems to follow the intuitive philosophy of Bergson. His minute and slow psychological analyses, in overburdened sentences, make him a difficult author for those outside the growing circle of his devoted followers.

Other notable novelists are Gide, Mauriac, Rolland, and Jules Romains.

*   *   *

The preceding account of the nineteenth and twentieth centuries is like a conducted tour, in half an hour, of a great museum of art. The guide can only indicate with a gesture the size of the halls and hurriedly affirm the richness of the contents.

BIBLIOGRAPHY

HISTORY OF LITERATURE

BÉDIER, J., and HAZARD, P., eds. *Histoire de la littérature française illustrée* (Paris, 1923), 2 vols.

BRUNETIERE, F., *Manuel de l'histoire de la littérature française,* 2nd ed. (Paris, 1899).

DES GRANGES, CH.-M., *Histoire illustrée de la littérature française,* 13th ed. (Paris, 1933).

LANSON, G., *Histoire de la littérature française* (Paris, 1938).

MORNET, D., *Histoire de la littérature et de la pensée françaises* (Paris, 1925).

NITZE, W. A., and DARGAN, E. P., *A History of French Literature* (New York, 1927).

PETIT DE JULLEVILLE, L., ed., *Histoire de la langue et de la littérature française, des origines à 1900* (Paris, 1896-1899).

SAINTSBURY, George, *A Short History of French Literature,* 7th ed. (London, 1917).

WRIGHT, C. H. C., *A History of French Literature,* 2nd ed. (New York, 1925).

9

Spanish and Portuguese Literature

RUDOLPH SCHEVILL
UNIVERSITY OF CALIFORNIA

RUDOLPH SCHEVILL (1874-1946) *grew up when every serious young Middle Westerner knew that one got an education by going to Europe after it. With a B.A. degree from Yale he earned his doctorate at Munich, and went on to the Sorbonne in Paris and the Universidad Central in Madrid. He returned to teach at Yale, and went to the University of California in 1910, where for thirty-five years the teaching of Spanish and the pursuit of Spanish studies were associated with his name. American Hispanists are sometimes twitted by their colleagues for untempered enthusiasm for their subject;* PROFESSOR SCHEVILL *was never open to the charge. Supported by impeccable scholarship, his writings carried always the mark of an alert, critical, and penetrating mind. Nothing better of their sort has been done in this country; they include* The Dramatic Art of Lope de Vega (1918); Life of Cervantes (1919); *and his lifetime work, the* Obras Completas . . . *of* Cervantes (1914-1941), *18 vols. When, in 1942, the Hispanic Society of America honored him with the medal of arts in literature, there could have been few to doubt the justice of the award. His eldest son, Dr. Karl E. Schevill, who prepared his father's essay for the press, has his Ph.D. degree in Spanish literature from the University of California, and now teaches at San Diego State College, in California.*

Spanish and Portuguese Literature[1]

THE Iberian Peninsula looks everywhere upon the sea, except in the north, where the wide neck of the lofty Pyrenees separates it completely from the rest of Europe. The significant section of its long coast-line forms a part of the western border of the Mediterranean basin, from which *Hispania* derived the most permanent elements of her race and language, that is, the essence of the civilization and the culture so peculiarly her own. From the Mediterranean came various foreign peoples in successive waves. Asia Minor and Egypt, Greece, Carthage and Rome, and lastly, the Moslem world sent armies that in turn afflicted the Peninsula with wars of conquest lasting over two thousand years, and leaving their imprint on the diversified history of Iberian life and thought. The Pyrenees, on the other hand, have served rather as a helpful barrier against Europe whenever its progress or its innovations were viewed as a danger to the established ideas of Church and State. Some of the early incursions from the north—for example, the prehistoric inroads of Celtic tribes, or the Germanic invasions of the fifth century of our era—left only a slight trace in the life, customs, or speech of the Iberian peoples.

With the coming of Christianity relations between the Peninsula and the rest of Europe became more established and were vigorously maintained, through a common Faith, up to the close of the Middle Ages (1500). The history of medieval Spain is the history of the gradual reconquest of her invaded soil. It is the triumph of institutional Christianity and, specifically, of the Spanish religion and race over the Islamic and Jewish religions

[1] This essay was one of the last works of the late Professor Schevill. It was left in rough draft, and revised by his son, Dr. Karl E. Schevill, who also provided the bibliography. Ed.

and races. When the Peninsula ceased to be a frontier of expanding Western Christendom the complete elimination of Moor and Jew gave the people a sense of religious unity that served to replace their lack of political unity; it imbued them with a fixed purpose of preserving Church and Monarchy with all the vitality and power they had derived from the victorious *reconquista* of eight hundred years. Out of this persistent struggle along the slowly receding frontier held by Islam was born the Spanish conception of ecclesiastical and monarchic government, held at first in common with other rising nations of Western Christendom, but becoming at the close of the Middle Ages the bulwark of a distinct conservative theocratic State.

BACKGROUND OF THE GOLDEN AGE

From the dawn of the Renaissance, close relationship of the Iberian Peninsula with the northern nations had lost its historical necessity and thus became more incidental; that is, currents of political or literary history have rather intermittently brought the Spanish and Portuguese people into contact with the full stream of European thought. Even the international character of the flowering Renaissance which profoundly affected the spiritual trend of Europe did not further genuine understanding between the Peninsula on the one hand, and France, England and Germany on the other. Not only recurrent wars with those nations, but the basic political and economic interests of Spain and Portugal turned the vision and the energies of the people from the North to new conquests in the Far East and in America, those absorbing and exhausting realms beyond the unexplored Atlantic. Instead of sharing the intellectual ferment and the new freedom of the age, the Peninsula had to assume the burden of administering territories twenty times the extent of the homeland, inhabited by primitive tribes to whom it carried its government, religion, and law, as well as arts and letters, but from whom it received no compensatory incentive to cultural growth.

In the sixteenth century Spain still retained much of her political prestige, and the genius of her people, as will be clear presently, expressed itself in many brilliant creations in art and in letters. But with the overthrow of the Islamic frontier, which had been the driving force of her national achievement, her dynamic rôle in Europe had been fulfilled. Her chief interests being confined now to the Mediterranean area and to America she was destined to play no kindred part in the religious revolts, in the scientific expansion, or in the birth of critical philosophic movements. Nor did she have a prominent share in the dawning industrial age after the mass expulsion of Jews and Moriscos, which hastened her economic decadency. Her fecund Golden Age at last burned itself out, and by the end of the seventeenth century her political power and her social vitality were drained out of the shell of her long static institutions. But the Iberians have always evinced a gift of resurgence, of developing forceful qualities of action rather than speculation, so that even Iberian productions in art and letters bear the stamp of something lived or enacted, with a distinctiveness peculiarly "Spanish."

The course of Iberian civilization was greatly influenced by features of geography and peculiarities of climate. Wide mountain ranges in the south, the center, and the west divide the whole land into isolated regions and independent social groups which have, from the earliest records, been inclined to separatism in their communal life and in their political aspirations. These geographical disparities have found expression at various times in a conspicuously regionalistic literature, reflecting local idioms and even a concept of patriotism restricted to a beloved locality known as *mi tierra* (patria), and seldom enlarged to the concept of a national polity. Extensive variations of climate have produced every product of the earth, scattered capriciously over the land from the lavish fruitfulness of the Mediterranean coastal areas to the sparse returns of the semi-arid central plateau, or the toil-exacting, stony mountain regions of the north and west. Even the rivers with their scant waters have yielded no communications comparable with the vast streams of other lands. The ensuing lack of transportation and the restrictions on essential trade have above all hampered the economic development of Spain and Portugal. Provincial fragmentation, therefore, has persisted in the form of regional antagonisms fostered by variations of speech forms and by a self-reliant independence of character that comprises the particularly Iberian concept of liberty.

Ancient writers of history and geography were already aware of these uncommon traits of the Hispanic character, which, they averred, made difficult a just and accurate analysis of its inherent complexity. It follows that a conscious expression of national unity very rarely enters into the history of Spanish thought, that the political history of Spain must also envisage a loosely related number of municipalities with their own charters or *fueros* that constitute the legalized form of a vigorous local patriotism. The tendency to disunion was long ago discerned by Strabo, who pointed out the inability of the particular tribes he had studied to find a common ground of harmonious thought or action. Hispanic esthetic ideas have in consequence derived their inspiration from modest local environments; poetry and novel have not required the creative impulse of a great metropolis like Paris or London. Even today, many writers throughout the Hispanic world are inclined to gather their material from their own towns or provinces, thus presenting the particular phase of the national soul with which they are most familiar, and which they can record with the greatest sincerity and skill. Emphasis on a local and, therefore, confined approach to life has marked the Spaniard with a reserve, born of hesitancy to accept currents of thought from the outside. He has been inclined to suspicion of novel ideas and of foreigners, or strangers in general. Traditional conservatism has created in him a preference for the good inherent in what is familiar, and a sense of mistrust in what is strange. Objectively viewed, then, the Spaniard's individuality in religious, social, and political concepts is rooted in a simple innate dignity; it is well illustrated by the common saying: *Cada cual tiene el rey en su cuerpo,* Everyone is a king in his own right.

Having found within themselves the most ample resources of expression the Iberian people have given special prominence to those concepts of honor and racial pride so frequently commented on by foreigners in the wake of numerous international conflicts. Spaniards and Portuguese alike could vindicate this proverbial pride by pointing to the extended sway of their religion and the vast dominions embraced in their conquests. Literature supported the boast of the soldier in glowing allusions to an empire on which the sun never set, and to a unity of faith that constituted the quickening spirit of a world-power. Thus the idea of Church and Monarchy united in harmonious rule remained the nucleus of political thought in the Peninsula, an idea, however, that was unhappily destined to receive elsewhere a narrow and prejudiced interpretation. More intimate acquaintance with the varied life of the people in town and village, with their intrinsic love of liberty, would have awakened in Europe a more just and balanced appreciation of the genuine character of the Peninsular people and of the range and nature of their literature. It would have qualified the satirical strictures of Montesquieu who, in dissembled sincerity, ridiculed the books of Spain as a whole, or the severe generalizations of the English historian H. T. Buckle, who in a sweeping verdict held all Spanish thought to be shot through with primitive superstition. These are but examples of the difficulty which English, French, and German nationals have experienced when required to judge a typical work of the Spanish genius, peculiar, remote, and a law to itself. An additional disadvantage has generally been insufficient acquaintance with a singularly rich and varied idiom, though at times infelicitously affected by the changing caprices of style.

Political thought in the writings of historians and of philosophers has reflected the traditional suppression of the essential freedoms of popular government. This deserves emphasis because of its inhibiting effect on the history of criticism. The frequently voiced concept of liberty as something that contrasts narrowly with its opposite, slavery, must not be confused with the modern concept of freedom of the mind. Its primal source was Aristotle, whose teachings had penetrated many fields and persisted long after medieval scholasticism had given ground to the light of the Renaissance.

Religious thought is much illuminated by comparing trends in England and Germany, notably as regards opposition to the Church of Rome, and especially, as regards the significant part played there, in the life of the common people, by the Bible. In Hispanic lands no vitalized heterodox movement, whether inspired by the dynamic tenets of Luther, or by the humanistic doctrines of Erasmus, or by the fervent aspirations of the *illuminati* (*alumbrados*), who advocated worship unencumbered by ritual, gained any secure hold. Direct knowledge of the Bible was not countenanced, and it has remained a book unknown to the common people. The teachings of Erasmus in favor of a purer faith based on "inner piety" and on personal acquaintaince with the Gospel through translations had been accepted by a group of fervent disciples. They can have comprised only a meager following recruited from a limited reading public, the sole ones susceptible to a timid religious reform. The Inquisition or *Santo Oficio* quickly ferreted out all heresy implied in the movement, and the enlightenment inspired by Erasmus faded with the suppression of every work connected with his name. Subsequently, traces of his thought are to be found solely in matters removed from all controversy. As regards the fate of the Bible, the Vulgate continued to be printed with its orthodox commentary, and preachers retained the tradition of quoting only the Latin original, unintelligible to the common people.

Hand in hand with the profound influence of the Bible in England and Germany went liberty of anti-papal criticism and of strictures on the clergy. Outside Spain a typical voice was that of Robert Burton, who in his *Anatomy of Melancholy* characteristically expressed the heterodox view that a priesthood may "deliberately" keep the public in ignorance, an idea greatly expanded by the eighteenth-century philosophers, with the implication that an uneducated populace by reflection created an equally uneducated priesthood. No such opinion could have been voiced in the Peninsula, even when the French Revolution was at Spain's door with its vital concepts of the rights of man, or equally fundamental issues of economic reform. The clergy were still engaged in the purification of the faith and the censorship of the printed word.

A genuine endeavor, characteristic of the age of humanism, had been made by the universities to achieve a freer atmosphere together with a reform of their life and teachings. This occurred at the outset of the sixteenth century, before the reaction of the Counter Reformation had definitely curtailed freedom of thought. In that brief period many distinguished scholars and teachers adorned Salamanca and Alcalá, Spain's leading universities, and their classical and humanistic studies occupied a recognized place in the forefront of scholarship of the Renaissance. But when the channels of ventilation in the world of teaching had been narrowed by a reaffirmation of the scholastic doctrines of Saint Thomas Aquinas and of fundamental Catholic dogma as it had been set forth by the Council of Trent (1563) and incorporated in the curricula of higher learning, not only the course of general education in the Peninsula was thereby affected, but, more especially, the important fields of philosophic speculation and of social criticism faced a much hampered development. As a result the Spanish genius turned to the observation of manners, to moral criticism, and notably to the satirical analysis of an enigmatic irrational world in which it found a rich, though circumscribed, field of brilliant expression. Finally, the various prohibitive expurgating indices constitute a detailed record of forbidden ideas.

One more influence of significance in the history of sixteenth century thought deserves mention, that of the Society of Jesus, founded by a Spaniard, Ignatius of Loyola. That it strengthened the religious foundation of the Spanish and Portuguese States is clear. But the successful intervention of the Jesuit order can be ascribed chiefly to their effectiveness as teachers and humanists in an age in which the varied learning that they fostered so skillfully was in greatest vogue. The course of the Society did not always run smooth because of disputes with rival orders, notably the Dominicans, who contrasted sharply with the Jesuits in their educational and social functions. The latter educated a more select class; the Dominicans moved among the common people as missionary preachers. But the first great scholastics had also been Dominicans whose followers exercised a profound influence at the universities, where the Jesuits with their greater flexibility and more practical Renaissance culture did not always receive a cordial welcome, and even roused embittered controversies. The Society left a marked impression on Spanish and Portuguese thought also because famous Peninsular members of the order gave it added prestige. The historian Mariana, the dramatist Calderón, the philosopher and moralist Gracián, the theologian Luis de Molina, who taught at the University of Coimbra, and the missionary Saint Francis Xavier were among the most noted of its sons. In the extended controversy between the advocates of free will and those of divine grace, Spanish Jesuits, notably the above mentioned Molina, a foremost voice of the Society, were especially prominent in espousing the freedom of the will. But the society also mingled with its practical educational activities an interest in government and politics, thereby strengthening the Church in its policy of having a hand in civil affairs at both Lisbon and Madrid.

The panorama of contributions which literature and the arts made to Iberian thought can now be reviewed. It is important at the outset to take cognizance of the unbroken continuity of an indigenous culture that was on the whole affected sparingly by the importation of foreign influence. Within that culture the spontaneous voice of the people occupies a unique place: it has expressed itself quite independently of the literature produced by the upper classes who not only enjoyed the benefits of higher education, but were also the chief recipients of whatever foreign ideas had penetrated the Peninsula. During the Middle Ages the productions of the people, often anonymous, form the most enduring element of the literary history of Spain and Portugal. In Spanish the most noteworthy monument is the vigorous realistic *Poema de mío Cid* (1150), a noble epic of that hero, felicitously mingling legend and history. Subsequent centuries produced an extensive body of popular verse of which the most famous are the *romances* or ballads, which grew to be the richest and most genuine of all poetic utterances. Prose also brought forth a number of didactic works that were indebted to Oriental sources now rooted in the Peninsula, and a variety of exemplary tales such as the *Libro de Patronio* (1328), by Prince Juan Manuel, nephew of King Alfonso X, known as *el Sabio*, who led historiography with his *Crónica general de España* (1275) and directed the compilation of the great code of law *las Siete Partidas*. Books of travel and adventure, like González de Clavijo's journey to Samarcand, recorded in his *Historia del gran Tamorlán*, revealed Spain's continued live interest in the Near East, and biography was born with the realistic pen-portraits of Fernán Pérez de Guzmán's *Generaciones e Semblanzas*, a remarkable gallery of noted contemporaries. In the field of medieval science cultured centers like Córdoba and Toledo became during the twelfth and thirteenth centuries a clearing house for Oriental and Christian thought through epoch-making translations of Arabic and Greek works. Spain played a significant part in the recovery of the genuine Aristotle, her Arabic scholars furthered a scientific rebirth by spreading the mathematics, the astronomy, the philosophy, and medicine of Arabs and Jews whose manuscripts were eagerly sought throughout Europe.

As we approach the dawn of the Golden Age (1450-1650), the significant embodiments of Spanish and Portuguese thought stand forth in well defined types of literature in which it is important to signalize peculiar extremes of idealism and realism. A specific exposition of sixteenth century thought was the profuse writing in the field of mysticism. It was for the most part the fruit of the Counter Reformation, which, as a reaction to humanism and to the freer mundane spirit of the Renaissance, fostered a return to purer medieval contemplation and introspection. In their religious ardor the mystics represent a passive militia comparable with the active religious zeal of the *conquistador*, who having overcome the Moslem carried the banner of the Faith to America. Music, painting, and sculpture also reflected the spirit of mysticism in typical profusion. Furthermore, the unrealistic literature of the mystics was contemporaneous with another copious type, the equally unrealistic books of chivalry embodying the adventures of a medieval knight.

Their vogue was presently superseded by a vigorous and more genuinely national expression of realism destined to reach a flourishing period in the seventeenth century. In essence the opposite of the fantastic romance of chivalry, it is represented by the novels of adventure known as the picaresque or rogue story, the first of which is the popular anonymous *Lazarillo de Tormes* (1550), and by a group of novels in dialogue inspired by the oldest and greatest of its kind, the famous *Celestina* (1499). This internationally known work, attributed to Fernando de Rojas, gave realism its most forceful utterance. The contrast which the unvarnished human character of these writings afforded with the mystical or chivalric world is obvious, and shows the extremes to which the imagination of the Spanish mind was impelled in the transient unreality of the one, and in the living pages of the other, based as they were on observation and on

satirical interpretation of everyday life. This realistic vein re-
affirmed a traditional art presently to be crowned by a masterpiece, the *Don Quixote* (1605).

Poetry

It is equally informative to contrast the manifold anonymous
voices of popular verse which happily had never been silent since
the Middle Ages, with the less varied artificial muse of known
poets of the Renaissance, who created a vast body of poetry, inspired in Italian metrical forms and drawing much of the content and idiom from the Latin and Greek classics. Thus, on the
one hand, the flow of balladry, already referred to, and the great
variety of popular roundelays and of *cantares* preserved a Peninsular art derived from the living themes deeply imbedded in folklore and native life. On the other, sonnets, Petrarchan *canzoni*
(*canciones*) or lengthy epic poems, like Ercilla's *Araucana*
(1569), on the conquest of Chile, during the composition of
which the poet had an eye on the *Aeneid,* also adopted mythological machinery from Ovid. Lyric poets such as the mystic
Luis de León (d. 1591) even applied Horatian imagery of nature
to their own environment in response to humanistic reverence for
classical models. Indeed, the current concept of the world of
nature, supposedly created for the special benefit of man, was the
fusion of a classical heritage with current religious teaching,
exemplified in the noted treatise *Del menosprecio de la corte y
alabanza de la aldea* (1539), by the popular Bishop Antonio De
Guevara, whose works could be read in numerous translations. In
Spain, Garcilaso de la Vega had effectively pointed the way in
the use of Italian metrics, thereafter skillfully adapted by both
Spanish and Portuguese poets. In Portugal, *Os Lusiadas* by
Camoens stands alone in epic grandeur. The poet himself was
inspired by the chronicles of Portuguese explorers, among which
the history of the Fernão Lopes occupies first rank for its moving
dramatic vigor.

Castilian influence had dominated the lyrical field, keeping pace with the political hegemony of that kingdom, attained under the union of Ferdinand of Aragon and Isabella of Castile. This leadership was maintained during the sixteenth century. Among novel metrical contributions to the history of Peninsular verse the foremost, because of its revival and influence on modernist trends, is the much debated poetry of Luis de Góngora (d. 1627). His strange genius reflects two extremes of metrical form: first, a continuation of the popular vein in ballad and simple song; and, second, a peculiar invention or experimentation known as *gongorismo*. It is a metrical process including every tour de force that an ingenious violation of syntax can devise, a capricious word order with unexpected inversions and a dispersal of ideas that normally belong together. Appeals to metaphor and metonymy are voiced in a latinized vocabulary requiring extensive acquaintance with the classical source of Góngora's lexicon. A theory that may best explain the obscurity of Góngora's last compositions may be that, actuated by the arrogance characteristic of the humanist, he purposely scorned writing any further for the unlettered mind. Cultured readers might at any rate guess at the meaning of his cloud of enticing imagery, a process continued by modernist admirers today. Consequently the technical effort of such a work as his *Soledades* deserves a prominent place in the history of metrical art not only in Spain, but also in Portugal, where Góngora had captivated a number of followers.

Drama

The contrasts which set off the spontaneous poetry of the people from that of the conscious "art-lyric" also characterize the history of the Spanish stage. As in England, the basic elements of the development of the theatre came from the material which engaged the interest of the common people. The scattered efforts of schoolmen or humanists to create entertainment based on artificial revivals of ancient models gained no ground. The successful ventures inspired by the simple folk of town and country reflected their own lives and their native speech. The trend from the outset was away from pure comedy or tragedy to the mixed concept with an accompanying disregard of the unities of time, place, and action.

Peninsular dramatic art presumably began with simple Biblical themes and plots of rustic life, of which medieval records are scant indeed, a unique survival being the fragmentary *Auto de los reyes magos* (1200). The compositions of the early Renaissance, however, suggest the nature of the artless stage from which they sprang. Fortunately, several playwrights have left us specimens of what was best in their day. The rustic Eclogues of Juan del Encina, the plays of Lope de Rueda, a keen observer of his fellow-men, and Gil Vicente, a genuine poet of varied inspiration, have preserved phases of daily life in Spain and Portugal with the living breath of entertaining scenes marked by wit and pleasing action. So influential was the art thus early achieved that Cervantes himself was led to call attention to the deserved popularity of Rueda, and to follow in his footsteps by perfecting the genre in his own *Entremeses*.

The history of stage-craft and of dramatic art in general up to the years of their decline and transformation at the end of the seventeenth century can be epitomized in a rapid summary of the contributions of the two Spanish writers whose names have successively occupied the highest rung in the ladder of theatrical fame. They are Lope de Vega and Calderón. A complementary study of their numerous contemporaries would have to pay regard only to the minor dissimilarities and the novelties of their plays, but it would not essentially alter the picture of the theatre of the Golden Age gained from the two foremost figures of that creative period.

In keeping with his fertile genius, Lope expressed greater pride in the varied and unbelievably large number of his plays than in the excellence of any particular one. Since other playwrights, in competition with Lope, whom Cervantes had called *monstruo de la naturaleza*, have likewise stressed quantity rather than quality, the many plays written during the seventeenth century have created an insuperable problem, not only of disentangling authorships in an age in which plagiarism sat lightly on the shoulders of the poets, but also of definitely selecting the vastly diminished number of truly good plays, for the detection of which hundreds of inferior compositions have to be read—a task no one would lightly undertake. Lope's exuberant creative art, for which there is no parallel in any stage, was, in essence, a pure improvisation. He himself has asserted that many of his plays were composed in a single day. Under such circumstances, the concept of action completely overshadowed contemplation; the unfolding of a rapidly moving plot nullified the careful development of any individual character. Impulse superseded reason, no time being left for a profound analysis of personality or of the motive for a particular action. Based on a free technique which stressed the doing rather than the thinking of the protagonists, the result for the typical play of the Golden Age was an unqualified sacrifice of the rounded drawing of distinct individuals and of originality of plot. The panorama of so prodigious a theatrical mass production was bound to present, with few exceptions, a hurried procession of two-dimensional dramatis personae, similar plots and stereotyped concepts of the moral causes behind the action. A definite pattern of ideas embraced questions of honor, loyalty, religious piety, to say nothing of the dominant voice of blind passion, in which woman's beauty is her marked distinction, and man, as a hunter in quest of self-gratification and pleasure, seems indifferent to the importance of mind or beauty of character. Love had been defined by some Renaissance moralists tinged with neo-Platonism as "a desire of beauty," an esthetic note repeated by both Lope de Vega and Cervantes. This narrow concept of the woman's rôle was worked to death in love stories on the stage and in fiction, making the heroine little more than a designing schemer or the innocent victim of masculine wiles.

Owing to its sketchy portraiture of character, the Spanish *comedia,* as all plays were designated, does not yield a list of individual personages comparable with a Hamlet, a Lear, a Macbeth; or a Juliet, a Cleopatra, a Cordelia, or a Rosalind. But the stylized formula of that *comedia* can be imputed to the genius of Lope only in part, since he revitalized a timid and circumscribed art that he had inherited by adding the vivacity and motion so characteristic of his facile invention, and the never languishing freshness of his poetic vein. The drama of the sixteenth century had passed through a long period of transition in both Spain and Portugal, expanding from modest medieval conceptions, by dint of experiments and modifications in language, versification and plot, of which many features had remained crude up to Lope's time. The sixteenth-century play had attempted a number of artificial patterns, including infelicitous plots conceived in imitation of classical models, chiefly Seneca in tragedy and Terence in comedy, resembling the humanistic ventures at the universities, and finally adopted three acts as the norm. The language of prose was left to playlets and interludes, and verse became the language of the *comedia* throughout its flowering and decline. The facility of the Spanish genius in that medium prompted a complete liberty of metrical scheme, and the versification of the drama came to embrace every kind of native or Italianate form, short or long, strophic or unconfined verse sequences (*silva*), rhymed or not, as in blank verse.

Lope's genius matured in easy conformity with the intellectual atmosphere of the Counter Reformation, in general, and of Madrid, in particular. As a dramatic poet he turned, as did the lyric poet, to a vivacious presentation of the life before his eyes, unencumbered by social criticism, or by weighty monologues or thoughtful pauses which would have hampered the action of his play. He broached no controversial subject, he never speculated in matters of religion or politics, nor touched on problems of education or the existing extremes of wealth and poverty in the world around him.

In the development of dramatic art of the seventeenth century, Calderón came immediately after Lope de Vega, and his concept

of the drama left its mark on the theatre during the fifty years that
followed Lope's death. His genius as well as his intellectual outlook were too decidedly his own to permit his art to become an
unqualified imitation of that of Lope. Both were supremely endowed in the lyric and dramatic fields, but where the facile pen
of Lope, a man of the world, swept him on through plot after
plot, that of Calderón, who in later life entered the priesthood,
left the imprint of a sacerdotal mission derived from his education
by Jesuits, and fostered by his philosophical and theological interests. He did nothing to modify the three-act frame of the
comedia, but by greatly slowing down the rapid action of Lope,
by embodying in the pursuits of his protagonists specific ideas,
by introducing long narrative monologues to explain the course
of events, and by abandoning the simplicity and directness of
speech of his predecessor for the colorful and artificial idiom of
the *culto* and *gongorist* style, he lessened the popular acclaim
of the *comedia,* and in disdain of the vulgar preferences of the
public, turned for a more satisfactory appreciation of his intricate
art to the upper classes of society.

Of the various themes which Calderón uses with dramatic
skill, but not without the monotony of repetitiousness, is that
of *pundonor,* an artificial concept of conjugal or family honor,
allied with the overworked motives of jealousy and revenge, altogether the most typical of Spanish concepts. His most famous
plays also turn on specific ideas: in *Life Is a Dream,* the triumph
of intelligence and reason over instinct; in *The Constant Prince,*
the unshakable religious faith of the hero; in *Devotion to the
Cross,* the protagonist's salvation after a life of crime because of
that devotion; in *The Wonder-working Magician,* the conversion
and martyrdom of a pagan, and many others which are an index
of the thought of Calderón. Clearly in all this the playwright is
a child of his age paying homage to dogma, and to theology,
called "the queen of all learning" in the academic world. After
embracing the priesthood, Calderón devoted his finest poetic
gifts to *autos sacramentales,* plays with an allegorical content that

deals with the Sacrament of Corpus Christi. This *auto* had had an honorable history in the Peninsula, having been fostered by the Church to enlist the public in the observance of important religious festivals. In the latter decades of his long life Calderón introduced musical features into his plays. His religious dramas absorbed elements of church music, his profane plays, for their part, introducing songs, the music of which represents the beginnings of opera, gradually developed under the influence of Italy in both Spain and Portugal.

To resume, just appraisal of a dramatic art so wholly nationalistic must be based largely on an understanding of the social background and of the thought which it reflected. The plays of the Golden Age, which closed with the seventeenth century, are rich in flashes of genuine Spanish life and customs, in pictures of homely urban and rural manners, in valuable records of popular speech forms and vocabularies, in passages of poetic charm, all contributing abundantly to the history of ideas current among the people. In the face of this rewarding field of investigation, it is a matter of regret that current study of these dramatic authors has entered on the misguided course of disregarding the claims of life and of ideas, preferably pursuing the conclusions to be drawn from mechanical analyses.

Satire and Realism

As has been stated, realism achieved very great significance in Spanish letters. Since careful observation of life and of human character discloses the foibles and blemishes of mankind more abundantly than its virtues, the confusing weft of broken purposes more commonly than records of success and of enduring faith, it follows that the Spanish type of realism could readily make satire the essence of its most effective utterance. The long list of satirical authors reveals that this supreme national voice was already vocal in the Middle Ages; it was abundantly fruitful in the Golden Age, and has persisted, with brief periods of silence, to our day. Medieval satire had in Spain as elsewhere a cheerful aspect. It produced in England the easy moods of gaiety in Chaucer, and in Spain the rollicking humor of his counterpart and contemporary, the archpriest Juan Ruiz, who played with the aspects of earthly love, ironically called *buen amor,* to show how piety, morality, and virtue quite generally tend to be only skin-deep. In the grim kaleidoscopic picture of court life, known as the *Rimado de Palacio,* drawn by the fourteenth century statesman and poet, the Canciller de Castilla, Pero López de Ayala, satire donned a garment of moral anger and cynicism which it has continued to wear intermittently with slight differences of degree. Some Peninsular historians have called this typically national outlook by the softer term of stoicism, which was, to be sure, a genuine inheritance from Roman times through such eminent Spanish-born figures as Seneca. Nor would ancient indebtedness be complete without mention of the satirical contribution of Martial, likewise a Spaniard. The very ancient origin of the satirical bent presaged its persistence in many famous writers, and even touched lightly the pen of Cervantes. But in his case it went hand in hand with a personal kindliness and with that tolerance of spirit which marked the Renaissance elsewhere. This human sympathy was not present in the above López de Ayala and it was quite foreign to such outstanding moralists of the Golden Age as Mateo Alemán, Francisco de Quevedo, and Baltasar Gracián.

The concept of satire took shape in these three prominent literary figures in a loosely conceived series of individual portraits interspersed with anti-social and, at times, bitter moral observations. In Alemán's picaresque story of adventure, *Guzmán de Alfarache,* the plot is woven from drab, often sordid skeins, packed with scenes from urban and rural life; it is marked by the absence of moral wholesomeness as well as domestic hygiene typical of that primitivism which Spanish customs have never wholly shaken off, and which the novel today continues to reflect in some of its pictures of crowded city life. This undisguised process passed into the mockery of Quevedo's many biting witticisms, especially into his *Buscón,* another story of adventure that mingled boisterous laughter with varying shades of vulgarity, indecency and bad taste, according to our more sensitive notions of the human body and its natural functions, especially as regards the lack of domestic appointments, in which centuries of humor had sought to find sources of innocent merriment. If this suggests traits of Rabelaisian humor, the comparison breaks down at once, owing to the fact that the coarse grotesqueries and exaggerations of Rabelais can arouse hilarious laughter which is seldom or never the response to a page of Quevedo, especially of his impressive *Sueños* or visions. In these he recorded, with little shading, a stern and mordant commentary on all society. It is a moral analysis, scrutinizing the actions and motives of individual types of men and women, set up only to be knocked down; it is a pattern of life in which evil is not compensated by pictures of virtue, nor the revolting and ugly by the beauty in some one individual, or in some isolated aspect of nature.

This uncompromising phase of satire reached its most comprehensive voice in the noted moralist Gracián, who completely captivated Schopenhauer by his unequivocally adverse judgment of man. It takes courage to master the pessimistic allegory of his masterpiece, *El Criticón,* the story of the life of Andrenio, a solitary boy reared on an island in the midst of wild beasts and later returned to the society of men where he has the opportunity of analyzing the sorry panorama of "civilization" that passes before him wherever his adventures carry him. The obvious theme is that he can everywhere ponder the superiority over men of that animal stage from which he sprang, a philosophy that invites a comparison with Rousseau's concept of the natural man: the widespread notion of the Noble Savage. There is great genius in Gracián's unstinted variety of imagery and of personification, in the progressive experiences with which he fills Andrenio's associations or conflicts with mankind. Prominence is especially given to the irrational acts of our daily lives, either ridiculous or mad, our inability to have will-power act in conformity with reason.

Gracián further presaged Schopenhauer's philosophy in presenting the continuity of our follies from youth to old age, with their inescapable harvests of wars, diseases, and other fruits of inherent vice. In this mingling of cynicism with much wisdom, in its brilliant idiom of never-flagging vigor and originality, much of the history of Spanish thought of the seventeenth century is epitomized. But the present neglect of the writings of Gracián and of his philosophy was decreed by the linguistic difficulty of the text and by the unrelieved pessimism of his point of view, intelligible only to those favored with the specialized learning required by his overburdened pages.

However meaningful the moral criticism of the seventeenth century turns out to be, in the works mentioned it neither attempted to be constructive nor boldly to point out, except by implication, the obvious sources of current social corruption or backwardness. Nor could the idiom in which this criticism was clothed contribute to its effectiveness. Known as *culto* and *conceptista*, it developed artificial tricks and devices which reacted prejudicially on Spanish prose for more than a century, and sealed off Peninsular thought in so effective a manner that its hard surface was only slightly sprung by the enlightening trend of the eighteenth century, and not broken until the dynamic results of the French Revolution began to be felt in the nineteenth century. The artifices and perversities of this prose style formed a striking parallel to the idiosyncrasies of gongoristic verse. There are hints in the pages of both Quevedo and Gracián that they chafed under the enforced control of ideas and felt obliged to vent their spleen in general social satire. But to the cautious reader the query will occur, why show so much contempt for all mankind? He will ask why these moralists did not turn their darts on those responsible for the national decline, on the unjust process of the law, on the sorry state of education at the universities which were drifting from stagnation to extinction as in the case of Alcalá, and, finally, on the privileged and their indifference to improving the lot of the common man. It is likewise necessary to recall that in their criticism of the world as they saw it, they shared with their own upper classes a contempt for the people—the reader will run across such phrases as *el pueblo vil, el pueblo ruin*—and to bear in mind that the arrogance of the Spanish moralists was in fact shared by men of rank elsewhere in Europe, where much blood was to be shed to substitute the proposition that all men are created equal.

The significance of Spanish realism of the Golden Age becomes obvious from its inclusion of the name of Cervantes. His unique position in all literature is also clear if the two strictures on the writings of Quevedo and Gracián be kept in mind: the limited scope of their pessimistic moral criticism, and the artificial prose which they used to express their ideas. The chief prose writers of Hispanic literature in that period were either humanists or theologians. There is no advantage derived from considering Cervantes from the angle of humanism. Although he is the foremost figure of an age upon which writers of antiquity left the impress of their thought and language, the classics have left a relatively faint trace on his pages. For humanism he substituted humanity, definable as a sympathetic interest in life everywhere, in the humor and pathos inherent in so rich a study as man. His masterpiece, *Don Quixote,* displays a happy fusion of careful observation with that aspect of the Renaissance which set no limits for the creative faculty and fostered an unwritten faith in a new kind of spiritual liberty. At a time when many writers clanked their chains, he speaks like one who is singularly free. He said what he had to say through the medium of humor, wit, and light irony mixed with the royal fooling of burlesque. He warmly disavowed the use of satire, and refrained from cynical analysis of society. He was aware of all forbidden subjects, but they had little to do with the limitless realm of his imagination, in which loyalty to the Catholic faith could be wholly sincere. The freedom of his fancy had nothing to do with liberty of conscience. The creatures of his imaginary world of adventure were drawn from the people, in whose thoughts criticism or speculation would have been quite artificial, and social, religious, or political puzzles could have had no place. This fact makes the work of Cervantes both timeless and universal.

As regards his language and style, they are wholly alive today. Some aspects of his prose as well as his verse disclose the use of traditional features of the novel and of the drama, but they do not prejudice the high level he reached in the genuine originality of his dialogue and of his narrative gift. The stereotyped conceptions that are to be found in "romantic" plots, notably in the rôles played by women, represent idealized pictures, purposely designed by him as entertainment for the uncritical reader. They constitute the chief bonds of relationship between his otherwise original creation and the current idea of fiction. His innovations, or his gift of "invention" as he himself has qualified it, as well as the unmatched clarity and beauty of his Spanish idom inspired nothing commensurate among imitators or followers in his own land. Abroad his influence was felt sporadically, but, at times profoundly, especially in England and Germany where translations of *Don Quixote* followed each other, where the humor and parody of the two protagonists were reflected on the pages of fellow craftsmen in the novel.

THE EIGHTEENTH CENTURY

Satire and the criticism of morals and manners continued to imbue Spanish ideas during the eighteenth century. Expressions of genuine concepts of freedom continued to meet many obstacles during the regime of the Bourbon monarchs, whose dynastic ideology fostered only the concept of absolute rule in both Spain and Portugal. France, which furnished the dynasty, failed to include the enlightenment of eighteenth century thought. There was, to be sure, substantial awakening in the Peninsula in those years, but from the vantage ground of today, what it achieved seems limited and narrowly effective. The founding of Academies in imitation of French models, the publication of the excellent first edition of the Academy's dictionary, the issuance of various learned compilations, among other signs of marked progress, represent a new light in the intellectual world. But it was the world of the educated, chiefly, which benefitted, since the common people seemed more than ever abandoned to poverty and neglect.

The reverberating impact of the French Revolution with its new doctrines and slogans of the rights of man, of liberty, equality, fraternity, of a revised national economy with bread for the people, had swept over Europe north of the Pyrenees. It produced no comparable unrest in the Peninsula, and consequently no significant change in the situation of the lower classes. On the other hand, the Spanish uprising against the French invasion of 1808 caused wide repercussions throughout both Spain and Portugal. As a genuine movement it might have afforded the people an opportunity to join the liberal trend of European thought; the political stir which the masses were creating for the first time in many centuries seemed to embrace the possibilities of social regeneration also. The two nations, however, were paradoxically involved in cross-currents, some of which, in the field of literature, inspired imitations of the French and prompted a small group of French sympathizers called *afrancesados* to accept even French philosophical ideas. Opposed to these were the narrowly nationalistic, Roman Catholic conservatives who bitterly opposed every foreign influence. For their part, the various isolated mobs, which were presently organized into armies sufficiently cohesive to assist their English allies, were actuated by a wave of purely patriotic fervor directed against the stranger who had invaded the sacred soil of Spain. These armies of the people, generally *guerrilla* in their methods of making war, were hardly aware of the intrinsic meaning of the French Revolution and certainly ignorant of the trend of French political and social ideas. Finally certain conservatives, to be found chiefly among the clergy and among the land-owning nobles, sided for the moment with the partriotic armies in their effort to expel Napoleon. As a military achievement, it supported their purpose to nullify all infiltration of the ideas of the French Revolution. Nor did it take long, after the defeat of Napoleon, for the upper classes supported by the clergy to fall in with the reactionary attitude of the Congress of Vienna. The voices of liberty and equality, abroad in Europe, were too insistent not to be interpreted by them also as a threat to the stability of their absolutist and theocratic regimes, to the privileges of the wealthy and to the security of the Bourbon dynasty, already uprooted in France.

THE NINETEENTH CENTURY

The early nineteenth century thus disclosed the same picture of widespread poverty with little educational betterment owing to the havoc of a decade of war that had reached across the Peninsula. The vitality of the universities had been further drained, since no subsidiary school system had been established from which to draw the means of intellectual enlargement. Nevertheless, there came into play once again evidence of the people's inherent productive vigor, that took the form of revitalized literary criticism and of a remarkable resurgence in the fine arts. The fame of the painter Francisco Goya had begun to mount and the world could view in his portraits a realistic history of his time more potent than the printed page.

Spanish literature also turned to portraiture mingled with self-criticism, concentrating on types and professions exemplified by the phrase *los españoles pintados por sí mismos*. The general content of much of the writing was concerned with manners and earned the name of *costumbrista* literature. It made evident also that French style had influenced Spanish writers; prose developed new clarity and restraint—too long neglected—and refreshing simplicity. Critics like Larra (d. 1837), having recourse once more to detailed observation, included in their analysis of urban life and custom spirited attacks on the defects of

the nation's character, castigating the inherited traits of pro-
crastination (*Vuelva usted mañana* is one title) and of hostility
to new ideas, the political and social stagnation of a people
who were living like the provincial Batuecas in a far corner,
allowing a progressive world to pass unheeded.

The romantic movement entered the Peninsula in full force
later then elsewhere, warping the real genius of the people
sufficiently to make them forsake realistic observation tempo-
rarily in order to indulge in fantastic flights of colorful pageantry,
in romantic personages and episodes, and in exaggerated motions
and passions. The most enduring contributions are to be found
in the field of poetry in which the penetrating influence of
Byron, Hugo, Lamartine, and to a lesser extent of Leopardi and
Heinrich Heine made itself felt. Prose style reflected acquaintance with the rich and colorful vein of Chateaubriand and
Manzoni, notably in Portugal, where the illustrious Almeida-
Garrett, Alejandre Herculano, and Anthero de Quental worthily
represent Portuguese literature along a wide front. Their works
illumined the nineteenth century beyond the romantic period in
which they had their roots; as distinguished patriots they supported political liberation and suffered exile, as did many Spanish
liberals, but their residence in France and England brought new
vigor to the Peninsula, and stimulated an interest in European
culture. Under their compelling influence, the novel, drama, and
poetry, as well as historiography flourished anew.

In the latter half of the nineteenth century the most significant work is to be found in the novel and in the field of criticism.
Lyric poetry must lay claim to a lesser eminence, since Peninsular verse yields to the greater excellence and abundance of
Spanish American poetry. The theatre displayed great variety in
sparkling one-act plays, appealing chiefly to the people; comedies
and tragedies dealing with current social problems reveal keen
analysis and wit and show the influence of French *esprit*, as in
Benavente, or of Ibsen, as in Linares Rivas, but without sacrificing
a genuine Spanish note.

Fiction and criticism deserve a more extended word. Analysis of the novel brings to the forefront the preference of novelists to present the life of their particular region. Although they at times venture farther afield, they do so less convincingly. This fragmentation of social imagery actually gives regionalism its inherent vitality and sincerity. Here are reliable sources for a study of religious, social, or political ideas, and of characteristic manners within a limited horizon. When the reader has ᴜcquainted himself with life in some Cantabrian village, with the customs of an Asturian or Portuguese fishing town, with varied urban scenes of Madrid, of Sevilla, of Lisbon, he can then put together a larger canvas of the Iberian peninsula. But even such masterpieces of regionalism as Pereda's tales of *La Montaña,* the Cantabrian mountains, Alarcón's Andalusian pictures, Doña Emilia Pardo Bazán's Galician stories, Blasco Ibáñez's novels of the Valencian *huertas,* those irrigated orchards by the sea, give rise to the paradoxical circumstance that in spite of the invaluable records of native life preserved in these novels, they are none the less dated for today's readers, who are constantly hurrying onward in a world of fluid revolutionary changes. Even the prodigious quantity and generous scope of the production of Pérez Galdós, the least regionalistic of the novelists, yield only a select number of enduring works, such as may serve as trustworthy sources for students of the social and religious questions which agitated Spain during his long life.

On the whole, the novel of the nineteenth century pursued an independent course, and intrinsically owes very little to the many-sided achievement of fiction in France and England. The skeptical and immensely free Anatole France or the crusading and fearless Dickens could not have thrived in the soil of Spain. Nor did the doctrine of naturalism gain any significant following there, whereas in Portugal it is in evidence on the pages of the eminent novelist Eça de Queiroz. It remained for novelists of our own time, Pío Baroja and Pérez de Ayala to develop an unvarnished directness akin to naturalism, but their dissimilar art can claim no particular French models. The already mentioned Emilia Pardo Bazán had favored a modified form of naturalism adaptable to the Spanish taste, but she met with indifferent success, since the principles which she set forth in her treatise on the naturalist novel, *La Question palpitante* (1883), were presently cried down by the novelists Pereda and Valera, voices of greater authority than her own. But their opposition may have been inspired as much by her own aggressive masculinity as by the realism which she advocated in her writings. At all events, the *roman expérimental* of Zola, with the vein of pessimism which this genre of novel developed in France did not alter the course of the contemporary Peninsular novel which never countenanced excesses of earthy details or of ugly descriptions or of repugnant episodes. It is rather the most recent novelists who have made concessions to French and Russian realism, thus reaping the displeasure of conservative Spanish critics who deem it unsuited to the Hispanic concept of fiction.

In the fields of history, or criticism and of general philosophic thought, Michelet, Taine, Renan, and Sainte-Beuve represented a range of free inquiry and speculation which could not flourish with any comparable scope in the Peninsula, where the conservative intellectual and religious elements did not accord them the open welcome that they had received elsewhere in Europe. There was, however, a noble group of men in Spain who devoted themselves earnestly to constructive analysis and criticism, among whom Joaquín Costa, Leopoldo Alas, and Juan Valera deserved well of their country for their efforts to remold esthetic, literary and political ideas and to introduce ampler·conceptions of liberty and social betterment. In the newly won fields of scholarship and science, learned foundations acquired international repute, among which stand the *Centro de Estudios históricos,* directed by Spain's foremost philologist, R. Menéndez Pidal, and the active *Institut d'Estudis catalans* of Barcelona. Science contributed a figure of unique eminence in the famous histologist S. Ramón y Cajal. In the midst of the clamorous seesaw of two alternating and equally stagnant political parties, such intellectual progress gave promise of relegating the popular orator and the professional politician to a position of diminished leadership.

A single detached scholar stands forth in this world of social promise and enlightenment, Marcelino Menéndez y Pelayo. It was typical of the Spanish genius to gather the plenitude of its creative criticism in the literary and historical works of a single *polígrafo* of unlimited erudition. The significant portion of all literary studies published north of the Pyrenees, and attributable there to many, was here embodied in the collected works of a single brilliant expositor of Hispanic thought. Menéndez y Pelayo assumed the gigantic task of synthesizing the ideas of some seven centuries, in order to make his essays on novel, drama, poetry, philosophy, and criticism comprehensive and rounded in scope. He was, moreover, endowed with a lucid, rich, and eloquent style. His spirit was noble and tolerant, he was wholly indifferent to politics, but he was also a devout conservative. His encyclopedic productivity was bound to result in unevenness of criterion; the range of his thought, developed in an atmosphere of loyalty to Catholic dogma, reveals at times the stamp of a restricted approach to the history of ideas which must affect the enduring worth of his achievement as a whole. His interpretation of Spanish ideas was dictated by a fervent pride in his country, many of whose writers were known to him alone; he therefore spoke from a platform of commendable patriotism, mingled with a conscious Roman Catholicism, which, in spite of expressed and implied principles of religious tolerance, gave his concepts of history and philosophy an infelicitous influence in Hispanic criticism. His unquestioned authority has tended to encourage less tolerant conservatives and reactionaries in their rejection of the liberty of conscience enjoyed in England and France. Thus, even so great a mind as that of Menéndez y Pelayo reflected the Spanish heritage of conservative, clerical domination, under the influence of which Hispanic thought has upheld the tenet that "submission to the Church and loyalty to its faith constitute an inescapable necessity of Peninsular history."

THE TWENTIETH CENTURY

The opening of the twentieth century found Spain on the eve of a far reaching liberalizing rebirth. Social and political thinking was gradually inciting the people to substitute a republic that would be theirs for the defunct monarchy that had always functioned for the few. The chief incentive to reform was the low esteem to which Spain had fallen among European powers after the war with America, and her own consciousness of intellectual stagnation and of general backwardness in science. The center of this dynamic movement of enlightenment and progress was occupied by the "generation of 1898," so-called because the men of that decade of military defeat were first articulately united to proclaim the need of a national revival. The education which many of that generation had received furnished the groundwork for the movement and is connected with the name of a great teacher, Francisco Giner de los Ríos, from whose schoolrooms in his *Institución libre de enseñanza* numerous pupils carried into the world the motive force of a spiritual regeneration. Giner's conservative opponents saw in him only an enemy of the "old" Spain, which he was, and a perverter of fine traditional ideas, which he certainly was not. In the logical course of history any effective renascence had to be frankly non-religious and anti-conservative. At first obliged to wage his battle alone against Church and State, Giner succeeded largely through the words of those who believed in him, in bringing fresh air into Spanish social thinking, in creating awareness of the decline of the universities, and in urging a fruitful participation in the outside world of ideas. He especially stressed renovation in religious thought with tolerance of other creeds.

Before the military dictatorship of Primo de Rivera emerged

(1923), significant works of numerous Spaniards had begun to reach the world beyond the Pyrenees. The concepts of socialism, trade-unionism, communism, and the like had filtered into the consciousness of workers in field and industry and given them an inkling of the rights enjoyed in advanced democracies but denied in the Peninsula. Literature likewise accepted the challenge of foreign thought, and works in philosophy and criticism, in fiction and poetry were applauded in translations abroad. Ortega y Gasset's *Rebelión de las masas* (1929) gave expression to much debated social and economic problems; Unamuno reflected in his *Del sentimiento trágico de la vida* (1913) the deep emotions experienced by the Spanish people in the face of personal questionings and religious doubts. Bolder speculation had made wider inroads, and a new freedom appeared on the horizon with the birth of the Republic (1931). Novel and poetry acquired more spacious frontiers of style and idiom; they proclaimed new resources and techniques and evolved fresh concepts of beauty in prose and verse.

The poetry of our own time embodies every technique from free verse to the most flexible handling of nationally rooted forms. In latter years the chief poets in the Peninsula as well as in Latin America have reflected a marked influence not only of the greatest of French poets but also of the younger group of English poets. The illustrious Nicaraguan, Rubén Darío, and the Spanish poets who recognized his primacy have been artists interested in form, in graceful varieties of meter, in flexibility of melody— in short, in certain finely wrought verbal details which point partly to French models and partly to reciprocal influences exerted among Spanish and Portuguese poets themselves.

The Republic, founded on idealist doctrines that had been absorbed from the principles rooted in English, American, and French political freedom, launched a noble but impractical Constitution "de los trabajadores," designed to realize justice, universal betterment, a living wage for all, to build new schools and to inaugurate religious liberty. Utopias have ever roused the resistance of men about to be relieved of special privileges and of their property. The antagonisms set on foot by the proposed constitution were the logical reactions of all classes hit by the reform, who hastily joined forces in a second Counter Reformation constituting a second less compromising military dictatorship within a decade. The dark period of the Franco falangist regime derived its initial strength from infiltrations of Italian fascism buttressed presently by German intervention. The autocratic wheel of Spain's persistent political fate had completed another victorious turn, and the new constitution, with liberty of the mind, lay dead.

*   *   *

The tragic history of the Peninsula, which has involved Spain and Portugal in similar trends of political thought, was thus reemphasized with ever desired freedom once more deferred. But the vitality of the people has reasserted itself in other dark hours, and the conviction is justified that successful government in Spain and Portugal, as everywhere, will securely repose one day on the consent of the governed, pursuant to the recognized principle that a people, not permitted to think, speak, worship, and print without deletion and revision, is an enslaved people condemned to march in the rear of progress. The Iberians' inherited love of individual freedom has never yet been destroyed. The essence of Peninsular culture should again rise to view, when a theocratic supremacy ceases to hold hands with a personal dictatorship, and, especially, when the concepts of religion, theology, philosophy, and education are kept separate and permitted to function each in its own right. Hispanic thought can rise to new achievements only when international currents of culture are no longer shut off at the frontier, but, entering in complete freedom can invite the isolated country "beyond the Pyrenees." to join the common progress of all peoples.

BIBLIOGRAPHY

GENERAL BACKGROUND

ALMEIDA, F. de, *Historia de Portugal* (Coimbra, 1922-1929), 6 vols.

ALTAMIRA, R., *Historia de España y de la civilizacion española*, 4th ed. (Barcelona, 1929), 4 vols.
Indispensable history of Spain and Spanish civilization. Bibliography.

———, *A History of Spanish Civilization*, pref. by J. B. Trend (London, 1930). English translation of one-volume work by Altamira and not to be confused with the *Historia de España*.

BALLESTEROS, A., *Historia de España* (Barcelona, 1919-1936), 9 vols. Illustrated.

BUCKLE, H. T., *History of Civilization in England*, rev. ed. (London and New York, 1925-1931), 3 vols.
See the valuable chapter on Spain.

CHAPMAN, C. E., *A History of Spain* (New York, 1918).
A one-volume summary of the *Historia de España* of Altamira. Restricted in scope.

DESDEVISES DU DESERT, G. N., *L'Espagne de l'ancien regime* (Paris, 1897-1904), 3 vols.
An invaluable work on economics, religion, society, etc.

Enciclopedia Universal Illustrada (Madrid and Barcelona, 1905-1933), 70 vols. plus 10 vols. of appendices.
An essential reference tool for all matters relating to Spain. Bibliography. Commonly known as *Espasa*.

Historia de Portugal, edicão monumental, direccão literaria de D. Peres (Barcelona, 1928-1937), 7 vols. plus 1 vol. index.
Important and useful history.

HUME, Martin A. S., *The Spanish People, their Origin, Growth and Influence* (Cambridge, Eng., 1898). Several editions, e.g., New York, 1914.
A good one-volume survey.

PEERS, E. A., *A Companion to Spanish Studies* (London, 1929; 3rd ed. London, 1938).
A one-volume survey by different authors of race, history, literature, art, architecture, and music.

STEPHENS, H. Morse, *Portugal* (New York, 1903).

The Cambridge Ancient History, vol. VII, chs. 2, 24; VIII, chs. 2, 3, 10; IX, chs. 7, 17; X, chs. 12, 13; XI, chs. 11, 12 (New York, 1923 ff.). Bibliography.

The Cambridge Mediaeval History, vol. I, chs. 9, 11; II, chs. 6, 12; III,

ch. 16; V, ch. 21; VII, chs. 20, 22, 23; VIII, chs. 15 (Spain), 16 (Portugal) (New York, 1911 ff.).
Bibliography.
The Cambridge Modern History, vol. I, chs. 1, 2, 11, 15; II, chs. 2, 3, 12, 15, 18; III, chs. 6, 7, 9, 15, 16; IV, ch. 22; V, chs. 13, 14; VI, chs. 4, 5, 12; IX, ch. 15; X, chs. 7, 8, 9, 10; XI, ch. 20; XII, ch. 10 (New York, 1903 ff.).
Bibliography.
TREND, John Branch, *The Civilization of Spain* (London, 1944).
An excellent treatment of Spain and her literature.

LITERARY HISTORY AND CRITICISM

BELL, Aubrey F. G., *Portuguese Literature* (Oxford, 1922; Portuguese trans. Coimbra, 1931).
———, *Cervantes* (Norman, Okla., 1947).
A good critical study.
BOGGS, Ralph S., *Outline History of Spanish Literature* (Boston, 1937).
A brief but useful outline, with page references to Romera-Navarro, Northup, Mérimée and Morley, and Chapman.
BRAGA, Theophilo, *Historia de Litteratura portugueza*, in *Obras completas* (Porto, 1909-1918), 5 vols.
———, *Gil Vicente e as origens do theatro nacional* (Porto, 1898).
ENTWISTLE, W. J., *The Spanish Language* (London, 1936).
The history of the Spanish language.
FIGUEIREDO, Fidelino de, *Historia da critica, litteraria em Portugal da renascença a actualidade* (Lisbon, 1917).
FITZMAURICE-KELLY, J., *Historia de la literatura española* (Madrid, 1926; Eng. ed. Oxford, 1926).
Valuable bibliography.
MENDES DOS REMEDIOS, J., *Historia da literatura portuguesa, desde as origens, até a actualidade* (Coimbra, 1930).
Anthology.
MENÉNDEZ Y PELAYO, M., *Orígenes de la novela* (Buenos Aires, 1946).
Indispensable tools are the many invaluable works of this author, the greatest of Spanish scholars. See the bibliographies in the histories of literature. The most recent edition of the *Obras completas*, 34 vols. (incomplete), Edición nacional (Madrid, 1940-1947) is under the direction of Miguel Artigas.
MÉRIMÉE, E., and MORLEY, S. G., *History of Spanish Literature* (New York, 1930).
The most reliable history of Spanish literature.
NICHOLSON, R. A., *A Literary History of the Arabs*, 2nd ed. (Cambridge, Eng., 1930).
The standard work on Arabic literature, with a special reference to the prose and poetry written in Spain.

NORTHUP, G. T., *An Introduction to Spanish Literature* (Chicago, 1925; 2nd ed., 1936).
A brief but readable history of literature.

ROMERA, Navarro M., *Historia de la literatura española* (New York, 1928).
Contains good literary criticism.

SALINAS, P., *Reality and the Poet in Spanish Poetry* (Baltimore, 1940).

SCHEVILL, R., *Cervantes* (New York, 1919).

TRANSLATION

MENÉNDEZ, Pidal R., *The Cid and His Spain* (London, 1934).
A shortened English version of the original Spanish work.

MORLEY, S. G., *Spanish Ballads* (*romances escogidos*) (New York, 1911).

Oxford Book of Portuguese Verse (Oxford, 1925).

Oxford Book of Spanish Verse, 2nd ed. (Oxford, 1940).

PANE, R. U., *English Translations from the Spanish, 1484-1943* (New Brunswick, N. J., 1944).
A valuable list of titles of English translations of Spanish works.

UNAMUNO, Miguel de, *The Tragic Sense of Life in Men and in Peoples*, intro. by S. Madariaga (London, 1921).

SELECTED STUDIES

ALVAREZ DEL VAYO, J., *Freedom's Battle* (New York, 1940).
Concerned with the recent Spanish war of 1936-1939.

BORROW, George, *The Bible in Spain* (New York, 1908).
Travel in Spain in the nineteenth century.

BRENAN, Gerald, *The Spanish Labyrinth:* an Account of the Social and Political Background of the Civil War (New York, 1943).
An accurate historical analysis of the conditions which led to the Civil War.

CARLYLE, Alex. J., *Political Liberty:* a History of the Conception in the Middle Ages and Modern Times (Oxford, 1941).
Political thought in the sixteenth century.

CHASE, Gilbert, *The Music of Spain* (New York, 1941).
Survey of Spanish music, historical development and discussion. Bibliography.

FORD, Richard, *A Handbook for Travellers in Spain and Readers at Home* (London, 1845), 2 vols.

KANY, C. H., *Life and Manners in Madrid* (1750-1800) (Berkeley, Calif., 1932).

MERRIMAN, R. B., *The Rise of the Spanish Empire in the Old World and in the New* (New York, 1918-1934), 4 vols.

NEUMAN, A. A., *The Jews in Spain* (Philadelphia, 1942), 2 vols.

Post, C. R., *A History of Spanish Painting* (Cambridge, Mass., 1930-1941), 12 vols.
  Thorough study of Spanish fine arts.
Ramón y Cajal, S., *Reglas y consejos sobre investigación científica*, 7th ed. (Madrid, 1935).
  An account of the decadence of Spain.
Singer, Charles, *A Short History of Science to the Nineteenth Century* (Oxford, 1941).
Smith, Rhea M., *The Day of the Liberals in Spain* (Philadelphia, 1938).
  Clue to interpretation of modern Spain.
Spanish Art: An Introductory Review of Architecture, Painting, Sculpture. Textiles, Ceramics, Woodwork, Metalwork; R. R. Tatlock, et. (Burlington Magazine, Monograph II; New York, 1927).
  Bibliography.

10

German Literature

BAYARD QUINCY MORGAN
STANFORD UNIVERSITY

The American orientation for decades was: east to study, west to teach. BAYARD QUINCY MORGAN was born in Dorchester, Massachusetts, earned his Ph.D. degree in the University of Leipzig, returned to teach at the University of Wisconsin, and eventually at Stanford, where he was long professor and head of the department of German. Emeritus now, he still lives at Stanford, California. He was among the early scholars in this country to recognize the importance of close study of translations and of the art of translation; he offered a course in the subject for many years, perhaps the only one offered anywhere, and his A Critical Bibliography of German Literature in English Translation (revised 1938) provides both a model and a standard. His list of publications is long; readers of his essay on the German mind and nature may care to turn to an earlier volume of which he was editor and compiler, The German Mind (1928).

German Literature

A ONCE popular writer of the nineteenth century in Germany, Friedrich Spielhagen (1829-1911), entitled one of his novels *Problematische Naturen* (Problematic Characters). The term derives from Goethe, who furnished the classic definition of it: a problematic character is one who neither satisfies nor is satisfied by any situation in life. It seems to me that this term applies to the German people throughout its recorded history, and that it gives us a clue to that basic insecurity which characterizes the Germans to this day. Both materially and spiritually, the German lives in an unstable equilibrium, and it would be difficult to say whether this is the result of adverse fate, or of unresolved dissonances in the German soul. I think it may be pertinent to explore this matter briefly.

As early as the third century of the Christian era, many tribes of men speaking what we have come to call Germanic dialects began to invade the lands of the Roman Empire from the north and east. They came perhaps driven by pressures from behind them, but almost certainly impelled by some inner restlessness, which is commonly associated with an unstable temperament. Some of them went a long way—deep into the Iberian peninsula, and even across the Mediterranean into North Africa. They held none of their farthermost outposts permanently, and yet they never formally withdrew, but were either absorbed, like the Langobards in Italy or the western Franks in Gaul, or they were wiped out, like the Vandals in Africa and the Franks in northern Spain. And ever and again this ceaseless will-to-motion, for which the world has taken over the German's own formulation of it,

335

Wanderlust, has erupted into action, mostly in a westward direction. We can see it in the incessant piratical raids of the Vikings, in the Norsemen's fantastic excursion to Vinland, and even in our own days in the persistent migrations of German-speaking settlers across the Atlantic to all the Americas. But what is *Wanderlust,* at bottom? Does it not spring from what I have called the unresolved dissonances of the soul? Is it not a flight from dissatisfaction, a groping for some contentment which, like a mirage, keeps on retreating beyond reach, because it is merely a projection of the wanderer's own dream?

There seem to be good grounds for doubting that spiritually insecure men will or can achieve external security. I am inclined to see something more than accident in the fact that instead of anchoring their lands on the shore of the western ocean, and keeping the Rhine as their natural and impregnable eastern boundary, the tribes which finally merged into a German nation settled in the imperfectly defined rectangle between Rhine and Elbe, Danube and North Sea. Moreover, they straddled the Rhine, thus losing its strategic advantage, while on the east they never acquired a natural boundary of easy defence. As a result, the German people have always lived dangerously, and Central Europe has never known security from armed invasion, and but few extended periods of actual immunity from it.

Nor have the Germans been able to win the security which is the fruit of political union and concerted action. Only twice in more than a thousand years were all the German lands united under one leadership: first under Charlemagne (768-814), and again under Charles V (1519-56). In both cases, it was a personal empire, not an organized one, and it fell apart as soon as the strong hand that had molded it was withdrawn. Nay more: seldom if ever did a German Emperor strive for the welfare of the Empire, but only for the aggrandizement of his own house and state; the more powerful the Emperor, therefore, the less cohesion in the Empire as a whole. Instability in a medieval state is to be sure nothing extraordinary, and throughout Western

Europe civil strife has been a regular and seemingly inevitable concomitant of political stabilization. But in the end, in most cases, men who spoke the same tongue succeeded in forming political unions of great cohesive strength, as particularism yielded to communal solidarity. Not so the Germans. It seems to me significant that even when in 1871 a measure of unity was achieved by the founding of the second Empire, great bodies of Germans remained aloof and even hostile: the Austrians, the Flemish and Dutch, the German Swiss.

While it did not necessarily follow, it remains a fact of no little consequence that the Germans have never had a permanent cultural center, comparable to Rome for Italy, Paris for France, Madrid for Spain, or London for England. Surely no other European people has had such a motley series of "capitals": Aachen (ninth century), Cologne and Mayence (eleventh-twelfth), Frankfurt (fourteenth-eighteenth), Augsburg and Nuremberg (fifteenth-sixteenth), Prague (fourteenth-sixteenth—not even a German city, yet here the first German university was founded in 1348), Munich and Vienna (sixteenth-nineteenth). Finally, under the political ascendancy of the Hohenzollerns, Berlin arrogated to itself a cultural supremacy which it was far from possessing at the time, and which it has but recently begun to enjoy in fact. This lack of a fixed and universally recognized cultural focus is a third factor making for national and therefore international insecurity. What other European people would have thought of creating an artificial capital, as the Germans did in choosing Weimar as the spiritual center of their short-lived republic?

I think it is not fantastic to link with a persistent sense of insecurity the two polar and sometimes conflicting aspects of the German character which, not infrequently appearing side by side, still puzzle the non-German world. On the one hand, we note in the Germans a marked bent toward introspection, toward indifference or even hostility to the world of practical affairs: the quality which has helped to earn for them the designation of "a nation of poets and thinkers." On the other hand they may exhibit a blustering, arrogant bravado toward other nations which has often won them both dislike and fear in neighboring lands; it can be found in the Pan-German propaganda of the nineteenth century, as in the National Socialist chauvinism of the twentieth. Under close scrutiny, however, much of this bluster is seen to be really another form of insecurity: conscious of historically justifiable claims or expectations upon the world at large, yet aware of their inacceptability in the eyes of other nations, and unable or unwilling to play the international game, the German blusters to cover his own irresolution and frustration.

Summing up this oversimplified sketch of more than fifteen hundred years of German history, my thesis is that we see a national house, so to speak, perennially divided against itself, and therefore failing to present a consistent aspect to the world around it, or indeed to achieve any consistency in its own inner life. But as this is a highly gifted, even brilliantly endowed people, full of energy, tenacity, and ambition, what results is not the passivity of resignation, but the uneasy vibration of a powerful force that encounters heavy resistance; not the dull apathy of a broken will, but the savage if impotent rebellion of a chained Prometheus.

Fate or schizophrenia? My answer must be—both. On the one hand, the geographic configuration of Central Europe, the conflicting interests of neighbor states, and the religious, economic, or political aspirations of individuals or groups impinged upon Germany from without, exerting an often violently disrupting force upon her; on the other hand, the Germans' own inability to make up their collective mind, their incurable (and often admirable) individualism, their refusal to compromise or subordinate principle to expediency—these opened the way over and over again to some intruder who might have been halted by the firm policy of a united people. And this repeated victimization of the common man by an adverse destiny which he could not control, and which he frequently did not understand, has conditioned, as it were, the entire German people, unfitting them for confident and concerted action, tuning them to tragedy, turning them into problematic characters who are as discontented with their place and rôle in the world as the world is dissatisfied with them.

It may be remarked in passing that the problematic character is by nature given to introspection and self-analysis, and I think it is no accident that Germans have been uncommonly partial to the novel of development (German: *Entwicklungsroman*), and particularly successful with it. Even *Parzival* (thirteenth century) may be regarded as such, but the first prose novel of that type is Grimmelshausen's *Simplicissimus* (1668); Wieland's *Agathon* (1766) and Goethe's *Wilhelm Meisters Lehrjahre* (Wilhelm Meister's Apprenticeship, 1795) are outstanding for the eighteenth century; Keller's *Der grüne Heinrich* (Green Henry, 1854) is the most noteworthy nineteenth century example; more recent German literature abounds in such novels.

If the points of view set forth above are sound, we must be prepared for great and apparently irreconcilable extremes in the outward forms of German letters; or, it may be, violent shifts from one side to the other of the critical mean. Nowhere, I think, has classicism been more chastely subdued, romanticism more consistently irrational, naturalism more determinedly factual, or expressionism more explosively insurgent. Only the unstable character can be so swayed by a theory or an emotion as to sweep past the danger-line into the zone from which no return to the norm is possible.

HISTORIC AGES OF GERMAN LETTERS

Probably no literature moves through the centuries in a straight line; but certainly German literature is marked more than most by great cleavages in form and spirit, responding to the vicissitudes of the German people's life. For our purposes we may conveniently recognize the following great periods or divisions: (1) The Age of Chivalry, reaching the summit of its brilliance around 1200 under the Hohenstaufen dynasty; (2) The Age of the City (fifteenth-seventeenth century), whose chief energy goes into various phases of the struggle for power—political, economic, religious, or other; (3) The Age of Classicism (eighteenth century), laying the foundations for modern German literature; (4) The Era of Political Maturation (nineteenth century), climaxing in the founding of the second German Empire in 1871; (5) The Period of Disintegration (1890-   ), which seems now to have had its limits set by World War II. It should be illuminating to look briefly, yet not just superficially, at the literary output of these several periods; it will be our effort, however, to bring out, first, those aspects of German letters which seem typical rather than accidental, and which tend to throw light upon significant facets of the German soul, and, second, those international relationships which appear to be outstandingly important in German literature.

1. *The Age of Chivalry*, strictly speaking, witnessed the birth of German literature, just as German and French history proper begin with the breakup of Charlemagne's empire. But we are fully justified in tracing German letters to their earliest beginnings amid the tides of the great Migrations. Looking backward into that chaotic and (to us) obscure period, we become aware of genuine links connecting the writings of the German people with those of their migratory forefathers; and in the earliest poetic creations of which we have record or trace, we can lay our finger on at least two features which we may unhesitatingly claim as typically German. These are a taste and aptitude for the poetic exploitation of the heroic, and a virtually universal linking of nature and love. Thus we find softness and sentimentality in personal relations coupled with harshness and even ruthlessness in public affairs: a conflict and inconsistency which persists to the present day in German life.

It is not surprising that from the actual age of the Migrations virtually nothing has come down to us: doubtless little if anything was written down at the time, and the great collection of oral survivals made at the behest of Charlemagne succumbed to the hostility of the militant Church, determined to stamp out every vestige of paganism. Fortunate accidents, however, have preserved for us three documents from which the essential features of early Germanic poetry can be ascertained; these are the Anglo-Saxon epic *Beowulf,* the Old Norse *Edda,* and the Old High German *Hildebrandslied.* In all three cases, there are historic reminiscences going back to approximately the same period: that of the fourth to sixth centuries of our era. In all three, we have a poetic form—that of the alliterative long-line—which was peculiar to the Germanic tribes and only died out with what may be called their romanization. In all three, finally, we find a concept of the heroic which is tragic and bold at the same time. Thus in the fragmentary *Lay of Hildebrand,* written down about the year 800 in Old High German and preserved by a lucky accident, we find father and son pitted against each other in a death-struggle decreed by the heroic convention, and none the less inevitable because of the foredoomed triumph of the father, slaying his beloved son with bleeding heart, but with inexorable hand.

Though written down some four hundred years later, the great German folk epic, *Das Nibelungenlied,* still breathes out a spirit basically akin to that of the *Hildebrandslied,* having drawn to be sure a considerable share of its matter from the same historic and legendary sources. Disappointing in its outward form, which is marred by excessive prolixity and tediousness, disappointing too in its inconsistencies and its wholly uninspired tone, this poem contains what I believe to be one of the most powerful tragic themes in all literature. It is moreover palpably Germanic. Brunhild the matchless woman, her love scorned by her fore-ordained mate Siegfried, willing to see him dead rather than married to her inferior rival; Gunther the amiable weakling, forced to call upon Siegfried to subdue his queen Brunhild (whose physical power is then magically dissipated); Siegfried the shining hero, whose destruction is wrought not by flaws of character, but by the very best aspects of his own noble nature; Kriemhild the soft and timid girl, turned into a vengeful fury by the murder of the husband whom her own unbridled tongue has betrayed to his ene-

mies; and Hagen, a profoundly enigmatic and problematic character, the henchman .par excellence, who leads his lords to a
destruction he foresees but will not lift a finger to prevent or post-
pone—these are outstanding examples of a psychology which is
unmistakably blood-brother to that of the *Hildebrandslied* and
the *Edda,* and which makes this poem the unique document it is.
No wonder that as late as the nineteenth century Friedrich Hebbel (1813-63), that supreme master of the tragic, was able to
mould the matter of the *Nibelungenlied* without substantial al-
teration into a drama (*Die Nibelungen*) of unexcelled intensity
and power. Even to the sophisticated reader of today, parts of the
Nibelungen story are eloquent of a fiercely tragic realism which
can stir the soul to Aristotelian "pity and fear."

Nowhere else, I think, shall we find in the writings of the Age
of Chivalry such authentic traces of the truly Germanic. On the
contrary, in the court epic and lyric (as distinct from the folk-
epic and lyric) both matter and manner are predominantly ro-
manized, even to the abandonment of the rugged, irregular patterns of unrhymed alliterative West-Germanic verse in favor of
the regular rhythms and rhymes which mark European poetry to
this day.

All the court poetry reveals the results of a remarkable process
of cultural unification on the part of these politically disunited
and even mutually antagonistic Germanic tribes. On the one
hand, they have succeeded in the rather difficult task of merging
dialectal variation in a "literary language" which can be understood in Austria and Thuringia, in Munich and in Cologne—evidence of a feeling of racial or at least linguistic solidarity. On the
other hand, and even more significantly, they have achieved a
sort of cultural harmony, and apart from divergences in language, there is little or nothing in the writings of the court poets
to indicate whether a singer came from east or west, north or
south. The characteristic forms of this chivalric culture blossom
everywhere at the same time, so that the wonder is how their
transmission could be effected so rapidly and so thoroughly, and

how a "canon" of such complexity could find so universal an acceptance. Of the four main categories of poetic creation indicated above, only the court lyric acquired a specific and exclusive designation, that of *Minnesang;* to this name corresponds a conventionality, not to say artificiality, which is nearly unique in German literary history, and which can only be accounted for by foreign influences.

The minnesong, indeed, is a strictly exotic product, imported, so to speak, from southern France. Not only is the basic theme and conception of minnesong—that of an essentially hopeless yet eternally faithful and worshipful lover—contrary to typically German views of the natural relation of the sexes; it is contrary to general medieval folkways in that regard. Its nearly universal sway, during the few decades of its literary ascendancy, and its rapid and complete eclipse, when Chivalry had run its course, both point in the same direction. Only one bold and independent poet—incidentally, the greatest of them all—Walther von der Vogelweide (1170?-1230?), had the courage and the native skill to break through the confining conventions of the minnesong and to sing of love as Germans have always sung it. What held the minnesong to its prescribed lines, charming at its best, yet ultimately sterile because unrelated to real life, must have been the arbitary power of the aristocracy and the courts; one can find a distant parallel in the "pastoral" fad of the seventeenth and eighteenth centuries.

Not less artificial in its way was the epic as written for court circles by three significant poets of the twelfth-thirteenth century: Gottfried von Strassburg (*Tristan,* 1205-10); Hartmann von Aue (1165?-1210?); and Wolfram von Eschenbach (1170?-1220). These epic-like poems were artificial, like the minnesong, in their detachment from actual life, in their employment of narrative recital to exemplify and underline certain ideas and ideals held up for emulation. One characteristic, despite all their wide variation, they exhibit in common: none of them are purely tales of adventure, told for the sake of the excitement they afford, but each one is written with a central theme in mind, with a moral purpose, if one will, which in most cases is paraded to some extent by the poet. Moreover, I think these various themes can be reduced to one general idea, which runs through much of German narrative art to the present day. It is a sort of German pilgrim's progress; more exactly, the soul in conflict with itself, meeting defeat in Gottfried's *Tristan,* achieving victory in Wolfram's *Parzival.* The *forms* of the conflict, however, are again in large part not originally German, but derive along with subject matter and plot from the neighboring people with whom the Germans were thrown together during the Crusades.

In retrospect, it becomes clear to me why the German writing of the Age of Chivalry was bound to go into a total eclipse, and had no power to give birth to literary progeny—as the general course of literary history might lead us to expect. One part of this production derives from pre-German (*i.e.* early Germanic) folkways, which were essentially pagan and must yield to the victorious advance of Christian ethics. The *Nibelungenlied,* still basically unchristian, pays lip-service here and there to the forms of Christian ceremonial. When these forms have become infused with living spirit, "Germanic" themes will have lost their audience. The other part, as we have seen, was an importation, and as such unable to take root in German soil. Thus there was nothing left on which the poets of succeeding centuries could draw for subject matter or inspiration; nothing for poetry to do but to make a wholly new start. It was unable to do so for a very long time.

2. *The Age of the City,* as I have called it, comprising nearly five hundred years of German history, is almost barren of "comparative" literary values, and of this period it can scarcely be said either that the German spirit absorbed and re-formed in any significant way important influences from other lands, or that, with one great exception, its own genius radiated beyond its own borders to kindle the souls of men of alien races. This was principally due, I believe, to the political and religious instability of

the German people, whose energies were claimed by struggles without and within, by the preparations for wars and the reparation of their destruction.

The one great exception, of course, is the Protestant Reformation promoted primarily by Martin Luther (1483-1586), but shared in by Calvin (1509-64) and Zwingli (1484-1531), and very largely a creation of the German mind. Its repercussions upon literature both at home and abroad were varied and violent, and both destructive and constructive in character. Destructive in the stress upon the forms rather than the essence of religion, and in the intolerance which was substituted for tyranny. Constructive in the trend toward individualism as contrasted with regimentation of faith, and not least in the popularization of the Bible as not only the supreme document of the Christian faith, but an unexampled model of fine and effective expression, an inexhaustible source of poetic thought and imagery.

From time to time, during this long period, a critical eye might have discerned in various literary products of the German people evidences of the more or less constant forces which shaped its destinies and would eventually flower into exportable literary garlands; some of these products, indeed, have attracted favorable attention in our own days. Among them are the works of the great German mystics, Eckhardt (1260-1327), Suso (1295?-1366), and Tauler (1300?-61), who are again being read in an age which, like their own, encourages a flight from outward turmoil into the eternal refuge of the soul; among them is that startling bit of seventeenth-century realism, the story of *Simplicissimus* by Grimmelshausen (1624-76), with its unforgettable pictures of the Thirty Years' War; among them is that brilliant apolog of human foible and frailty, the story of *Reynard the Fox* —Dutch, *i.e.* Low German—which no less a poet than Goethe deemed worth the retelling, and which seems to be one of the imperishables in occidental letters.

More significantly indicative of the constant forces alluded to above, and more closely allied to the inner progress of the German soul, are three types of collective literary product, all of them lyrical in character, which form a sort of continuous literary accompaniment to the march of all these intermediate years: (1) the *Mastersong*, with its sturdy if unenlightened faith in the sanctity of art; (2) the *hymn* or religious lyric, raised to the status of ritual in the Lutheran church, but marked by a fervid piety which not seldom found truly poetic expression; and (3) the secular *folk-song*, always one of the most favored and fertile products of the German mind, and in all its recorded examples a golden treasury of the thoughts and ideals which have inspired the Germans from the earliest times down to the present day. Here if anywhere we can find *homo teutonicus*: essentially good-humored, basically optimistic, slightly sentimental, prone to jollity and to love, and naively addicted to feelings of national pride.

3. With the *Age of Classicism* and the eighteenth-century revival of German letters—paralleling the economic and social recovery from the destruction of the Thirty Years' War—Germans really begin their international phase, in which they are at first mere recipients and imitators, but later gain sufficient force to become exporters of spiritual wares. The first important outside influence to which they yield is the French brand of neoclassicism, as exemplified above all in seventeenth-century drama. Lacking a native drama of any stature, they were easily persuaded to adopt the French classical plays and their underlying dramaturgy (including the celebrated "three unities"). One of the byproducts of this emulation of Corneille and Racine (Molière had little vogue) was the adoption of the Alexandrine verse as the vehicle for most serious poetry, dramatic or other. It must be said, however, that French classicism proved sterile as a begetter or even stimulator of native German literature. No eighteenth century German drama in the French classical manner and tradition survives today, nor did any of them outlive the century of their birth; and even the Alexandrine, as we shall see, gave way before the superior merits of blank verse from Britain. The closest approach to a fruitful influence emanating from French classicism

is to be found in Wieland (1733-1813), who employed French gaiety, wit, grace, and even salacity to win aristocratic readers for his many narratives in prose and verse; but it was not so much a matter of imitation as of adaptation, and throughout his career Wieland created works which were genuinely German, not French. Romanic minnesong ran its course and died, leaving hardly a trace; romanic drama ran an even shorter course, then disappeared, and for the same reason—because it had no hold upon German life, and no integral relation to it.

On the other hand, the attempt to colonize German territory with a foreign element met in this case with early and significant challenge, in which we may distinguish three different modes of attack. The first one came from critics who disputed the theoretical basis underlying the French influence, preferred the claims of English literature over that of France, and founded the first of many "moral weeklies," patterned on those of England, which were to win the full adherence of the German reading public. These weekly magazines, of which the *Spectator* of Addison and Steele was the progenitor, became one of the chief agents of the second major international influence to which German letters were widely subjected: namely, that of British philosophy (Hume, Locke, Shaftesbury, Adam Smith, etc.); religion (Milton, *Paradise Lost;* Thomson, *The Seasons;* Young, *Night Thoughts,* etc.); morality (*Robinson Crusoe,* Richardson, Fielding, Sterne, Goldsmith, et al.), and drama (Shakespeare). Once the eyes of the German public had been focused upon this kindred people across the Channel, the flow (and the back-flow) of influence was never stopped again: here was not only consanguinity, here was a kinship of spirit which could not fail to assert itself in action. The pertinent phenomena are legion, and I merely call attention to one or two of the less widely observed items. Thus, it was George Lillo's *The Merchant of London* which furnished the pattern for the subsequently important "middle-class tragedy" in Germany; it was Milton and Shakespeare whose blank verse— first in the hands of Lessing (1729-81), then in the masterly ones of Goethe (1749-1832)—replaced the Alexandrine for German drama; and it was the misty emotionalism of Ossian which so closely paralleled typical eighteenth-century moods in Germany that Goethe incorporated in his *Werther* (1774) some of his own translation of the *Songs of Selma*. The rôle played by Shakespeare in Germany would require an entire essay; here it must suffice to say that modern German literature is unthinkable without him.

The second form of attack upon foreignism in German letters was the one inaugurated by F. G. Klopstock (1724-1803), who as a mere high-school boy felt the humiliation of Germany's lack of a worthy national literature of her own, and resolved to start filling the void himself. With Milton's great religious epics in mind, but with Homer's majestic verse in his ear, Klopstock set about narrating what he and a majority of his readers regarded as the greatest story in the world: the passion and death of Jesus Christ. The appearance of the first three cantos of the *Messias* in 1748 created a sensation which never wholly subsided during his lifetime; and when Klopstock died his body was conducted to the grave by the greatest popular escort that had ever signalized a German funeral. A not unimportant by-product of his lyric imitative epic was the effective introduction into German letters of the Homeric hexameter, a verse-form which has remained one of the permanent patterns of German poetry, used by J. H. Voss (1751-1826) for his still unsurpassed translation of the Homeric epics, by Goethe for his *Hermann und Dorothea*, by Goethe and Schiller (1759-1805) for their celebrated *Xenien*, and in our own day by Gerhart Hauptmann (1863-1946) for his postwar story, *Till Eulenspiegel*. Nor should we forget that Klopstock transplanted into German verse a great variety of the classic Greek and Roman meters, and derived from the odes of Pindar that "free verse"—unrhymed and rhythmically irregular— which has likewise permanently enriched German lyric poetry.

The third and most powerful assault upon French classicism, and the one which gave it the *coup de grâce*, was delivered in two-fold form by G. E. Lessing, the first of the eighteenth-century German writers whose towering stature can be said to cast its shadow at the feet of the present age. Not content with smashing argument proving the inadequacy of foreign themes treated in a foreign manner as a foundation for a national literature, Lessing proceeded to suit example to theory and created a serious comedy, *Minna von Barnhelm* (1767), in which for the first time German characters in a German situation solved a typically German problem. It was the first drama to achieve a permanent place in the German theatre.

In the meantime, a third foreign influence of a different sort, again deriving mainly from France, had been manifesting itself in various ways and without announcing itself as anything alien. This was rationalism, made popular and for a time virtually supreme by a philosophic teacher of uncommon talent, Christian Wolff (1679-1754). Rationalism, or, as the Germans like to call it, "enlightenment," saw in the human mind, in the reasoning power of the mind, a kind of final arbiter of taste, and a source of creative energy as well. To this extent Wolff was on the side of the French, and to a limited degree even Lessing—a rationalist to the core—would have subscribed to his theories.

It is a law of art as well as mechanics that every active force tends to set up an opposing one, and in few other people was rationalism so likely to meet with dissent as in Germany. Not only the latent individualism of the German temper was involved, but also, and more significantly, the natural and often violently impetuous emotionalism of the German soul. It would be an oversimplification to make rationalism solely responsible for the "storm and stress" movement which actually did express the most uncompromising rejection of the entire rationalist standpoint; but it seems likely that the calm arrogance of the defenders of rationalism contributed to the violence of the reaction.

Not that one can set up a chronological sequence in which a rational manifesto is followed by an emotional outburst. Actually, the roots of this reaction reach back rather far and wide:

into Pietism with its stress on the life of the soul, into Rousseau-
ian nature-worship, into J. G. Hamann's (1730-88) encomiums
on the freedom of Oriental literature, into Klopstock's impassioned emotionalism, and, back of all these, into the very heart
of the Renaissance, which gave birth to the modern conception
of the importance of the individual.

Individualism, indeed, is the watchword and the counter-
sign of that anti-rationalistic trend in German letters which, first
emerging around 1770 as "storm and stress," and then again
around 1800 as "romanticism," gave Germany in bloodless form
something akin to the political revolution of her sister state to the
westward. To this period belongs the inception of Goethe's great
masterpiece, *Faust,* with a typical storm-and-stress character as its
hero. For to these writers the heart is supreme, not the mind,
hence away with any moral code; the poet's inspiration (they all
called themselves "original geniuses") is sacred, hence a truce to
formal rules of every kind; nature is good, hence down with all
that might go counter to natural law. Thus, young Goethe's *Götz
von Berlichingen* (1773) not only lauds the self-righteous warrior who takes the law into his own hands, but also adopts a
dramatic form which violates every one of the conventions upheld by French classicism; and his Werther goes out of life
rather than relinquish his love. Thus too, Schiller in his *Robbers*
(1781) makes a hero of the youth who defies the state in open
banditry. The literature of German romanticism is full of the
amorphous, the fragmentary, the incomplete: since "inspiration"
is the criterion of art, the writer need not, nay, he must not continue when his inspiration is at an end.

In between these two phases of emotionalism in literature, the
second of which Germany shares with most of Western Europe,
and extending far beyond the latter phase of it, we have another
type of classicism, more fruitful for German letters than that
derived from France. Largely led by Goethe and (later) Schiller, stimulated by J. J. Winckelmann's (1717-68) "discovery" of
Greek and Roman art (especially sculpture and architecture),

and Goethe's own studies in Rome (1786-88), many writers of the late eighteenth century attempted to emulate that "noble simplicity and quiet grandeur" which Winckelmann believed to be the essence of classical art. In Goethe's *Iphigenie auf Tauris* (1787) and *Torquato Tasso* (1790), in Schiller's *Braut von Messina* (1803), with its effective use of a Greek type of chorus, we see outstanding examples of this form of classicism.

Thus the Age of Classicism in German letters is by no means all of one piece; instead, the pendulum swings from the rational to the irrational, from sobriety to emotionalism, from the unbridled license of youthful Goethean rebellion to the strong-willed self-mastery of mature Goethean control. And as Goethe the youthful revolutionary pokes fun at pedantic Wieland, so Goethe the classical reformer turns away from his critical door the greatest genius of the romantic school in Germany: Heinrich von Kleist (1777-1811). Kleist, it must be admitted, is a typically problematic character, gifted but unstable, incapable even of committing suicide without a fellow victim to keep him company.

Until the middle of the eighteenth century, it could hardly be said that German letters had attracted any significant attention outside of Germany. We must regard as more or less accidental the translation by Caxton of a Germanic (actually Dutch) *Reynard* and its publication in 1481; the spirited rendering by Thomas Barclay of Brant's *Ship of Fools* in 1508; and Marlowe's *Dr. Faustus* in 1588. In any case, they remained isolated and did not lead to any German "influence" on English literature. With the beginnings of modern German literature there sets in that "back-flow"· from Germany to England referred to above. Numerous translations from a variety of German authors appear in English, are referred to in the magazines, and discussed by the educated. At the turn of the century the dramatist Kotzebue (1761-1819)—now adjudged to be of very little merit—becomes a veritable sensation in London, and Sheridan's adaptation of his *Spanier in Peru* goes through 26 printed editions in 1799 and 1800. One may safely speak of a "boom" in German writings and writers during the last two decades of the eighteenth century. German letters have won their international place in the sun.

4. What I have called *The Century of Political Maturation* embraces, in the main, three major literary trends: romanticism, revolution, and realism. In a rather hasty generalization we may say that the fantastically dreaming romantics, looking backward into earlier periods of German history, laid the foundations for much of the political realism which seems the very opposite of "romantic," developing an ardent patriotism which is exemplified in numerous ways in the War of Liberation, for instance, in Karl Theodor Körner (1791-1813), *Lyre and Sword*; this patriotic temper helped to fan the flames of political agitation, which blazed up between the July Revolution of 1830 and the March Revolution of 1848; and the soberness, even somberness, which succeeded the bloody if brief struggles of the latter year was reflected in the sturdy but somewhat stodgy realism of the following decades.

In romanticism I am tempted to see characteristic examples of that remarkable polarity in the German to which attention is called in the Preamble. Take such a figure as E. T. A. Hoffmann (1776-1822), writer of fantastic stories, calling upon his wife to draw him back to reality from the horrors of the dream-world which his own imagination had created. Take the Grimm brothers (1785-1863; 1786-1859), founders of Germanic philology and models of exact and scrupulous scholarship, going to extraordinary pains to make their celebrated collection of folk and fairy tales, and creating one of the imperishable monuments of untrammeled fancy, a true bit of "world literature." Take Ludwig Tieck (1773-1853), a spinner of fanciful if sophisticated stories in his youth, then becoming one of the earliest producers of that type of serious novelette which has remained one of the specialties of German literature. Take the manifest failures and frustrations which greet us on every hand: Kleist a suicide at 34; Hölderlin (1770-1843) losing his mind at 32, yet continuing to produce snatches of real poetry for forty years; Bettina von Arnim

(1785-1859) "faking" as a sort of wish-fulfillment her *Goethe's Correspondence with a Child;* Schopenhauer (1788-1860) bringing out his major work (*The World as Will and Idea*) at the age of 30, and then waiting for over forty years for the recognition which was to come only after his death; Novalis (1772-1801), dead at 29, leaving behind among other evidences of genius an unfinished essay, *Die Christenheit oder Europa,* an almost programmatic document basic to the spirit of romanticism, yet unpublished and unnoticed till romanticism was already on its way out. Or consider such amorphous yet in part brilliant works as Brentano's (1778-1842) *Godwi,* Arnim's (1781-1831) *Kronenwächter,* Hoffmann's *Kater Murr,* Tieck's *Franz Sternbalds Wanderungen,* Novalis's *Heinrich von Ofterdingen,* source of the lasting romantic symbol of the "blue flower" of poetry.

Even more noteworthy and memorable, on the other hand, are the achievements of German romanticism, to the permanent enrichment of German letters, and through them of the Western world. Here we may mention *Des Knaben Wunderhorn* (1806), that invaluable collection of folk-songs edited by Arnim and Brentano (following in the path of Herder), which was to influence German lyric poetry, and through it German song, for a hundred years; the masterly Shakespeare translations of A. W. Schlegel (1767-1845) and Dorothea Tieck (1799-1841), especially the former, which made Shakespeare virtually a German author; the brilliant plays of Kleist, one of Germany's greatest dramatic geniuses, who anticipated Freudian psychology by nearly a century (*Penthesilea*), and preached a praiseworthy type of Prussian militarism (*Prinz Friedrich von Homburg*) far in advance of any general recognition of its existence; the lyrics of such poets as Chamisso (1781-1838), Eichendorff (1788-1857), Heine (1797-1856), Hölderlin, Kerner (1786-1862), Körner, W. Müller (1794-1827), Novalis, Uhland (1787-1862), many of them set to music by the greatest composers; the philosophy of Fichte (1762-1814), Hegel (1770-1831), Schelling (1775-1854), Schleiermacher (1768-1834), and Schopenhauer, which led among other things to the emancipation of woman and the liberalization of social life.

In its emotional extravagance and its fantastic imagination, in its preference for substance rather than form, in its creative drive and its restless roving, in its impulsiveness and instability, in short, in its strength and weakness combined, I find romanticism peculiarly suited to the genius of the German, and therefore perhaps more alive, in a literary sense, than any subsequent period of comparable length. Moreover, it seems to me less influenced from without, more indigenously and spontaneously generative, than any other literary period of modern times in Germany. Its influence, on the other hand, has been widespread and pervasive: the Grimm fairy tales have become international; Hoffmann kindled French enthusiasm and stimulated Edgar Allan Poe; the masterly novelettes of the romantics, translated by Carlyle, became widely popular in England and America; the lyrics set to music by Schubert (1797-1828) and Schumann (1819-56) and Franz (1815-92) carried German poetry into thousands of hearts and homes outside Germany.

It was to be sixty years before German letters were to make any further substantial contribution to the spiritual life of the Western world. However, this diminution was not due to a slackening of creativeness in Germany; it resulted largely from the diversion of attention inside Germany to political and economic affairs: notably the industrial revolution, the agitation for political rights which brought on the Revolution of 1848 and the founding of the second German Empire, the Wars of 1864, 1866, and 1870-71, and the financial disturbances which culminated in the panic and crash of the early seventies. These urgent affairs drained off a considerable share of the people's energies, reduced the critical responses whereby the production of literature is encouraged and guided. Austria had no ear for the genius of Grillparzer (1791-1872), Germany none for the greatness of Hebbel, and Gottfried Keller's (1819-90) Swiss background held back his general recognition elsewhere. In the German people's own relative indifference to their literary leaders we have a partial explanation for the failure of other lands to sense their full importance.

Influences on German letters from without, on the other hand, were neither few nor insignificant. I call attention, for example, to the vogue of the historical novel in the manner of Scott, to the novel of manners derived from Dickens and Thackeray, to the really tremendous influence of Shakespeare as a direct result of the Schlegel-Tieck translation, to the balladry which was encouraged in the late eighteenth and the nineteenth centuries by Percy's *Reliques of Ancient Poetry,* to the interest shown in such American writers as Cooper, Washington Irving, Poe, and Whitman—also Mark Twain in later decades—and finally, as the century drew onward, to the avid reading of Zola and Tolstoy and Ibsen, prophets and prototypes of literary naturalism.

Purely and typically German, and really understandable only from viewpoints within the German soul, are such writers as Theodor Storm (1817-88), with his genre vignettes of life in Schleswig; Fritz Reuter (1810-74), a capital and original humorist who wrote altogether in his native Mecklenburg dialect; Otto Ludwig (1813-65), portrayer of middle-class life in Thuringia; Gustav Freytag (1816-95), another exponent of middle-class life; Friedrich Hebbel, a dramatist of the utmost tragic power; Richard Wagner (1813-83), more composer than poet, yet touching literary mastership in his *Mastersingers of Nuremberg;* and Heinrich Heine, next to Goethe, I think, the greatest lyric poet of Germany, and certainly more widely read outside of Germany than any other German lyricist. Nor may we overlook the unique figure of Wilhelm Busch (1832-1908), artist and versifier, whose rollicking verse tales, admirably illustrated by himself, have supplied the German people with scores of mirthful and apt quotations, and are in their way truly deathless.

5. *The Period of Disintegration.* Notable as were the political successes of the Franco-Prussian War (1870-71), its effect upon literature was at first inconspicuous and later disastrous. In twentieth-century German letters, at all events, instead of the

polar oscillations of earlier periods, we find direct head-on collisions, so to speak, flat contradictions, irreconcilable conflicts, culminating after 1933 in a sheer cleavage which is without precedent or parallel in the history of Western civilization.

These conflicts are presaged and exemplified in the life and thinking of one man who bears more responsibility for the warring ideologies of this period than any other: Friedrich Nietzsche (1844-1900). Brilliantly original and tempestuously dynamic, Nietzsche is in no respect more German than in the violence with which his own mind wars on itself; and there is something profoundly symbolic in the fact that the tensions in his soul literally tore it apart and drove him into insanity in the very prime of life—just as the *Grossraum* of the German mind was to disintegrate in 1933.

Was this cleavage inevitable, one is compelled to ask? For there were German poets who met the challenge of the new era without outcry and without resentment: like Theodor Fontane (1819-98) with his tranquil wisdom and his sovereign irony, like Thomas Mann (1875-   ) in his grave and unemotional disillusionment.

But the Germans are not born to passive resignation, and not for nothing has Ricarda Huch (1867-1947) written in her *Storm Song:* " 'Tis only struggle, and though I fail, gives zest to life." The dissipation of their political energy, the divergences of their philosophic outlook, both derive from one of the most admirable qualities of the German mind: rugged individualism. No alliances from now on, only antagonisms: naturalism vs. impressionism vs. neo-romanticism vs. expressionism. The literary antitheses here are nearly as old as literature itself; what is new is the strength and the simultaneity of the competing claims.

Naturalism drew its authorization from the strongest and newest forces of the nineteenth century: from the expansion of scientific theories, from the rise of the plutocracy and the degradation of the proletariat, from the discoveries of Darwin and their application to human life and society. If man is largely determined by his heredity, let parents consider their responsibility (Hauptmann, *Before Dawn*); if man is a product of his environment, let society be admonished to reform, as in Frank Wedekind (1864-1918), *Spring's Awakening;* while admiring the technical advances in industry, let us not forget those whom the machine robs of a decent living (Hauptmann, *The Weavers*); in considering the wrongs of the underprivileged, remember that women share rights with men, as Helene Boehlau (1859-1949) reminds us in *Der Rangierbahnhof;* if society can be blamed for individual error, the "criminal" is not so bad after all, but shares in our common humanity (Hauptmann, *The Beaver Coat*); indeed, that society is itself the real criminal, as in Jakob Wassermann (1873-1934), *Caspar Hausen;* sex is ugly, but so is the denial of it (Wedekind).

Underneath and behind all these motifs and trends lay one fundamental ideal: the appeal to truth as such. The literary Naturalist took his place beside the exact scientist as one who sought to enlarge the knowledge of the world in order to make that world a better place to live in. Society could and should be made to see the errors of its ways, and correct them. Ye shall know the truth, they might have said, and the truth shall make you free.

But truth need not be ugly, retorted the literary impressionist, who was not so much concerned with truth itself as with the way in which it was sensually recorded on the poet's mind. Quite the contrary: it was the beautiful impression which seemed most worth while to these poets, who declined to undertake the reform of the world or the correction of social ills. If naturalism might seem to adopt the technique of the photograph, impressionism anticipated the moving picture, as in Liliencron's (1844-1909) picture-poem, *Die Musik kommt* (The Band Goes By), or Heinrich Mann's (1871-1950) novel, *The Little Town.* Schnitzler (1862-1931) compressed a life into an impressionistic monologue with tragic ending, *Fräulein Else.*

If naturalism and impressionism clashed to a large extent on technical grounds, they both encountered a more fundamental opposition in neo-romanticism. The very foundation of naturalism was an acceptance of the present world, and its most important affirmation lay in the conviction that the Golden Age lies in the future. Neo-romanticism, on the contrary, looked perforce to the past, and conjured up its ideal visions out of bygone days. Naturalism centered its interest on the common or even less than common man; neo-romanticism was aristocratic to the core.

Outspoken and specific is the neo-romanticist's rejection of the naturalist's formula and credo. Says Hofmannsthal (1874-1929) in a significant essay: "The betterment of the world and the dreams of philanthropy have nothing to do with poetry. No direct road leads from poetry into life, none from life into poetry. Naturalism has only made ugly what former writers only beautified."

What the neo-romanticists sought above all was beauty, not the "prettification" of life against which the naturalists had rebelled. To this pursuit Hofmannsthal devoted himself throughout (*Death and the Fool; The Marriage of Sobeide*). But its self-appointed prophet and worshipper was the lyricist Stefan George (1868-1933), who saw in it not merely an esthetic satisfaction, but a sort of sacred flame for the betterment and purification of mankind.

While the naturalists and the neo-romanticists were still engrossed in their essentially endless struggle, events in the political sphere went through one tension after another, until the entire Western world burst into flame in the summer of 1914. The World War had cast long shadows before it, and so the emergence of German expressionism, which was both echo and antinomy of the armed conflict, was not unexpected; antinomy too of the "patriotic" war-literature, which won adherents in every literary camp. Its violence and extravagance was partly that of reaction to its opponents, but in the main it reflected the excesses of the war itself. At the same time, it registered distinct and conscious opposition to all the contemporary schools of writing, while it revealed within its own body something of that disunity which marks this entire period in German letters. In its persistent inconsistencies, in its nobility and its depravity, in its fierce theorizing and its patterned procedure, in its intensity and its diffusion, it was the true child of its time and of the people from whom it sprang.

Its very outward appearance is arresting, showing a style and rhythm which may be called "baroque," and a restlessness which not seldom rises to frenzy (a favorite word and concept with these poets), a love of motion which may approach the grotesque in Kasimir Edschmid (1890-   ), *Frenzied Living*, and in Klabund (1890-1928), *The Six Mouths*. Mighty emotions, unbridled passions, sweeping gestures; passivity unthinkable. The basis of this restlessness is a ceaseless search for the inner essence of things, as distinct from their (accidental) outward forms. Truth as such is of no value; only the soul (of things) is worthy of attention. See Georg Kaiser's (1878-1944) trilogy *Gas*—no names of persons, only functions.

Spiritual opposition to war, one of the mainsprings of the entire movement, is revealed in an ecstatic cult of brotherly love (German: Güte). This is so in Franz Werfel's (1890-1945) collected poems, *Der Weltfreund* (*The World Friend*), *Wir* (*We*), *Einander* (*One Another*). Spiritual affirmation of constructive as opposed to destructive thinking underlies the expressionist's search for God, not through dogma and ritual, but directly, as the mystic has always sought the supernatural. It was Max Brod (1884-   ) who coined the phrase "the way to God" in his novel *Tycho Brahes Weg zu Gott* (1916). But twentieth-century literature has nothing to equal Rainer Maria Rilke's (1875-1926) *Stundenbuch* (Book of Hours) for breathtaking candor and directness, for immediate communion with God.

Expressionism had to run itself out rapidly. With the end of the war came depression, inflation of money and deflation of emotion, sober disillusionment and practical distress. The tensions and frenzies of battle gave way to daily cares and struggles, and outcries in the expressionistic manner would have seemed shrill and overdone.

The disunity which had cleft the German people even during the war was not to be ended by it. Before expressionism had run its course, poets and public split up into the internationalists on the one hand, the patriots and the regionalists on the other; with the former group most of the pacifists and the Jews allied themselves, while the anti-Semites and the nationalists made common cause and paved the way for the great schism of 1933. These regionally oriented writers, later to achieve notoriety under the half-ironic title of "Blubo Literature" (Blut und Boden, *i.e.* "blood and soil"), were for a time outshouted and outdone by the exponents of a so-called "new objectivity" (Neue Sachlichkeit). This movement started out with a kind of reporting; witness Erich Maria Remarque (1898-   ), *All Quiet on the Western Front;* Ludwig Renn (1889-   ), *War.* Now the war could be viewed in perspective, evaluated and appraised more calmly and dispassionately. If the result was negative, as Arnold Zweig (1887-   ) suggested in *The Case of Sergeant Grischa,* that was not surprising: the state of the German world did not encourage optimism.

Quite the contrary: the disastrous aftermath of the war, with poverty and unemployment and starvation at home, with humiliation and misprision abroad, without joy in the present or hope in the future, led to a new ferment which rejected the sobriety of the realists and insisted more and more upon the validity of an ideal world. Against the international vilification of the German people, the national socialists set up the doctrine of racial superiority; to counteract the attempt to hold the Germans in a lasting servitude, they envisaged a German hegemony in Europe; to overcome the armed might of powerful enemies, they preached the need of heroism, organization under leadership, and military prowess.

When they judged the time to be ripe, they staged one of the completest revolutions in occidental history: one which embraced every phase of the nation's life, and hence also its creative minds, its artists and poets. From the tenets and principles of the state no dissent could be or was tolerated (the burning of the books was a symbolic act of rejection), and gradually those who could not conform and would not hold their tongues were either silenced—by death if necessary—or driven into exile. This gave rise to a unique situation: an ideological cordon was drawn around a political unit, in which the gates opened only one way. Through this cordon ideas might issue outward, but none might enter; the literature of *Das dritte Reich* could be exported, but no importations were tolerated without passing quarantine. Thus, for more than ten years, German literature waged a kind of internecine warfare, each camp, the smaller, disorganized one of the *émigrés,* and the powerfully intrenched one inside the Reich, claiming to be the true representative of the German spirit. Guns at last breached the German *cordon sanitaire*—with what result?

EPILOGUE

In my Preamble I referred to the basic insecurity of the German temperament, the unstable equilibrium in which the German is condemned to live, and the unresolved dissonances in his soul which help to make him an internationally problematic character. And I see in the civil war just mentioned as striking and convincing a manifestation of the nationally problematic character as one could wish.

One might go even further and show that instability and insecurity are often revealed in those very Germans whom we would single out as peculiarly representative of their people and its life, and that these qualities may be spiritually characteristic of the highest type of German.

It should be instructive to examine from this point of view the four twentieth-century German writers whose figures tower above their national boundaries, who seem certain now to out-

live themselves in their works: Stefan George, Gerhart Hauptmann, Thomas Mann, Rainer Maria Rilke. In each of these truly
great poets there is this paradox: sureness of art and unsureness
of thought, utmost potency of expression and a doubtful legacy
of message. Let us look at them.

Gerhart Hauptmann's versatility has been diversely interpreted, his critics charging him with being a weather vane, his
admirers pointing out that he generally preceded the trends he
was supposed to be imitating. Quite objectively, it seems to me,
one must see in such extreme shifts of front as that from *The
Weavers* in 1893 to *The Sunken Bell* in 1896, back to *Drayman
Henschel* in 1899, and back again to *And Pippa Dances* in 1906,
some evidence of a temperament which is insecure, not quite sure
of what it wants. Of this Hauptmann has furnished significant
internal evidence in his works, namely by his development of the
so-called "half-hero," the central figure who does not dominate the
action but is carried along by it, and by the establishment of a
new type of tragedy, that of inadequacy. Both of these features
are strikingly exhibited in *The Sunken Bell,* whose hero personi-
fies Hauptmann's own sense of defeat in the (initial) theatre
failure of *Florian Geyer*.

George, supreme among modern lyricists for sheer mastery of
form and sublimity of thought, aristocrat to his finger tips, scorn-
ful of the common man, by whom he did not even wish to be
understood, building a cult of exclusive art-worship, a pursuit of
beauty in which only the elect might share, suddenly turned
"patriot" and wrote in *Das Neue Reich* poems which caused
the Nazis to acclaim him as their prophet—whereupon George
went into voluntary exile to avoid dying on the soil which he felt
the Nazis had polluted!

Rilke's shift in attitude, from the religious mysticism of his
early writing to an almost despairing denial of all the rational
bases for religion in his later poems, might be considered a form
of "development," in which Rodin played a decisive part. What
startles one into assuming "insecurity" in Rilke is really a striking

divergence in the critical approach to him. Praised and admired by many for his sincerity and his profound humility, he is severely attacked by an important and influential body of critics, granted skill and verbal adroitness, but accused of arrogance and egocentricity.

In Thomas Mann's case, the tragedy of indecision is written into the very fabric of his early writing, and finds classical expression in *Tonio Kröger*. In Tonio, whose two-way name symbolizes his warring heritage, who adores his slightly amoral (non-German) mother and admires his respectable father, who is condemned to be a writer yet longs for the raptures of the commonplace, we have a kind of spiritual portrait of Thomas Mann himself. For him this conflict and cleavage is inescapable in all art, and the barrier between artist and commoner is perpetual, and is maintained with equal zeal on both sides; for the artist, tragedy is the necessary consequence, almost the necessary condition (*Death in Venice*). Like Hauptmann, Mann shares the fate of the half-hero, and identifies himself with a tragic inadequacy (Hans Castorp in *The Magic Mountain*). Later in life, Mann was to espouse in his person and in writing the democratic principles which he had previously rejected, and today political discussion quotes Thomas Mann against Thomas Mann.

The term "disintegration" as used above implies an integration which one might expect to see exemplified in earlier periods of German literature. If I single out Goethe as the outstanding representative of an integrated German personality, it is not because he stands alone, but because he embraces in one person nearly everything that a man could be. No one can do justice to Goethe without noting first of all his universality, the fact that in addition to being a great statesman and a great scientist, a theatre director and an art critic and connoisseur, an essayist and a translator, a historian and a scholar, a biographer and an autobiographer, he created masterworks in all the categories of literature—in the lyric (where he is so great as almost to defy translation), the epic tale (*Reineke Fuchs, Hermann and Dorothea*), the drama (*Götz von Berlichingen, Iphigenia in Tauris, Torquato Tasso*), and the novel (*The Sorrows of Werther, William Meister's Apprenticeship, The Elective Affinities*).

But even if all these works did not exist, he would still be entitled to supreme rank as the author of *Faust*, a work which it is hard to discuss without invoking superlatives. Originally conceived as a storm-and-stress hero, as a passionate rebel, Faust passes through all the transformations undergone by Goethe himself in the course of his long life, and thus may stand equally for romanticism and classicism, for the utmost in turbulence of soul and the utmost in self-restraint, for the impetuosity of youth and the resigned wisdom of old age. And all this cast in a bewildering variety of poetic forms, so that it has been well said that *Faust* could serve as a textbook of metrics.

Neither before nor since has the German mind achieved such a complete mirroring of its essential character as in this dramatic poem, in which nothing less is at stake than the destiny of man and the integrity of the universe. Here the most gifted son of a gifted people has erected a deathless monument to the spirit of his age and of his entire nation. Here this great poet, whose definition of the problematic character attests his own propensity to become one, showed the Germans how such a self-destructive tendency could be overcome.

What will become of German literature? It would be premature to predict its future course. We can at most point out some of the factors which seem bound to make the end of World War II an axial point in any future treatment of this field. These are: (1) a complete revaluation of national socialism in all its aspects, in which voices both outside and inside Germany will participate; (2) the return—at least in part—of Jewish names to the German histories of German literature; (3) the restoration of contacts between German writers outside and inside Germany; and (4) the repercussions of the political and economic consequences of World War II, many of which are only now in the making.

All in all, I make bold to assert that German literature has entered upon a wholly new phase, whose manifestations it will be for future critics to appraise.

BIBLIOGRAPHY

GENERAL BACKGROUND

BITHELL, Jethro, ed., *Germany, a Companion to German Studies* (London, 2nd rev. ed. 1937; 3rd ed. 1942).

DIESEL, E., *Germany and the Germans*, trans. by W. D. Robson-Scott (New York, 1931).

PINNOW, H., *History of Germany* (New York, 1933; rev. ed., 1939).

REINHARDT, K. F., *Germany 2000 Years* (Milwaukee, 1951).

SHUSTER, G. N., and BERGSTRAESSER, A., *Germany, a Short History* (New York, 1944).

HISTORY OF LITERATURE

FRANCKE, Kuno, *History of German Literature as Determined by Social Forces* (New York, 1901); 4th ed. of *Social Forces in German Literature*.
Useful for its stress on the interrelationship of literature and life.

ROBERTSON, J. G., *History of German Literature*, rev. ed. (New York, 1931).
Standard work of conservative type; informative, reliable, somewhat conventional.

SCHERER, Wilhelm, *History of German Literature*, trans. from 3rd ed. by Mrs. F. C. Conybeare, vol. 2 (Oxford, 1886).
Excellent for all periods up to Goethe's death in 1832.

THOMAS, Calvin, *History of German Literature* (New York, 1909).
Compendious; still useful for quick orientation and independent judgments.

CRITICISM AND PERIOD STUDIES

BENNETT, E. K., *History of the German Novelle from Goethe to Thomas Mann* (Cambridge, Eng., 1934).

BERTAUX, Felix, *Panorama of German Literature, 1871-1931*, trans. by J. J. Trounstine (New York, 1935).
Extensive bibliography of recent and living writers.

BITHELL, Jethro, *Modern German Literature, 1880-1938* (London, 1939).

CLOSS, August, *The Genius of the German Lyric* (London, 1938).

Lange, Victor, *Modern German Literature, 1870-1940* (Ithaca, N. Y., 1945).
Bibliographies, including English translations.
Samuel, R., and Thomas, R. H., *Expressionism in German Life, Literature, and the Theatre* (1910-24) (Cambridge, Eng., 1939).
Stawell, F. M., and Dickinson, G. Lowes, *Goethe and Faust, an Interpretation* (New York, 1929).
Witkowski, Georg, *The German Drama of the 19th Century*, trans. by L. E. Horning (New York, 1909).

ANTHOLOGY

All translations published in book form up to 1935 are listed, many of them with critical ratings, in B. Q. Morgan, *Critical Bibliography of German Literature in English Translation, 1481-1935* (Stanford, Calif., 1938). A few items are listed here for special reasons.
Bithell, Jethro, *Contemporary German Poetry* (London, 1909).
One of the best collections of late nineteenth-century German verse.
——, *The Minnesingers* (New York, 1909).
Style and spirit are excellent, but he takes liberties with the form of the different originals.
Carlyle, Thomas, *German Romance* (Edinburgh, 1827), 4 vols.
Musaeus, Fouqué, Tieck, Hoffmann, Richter, Goethe. Superior translations.
Dwight, J. S., *Select Minor Poems of Goethe and Schiller* (Boston, 1839).
On the whole, the best translations of Goethe's shorter poems in one volume.
Francke, Kuno, *The German Classics of the 19th and 20th Centuries* (New York, 1913-15), 20 vols.
Nearly indispensable for the English-speaking student of German literature. Excellent translations and competent critical essays.
Hedge, F. H., *Prose Writers of Germany* (Philadelphia, 1849).
Extensive selection in excellent translation.
Merivale, J. H., *Poems Original and Translated* (London, 1844), 3 vols.
Vol. 3 contains unsurpassed translations of Schiller's shorter poems.
Morgan, B. Q., *Nature in Middle High German Lyrics* (Göttingen, 1912).
A number of nature poems in metrically faithful translation.
Pierce, F. E., and Schreiber, C. F., *Fiction and Fantasy of German Romance* . . . *1790-1830* (New York, 1927).
Excellent translations from the romantic school, some not found elsewhere.
Rothensteiner, John, *A German Garden of the Heart* (St. Louis, 1934).
Some fine translations of German lyrics, including twentieth-century poems.

WARNER, C. D., *Library of the World's Best Literature*, new ed. (New York, 1917-18), 30 vols.

Largely independent in both essays and translations, still quite valuable. In 1928 the German material was combined in vol. 9 of the *Columbia Course in Literature* with critical essays and many original translations by B. Q. Morgan.

II

Scandinavian Literature

ADOLPH B. BENSON
YALE UNIVERSITY

Anyone who cares to check through the pages of the forthcoming Guide to Comparative Literature *will find that for more than a quarter of a century* ADOLPH B. BENSON *dominated the study of American-Scandinavian literary relations as though the field could afford only one student—and indeed, it needed little more. Anyone who has followed the excellent and growing list of publications by the American Scandinavian Foundation will find further evidence of the activities of this same Adolph B. Benson. And a generation of Yale students have their Old Norse from him. He was born in Skåne, Sweden, but educated in this country, finishing with the Ph.D., Columbia (1914). His publications—criticisms, scholarship, translations—are legion; he has traveled extensively, often as an official representative; he is a Commander, Royal Order of Vasa, Sweden, 1941; but his friends know that these distinctions do not keep him and Mrs. Benson from preparing an excellent smörgåsbord. He is now emeritus, living in Berlin, Connecticut.*

Scandinavian Literature

THE Scandinavian countries, in northernmost Europe, comprising Denmark, the Swedish-speaking part of Finland, Iceland, Norway, and Sweden, have all distinct national individualities of their own, but form historically, geographically, and racially, a cultural unit. For thousands of years their peoples have inhabited the Danish and Scandinavian peninsulas and neighboring islands, speaking to the end of the Viking Age practically the same tongue, the North-European branch of the Germanic languages. Even today, except for the modern Icelandic and certain provincial dialects, the various Northern languages are sufficiently alike, especially in their written forms, to be understood by most Scandinavians. To remember this is important for an understanding of their literature. It must also be emphasized that, historically, despite quarrels and wars of the past, many of them local, the Scandinavian peoples have never been conquered permanently or absorbed by a foreign power, and no Scandinavian nation has fought against a sister nation since the Napoleonic era, when through unfortunate circumstances Denmark took the part of Napoleon and Sweden was drawn in on the opposite side. Freedom and independence, personal and political, have been the ruling motives since time immemorial, and these are reflected in the literature of the North.

Geographical location and climate, also, have played a significant part in the molding of Scandinavian literature. While the beauty and majesty of the natural scenery in the North have produced a large number of outstanding nature poets, the relatively severe winters, with their social and economic consequences, and the sombre, soughing pine and spruce forests have, consciously or unconsciously on the part of writers, intensified the general seriousness of Scandinavian letters, and have often made them heavy, gloomy, dark, and tragic, for life itself was a greater struggle in the North than in the warmer climes: it was literally a constant battle against the Frost-Giants which we meet so often in Norse mythology. On the other hand, the environment demanded unusual vigor, exertion, organization, and deeds of heroism. And during the long winter evenings the ancient Scandinavians had plenty of time to ponder the problems of the universe and determine a sense of relative values. So they developed a profound and complex religion, in which reigned, for example, a special god of poetry (Brage), and their chief divinity, Odin, was willing to pawn for lifetime one of his own eyes for draughts of wisdom—facts worthy of note for later literary evaluation.

But the regions of the North also produced a definitely sunny background. The white birches, the smiling lakes of Sweden, the fertile plains of Skåne and Denmark, and the awe-inspiring fjords of Norway stimulated hundreds of writers to record their esthetic enthusiasms in faultless verse, with genuine feeling. The forests and streams, ocean and mountains were densely peopled by trolls, nixes, wood-sprites, mermaids, and innumerable supernatural creatures, good, bad, but seldom indifferent, and most of them of a special Scandinavian character. They often appeared, and reappeared, in literature. It was on the whole an atmosphere highly favorable to superstition, witchcraft, ghosts, mysticism; hence a rich soil for folklore and religion. Also, the northern isolation suggested meditative works of solitude, and brought the ancient Scandinavian people, when they met at all, into more intimate contact with each other, and with their pagan gods. For, as in *Thrymskvida*, they knew their gods so well that without disrespect they even made sport of them, and humor was born, which, in turn, fostered pure entertainment as a purpose of literary production. Narration became an art. Humor, gaiety, song, and comedy alternated with gravity. Philosophically, the

Scandinavians, ever observant and thoughtful, first became Stoics and fatalists, but always remained fundamentally realists, with idealistic trends.

In religion, Northern mythology had essentially much in common with Christianity, and this together with perhaps an unconscious, inborn, Northern tolerance of all religions, and the dim realization that divine worship was a very personal matter, served to make the transition from paganism to Christianity in the Scandinavian countries a relatively peaceful one. Maybe indifference played a part. Purely practical matters were also considered, as in Iceland. Therefore, since heathen literary material was bone and sinew of the common people; since it was largely based on an abundance of native exploits, Viking or otherwise, and upon native religion and philosophy; and since the future literary recorders of the ancient traditions, though often Christian priests, were of the people (instead of constituting a special caste) and had a strong national historic sense and taste, the pagan literature of the North, and heathen traditions of the whole Germanic world, elsewhere destroyed, were preserved in Scandinavia, especially in Iceland. The resulting enrichment of the future literatures of such countries as England, Germany, and Scandinavia is well known. The point to make here is that the Northern people, many of whom were isolated near the Arctic circle, were intelligent and educated enough to recognize the value of their raw material and, as we shall see, knew early how to give it artistic form.

Officially, the Scandinavians were slow and cautious in adopting Christianity. Not until about 1150 was Finland Christianized, though Denmark, Iceland, and Norway, for instance, had much earlier succumbed to the new ideas, in part for geographical reasons, and Sweden had permitted the Christian missionary Ansgarius to preach his religion there in the ninth century. This religion was, of course, Catholic. The Protestant Reformation came in all the Northern countries in the sixteenth century, from Germany, and again the complete transition was gradual and closely allied with national trends and desires for political independence, without any foreign masters, cultural or otherwise. While during the Catholic period the medium of expression in the learned and ecclesiastical circles of Denmark and Sweden particularly was, as elsewhere, largely Latin, in the Reformation era the native vernacular came, as in Germany, to the fore, except in the field of scholarship. But the conversion to Protestantism in Scandinavia, where it meant national freedom of faith, thought, language, and politics, was more complete than in most other lands. Today the state religion in all Scandinavia is Lutheran, though with religious freedom for all other denominations. In the study of its literature this must be borne in mind.

There are other factors to be considered, especially by the student of comparative literature. There has not for many decades been any illiteracy worthy of mention in any of the Scandinavian countries. Not only everybody *can* read and write, but a disproportionally large number of people, it seems, *do* read and write to an astonishing degree. Education is compulsory, of course, and schools and higher institutions of learning of all kinds are numerous. From Sweden come the Nobel prizes in science and literature. Social, historical, industrial, and cultural changes or movements all over the world are followed closely and reflected in writings. The absolute freedom of press and speech makes this possible. All Northern lands are, like England, definitely democratic, and without any mental reservations, with parliamentary governments *in fact,* although Denmark, Norway, and Sweden still retain their monarchies and kings. Sweden, however, the largest and probably the oldest of the Scandinavian nations, is more conservative and aristocratic than Norway, for instance, but its government is in the best sense socialistic, and thoroughly progressive. It is a matter of relativity.

Still another general characteristic must be understood before we even mention a survey of its literature. The Scandinavian scholars and literateurs are excellent biographers, belles lettres interpreters, reviewers, polemic writers, and literary historians, but, with few exceptions, they care comparatively little for extensive original *theories* of criticism, for pure psychologizing as such, or for speculative metaphysics. They prefer more often to let their ideas or philosophies appear in their creative writings. They may follow or reject certain critical, esthetic, or philosophical theories advanced by others, and express themselves violently for or against them, but will seldom endeavor to create a new, epoch-making philosophy in the abstract. They keep for the most part their feet too close to terra firma. Only in the field of religion, with names like Swedenborg, N. F. S. Grundtvig, and Kierkegaard, have the Scandinavians made contributions to philosophy of international interest. In the field of criticism only George Brandes, of Jewish descent, is well known to the Anglo-Saxon world—partly because of the languages in which most of it is written—and Brandes was perhaps more of a cultural agitator and international copyist and intermediary than a pure critic. But Scandinavia is rich in creative literature, and it extends from about the beginning of the ninth century, when oral tradition took form, to to the present time.

MEDIEVAL LITERATURE AND CRITICISM

The Runic inscriptions, so common in certain parts of Scandinavia, and going back to the early Christian era, had only a historical and linguistic significance. But the intellectual heritage, brought orally (*ca.* 874-930) to Iceland from Norway, by the highly cultured nobility, and others, was distinctly literary, critical, religious, and philosophical. In fact, Iceland soon developed a unique classic literature, in both verse and prose. The poems of the *Elder Edda* (from *odhr*: poetry) presumably were composed anonymously several centuries before they were collected and written down in the thirteenth century. Their contents were mythological, heroic, and didactic, and their artistic form followed definite ancient patterns, with alliteration and poetical paraphrases. The high quality and popularity of the

Edda songs led to imitations, skaldic poetry, by over two hundred known authors. This required a written guide, hence the *Prose Edda*, undoubtedly written by Snorri Sturluson (d. 1241), which is a handbook for poets, and provides the necessary mythological background, metrical rules, and metaphorical paraphrases (*kennings*). But after a time, skaldic verse, long popular at many royal courts of Europe, degenerated, because of its increasingly metrical complexity, artificiality, and surcharge of kennings; also, it became oldfashioned, since the circumstances demanding it— such as the relation between the eulogizing skald and his patron lord or prince—had largely disappeared. It was followed in Iceland by the much less artistic but more popular *rima*. As for the extraordinary prose sagas—mythological, royal, family, Christian, and purely fictional (the latter influenced by medieval European romances)—they were also at first transmitted orally by unknown but highly skilled sagamen and written down in Iceland, principally in the thirteenth century. Their terse, objective descriptions of actions, people, and character, and their dramatic intensity in the telling of tragic events are probably unequaled in any literature. The Icelanders knew how to tell a story. Historical sagas, written with an exceptional effort to record events truthfully, had appeared in the twelfth century. The zenith of historical sagas is Sturluson's *Heimskringla*, the tale of Norwegian kings down to 1177, generally considered, both in subject-matter and style, the most outstanding prose work in Old Norse (Icelandic) literature. In Denmark Saxo Grammaticus (d. ca. 1208) wrote in Latin a remarkable *Historia danica*, in sixteen books, based on myths, legends, oral tradition, and poems (some of which are preserved in Old Norse form), which among other matter contained the story of Hamlet (Amblet). First published in Paris, 1514, a classic Danish translation appeared in Copenhagen, 1575. This work is of momentous consequence for students of comparative literature.

The foremost Catholic personality in the Scandinavian North was St. Birgitta of Sweden (1303-1373); canonized, 1391, founder of the Brigittine Order, whose *Revelationes* (Lübeck, 1492), based on allegedly divine "revelations," were first widely circulated in manuscript all over Europe. Through numerous later translations of this work, and her Order, she has exerted, especially in Catholic circles, an influence down to our own time. She was a persistent critic of the prevalent social order in court and ecclesiastical groups—not even the highest Catholic prelates were spared—but there was no doubt about her sincerity and religious, Catholic devotion. She had been a married lady and Saint Katherine of Sweden was her daughter.

In the interim literature declined. Kings, courts, lords, were after 1300 occupied with practical matters; the clergy themselves with ecclesiastical affairs, and wrote mostly in Latin; the rising industrial classes were not interested in classic culture; and the German Hanseatic League, which monopolized most of the late medieval foreign trade in Scandinavia, threatened to monopolize the Northern culture as well. Iceland had been joined politically to Norway (1262), and both passed to Denmark (1380). Hence the term "Dano-Norwegian" as often applied thereafter to literary and linguistic matters. It was a period of turmoil, war, and instability. An experiment to unite all Scandinavian countries under one ruler (Queen Margaret, 1353-1412) proved a failure. Hence the Northern literatures from about 1300 to 1500, in Denmark and Sweden particularly, consisted largely of rhymed chronicles in popular verse, Latin and religious writings, provincial laws (though these had also a cultural importance), and translations of South-European romances. Only the native ballad and folk-song flourished, a field in which Scandinavia, especially Denmark, has made a lasting contribution to world literature and criticism.

THE PERIODS OF REFORMATION AND LEARNING

The spirit of the Renaissance in the North is at first best exemplified in the Reformation, which not only broke all ties with Rome and through such reformers as Olaus Petri (1497-1552) of Sweden produced Protestant hymns and other religious works, but proved through complete translations of the Bible (in Sweden, 1541; Denmark, 1543; Iceland, 1584) that the vernacular could be employed for literary production. Historical criticism and the school comedy in Swedish were introduced by Petri. With acknowledged languages of their own, national feeling was stimulated; ardent Danish Protestant patriots composed biting satirical poems on the papacy and Catholicism; and G. Messenius (1579-1673) wrote Swedish historical plays. In the seventeenth century successful native experimentations in hexameters (as in the Swedish court-poet G. Stiernhielm's *Hercules*) and Alexandrines followed; and critical Danish and Swedish treatises on linguistic, phonetic, and rhetorical problems resulted. Verse-technique was discussed; in 1650 the Swedish court of Queen Christina was graced by several foreign writers, artists, and thinkers (including Descartes), writers who had at least a superficial influence on Swedish letters, particularly in matters of form and sometimes in thought; a Swedish work on poetics, based on Opitz, appeared in 1651; dramatic interest was heightened by the performance of U. H. Hjärne's tragedy *Rosimunda*, 1665; an endeavor to improve Swedish words came, 1670, and Scandinavian grammars and dictionaries began to be published. The appearance in Denmark and Sweden of medieval Icelandic manuscripts prompted an intense study of Scandinavian antiquity in all Northern lands; humanists debated Christianity and Neo-Aristotelianism; and the Swedish victories in the Thirty Years' War not only heightened the national spirit but created and accelerated in Sweden a form of uncritical superpatriotism in Swedish literature, as in the polyhistorian Olof Rudbeck's *Atlantica* (1675-1702), a work which acquired a European reputation. This fantastic, nationalistic tendency to exaggeration was in the eighteenth century ridiculed by O. Dalin and, more recently, by Strindberg. In the meantime Marinism and the influence of the Second Silesian School had reached Scandinavia. A bombastic but notable panegyric on King Charles XI by G. E. Dahlstjerna (1661-1709), the representative of the movement in Sweden, was printed in 1697, and introduced a meter new to Swedish writers, the *ottava rima*. About the turn of the century (1701), T. Reenberg of Denmark, in *Ars poetica*, urged the need for literary criticism.

Among the polyhistorians—and there have been several in Scandinavian history—were many real scientists, including Rudbeck, who had distinguished himself in various scientific fields. And this leads to another feature of Scandinavian letters, which is perhaps more prominent in the North than elsewhere—the close relationship of science, history, law, and literature, *and the recognition of that fact*. Some Swedish histories of literature, for example, include without hesitation important works which seem far removed from belles lettres. The term *literature* has often a much broader meaning in Scandinavia than elsewhere. Hence, at the threshold of the eighteenth century we must stop and recall the traditional Northern fondness for research and scholarship. Long before the Scandinavian universities were founded (Uppsala, 1477; Copenhagen, 1479), students from the North, despite distances and difficulties of travel, frequented foreign institutions in large numbers—Heidelberg, Padua, Bologna, Paris. Apparently most Danish and Swedish students in the Middle Ages attended the University of Paris. Several Scandinavian scholars became professors in Paris, and one Dane at least rector of that university. So, learning, with or without the attachment to polite letters, found in the seventeenth and eighteenth centuries a ready welcome in Scandinavian lands. Now for a time the chief cultural background is erudition.

The Scandinavians have long been noted for their historical, antiquarian, and scientific research, of which the following may serve as examples: history by Icelanders, beginning in the twelfth and thirteenth centuries; ballad compilation by a Dane, A. S. Vedel, at the end of the sixteenth century, and continued by other Northern scholars into the nineteenth; and early investigations in the natural sciences by Danes and Swedes, especially in astronomy, botany, chemistry, geology, and anatomy. We need but mention by way of example such names as Are Thorgilsson (*ca.* 1120, in history), Ole Worm (1588-1654, antiquity), Tycho Brahe (1548-1601, astronomy), Linné (1707-1778, botany), Anders Celsius (d. 1744, physics), K. W. Schéele (1742-1786, chemistry), and Swedenborg (1688-1772, mining). All except the first reported their experiments almost exclusively in Latin, for during the "Period of Learning" (*ca.* 1600-1775), and for a long time thereafter, Latin remained in Scandinavia, as generally elsewhere, the language of scholarship. Only popular and purely literary classical works, such as lyrics, appeared in the vernacular. Yet, there were notable exceptions, and Linné in some of his scientific travelogues of the eighteenth century became a master stylist in Swedish prose.

THE PERIOD OF ENLIGHTENMENT

In 1700, therefore, as in other European lands, Northern literature was already submerged, as one might say, in a scientific spirit. Hymns and other religious poems on the creation and related Biblical subjects had continued to appear, but both an esthetic and a philosophical change was in the offing, ushering in the Age of Reason, skepticism, and enlightenment. It came about, of course, in part, under foreign influence.

Previously the impulses from abroad had, as during the Reformation, been largely German, with some Italian (Marinism) and French. During the eighteenth century, except for the German influence in Denmark during the latter half, it became predominantly French and English. Criticisms extolled not only Boileau, Voltaire, and earlier French classicists, but Addison, Pope, and Swift, and in Sweden Olof Dalin (1708-1763) led the new movement by creating a modern Swedish literary prose based on the English *Spectator*. In general, throughout the whole century, the more outstanding Swedish writers, for example, endeavored, with some exceptions, to mold even the most national Swedish subjects into French form. A poem by Dalin on Swedish freedom was modeled on *La Henriade*. His colleague, Fru Charlotta Nordenflycht, wrote on the utility of poetry, and opened her home to establish the first literary salon in Sweden. N. V. Rosenstein, who had adopted Locke's system of philosophy, drafted a treatise on enlightenment (1793); G. F. Gyllenborg, an imitator of Thomson, defended reason and good taste à la Pope (1798); and J. H. Mörk wrote discursive novels on national themes. Pastorals, elegies, epics, idylls, heroic poems, historical dramas, and tragedies poured from the Scandinavian devotees of French classicism, whose uncompromising leader in Sweden was K. G. av Leopold (1756-1829). The latter presented his critical views in an article entitled "Genius and Taste" (1786), and in the same year the Swedish Academy of Letters, on the model of the French Academy, was established with a motto of the same title. A witty, satiric, and enthusiastic but more pliable follower of the French school was J. H. Kellgren (1751-1795), who in 1787 published a crushing critical paper, *A Person is not a Genius Because He is Crazy*. Nor should it be forgotten that King Gustavus III was himself a patron of arts and letters, and an author of some ability. Hence the term "Gustavian Period" (1780-1809), and the designation "Gustavians" for its conservative adherents, or "Academicians," since the King had founded the Swedish Academy which attempted to dictate literary taste during that period. Gustavus III, himself an actor, was especially interested in the drama of the French style, and founded the Swedish national theater and opera; had made his court into a miniature of Versailles; and had among other innovations built an open-air theater at Drottningholm (outside of Stockholm) which already possessed a large, well-equipped regular theater. One of the better known Swedish poets under French influence was G. P. Creutz (1731-1785), who was Swedish ambassador to France during the American Revolution, the senior diplomat at the French court, who kept an open house in Paris for all literati, spoke French like a French-man, and knew Benjamin Franklin personally.

But the first truly great post-medieval Scandinavian writer of international scope was the Norwegian-born Dane Ludvig Holberg (1684-1754), professor, historian, moralist, satirist, and dramatist. He found poetry, as such, distasteful and made his debut in history. As a rationalist he championed the new and use-ful, and while he belonged definitely to the Age of Reason, he followed his own independent style of writing, though drawing inspiration from Cervantes, Molière, and Shakespeare. He visited many European countries, studied their life, laws, literature, and social conditions, which resulted later, among other cultural effects, in a remarkable satire on all Europe, *Nils Klim's Under-ground Journey,* a work like *Gulliver's Travels,* which was written in Latin (1741) but which was soon translated into most European languages. His greatest fame, however, rests on his inimitable comedies written in Danish for the Copenhagen theater. He possessed an unusually keen eye for the distorted and ridiculous in society, had a delicate sense of humor, and became in his creative work a potent but pleasant critic of his time. Later, the Norwegian Student Society in Copenhagen be-gan (1772-1774) actively to foster French classicism and pure poetic expression. Stimulated by French and English models, the Norwegian C. B. Tullin (1728-1765) accepted critically the genre of pastoral poetry, since it was, allegedly, founded on nature and man's oldest mode of life. In Finland, H. G. Porthan (1739-1804) studied native folk-songs and history.

PRE-ROMANTICISM

But French classicism was not the only dominating literary trend in the eighteenth century, and while the *form* of expression might be English or French, the subject-matter was more fre-quently national. Holberg had created a Danish drama, played in a Danish theater. Foreign plays and foreign troupes of actors were not in the future to hold the same attention as in the past. To be sure, they still played a part, particularly in Sweden, but in general the tendency was to focus literary efforts on native material, and every writer independently reserved the right to do as he pleased, in the selection of both form and content. Experiments in rhyme-free verse and irregular meters had been made in Sweden in the seventeenth century. Feeling and freedom could not long be suppressed in Northern lands or minds. Many poems of Fru Nordenflycht (d. 1763), "The Mourning Turtle-Dove," as she had been called, were intensely melancholy and subjective, reflecting personal sorrows. So before the French school was fairly started, there arose a clear undercurrent of Pre-Romantic opposition to any prescribed literary dogmas. Fresh impulses, or encouragement, came, as in France, Germany, and England, from Klopstock, Ossian, and Rousseau.

Thus it happened that emotion, pietism, nature, and freedom of form vied simultaneously for supremacy with rationalism. It was in Denmark that the German Klopstock completed his *Messias* (1773); P. C. Stenerson, a Norwegian admirer of Klopstock, wrote a treatise on unrhymed verse as exemplified in his *Odes*, 1752; and another Norwegian, Johan Wessell (1742-1785), while a student of French classicism, pleaded for feeling and native ability in poetry, and in a tragedy-parody attacked imitation, affectation, and French rules of form. In *De poesi tragica* (1774) the Swedish critic J. F. Neikter proclaimed his faith in native individual genius, and asserted that "rules never made a poet." Looking forward to a national Swedish drama and theater —since subsequent to the medieval morality and miracle plays, followed by the usual school comedies, the Swedish stage productions had been largely imitations or adaptations of foreign plays— a Swedish translator of ancient classics, G. Regnér, attacked French taste in *Thoughts on the Swedish Theater* (1780). Bengt Lidner (1758-1793), a dissipated genius, treated dramatically with strong unbridled feeling and original style themes on King Eric XIV of Sweden, Medea, the earthquake of Messina, the destruction of Jerusalem, and "Messiah in Gethsemane." Thomas Thorild (1759-1808), a worshipper of Rousseau, Ossian, and Klopstock, answered attacks by Kellgren in his *Criticisms of Criticisms* (1791). The general result was a violent controversy between feeling and independence on one hand, and reason and rules on the other. Strange to say, in this period one of the most gifted lyrical poets in Sweden, and one of the most original geniuses in any literature, a protegée of the French-loving Gustavus III, immortalized in song the drinking tavern folk of Stockholm (*Fredman's Epistles*, 1790; *Fredman's Songs*, 1791). This unique personality was Carl Mikael Bellman (1740-1795), a poor, often unhappy consumptive. Never have the Bohemian classes been more faithfully, sympathetically, and humorously portrayed as human characters. With a mingling of realism and idealism, tears and joy, his bacchanalian creations preached music, song, and happy resignation. Drain your glass today, for tomorrow you may die. This was his gospel. Like so many others who wrote drinking songs in the evening, he also wrote hymns, presumably in the morning after the night before. As for forms of composition, he was a rule unto himself, and his best songs must be sung, not read.

We have already mentioned that extraordinary versatile character Emanuel Swedenborg, who in himself represented two supposedly contradictory European tendencies of the eighteenth century—science and religion; first science, including mathematics and inventive mechanics, then spiritual or speculative philosophy. His knowledge of physiology had made it possible for him, it is claimed, to put himself into a trance almost at will, through a system of suppressed breathing, and thus commune with the spirits, even God himself. At least he seems to be sincere in his conviction that he did. He became a seer and theosophist, unconsciously probably, the founder of a new church, who was to exert marked influence over the whole Western world, especially in England and America, particularly during the nineteenth century. He was at first much more widely read outside than inside his native Sweden. When he died (1772) in England, where he had resided for many years, he was buried there: today his remains rest in Uppsala Cathedral. His emphasis on universal, divine love; on the unbroken continuity of life beyond the earthly death; on the moral freedom of man; on his theory of "correspondence of all material things with the spiritual principles, good or evil, of which they are outgrowths and manifestations," these and many other Swedenborgian ideas appealed greatly to the transcendentalists of New England, especially to Emerson, who in his *Essays* made him the world's representative mystic, and proclaimed him to be one of the five great poets of the world, the others being Homer, Dante, Shakespeare, and Goethe. Scores of other Americans, like Walt Whitman, read Swedenborg and waxed enthusiastic over him, a mortal who believed himself to be the divinely appointed herald of a new religious dispensation. His literary or spiritual influence is, literally, inestimable, because to many it is too intangible. Swedenborg wrote a tremendous number first of scientific and then religious-philosophical books, all in Latin, but which were soon translated into most well-known languages. His chief theological and mystical work is *Arcana cœlestia* (1749-1756). Best known in English probably are *Heaven and Hell* and *The Divine Love and Wisdom*.

In the interim, the Danish poet Johannes Ewald (1743-1781) had, after a few satirical dramas and excellent lyric poems, published a tragedy, *Balder's Death*, 1773, and in the *Fisherman*, 1779, a dramatized picture of the people on the Danish coast, had included a poem, "King Christian Stood by the Lofty Mast" (translated by Longfellow), which became the favorite national song of the Danes. The Scandinavian literature was ready for nationalism and romanticism.

NATIONALISM AND ROMANTICISM

The Scandinavians are both progressive and, notably the Swedes, conservative. Sensitive to every wind that blows, near or distant, in practical or cultural matters, they seldom adopt hastily *in toto* any foreign policy or follow at once any cultural movement or event from across the Baltic or other points. While the Swedes particularly are in general said to have a predilection for things alien, they are slow to accept any new philosophy of life or letters without some proof of its right to existence. Consequently, the revolutionizing speculative ideas from Germany, at the end of the eighteenth century, did not reach Sweden, in force, until about 1810, partly also, no doubt, because of its relatively remote geographical location. But when the romantic philosophies did appear, they came via Denmark, and with an accumulating intensity, resulting in some exquisite lyric poetry and violent polemics, the latter often far more interesting and intelligible than the obscure and cosmic but beautiful verse. In Sweden a battle royal developed between pseudo-classicism and romanticism, between form and fantasy, the foreign and the native. As usual, in the long run, the new ideas were victorious.

A Swedish philosopher, B. C. H. Höijer, sponsor of beauty in poetry, had introduced Kant and Fichte; Henrik Steffens, a Dane born in Norway, had glorified pantheistic philosophy (1801), and as a literary mediator converted a Dane, Adam Oehlenschläger (1771-1850), to the romantic ideas. In general there were two main tendencies in Scandinavian romanticism: the philosophical, under German influence, which followed Tieck, Novalis, and Schelling as its models; and the national group, who chose their subjects from native sagas and traditions. In Denmark these trends were at first fused in one author, the versatile and prolific Oehlenschläger, who after having dramatized the Alladin theme (1805) turned to tragedies from legendary Danish history and to a great cycle of epic poems, *The Gods of the North* (1807-1819). Adherents of the old school of reason felt he had gone too far in his independence, and its eminent Danish sponsor, Jens Baggesen (1764-1826), a rationalist of the Wieland type, violently attacked the new ideas in a series of bitter polemics that have assumed historical importance. In some features Baggesen was undoubtedly right; but Oehlenschläger and his many friends not only won, but practically drove Baggesen from the country. In Denmark the critical struggle for supremacy had been waged chiefly between two men: one a creative writer who himself took small part in the controversy; and the other, a real controversialist of restless, polemic caliber. In Sweden the esthetic and literary battle raged more or less violently from 1809 to 1821, and many able conservatives and young, promising radicals joined the fray. In Sweden, as inferred, the two groups of the new movement were separated into the philosophical "Phosphorists" (from their journal, *Phosphoros*) and the so-called "Gothic," or primarily Swedish, Society, which specialized in native themes. Their interests, to be sure, sometimes coincided, and often overlapped, but generally were quite far apart. The former group promoted its ideas polemically in *Polyfem,* and, creatively, in *Phosphoros, Poetisk Kalender,* and *Svensk Litteratur-Tidning,* while the latter sent its contributions to *Iduna* (1812-1824). The leader of the New School, as the Phosphorists were called, was an optimistic, insolent youngster, P. D. A. Atterbom (1790-1855), a very gifted lyric poet and editor, later professor of esthetics and philosophy, who reveled in allegory, imagination, and symbolism, wrote sonnets by the score, and long after the worst polemics of the literary battle were over produced a truly remarkable dramatized fairy-tale, *The Isle of Bliss* (1824-27). Atterbom was ably assisted by other young enthusiasts, notably Lorenzo Hammarskjöld (1785-1827), who was the first in Sweden to herald the new ideas from Germany (*ca.* 1804) and did good service as an historian of art and literature, and as an esthetic critic.

The cudgel for the Old School, or Gustavian Academicians, was forcefully wielded by P. A. Wallmark in *Journal för Litteraturen och Teatern,* later called *Allmänna Journalen,* where he attacked the vagaries of the Germanized New School, while J. M. Stjernstolpe ridiculed the super-patriotic "Gothomania" and the old Scandinavian gods (1820). The story of this ridicule is interesting and illuminating. It was called "The Mythologies, or the Dispute of the Gods," and deals in a comparative way with the assumed characteristics of both Northern and Southern systems. It is a clash between two religious and esthetic philosophies. Naturally, the Greek mythology is taken as the standard. The weapon of attack is satire. The Scandinavian divinities from Valhalla are sent on a visit to the gods on Mt. Olympus, bringing along their customary retinue—attributes of cats, goats, ravens, and serpents. The immediate result, according to the Old School satirist, is a devastating social humiliation for the Northern visitors, not to speak of great physical consternation and illness among the Olympians. Venus is thrown into convulsions over the grotesque appearance of the Scandinavian barbarians, and Juno gets a stomach-upset. Besides, Jupiter, as a god, insists on chronological priority over the Asas or Northern gods.

If the conservative satirist thought he had forever silenced the opposition, he was mistaken. The reply from the New School came quickly. It was pointed out that though the Old Norse gods had perhaps been crude, they had been *natural;* and the Olympians were at once, presumably to be courteous, sent on a return visit North. And behold! Jupiter, or Zeus, appears with a hawk's head and horns; Pan, of course, has ram's legs; and it is pointed out that "no maiden with a hundred breasts like the Ephesian Diana" ever appeared in Norse quarters. In fact, it turns out that very few of the Greek divinities were of legitimate birth. They never reach their Northern destination at all. They get no further than Eleusis, when they encounter a herd of sacrificial pigs. An ass, "who understands them without an interpreter, leads the conversation for the Olympians, and immediately thereafter Jupiter and his retinue return home, disgusted." Thus the new ideas fought the old in Sweden, 1820. Incidentally, even a member of the new national Gothic Society, E. G. Geijer (1783-1847), had apprehensions lest the boisterous supporters of the new mythology should go too far in their enthusiasm, and warned against excessive use of Norse gods in art.

The creative leaders of the national group, besides Geijer,

historian and lecturer, who, following Rousseau's philosophy, lauded in excellent popular verse the occupational virtues of ancient Scandinavia, there were P. H. Ling (1776-1839), founder of the Ling system of gymnastics, and E. Tegnér (1782-1846), the first Swedish poet to become known internationally and the greatest of his generation. Some of his poems, including a few fragments from *Frithiofs Saga* (1825, of which there are fifteen complete English translations), were later translated by Longfellow. Tegnér was an apostle of clarity and pure rhetorical form, and attacked the Phosphorists for their obscurantism. His contention was that a misty expression implied a misty thought. Yet many of his own poems had a distinct romantic coloring. As teacher of Greek, orator, patriotic poet, and broad-minded Lutheran bishop, he exerted a widespread influence on his period.

An ardent enthusiast, who so far as the Scandinavian gods and heroes were concerned, desired to become the Swedish Homer, was Ling. He published (1816 ff.) a gigantic epical work in thirty songs *Asarne* (The *Asas; the* Norse Gods), which proved unreadable, and in 1819 a *Symbolism of the Eddas*, a work of unmistakable romantic stamp, where he "revels in the Norse myths like a child in a fairy story," and attempts to show by comparison that many characters in classic mythology, like centaurs, satyrs, and cyclops, were "as little adapted [in art] for the chisel as 'our formless trolls.' " Worthy of note, in this connection, is the fact that Geijer, who, as we have seen, was also interested in the subject of Norse gods in art, published in 1820 a philosophical treatise, in which he expressed rather free opinions about the dogma of redemption and the Trinity in the Christian religion. He did not "approve of a blind faith based simply on authority," an echo of the ideas of Enlightenment and simultaneously an anticipation of liberalism.

More or less independent Swedish poets of the period were Vitalis (1794-1828), satirist, humorist, and withal a profound elegiac and philosophical, religious poet, who as a critic attacked both branches of the romantic movement; and that strangest phenomenon in Swedish poetry, E. J. Stagnelius (1793-1823), who wrote tragedies in the antique style with Old Norse motives, and ornamental, gnostic, mystic-pantheistic poems. He loved to portray "the human soul as a prisoner in the hall of the princes in the world, and longing for heavenly splendor, whence it came." K. A. Nicander (1799-1839), friend of Longfellow, depicted in *Runesvärdet* (*The Rune Sword*, 1821), in pentameters, the conflict between heathenism and Christianity. J. O. Wallin (1779-1839), archbishop of Sweden, wrote one hundred and twenty hymns and translated or adapted many others for the Swedish psalmbook, and penned a glowing dithyrambic song, "George Washington." F. M. Franzén (1772-1847), born in Finland, and later bishop, an original, didactic, and lyric poet, who seemed most at home in the idyllic element, had in 1797 received a prize from the Swedish Academy for a poem in honor of the above-mentioned Creutz, but had not won the unqualified approval of the Academy, "since the poem had been treated with more freedom than seemed desirable." Franzén, too, had, perhaps unknowingly, helped to inaugurate a movement which disregarded strict observance of poetic rules.

This new school of poetics brought into Sweden, as to other lands, many new South-European verse-forms. But the most positive acknowledged gain for the so-called romantic revolt was the interest in and the collection of folk-songs, an interest which was shared by all literary parties. In 1814-16, therefore, Geijer and A. A. Afzelius published a notable group of *Svenska folkvisor* (folk-songs). Needless to say, also, some of the choicest pearls in Swedish poetry stem from the second and third decades of the nineteenth century. The younger group had been victorious, and the result was a definite enrichment of poetic literature as an art, and the conception of art, for its own sake. No good novels had yet appeared. As for the violent criticisms that were hurled in all directions, it might be contended that the extremes often balanced each other, which eventually brought moderation, sanity, and progress. As the period was drawing to a polemic close, a strange, bizarre figure, the only Scandinavian genius of his kind, had left his home in Stockholm to seek in the forests of the province Värmland that return-to-nature ideal which Rousseau had preached. He failed. This was K. J. L. Almquist (1793-1866), who in "free fantasies," as they were called, wrote poems and dramas of the most varied and imaginative kind. In a sense he is the most capricious, fantastic, arbitrary, inventive, and grotesque writer in the whole era, yet he has produced some of the best, and certainly unique works in Swedish letters. It was he, a transitional figure, who in the thirties, in part through observation and practical experience in life, burst into realism, socialism, and feminism. He was not alone in this movement, but more of this later.

DANISH RELIGIOUS ROMANTICISM AND LIBERALISM

In Denmark a national, religious, idealistic romanticism predominated, on the whole, throughout the first half of the nineteenth century. Oehlenschläger had many admirers and followers, and, despite literary feuds and criticisms, poems, dramas, translations, satires (often in dramatic form), and controversial writings, by exceptionally able authors, appeared in great abundance. Verse still held its own, but also prose tales and historical novels based on native themes became popular. The most potent figure of the period was undoubtedly N. F. S. Grundtvig (1783-1872), who though an ardent opponent of infidelity and rationalism, opposed the doctrines of the Established Church and apostolic or post-apostolic views. In religion he preached "the living word," and a "joyful Christianity." It was a personal faith, with Christ as the central figure in the world's development. Grundtvig wrote over a hundred volumes, in all branches of literature, and had a tremendous influence on the intellectual and spiritual development of Denmark. He cared little for form; thoughts were uppermost. He translated Saxo's *Chronicle of Denmark* (*Historia Danica*), from the Latin, Snorri Sturluson's *Heimskringla,* and *Beowulf* into Danish; called attention to Anglo-Saxon literature; and published a work on Norse mythology (1808). The latter was later abridged under the title *Symbolic Language of the North* (1832), an original historical-philosophical interpretation. He founded the now well-known folk high school, a peculiarly Northern type of popular institution for adults, which was to represent a fusion of national and Christian elements. These schools for primarily common, non-academic citizens are now numerous in Denmark, Norway, and Sweden, and are established in many other countries. Grundtvig strengthened national feeling, furthered the cause of the people, and revived religious life in Denmark. Despite violent secular and ecclesiastical opposition, he died a bishop. In a sense, he, like Geijer, anticipated liberalism in thought and religion.

THE DAWN OF DANISH REALISM

A stimulating influence on the Danish people was exercised by the exceedingly popular B. S. Ingemann (1789-1862), author of lyric and religious poems and legends, one epic on the Danish Valdemar the Great, and four historical novels based on popular ballads of the Middle Ages, with Walter Scott as the model. In spite of attacks by Heiberg (*q.v.* below) for "abstract mannerism" and lack of substance, he became a real national poet. Mention must be made here, too, of the Norwegian-born J. C. Hauch (1790-1871), follower of Schelling and Oehlenschläger and author of dramatic poems, tragedies, and historical novels, who after Oehlenschläger's death became his successor as professor of esthetics in Copenhagen University. As painter of nature and common people, especially of the heaths of Jutland, where he was pastor, S. S. Blicher (1782-1848) is unexcelled. His descriptions of the native villagers are realistic masterpieces, especially *The Parson of Vejlby*, the tragic story of which Mark Twain Americanized, with a happy ending, in *Tom Sawyer, Detective*. Blicher had in 1807 translated Ossian.

In this brief sketch of Scandinavian tendencies in literature and criticism we need only recall that Hans Christian Andersen (1805-1875) was a Dane. He needs no introduction to anybody, anywhere, for he is known the world over for his fairy-tales that began to appear in 1835. In this field he has no peer. Some of his tales he invented himself; others he borrowed and adapted from popular traditions and old ballads. Except for an autobiography, he was not so successful in other genres. In connection with Andersen we are reminded of that bourgeois-born Danish "Bohemian" Holger Drachman (1846-1908), lyric poet, sponsor of social justice, and author of some sixty volumes, who wrote the intensely popular Danish fairy-tale play *Once Upon a Time*. In the interim R. C. Rask (1787-1831) had through a prize essay on the Old Norse or Icelandic language, and other linguistic works, laid the foundation for a comprehensive and systematic study of the Old Scandinavian tongue.

The foremost Danish critic of the era was J. L. Heiberg (1791-1860), a reflective mind and a stickler for form, who in dramatic satire (1815) scathingly attacked the ideas of the Romantic school, and made a great stir in Danish esthetical circles by introducing from the French a "new dramatic species," the vaudeville. In Heiberg's hand it became a Danish creation, an ambition to foster Danish humor and comedy for his own people. He had published a work on the marionette theater in 1814, followed later by a dissertation on vaudeville as dramatic art. He was, according to Winkel Horn, "the poet to proclaim the Hegelian philosophy in Denmark, both in purely philosophical essays and in connection with his esthetic criticisms, which, though scattered in a multitude of articles and short papers, still taken as a whole, constitute a scientific system." His polemic writings were directed principally against Oehlenschläger, Grundtvig, and Hauch. "He battled for the unity of rationalism and idealism against feeling and imagination." Small wonder that he had no sympathy for the works of Hans Christian Andersen.

NATIONAL ROMANTICISM IN NORWAY

Norway developed a form of national romanticism all her own. In 1814 she had been separated from Denmark—she had already her own university (1811)—had obtained her own constitution, and without her consent had been united to Sweden through the political manipulation of other powers. These changes engendered such a feeling of liberty and independence that in most writings, for nearly a century, nationalism in some form overshadowed other motives. Not that everybody felt or thought alike either in political or cultural matters; on the contrary, there ensued a contest between the moderate and super-nationalistic elements which in matters linguistic, esthetic, and literary is still going on, though in a more sympathetic, coöperative form. The leading spirit for the national movement was the reckless patriotic enthusiast Henrik Wergeland (1808-1845), who advocated absolute freedom from everything foreign, especially Danish, and scorned any coöperation with or impulses from other cultures. His sense of freedom, however, extended to the Jews, who at that time were prohibited from settling in Norway. And he was an able poet.

Led by J. S. C. Welhaven (1807-1873), the moderate opposition formed the so-called "Intelligence Party," which recommended that the cultural relations with Denmark and other nations be continued. In 1834 Welhaven in a series of sonnets scourged the "one-sided, narrowminded patriotism" of his day, and exposed the shortcomings of the Wergeland group. After all, it was possible to portray Norwegian scenery and native culture without breaking all ties with the outside world. Welhaven's special field was philosophy, but he also lectured on the history of literature and published essays on Dano-Norwegian letters.

Still the national movement gained ground, and it was definitely established and universally recognized through the publication, 1841-1844, by P. C. Asbjörnsen and Jörgen Moe of *Norwegian Fairy Tales*, perhaps the greatest event in the whole movement of that generation toward a more truly national culture. "Danish bondage" was thrown overboard, for these tales "gave a certain dignity to vernacular literature and revealed the poetry of popular tradition." They were followed in 1845-1848 by two volumes of Norwegian folk-legends.

SWEDISH REALISM AND LIBERALISM

Scandinavia has always had an abundance of good poets, and this is particularly true of Sweden, which can probably boast of at least a dozen first-rate lyricists. But in Sweden a more frequent use of realism and prose came relatively early in the nineteenth century. G. W. Gumälius, 1828, introduced a genre which is rich and popular in Swedish literature, the historical novel, in the style of Walter Scott, as in Denmark; Fredrika Bremer (1801-1865), feminist, wrote a number of domestic novels that became extraordinarily popular in English-speaking countries, and in the fifties published about thirteen hundred pages on her travels in America; under eminent leadership, *Aftonbladet* became in 1830 an outstanding organ for realism and liberalism; in 1839 the aforementioned Almquist boldly published his shocking, feministic, *Det går an (It Will Do)*, picturing a heroine who could take better care of herself than her contemporaries either admitted or permitted. Closely allied with the realistic trend was the movement of Scandinavianism, a plea for Northern unity, which was sponsored by both Danish and Swedish writers.

Svend Grundtvig had begun in Denmark, 1853, to edit and publish the Danish ballads and folk-songs on the more realistic principles of reproducing the exact form of the original. The foremost Swedish champion of liberalism of the time was Viktor Rydberg (1828-1895), a classic idealist, Hellenist, and humanist, who in *The Last Athenian,* for instance, a novel localized during the early struggle of paganism with Christianity, defended liberal ideas in religion. Because of mastery of both form and thought Rydberg wrote some of the best poetry in Swedish literature.

SWEDISH-FINNISH LITERATURE

Of authors previously mentioned, Bremer, Creutz, and Franzén, though writing in Swedish, were born in Finland, which had belonged to Sweden from about 1150 to 1809, when it was lost to Russia. Its culture on the seaboard had been largely Swedish; a Swedish university had been established by Queen Christina at Åbo (now Turku) in 1640; and dozens of able Swedish-speaking writers subsequently came from Finland. Still a strong national feeling for the native Finnish (of the Finno-Ugrian group of languages) developed during the nineteenth century, the culmination of which came with the publication, 1835, of *Kalevala* (The Land of Heroes), the Finnish national collection of mythological and heroic traditions, from the form of which Longfellow borrowed the meter for his *Hiawatha.* (Longfellow was in Sweden in 1835). Finnish mythological poetry had also been published in 1822 by Zacharias Topelius, Finnish author of the famous Swedish *Surgeon's Stories.* But the greatest Swedish-Finnish literary figure was J. L. Runeberg (1804-1877), who besides idylls, epigrams, epic poems, and lyrics, wrote the immortal work, *Songs of Ensign Stål* (1848-1860), a collection of poems, each in a different meter, and based on the events in the Finnish War of 1809. Through their beauty, power, pathos, simplicity of style, realism, and glowing patriotism, Runeberg exerted great influence, and is by many considered the greatest of all Swedish poets before Fröding. Fredrik Cygnäus (1807-1881), the first outstanding critic in Finland, interpreted the "democratic realism" of Runeberg, and studied folk literature and the tragic element in *Kalevala*.

RELIGIOUS PHILOSOPHY—KIERKEGAARD

By this time faithful translations of Dante, Homer, Euripides, Byron, and Shakespeare had appeared in Danish, and of Tasso, Ariosto, Camoens, Dante, Milton, and Shakespeare in Swedish. The Dane Christian Arentzen (b. 1823) wrote valuable works on Baggesen and Oehlenschläger; a great Danish theologian and bishop, J. P. Mynster (1775-1850), discussed the Christian faith; H. N. Clausen (1793-1877) represented in his writings the critical tendency in theology; and H. C. Oersted (1771-1851), the discoverer of electro-magnetism, wrote a brilliant work on *The Spirit in Nature* (1850). In Sweden K. J. Boström (1797-1866) had about 1840 begun to develop an independent philosophic system of a personal, idealistic character, which in religion was "directed against the prevailing orthodox conception" (R. Steffen). But the leading Scandinavian religio-philosophic personality of the period was the Dane Søren Aaby Kierkegaard (1813-1855), often considered the greatest thinker Denmark has produced.

Kierkegaard was a link between theology and philosophy, was interested in fundamental principles of Christianity rather than in dogma, and set forth its ideal claims accordingly. He had little use for the official, communal form of it. To him "life in faith" was exclusively a union between God and *individuals*. Christendom was a union of Christianity and the world; whereas real Christianity meant a renunciation of the world. So he attacked official Christianity and its priests in numerous works, contrasted esthetic and ethical views with the Christian, and developed peculiar concepts of his own. His often vague and trying writings

—one has to be patient in reading them—are distinguished "for their refined and brilliant dialectics combined with passionate enthusiasm for the maintenance of Christianity as the 'Gospel of suffering.' " Christianity is not a doctrine at all, he says, and since it centers about Jesus, the "God-Man, the sign of contradiction," and since he (Jesus) was not by most of his contemporaries considered as a god, one must have faith that he was something which really had to develop later. Because of the recent interest in Kierkegaard, as a parent of the subjective, extrarational Existentialism, he has now been made available in excellent English translations.

MODERN NORWEGIAN NATIONALISM—BJÖRNSON

Meanwhile Norwegian nationalism assumed a new and interesting form. About 1850, in connection with the so-called "agrarian awakening" in Norway, Ivar Aasen (1813-1896) "created a new Norse language, the landsmål, based on the old Norwegian country dialects, as contrasted with the prevalent standard literary medium, the more Danish riksmål" or Dano-Norwegian, and creative writers like A. O. Vinje (1818-1870) and Arne Garborg (1851-1924) established its rights as a literary language. A Norwegian journal of esthetic criticism, the *Andhrimner*, was founded by Ibsen and others, 1851. But the most influential Northern patriot of his age was that emotional firebrand and towering orator and literary figure Björnstjerne Björnson (1832-1910), the emperor of Norwegian nationalism and realism. Both in his unexcelled descriptions of native peasant life (as in *Synnove Solbakken*, 1857) and in his early dramas from the history of Norway, it was easy to see where his abilities and sympathies lay. The same proved true of his poems. Björnson wrote the Norwegian national anthem. His later social and political plays, such as *The Editor* and *A Bankruptcy*, both of 1875, were perhaps not so successful; but his epic-lyric *Arnljot Gelline* (1870) and *Beyond Human Power* (1883), a tragedy of faith and an attack on Christianity, are masterpieces. Curiously enough, despite his nationalism and early advocacy of the landsmål, he remained a conservative in form and wrote in the Dano-Norwegian *riksmål*. But he is the "inspired prophet," the friend of the common people, the teacher and preacher to whom art is a medium for ideas, and seldom, if ever, existent for itself alone.

In distant Iceland, the editor of *Fjolnir* had perfected (1835-1847) its poetic language with patterns from the sagas and the country vernacular.

IBSEN

While Björnson was a chauvinistic nationalist and leader, Henrik Ibsen (1828-1906), dramatist extraordinaire, was an individualistic cosmopolite, the "secluded Sphinx of the North," the rebel, fighter, moralist, and skeptical critic who went through life scattering profundities of thought, riddles, and problems, and asking questions that neither he himself nor anyone else at that time was expected to answer. His works, most of them written abroad, are, as is well known, world literature, the influence of which soon spread over the rest of Europe. Ibsen's romantic period, which included the tragedy *Brand* (1866) with its philosophy of everything or nothing, and its counterpart, *Peer Gynt* (1867), often called the *Faust* of Norway, was followed by nothing less than war on society, as declared by *The Pillars of Society* (1877), an attack on conventional hypocrisy, with a plea for truth, liberty, and honesty. In 1870 Ibsen had invited Georg Brandes to join him in "the revolt of the soul of man," and the result was a series of dramatic assaults on social hypocrisies which are known the world over: *The Doll's House* (1879), a plea for real companionship in marriage and technically considered Ibsen's first masterpiece; the Darwinistic *Ghosts* (1881); and *An Enemy of the People* (1882), which condemns the self-interest of "the compact majority," asserting that he is the strongest who stands alone. Later Ibsen abandoned social problems and sought themes in great psychological personalities and in symbolism, like *The Master Builder* (1892). Ibsen, the titan of Norse letters, and Björnson created the modern Norwegian drama. Both started as national romanticists, but after a time pursued ardently the realism, or naturalism, of social problems.

NATURALISM

With Björnson, Jonas Lie (1833-1908) is the creator of the modern realistic Norwegian tale or novel, often localized in Nordland, in a shipping town, as *The Pilot and His Wife* (1874). His classical work is *The Family at Gilje* (1883), the home of a government official, a captain, in 1840. Lie has truth, humor, and sympathy. In 1876 the Danish Darwinian and psychologist J. P. Jakobsen (1847-1885) published his objective *Marie Grubbe, a Lady of the Seventeenth Century*, where the heroine shows the personal influence of heredity and environment, followed (1880) by *Niels Lyhne*, a problem novel about a dreamer who "learns how to resign himself to reality." Meanwhile he had already (1872) written *Mogens*, the first naturalistic novelette in Danish literature, where milieu, nature, soil, become the determining molding factors.

The modern period, beginning with naturalism, about 1870, was formerly inaugurated by that pioneering, prolific Jew, the critic Georg Brandes (1842-1927) in *Main Currents in Nineteenth Century Literature* (1871-1875; English version, 7 vols., 1901-1905), which was based on the radical European literary movements. The trend was followed in Denmark by H. Bang (1857-1912) and Henrik Pontoppidan (b. 1857), Nobel-Prize winner. Bang published a collection of essays, *Realism and Realists* (1879), soon followed by *Critical Studies and Sketches*; and Pontoppidan's best work, a novel, is *Lucky Pehr* (1898-1904; 8 vols.), an ironic title, the story of a minister's son whose life is thwarted by racial inheritance. In Norway, besides Ibsen, naturalism found sponsors in A. Kielland (1849-1906), and Amalie Skram (1847-1905), the latter, allegedly, the most complete pessimist and most consistent exponent of naturalism in the North. *Offspring* (1890) is Fru Skram's chief work.

The greatest writer in Swedish naturalism, is, of course, August Strindberg (1849-1912), Sweden's only internationally-important dramatist, and "probably the most noteworthy figure in Northern literature of the last fifty years," said Topsöe-Jensen in 1929. His novel, *The Red Room* (1879), introduced the movement in Sweden, followed by such cynical, mocking attacks on women as *Married* (I, 1884; II, 1886) and the plays *The Father* (1887) and *Miss Julia* (1888). Strindberg, who published some sixty volumes of all modes of writing, of which about a third are available in English, is the personification of contradiction. He is an atheist and a believer, a socialist and an anti-socialist, a friend of man and an apparent hater of women, a naturalist, deist, Swedenborgian, romanticist, symbolist, expressionist, and superman. He wrote dream plays, short stories, novels, one-act plays, and historical tales and dramas—all more or less self-confessions. Chief foreign influences came from England, France, Germany, and America. Incidentally, he ridiculed the characterization of Nora in Ibsen's *A Doll's House*.

In Iceland the most famous prose writer to come under the influence of Brandes was perhaps Gestur Pálson, who studied in Copenhagen from 1875 to 1882, and whose work is characterized by a profound pessimism, with bitter satire on existing social conditions. He paved the way for H. K. Laxness (b. 1902), the creator of modern realistic prose in Iceland, such as *Salka Valka* and *Independent People*, and T. Thordarson, the exponent of radical modernism and soul analysis.

NEO-ROMANTICISM

But the North, essentially lyric and psychological at heart, could not long endure exclusively the "fare of sordid realism, even if termed 'scientific truth.' There came a reaction, therefore, *ca.* 1890, neo-romanticism and symbolism, which sought to restore imagination and artistry for its own sake. The Danes Jörgen Bukdahl and H. Rode attacked Brandesianism, and the Norwegian Knut Hamsun (b. 1859), Nobel Prize winner, wrote (1917) the national, wholesome *Growth of the Soil.* In Sweden the opposition was consciously sponsored creatively and theoretically by Verner v. Heidenstam (1859-1940) and the extremely popular Selma Lagerlöf (1858-1940)—both Nobel Prize winners—and by Gustav Fröding (1860-1911)," Sweden's greatest poet, while the leading critics were O. Levertin (1862-1906) and the post-romanticist and secretary of the Swedish Academy C. D. af Wirsén (1842-1912). Miss Lagerlöf's *Gösta Berling's Saga* (1891), inaugurating a long list of imaginative, idealistic fairy-tale-like stories and novels of rare artistry, broke definitely with positivism and naturalism.

"The romantic revival assumed various forms: Oriental exoticism, nationalism, and stoic moralism (Heidenstam); estheticism (Levertin); symbolism and mysticism (O. Hansson); expressionism (Strindberg himself); artistic realism plus medieval Catholicism (Sigrid Undset, b. 1882, Nobel Prize winner); and Hellenism (V. Ekelund). Of these Hansson and Ekelund were from Skåne, Sweden. In Iceland the scholarly critic Sigurdur Nordahl introduced a new romantic spirit, and the Danish novelist Johannes V. Jensen (recent Nobel Prize winner) in a monumental work, *The Long Journey* (1909-1921), exploited Darwinism in literature." Other less romantic currents have included communism and proletarianism (M. A. Nexö). To these should be added E. A. Karlfeldt (1864-1931), posthumous Nobel Prize recipient, the "singer of Dalecarlia," a pure lyricist.

MODERN REALISM AND SOCIAL CRITICISM

In the twentieth century Scandinavia has been extremely productive in all fields of literature, in the novel, short story, essay, biography, poetry—in which there has been a veritable renaissance, especially in Sweden—and in new forms of the drama. Peasant life, provincial scenery, national movements, and world events have been favorite themes, with a tendency toward more realism and social criticism than immediately before. We can add only a few names and works. In Denmark J. Knudsen (1858-1917) reveals the ideal of his novels in a collection of essays, *Philosophy of Life;* in Norway the aforementioned Fru Undset wins first rank among novelists by depicting the social civilization in the Norway of the fourteenth century, in the three-volume historical novel, *Kristin Lavransdatter* (1920-1922); J. Bojer (b. 1872), in a long, popular series of novels issues "a call to arms in defense of the world of inner values"; and J. Falkberget (b. 1879) deals with the vagabond laborer. In Sweden Per Hallström (1866-1944) becomes master of the short story; Albert Engström (1869-1940), of humor; Vilhelm Moberg (b. 1898), of bold realism in prose; Pär Lagerkvist (b. 1891) of the impressionistic drama; Frans G. Bengtsson (b. 1894), of the portrayal of colorful historical personalities, real or fictional, such as Charles XII and the Viking Red Orm; and Hj. Bergman (1883-1931) of the appealingly bizarre in the human character, both in fiction and in comedy. Ellen Key (1849-1926) wins world renown as a champion of feminism and individualism; and the city of Malmö, Sweden, builds during World War II the most modern theater building in existence.

As for critical evaluations, the number of able Scandinavian critics, including creative authors, has been incredibly large. And while much Scandinavian criticism, it is true, has since the eighteenth century constituted a national record of appreciation, description, and interpretation of the creative efforts of others, rather than one of a direct, theoretical, causative type, it reveals, on the other hand, as the writer has stated elsewhere, "an unusual independence of judgment, marked individuality and eclectic power in the study and adoption or rejection of foreign trends. . . . Despite the prevailing sensitiveness to alien influences of form, taste, and philosophy, particularly in Sweden, Scandinavian criticism has, like its literature, always preserved a balance and national character of its own."

BIBLIOGRAPHY

BIBLIOGRAPHY

American-Scandinavian Foundation, *A List of Books by Scandinavians and about Scandinavia*, 4th ed. (New York, 1946).
Guide to Information about Sweden, Naboth Hedin, ed., American Swedish News Exchange, Inc. (New York).

LITERARY HISTORY AND CRITICISM[1]

American-Scandinavian Foundation, Introduction to *Norwegian Fairy Tales* (New York, 1924).
BACH, Giovanni, et al., *The History of the Scandinavian Literatures* (New York, 1938).
Selected bibliographies of all Northern literatures, giving a fine treatment of Icelandic and Finnish writing especially.
BECK, Richard, *History of Icelandic Poets: 1800-1940*, vol. (1950), *Islandica* (Ithaca, N. Y.).
Scholarly and lengthy treatise. A complete bibliography of Islandica, covering all periods, may be found at the end of the above-mentioned volume.
BENSON, Adolph B., *The Old Norse Element in Swedish Romanticism* (New York, 1914).
———, "Scandinavian Criticism," *Dictionary of World Literature*, Joseph T. Shipley ed. (New York, 1943).
Columbia Dictionary of Modern European Literature (New York, 1947).
Includes many up-to-date articles on Scandinavian writers and cultures.
EINARSSON, Stefán, *History of Icelandic Prose Writers: 1800-1940*, vol. (1938), *Icelandica* (Ithaca, N. Y.).

[1] In a not too distant future The American-Scandinavian Foundation of New York will publish histories in English of the various Scandinavian literatures. The Foundation has to date published about seventy volumes of biographies, monographs, literary classics, anthologies, travelogues, and other works dealing with the history and outstanding cultural personalities of the Scandinavian countries, many of the classics containing in introductions comprehensive critical and biographical material.

GUSTAFSON, Alrik, *Six Scandinavian Novelists* (New York, 1940).

HORN, Fredrik Winkel, ed., *History of the Literatures of the Scandinavian North* (Chicago, 1895).
Contains an excellent bibliography, prepared by Thorvald Solberg, for the period up to 1880.

HUSTVEDT, S. B., *Ballad Criticism in Scandinavia and Great Britain* (New York, 1924).

JORGENSON, Theodore, *History of Norwegian Literature* (New York, 1923).

TOPSÖE-JENSEN, H. G., *Scandinavian Literature from Brandes to Our Day* (New York, 1929).
Although sketchy, gives an idea of the quality and magnitude of recent belles lettres.

ANTHOLOGY

LEACH, Henry Goddard, *A Pageant of Old Scandinavia* (New York, 1947).
An anthology of translations of medieval Scandinavian writings—poetry and prose—and of international references to the Viking North from Greek, Arabic, and other sources.

12

Slavic Literature

J. A. POSIN
STANFORD UNIVERSITY

Born in Russia, J. A. POSIN was educated mainly in this country, earning the Ph.D. degree at the University of California. During the late war he was director of the intensive Russian program at the University of Iowa, and head of the Russian department, Navy Language School, at the University of Colorado. He has taught, also, at Cornell University, at the University of California in Los Angeles, and is regularly on the staff of Stanford University, teaching Russian language and literature. In addition to critical, bibliographical, and scholarly writing, PROFESSOR POSIN *has published Russian prose and poetry in translation; see especially* Poet Lore (*1941*), American Slavonic Review (*1942-44*), The Russian Review (*1948-50*), The Pacific Spectator (*1951*).

Slavic Literature[1]

EXCELLENCE of form, that is, style or technique, and the depth of content appear to be peculiarly well combined in Russian literature. With very few exceptions, there has been no tendency on the part of the Russian writers to emphasize either of these phases at the expense of the other. A writer in Russia has always been aware, consciously or subconsciously, of the fact that the knowledge of the technique of his craft is of supreme importance, and that, on the other hand, he should invoke his gift only in the service of meritorious causes.

THE GROWTH OF FORM

In considering the form, one must bear in mind that the time allowed to Russia by circumstances for the development of her literary art was comparatively short, much shorter than with other important literatures. The Slavic (Cyrillic) alphabet itself has been known only since the ninth century, having been invented by two Greek monks, brothers Cyril and Methodius. The providing of literary language for any Slavic country was not their chief concern. They were primarily interested in evolving a written language in which they could fix prayers, translations of the Gospel, and other church literature. They provided a powerful stimulus for the development of literature even though the literature as such was only a by-product.

This situation continued, in the main, until the time of Peter

[1] Although this essay is entitled *Slavic Literature*, it deals overwhelmingly with Russian literature, and only cursorily and incidentally with the literatures of other Slavic countries. The limitations of the present volume permitted the more or less detailed treatment of only the most prominent literatures. No one individual—least of all the author of this essay—is to blame for this condition.

the Great (1689-1725). The relatively few works up to that time were dedicated to non-literary tasks: Chronicles; *The Lives of Saints*, and other church writings; and the *Domostroi*, a set of rules and regulations pertaining to the household and family affairs of the seventeenth century. Somewhat apart from these stands the one alleged monument of the late twelfth century, *Slovo o Polku Igoreve* (*The Story of Igor's Army*), known only through a presumed sixteenth-century version, discovered late in the eighteenth century and later destroyed by fire. Neither its value, nor even its authenticity can now be ascertained. Another form of popular expression, Russian sagas, the *byliny*, could hardly be called literature in the modern sense because they were, together with popular tales of anonymous folk origin, rendered orally at first. It must be borne in mind at all times that, until very recent times, the percentage of literacy in Russia was extremely small.

With Peter the Great, as in the case of Cyril and Methodius, literature per se played a subordinate rôle. The monarch was primarily interested in building a powerful state and a powerful and modern army. Out of these considerations grew the necessity for greater literacy. But, though merely a by-product, the literary expression, once started, continued a life of its own. Peter's contribution to literature consisted primarily in modernizing the Church-Slavic alphabet and evolving the so-called civil alphabet (*grazhdanskaya azbuka*) which allowed a much greater flexibility and conformance to the spoken popular language.

The eighteenth century saw the gradual liberation of the literary Russian language from the shackles of non-Russian Church-Slavic forms, or *slavianshchina*, and the emergence of a modern Russian literary language which came much closer to the popular Russian speech, a process distantly resembling the struggle in the West during the European Renaissance with its insistence on the use of native languages in preference to the Church-sponsored Latin. A writer like Karamzin (1766-1826) was, in effect, a bridge between the Church-Slavic construction of the eighteenth century and the first thoroughly modern Russian writer, Alexander Pushkin (1799-1837).

The significance of Pushkin as a reformer of the Russian literary language far outweighs all other considerations of him. That is why it is so difficult for non-Russians to understand his importance even when there are competent translations of his work, which, incidentally, are pitifully few. Other writers came later, and, using Pushkin's heritage, his free and unfettered Russian language, brought their own content. But the greatness of Pushkin consists in this "giving the language" to the Russian literature, in serving as a fountainhead for later writers. The fact that, more than a hundred years after his death, Russian literary language has not evolved any essentially new forms, is not a testimony to its poverty, for these forms were sufficient to win for Russian literature a foremost place among the European literatures. Rather, it is a testimony to the genius of Pushkin who could project his contribution a century and a quarter ahead. Pushkin's works read as though they were written only yesterday. It was fortunate, also, that, contemporaneously with Pushkin, there lived in Russia a most astute and penetrating critic, Vissarion Belinsky (1811-1848), the father of Russian materialist criticism of the nineteenth century. He was able to discern almost immediately not only the greatness of Pushkin as a poet in his own right but also his significance for the Russian literature as a whole. Belinsky's authoritative appraisal went far toward early establishing Pushkin as the greatest Russian writer.

From the standpoint of the forms of literary language, nothing even remotely comparable to Pushkin happened in Russian literature since his time. He definitely closed one epoch and just as definitely opened another. This literary epoch, opened by Pushkin, still continues, in spite of radical changes in Russian political and social life.

THE IMPORTANCE OF CONTENT

Having thus briefly traced the evolution of the modern forms in Russian literature, let us now turn our attention to content. That aspect of literature has been more important in Russia than in many other countries. By force of historical circumstance, Russia was denied any outlet for progressive thought, except literary fiction. There was no parliament, no free pulpit, no forum of any kind, no press, even, deserving the name. The only place where there would be occasionally a breath of fresh air was fiction. The reasons are not far to seek. The total literacy of Russia was very low, and the percentage of people who could read and enjoy sophisticated works of literature was smaller still. Thus works of fiction presented—or so the authorities thought— the least danger to the existing order. Another reason was that many of those works were couched in such subtle and figurative language that the censors frequently could not detect the "dangerous" thought contained in a book.

With the reign of Peter the Great, literature begins to speak in the Russian language, and the Russian reading public begins to read works written in Russian, instead of subsisting almost exclusively on French literature. The eighteenth century may be called the age of satire. It began and ended under two enlightened reigns, that of Peter the Great at the beginning of the century, and that of Catherine II at the end. Both reigns represented, in a measure, a break with the old way of life. Peter was a revolutionary on the throne, reversing the usual process of revolutionary activity stemming from below. Satire is a logical weapon of a revolutionary; he must make his adversary and his adversary's works appear ridiculous. Thus, in a sense, satire received royal sanction, for Peter was surrounded by the hostile crowd of hereditary reactionary noblemen, the boyars, against whom he sought and found allies among the progressive elements, particularly the satirists.

Catherine II (1762-1796), originally a German princess, also needed allies, and found them outside the circle of the hereditary nobility. In addition to the people who directly helped her to depose and assassinate her husband, she sought and found allies among the less illustrious by birth, champions of the common people, particularly the satirists. Here again, though in a smaller measure, was the revolution from above. The most noted satirist of Catherine's time, Fonvizin (1744-1792), wrote two comedies: *Brigadir*, which ridicules the excessive aping of everything foreign, particularly everything French; and *Nedorosl* (*The Young Hopeful*), a much more mature work. The target of this comedy is the ignorant and arrogant class of serf-owners, and, by implication, and sometimes by direct statement, Fonvizin presents the plight of the serfs, virtual slaves. Parenthetically, it matters little to literature that Catherine herself was not strongly concerned with the plight of the serfs and, indeed, did much to increase their number and their burden. Once uttered, the protest against serf economy grew ever louder in Russian literature, and formed the leitmotif for the following years.

THE GROWTH OF SOCIAL PROTEST

At first, this protest is based entirely on idealistic and ethical considerations. Alexander Radishchev (1749-1802) was spurred by the ideas of the French Encyclopedists. His *Puteshestvie iz Peterburga v Moskvu* (*The Journey from Petersburg to Moscow*), despite its innocent title, sounds a passionate plea for the rights of the underprivileged, the serfs. To judge the material of the book, one need only notice some of the chapter headings. They proceed from "Bad Condition of Peasants" and "Cruelty of an Official" to "The Sale of the Serfs" and "The Horrors of Peasant Life," with the conclusion "Project of Liberation of Serfs." This last chapter was the cause of the drastic treatment accorded to the author. The Catherine of 1790, the date of publication of the book, was not the Catherine of 1770 who had encouraged the young Radishchev to study the enlightened French writers and "moral philosophy." The Empress had seen the "horrible example" of the French Revolution of 1789—and before that the American Revolution—which showed her what happens when people take moral preachings seriously. Radishchev's book was burned, only a few copies escaping, and the author sentenced to hard labor in Siberia. He had made the mistake of believing that if only those in power could see the light of reason, the remedy of injustice would be brought about by the simple application of logic.

This idealistic outlook persisted in Russian literature until the beginning of the 1840's. One of the most brilliant comedies in the Russian language, *Gore Ot Uma* (*Woe From Wit*), by Alexander Griboiedov (1795-1829), ridicules the corruption of the highest court nobility, and makes an impassioned plea for honesty and integrity in government. The comedy coincided in time with the unsuccessful revolutionary uprising in Petersburg in December, 1825. Although Griboiedov was not arrested, his comedy was prohibited from print or public performance for many years to come. Nicholas I and his government quite correctly judged that here was "literary Decembrism"—the participants in the uprising of 1825 were known as the Decembrists—consisting of an attempt to laugh the autocracy out instead of shooting it out. *Woe From Wit* was first produced and published long after its author was dead, but the work enjoyed tremendous surreptitious circulation in manuscript from the start, being copied and recopied by voluntary hands.

The period of the reign of Nicholas I, from 1825 to 1855, was one of the most gruesome for Russia and for Russian literature. Frightened by the outbreak of 1825, the Tsar acted to forestall any similar movement or action. Everyone and everything that had any suspicion of progressive thought was persecuted. Literature suffered in consequence as it was suspected, not without foundation, that the majority of literary men had very little affection for Nicholas. One of the results of this policy was a wave of pessimism, whose most brilliant exemplar, Mikhail Lermontov (1814-1841), set forth his doubts and misgivings in a series of gem-like poems and in a prose narrative, *Geroy Nashevo Vremeni* (*The Hero of Our Time*).

But even in the Russia of Nicholas I the urge for a greater measure of freedom could not be entirely stifled. It was expressed through literature of both fiction and criticism, the latter led by Belinsky. His early work was influenced by the German idealistic philosophers and the right-wing Hegelianism, but toward the end of his brief life he tended more and more toward radical materialism, left-wing Hegelianism, and Ludwig Feuerbach. He cleared the path for his followers—Chernyshevsky, Dobrolyubov, and Pisarev—so that Russian literary and social criticism played an unique and important part in Russian literature. In fiction there was a shift in values. Whereas, before the 1840's, the ideas of "pure art" and "art for art's sake" were still very fashionable, beginning with the 1840's, partly under the influence of Belinsky, those values gradually give place to another set: utilitarianism, rationalism, and materialism. Related to this change was a significant development, which later received the name of the "Gogol trend," *gogolevskoye napravlenie*. It was the beginning of the "literature of exposé," something in the nature of the muckraking literature of the beginning of the twentieth century in the United States. It started from the short story *Shinel* by Nikolai Gogol (1809-1852), variously translated into English as *The Mantle, The Cloak,* and *The Overcoat*. It shows "the little sorrows of a little man," in a humorous fashion; and, what is of great importance, the remedy of the sorrows that suggests itself is plausible and socially logical. Here there is no individual problem of peculiar and unusual circumstances, but something which can be solved by common, albeit gigantic, effort. Within the peculiar Russian context, this advantage contained a tremendous handicap, the opposition of the Tsar's government to any progressive step which made even talking and writing about social problems a crime. But the issues were clear. Gogol's other works in the same vein, the long narrative *Myortvye Dushi* (*Dead Souls*) and the play *Revizor* (*Inspector-General*) helped to establish the trend more firmly. The fate of these works was better than that of Griboiedov's play; the one was published and the other produced on the stage during the lifetime of their author. The difference in treatment accorded to Griboiedov's and Gogol's work was undoubtedly due to the fact that the target in Gogol's satires, unlike that in *Woe From Wit*, was the small fry of petty gentry and the petty provincial officialdom. Of course, the censors miscalculated. The real target, though probably an unconscious one so far as Gogol himself was concerned, was the whole way of life based upon serfdom. Consequently, the target was the group of people who bore the responsibility for managing Russian affairs, and chief among them was the Tsar. Nicholas grasped this point immediately, for, after the premiere of the *Inspector-General*, he remarked that he himself was the chief culprit of the play.

In 1845, a young novelist Feodor Dostoevsky (1821-1881) wrote a short novelette in the form of letters called *Bednye Liudi* (*Poor Folk*). Like *Shinel*, it showed the life of a petty government official of the capital, and the problems, of course, are the impecuniousness and insecurity. It thus continues the Gogol trend, although the term had not yet been coined. Some fifteen years later, Dostoevsky produced another work, *Zapiski iz Myortvovo Doma* (*The House of the Dead*), which belongs with the earlier work in that the sociological motif predominates in it also. While describing the life of prisoners in Siberian hard-labor camps, it simultaneously sounds a protest against ignorance, cruelty, and poverty, conditions which seem to have a strange affinity for one another. By skillful identification of the prison population with the population on the outside, Dostoevsky includes in his indictment practically everyone in Russia who has any power at all over the serfs.

THE IMPACT OF REVOLUTION

After 1848, the year of European revolutions, and until the death of Nicholas in 1855, following the disastrous Crimean War, two conflicting currents permeated Russian public and social life. On the one hand, the breath of European unrest found its way into Russia in the form of smuggled publications from abroad, principally those of the *émigré* writer, Alexander Herzen (1812-1870). On the other hand, as a counterbalance to the influence of these publications and the whole tenor of European life, the government increased still further its pressure on all liberal elements. In 1849, Dostoevsky, together with many others, was arrested and sentenced to death. The legal pretext for the sentence was Dostoevsky's participation in the so-called "Petrashevsky circle," an innocuous group engaged in the discussion of the ideas of the French Utopians. At the last moment, the sentence was commuted to hard labor in Siberia.

The defeat of Russia in the Crimean War (1854-55) emphasized the inadequacy and inefficiency of the autocratic regime. The logical question arose. What was the good of the government which did not want to grant internal reforms, and failed in its self-assumed task of warding off the external blows? The answer could no longer be postponed. There was, however, no answer to be given. Fortunately for himself, as well as for Russia, Nicholas did not survive the year of the Crimean defeat. Although the new Tsar, Alexander II (1855-81), differed little from his predecessor in his personal outlook, he was called upon to play a far different rôle. The liberal and progressive intelligentsia demanded recognition of its rights, and the peasants were rioting all over Russia. Faced by the prospect of having his hand forced from the "bottom," the Tsar decided to relent at the "top," setting the serfs free. For the liberal intelligentsia, the writers prominently among them, this represented a culmination of over a century of conscious struggle on behalf of the peasants. The initial enthusiasm over the momentous measure was so great that even the bitter foe of autocracy, Herzen, exclaimed in the pages of his publication abroad, "Thou hast won, O Galilean!" The enthusiasm was short-lived, however. Once started on the road of reform, Russian public opinion demanded much more than the half-measures of the government, calculated on an irreducible minimum, could provide. The peasants were freed, that was true, but they were not granted sufficient land, and what land they did get had to be paid for in the so-called redemption payments, *vykupnye platezhi*, stretching over decades. Moreover, the reforms in civil life, trial by jury, a measure of local self-government, or *zemstvo*, and others, were not sufficiently broad in scope. Many of the old sores of corruption remained, and these, together with inefficiency and ignorance in high places, presented a convenient target for satire, this time from "below."

"The Gogol trend" in literature continued to promote civic betterment by ridiculing the seamy sides of Russian life. The satirical poet Nekrasov (1821-1877) sets out to answer the question implicit in the title of his long poem *Komu na Rusi zhit' khorosho? (Who Lives Well in Russia?)*. Various classes and occupations are examined—landlords, officials, the clergy, the merchants. All the groups give a discouraging answer that they do not "live well." The satirist Saltykov (1826-1889) did in prose what Nekrasov did in verse. His particular target was the administrative officials of various Russian provinces, the governors and their assistants. He knew those people well, for he had been one of them. He exposes them in books like *Pompadury i Pompadurshi (He-Pompadours and She-Pompadours)*, describing, with satirical exaggeration, the lives, loves, and the antics of the provincial society.

In criticism, similar motifs are discernible. Continuing the tradition established in the forties by Belinsky, the critics of the sixties promoted civic improvement, utilitarianism, and materialism as did the fiction writers. Among them were Nikolai Chernyshevsky (1828-1889), Nikolai Dobrolyubov (1836-1861), and

Dmitry Pisarev (1840-1868). They were not merely literary critics, in the Western sense. Because of the peculiar Russian conditions, the discussion of every literary topic inevitably involved the consideration of social, economic, and, so far as possible, political problems. Often they were linked to literature only in that, technically, their articles were written in connection with some literary work or writer. What was the essence of their writings? Briefly stated, it was a passionate demand for a better chance for most of the Russians. In economics, they went one step beyond the emancipation of the serfs. They insisted on greater economic opportunities for the peasant, more and better land and better conditions of life, and for the city dwellers, particularly the workingmen and the so-called intellectual proletariat, better living conditions and greater security. In philosophy, they were materialists of Feuerbachian type, impatient with mild liberalism, idealism, and conventional Christianity. Pisarev went so far as to reject all esthetics, alleging that they contributed nothing to the material welfare of man. In politics, veiled as of necessity their pronouncements had to be, they were not satisfied even with the ideal of constitutional monarchy, but exhibited a definite preference for a republic.

WESTERNITES AND SLAVOPHILS

Though most vociferous for a time, the materialist critics did not monopolize Russian thought in literature. Since the thirties of the last century, there were two currents in Russian thinking and, consequently, two definite currents in literature, Slavophilism and Westernism. The latter was in the ascendancy until the reaction of the middle sixties; the former gained strength coincidentally with that reaction. The Slavophils, in general, were distrustful of the European West and its influence. Tracing the beginning of Westernism to Peter the Great, they urged a return to pre-Petrine days, and put their trust into three phenomena which they accepted as typically Russian, religious orthodoxy, autocracy, and nationality. These three entities made the Slavophils more acceptable to the autocratic regime than were the Westernites, for the ideas of the Slavophils and those of the advocates of the autocratic rule dovetailed. If the dogmatic concept of nationality was to mean anything in the presence of various actual Russian nationalities, a religious yardstick was necessary which would automatically dub "Russian" only a person of Greek Orthodox faith. But in order to preserve this highly arbitrary and artificial status, a strong governmental support was necessary for the traditional Greek Orthodox church. Hence, in order to preserve the first two, dogmatic nationality and orthodoxy, the third factor, autocracy, was indispensable. The cardinal practical point of the Slavophil frame of mind was that Russia was an entirely different entity from Western Europe, and had to develop according to its own peculiar pattern. Slavophils denied that Russia could profitably imitate or adopt anything from the West, either intellectually or materially.

The Westernites went to the other extreme. Impressed by the progress of Western European countries in philosophy, the arts, and industry, they believed that Russia could use Europe as a pattern. In economics, they trusted not the peasant with his own peculiar communal organization, but the emerging industry with its class of industrial proletariat, a concept which paralleled the Western social progress. To the extent that they denied the mystical significance of the Slavophil trinity, particularly autocracy, they were unpopular with the Tsar's government.

A good example of the Slavophil-dominated thought in literature is provided by the works of Dostoevsky in his second period, after *The House of the Dead*. Having undergone a complete reversal of his former radical beliefs during his Siberian exile, and a conversion to the conservative, not to say reactionary, mode of thinking, he embraced the essentials of Slavophil philosophy. In his four major novels, *Idiot* (*The Idiot*), *Prestuplenie i Nakazanie* (*Crime and Punishment*), *Biessy* (*The Possessed*), and *Brat'ia Karamazovy* (*The Brothers Karamazov*), the same note recurs insistently. The human mind is the work of the devil; love (charity) is the creation of God. What really matters, according to those works of Dostoevsky, is the divinely inspired love for one's fellow man, preferably of Greek Orthodox faith, without any interference from the intellect. That was precisely what some of the Slavophils preached. According to them, the education of the peasant was not only unnecessary but even harmful. It was much better to leave him in the state of blissful ignorance. If love is all that matters, then indeed the West can offer little or nothing to Russia. What the West had to offer, according to Dostoevsky, was the "soulless arithmetic," the solution of social problems in statistical terms, per capita. That, in his opinion, reduced everything to mere mechanics of living, leaving out the human soul. This latter entity, being highly individual with every person, would not lend itself to mass treatment, as, for instance, the problem of food or shelter. Since every soul has its own troubles, and should be treated individually, there is no room in the Slavophil-Dostoevskian scheme of things for social thinking or for socialism. And indeed, as we shall see further, this indifference to social problems—to problems which touch the whole society, and which leave the individual and specialized problems out of consideration—this indifference constitutes the chief characteristic of the writers in the Slavophil camp. The attitude of writers to socialism may serve as a chemical indicator, a litmus paper, in determining their stand in regard to Slavophilism or Westernism. It is safe to say that there was not a single writer among the Slavophils who was sympathetic to scientific, or even to utopian socialism. Whether this attitude resulted from the fact that socialism was a Western emanation, or from some other conservative influence like governmental preference, need not interest us now. In the four novels of Dostoevsky mentioned above, the scheme and design of the author are clearly discernible and very similar, not to say identical. In *The Idiot,* the one "good man" is Prince Myshkin—an epileptic person, not very stable mentally. His being "good" is quite sufficient. In *Crime and Punishment,* Myshkin's counterpart is the streetwalker Sonia Marmeladov, also a mental lightweight, who has human charity in abundance and through whom the clever and therefore sinful Raskolnikov is saved. In *Brothers Karamazov*, of the four Karamazov brothers, including Smerdyakov, only one is unquestionably deserving the kingdom of Dostoevsky's heaven, Aloyosha. He is similar to Myshkin and Sonia, and is thus the author's symbol of his peculiar brand of "goodness," rather than a living person. Dmitry Karamazov may be the next on the list of candidates for the heavenly kingdom; he is not very bright. We feel that if we search further, we may find Smerdyakov and Fedor Karamazov, the father, on the list. But never Ivan Karamazov, the brain of the Karamazov family. He would be joined by Svidrigailov from *Crime and Punishment* and Pyotr Verkhovensky from *The Possessed*. These men are outside the Dostoevsky pale. They rely too much on reason and have no spark of divine love.

Leo Tolstoy (1828-1910) also fits into the Slavophil pattern. He was indifferent to the revolutionary movement and he was opposed to westernization. In his best-known work, *War and Peace,* he is imbued, partly subconsciously, with the glory of Russia in the person of Prince Kutuzov as opposed to the West in the person of Napoleon. The true explanation of why he never achieved his original design of depicting the Decembrist movement which came on the heels of Napoleonic wars was, most likely, that he could not find it in himself to sympathize with that movement. It was a Western movement. The basic idea of *War and Peace* is far removed from Westernism. It is expressed through the person of Platon Karataev and is not very different from the principal idea of Dostoevsky: simplicity and ignorance, if only they are accompanied by the all-powerful divine agent, are higher and better than sophistication and knowledge. In the same vein, and according to the same pattern, is Tolstoy's best-known play, *The Power of Darkness*. Here again, conflict develops between the forces of good and evil, represented in husband and wife respectively. It is *Crime and Punishment* of Dostoevsky all over again. The clever and criminal woman in the play fails, and triumph comes to the simple inarticulate Akim, her husband, plus divine agency, which is on his side. In their efforts to make clear that the social position of their chief characters is of no consequence, so long as these characters are called or chosen by God, both Dostoevsky and Tolstoy select for the carriers of their idea the most lowly occupations: Sonia in *Crime and Punishment* is a prostitute, and Akim in *The Power of Darkness* is a cesspool cleaner. There is parallel of unusual degree in the central idea and characters of both works.

Anna Karenina, the second best-known work of Tolstoy, has essentially the same central theme: the sophisticated, artificial, and insincere atmosphere surrounding the life of Anna is contrasted with the wholesome, back-to-nature existence of Levin. The artificiality and sophistication of Anna's life lead her into sin, while Kitty and Levin, like Pierre and Natasha in *War and Peace,* are left to lead godly, though unexciting, lives.

Tolstoy's non-fiction works are mere extensions of his novels and plays. Their central themes are: "non-resistance to evil by force," and "the kingdom of God is within you," which, in effect, are one and the same thing. If one is self-sufficient to the point of carrying within him the ultimate good, why resist the evil that dwells outside? Therefore, Tolstoy's chief concern is the salvation of his own soul, a procedure which he recommends to everyone. Save your own individual soul, and there will be no necessity to worry about social problems. Tolstoy intensely dislikes the complications of modern life. Throughout the whole of his works goes the fear and hatred of the city, of the machine, of mechanical progress. He conceives his ideal in terms of rural, patriarchal relationships between a "good" landlord and a God-fearing peasant. There is no room in his ideal scheme of things for the more complicated industrial relationships of a modern city. When he is confronted with the problem of the city, the best he can do is to advise the people to return to the village, back to the soil. It is the romantic ideal of Rousseau, whose great admirer Tolstoy was from early adolescence.

This outlook does not interfere with Tolstoy's preoccupation with eternal questions: the question of what is life, or what is death, problems which transcend any one epoch and any one country. The portions of *War and Peace* dealing with them, and the entire short story *The Death of Ivan Ilych* could be written by a writer of any epoch or any country. Tolstoy's popularity and universality stem from precisely these aspects of his work—timelessness and spacelessness.

ECONOMIC AND AGRARIAN PROBLEMS

The Westernite writer Ivan Turgenev (1818-1883) was less fortunate in that respect. His works are tightly bound with his own epoch and reflect the changing moods of Russian public opinion for the thirty years, from the middle forties to the middle seventies of the last century. He made his debut in literature with a series of short stories published in contemporary journals and later collected under the title *Zapiski Okhotnika* (*The Sportsman's Sketches*). Like Radishchev's *The Journey from Petersburg to Moscow* they concealed dynamite under an innocent title. The central theme is the same protest against serfdom, although there is a difference in method and in fundamental purpose. *The Journey* deals chiefly with the *abuses* of a serf-owning order of society, and anything which depicts the abuses of a social order is thereby relegated to the realm of reformist literature, as the obvious conclusion is that there is nothing fundamentally wrong with the system, provided the abuses are corrected. From that standpoint, the character of Simon Legree in *Uncle Tom's Cabin* (which has been compared to the *Sportsman's Sketches* continually since the appearance of both works) weakens the effectiveness of Harriet Beecher Stowe's novel. Not so with Turgenev's *Sketches,* which are more subtle and more radical. Here the author does not make conscious propaganda and he does not preach. In a series of excellently done character sketches, he presents, for the most part, simple, guileless folk, with their hopes, their loves, and their problems. Some of them possess practical intelligence and are substantial members of the community, like Khor in the sketch "Khor and Kalinych"; some are poetically endowed; some are talented singers. Turgenev presents the whole gamut of human emotions, and the reader readily identifies himself with various characters and their problems. Eventually the truth comes as a shock to the reader, that these people are slaves. They can be flogged at the least whim of their master; they can be sold like cattle, separated from other members of their families; they can be bartered, or gambled away at the turn of a card. When that realization became widespread in Russia, the days of serfdom were numbered, for it was obvious that even the kindest slave-owner was not to be tolerated. Not merely the abuses, but the institution itself was wrong. One might add that the time was ripe for the reform anyway. The old feudal economy was proving too costly, with its antiquated, forced, and inefficient labor. Both the economics of the situation and the aroused public conscience were headed in the same direction, toward the Western solution of allowing free individual enterprise, with employers, not owners, of labor, and personally free, hired laborers. In 1861, with the signing of the manifesto freeing the serfs, serfdom was no longer an issue. But there were other issues, political and economic and they were accentuated by the removal of serfdom.

The economic issue, owing to the still predominantly agricultural character of the country, was the obtaining of more and better land for the peasants. This issue dominated the economic life of the country up to the Revolution of 1917. The chief political issue was the granting to the people of fundamental democratic rights, and this issue has not been satisfactorily resolved to this day. Turgenev's other major works deal primarily with that political issue, particularly his novels *Nakanune* (*On the Eve*) and *Otzy i Deti* (*Fathers and Children*). In *On the Eve*, very appropriately titled in that it appeared shortly before the Emancipation Manifesto, the author observes the apparently discouraging fact that there is no one in Russia among the educated classes who would be able or willing to undertake the struggle for freedom. The hero of the novel is a Bulgarian who is burning with only one desire, to free his country from the domination of the Turks. He seeks a temporary refuge in Russia, meets an idealistic Russian girl, marries her, and departs with her for Bulgaria to wage his war against a foreign oppressor. But that has nothing to do with the problem of Russia and with Russia's effort to get rid of the domestic "Turks," that is, the autocratic regime. A question inevitably arose: are there really no people in Russia willing and able to undertake that task?

The answer came in Turgenev's masterpiece *Fathers and Children*, which was published immediately after the Manifesto of 1861. The hero, Bazarov, dominates the novel, which, in essence, is a delineation of that character and not a novel in a conventional sense. Turgenev called Bazarov a "nihilist," and this name has been applied to Bazarov and his generation ever since. If we take the epithet literally, a nihilist being a believer in nothing, we do a grave injustice to that character. He is simply a materialist of the Pisarev or Dobrolyubov type. He is indifferent to divine power, although it would be an unauthorized assumption to call him an atheist. He believes in the power and efficacy of science—he selects medicine and medical research as his career. His other characteristics must be inferred, since the plain statement of them was impossible under censorship. There are unmistakable indications that he believes in a thoroughgoing reorganization of the entire political organization in Russia, achieved if necessary by revolutionary means. His ultimate goal is difficult to discern. Turgenev could not possibly foresee it, and indeed it is not clear even to Bazarov himself who says, "our task is only to clear the space; others will come and will build upon it." But there is nothing to suggest that his immediate purpose is very different from that of the founders of the American republic, who could not see too far into the future either, being content to win independence and leave behind them a flexible instrument for any future contingency, the Constitution of the United States. In other words, *Fathers and Children* is a bid for the benefits of Western progress as expressed through the American and French Revolutions.

In the intensified tempo of life in the early 1860's, social processes took much less time to crystallize than would normally be the case. By 1863, the Bazarov type, an exception three years before, became a common phenomenon. We have testimony to that effect in Chernyshevsky's only novel *Shto Dielat? (What Is to Be Done?)*. It is definitely inferior from the standpoint of literary technique. Chernyshevsky himself had no illusions about its literary merits—he wrote it while·a political prisoner in the fortress of Sts. Peter and Paul, and his critical review *Sovremennik (The Contemporary)* had been closed—but it had great influence upon the growing generations of public men, revolutionaries and writers. Ignoring its quite impossible plot, we see at once that it presents some new people, new, that is, to Russian literature. Our old friend, Bazarov, appears here under a different name, Lopukhov, but there is also a new type, Rakhmetov, the revolutionary Populist. He was a wealthy landowner who refused to use his wealth for his own benefit. He lived on only four hundred roubles a year and devoted all his time to study in preparation for revolutionary activity. He used the bulk of his fortune for philanthropic purposes, paying tuition and expenses of five other students. He consciously practiced the most rigorous asceticism and frugality, living like a common peasant because only in that way might one gain the confidence of common people. Unlike Turgenev's Bazarov, Rakhmetov does not possess a single human weakness, and accordingly he impresses one, not as a living human being, but as a walking symbol of the movement later known as Populism, and this in spite of the fact that the ideas put forth in the novel do not follow the Populist line. The central idea is that the future of Russia rests on coöperation and coöperative effort both in the city and on the farm. This is definitely a

Western idea, including as it does the coöperative movement in the West and the development of trade unionism. All this, of course, represents wholesale borrowing from the West. Thus, Chernyshevsky reflects in his fiction, as well as in non-fiction works, the mixed ideologies of Slavophilism (the Populists) and Westernism (the coöperatives), with a strong leaning toward the latter.

The case of the Westernites was carried further by the critic Dobrolyubov, making use of the works of two other writers, Ivan Goncharov (1812-1891) and Alexander Ostrovsky (1823-1886). In the first, Dobrolyubov draws his conclusions from Goncharov's famous work, *Oblomov*. Il'ya Oblomov, an impoverished landowner, emerges from Goncharov's pen as an amiable though inefficient misfit, and the entire village of Oblomovka is presented with gentle humor and unmistakable affection. The characters, as drawn by Goncharov, are lovable lazy people who refuse to worry about important problems, and confine their activities to eating, sleeping, and procreation. It is only after Dobrolyubov strips the modifying drapes of amiability that the true nature of Oblomov and the Oblomovs begins to appear. In his essay *Shto Takoe Oblomovshchina* (*What Is Oblomovdom*), Dobrolyubov shows that the amiable Oblomovs are in effect parasites whose existence is possible only because there are underprivileged people who do all the work for the Oblomovs. The tragedy of Il'ya Oblomov is that he happened at the wrong time, when the emancipation of the serfs was already impending, and so, prepared for one type of existence, he had to lead quite another. Dobrolyubov then generalized the isolated case of Oblomov to include all "Oblomovs," no matter where and when and under what name. Dobrolyubov's definition of Oblomovdom is "a nasty habit" of obtaining and using the fruits of someone else's labor without giving in return the equivalent in useful labor. Thus the novel was raised to the status of a social phenomenon.

Dobrolyubov did even more for Ostrovsky and his work. Ostrovsky was an amiable Moscow resident who by his origin and early occupation knew the Moscow merchant class very well. In a series of talented and vivid plays he gave an unforgettable picture of the merchant life, with its boorishness, ignorance, and cruelty to underlings and members of the household, as well as its cynical attitude to the customers: "if you don't cheat, you won't sell." Dobrolyubov's penetrating analysis showed that, in reality, Ostrovsky's picture applied with full force to the entire edifice of Russian life at the time. In his famous essay *Tyomnoe Tsarstvo* (*The Realm of Darkness*), Dobrolyubov managed, in spite of censorship, to raise and to answer the question: what was to be done in order that the phenomenon of the "realm of darkness" would disappear forever in Russia? His unmistakable and far-reaching conclusion was that nothing short of the thoroughgoing reshuffling of all social forces, that is, a social revolution, would do. He further discussed this problem in a companion essay, *Looch Sveta v Tyomnom Tsarstve* (*Ray of Light in the Realm of Darkness*), and thus the works of Ostrovsky, regardless of the sympathies and inclinations of Ostrovsky himself, bear a pronounced Westernite character. As they were interpreted they imply the reorganization of Russian life on the more enlightened, Western pattern.

POPULISM, GUILT, AND FUTILITY

The honeymoon of the epoch of reforms was quickly over. The dissatisfaction with the limited scope of liberal measures granted by Alexander II crystallized soon after the Emancipation Manifesto. Herzen took back his enthusiastic words. The government retaliated. In 1862, the publication of *The Contemporary* was suspended and its mainspring, Chernyshevsky, arrested. The arrest was followed by a prejudiced trial and banishment of the critic to Siberia for twenty-five years.

In the second half of the sixties, at the instigation and with the encouragement of Herzen from abroad, the so-called Populist movement developed. It combined the Westernite-socialist sentiments with the Slavophil outlook of seeking a separate and distinct road for Russia. It preached a peculiar form of agrarian socialism based on the existing agricultural unit, *obshchina*, and on the so-called *mir,* a crude form of collective organization on the farms. Thousands of enthusiastic young men and women of education and culture went *v narod* ("into the people"), mingling with peasants, living among them, eating and dressing like peasants, and all the time preaching their gospel of agrarian socialism. This social movement shortly gave birth to a political group, an underground terrorist organization called *Narodnaya Volia* ("People's Will"), which used assassination as its chief weapon. Its development was aided by the fact that the government greatly hampered the work, and persecuted the personnel, of the peacefully minded Populist propagandists in the village. In the late sixties, the People's Will tried Alexander II—in absentia, of course—and condemned him to death. Execution of the sentence required fifteen years and four unsuccessful attempts, but on March 13, 1881, the Emperor was blown up with a bomb.

Alexander III (1881-1894), the son of the assassinated monarch, continued and aggravated his father's policies. The plea of the aging Tolstoy to spare the lives of the assassins in the name of Christian mercy was disregarded, and police rule was so strong that social and political activity reached the lowest point since the days of Nicholas I. Many of the intelligentsia were willing to compromise with what seemed the inevitable. Many preached the gospel of "small deeds," that a crumb is better than no bread at all. In this atmosphere of social and political stagnation, prose writers turned to the solution of ethical problems, to problems of the human conscience, and to bewailing the unfortunate lot of the Russians. In poetry prevailed symbolism which was borrowed from decadent writers of Western Europe.

The best exponents of the typical Russian conscience, the feeling of guilt on the part of the privileged classes before the underprivileged and disfranchised peasants, were Vsevolod Garshin (1855-1888) and Vladimir Korolenko (1853-1921). In *Chetyre*

Dnia (*Four Days*) and other works, Garshin asks: what is a person to do when he feels that hundreds of thousands of meek, docile, and ignorant Russians are driven to slaughter in a war that has nothing to do with their wishes in the matter? The answer is characteristic. He joins the army, not to kill but to be killed. He regards war as a natural calamity, like plague or pestilence, and he would consider himself dishonorable if he were to run away, or to stay away, from it. A similar attitude appears in *Khudozhniki* (*The Painters*). A young and talented painter gives up his career in order to be a village schoolteacher partly because he considers it dishonorable to enjoy the fruits of culture when people around him are suffering from lack of bare necessities of life. Korolenko, too, felt his "guilt" before the people. *Son Makara* (*Makar's Dream*) is an eloquent plea, not merely for formal justice, but for understanding and mercy as well. The ignorant Siberian peasant, Makar, commits many sins but, the author argues, he had never had a chance to live decently or to develop even a sense of distinction between right and wrong. He should be, and is, forgiven. Defense of the underprivileged formed the basis also of Korolenko's articles published in the *Russkoye Bogatstvo* (*Russian Wealth*), a monthly review of which he was a co-editor. A good example will be found in the long article "Dom #13" ("House #13"), which discussed a Jewish pogrom in gruesome detail. Korolenko visited the scene of the massacre, and substantiated with witnesses' accounts the criminal negligence of the police and its active coöperation with the hoodlum element.

The most talented writer who attained his maturity in this period was Anton Chekhov (1860-1904). His mental development took place during the late seventies and the bulk of his work was done in the eighties and the nineties, the period of ennui, sickness of the spirit, and general gloom for the Russian intelligentsia. The epoch did not fail to leave its imprint on Chekhov's work. His early stories, most of them very short, present with mild irony the life of the provincial intelligentsia and semi-intelligentsia. It is a dismal picture. Gone are the fire and enthusiasm of the sixties. In their place, there are gluttony, concern with the petty successes in the civil service, and the small worries of small men. Chekhov is not sarcastic, he is not a satirist. He does not laugh at his characters. With good-natured sadness, he seems to laugh at himself more than at anyone else, and to say: "We certainly have made a mess of things." His stories suggest no solution; there is no rebel spirit, and in only one, *Kryzhovnik* (*The Gooseberries*), is there a mild sort of impatience with things as they are. But if he does not laugh at his characters, he sometimes laughs with them. He is so thoroughly Russian in his themes and idiom that much is lost in translation, and frequently stories which are full of sparkle and humor in the original possess neither in translation.

In later life, Chekhov wrote his four best-known plays, two of which, *Tri Sestry* (*Three Sisters*) and *Vishnyovyi Sad* (*The Cherry Orchard*), are chiefly responsible for his reputation in the United States. *Three Sisters* is a symphony of futility, and in this it reflects the spirit of the time among the petty bourgeoisie. Beginning with the three sisters themselves, not one character in the play knows what he wants, let alone how to get it. The sisters were nice enough persons, practically everyone around them was just as nice a person as they, and yet no one was able to arrange his life to his own satisfaction. A companion piece to *Three Sisters* is Chekhov's story *Chelovek v Futliare* (*The Man in a Case*). Here are the same futility and lack of purpose. The "man" was frightened of everything, not externally but from the inside, and he invented barriers and obstacles out of his panicky imagination. When he died, the author tells us, he seemed to reach calm and contentment; he had fitted into a "case" from which it would not be necessary to emerge again. *The Man in a Case* may be regarded as a symbol of thoughts and feelings of the Russia of the 1880's.

The Cherry Orchard was written and first produced early in this century. It has its share of people for whom there is no hope —the owner of the orchard and her brother, for instance—and if there is also a note of optimism, it is to be heard in the by-play of an impecunious young couple, the daughter of the orchard-owner and a student-tutor. The dominating note is the sound of the cherry orchard being cut down. The merchant, Lopakhin, who had bought the orchard, decided to cut it down, to subdivide the property, and make more efficient use of it. This is, of course, symbolic. All of Russia is a Cherry Orchard, beautiful but useless, and the builders of the new life—the merchant and industrial class, in Chekhov's estimation—were establishing their new law. Although Chekhov, as the subsequent events proved, was conspicuously wrong in believing that the aristocracy would be followed in power by the merchant and industrial class, his guess was the logical one considering what had happened in Western Europe.

In poetry, the civic motifs gave way, first, to "poetry for poetry's sake," and later, toward the end of the century, to symbolism. The technical revolution produced in Russian poetry by Pushkin was so great that, after him, many very minor poets had a degree of technical perfection which would have been considered phenomenal before him. During the eighties and the nineties a large number of people could write passable verse in Russia, and most of them did. In a relatively short time, preoccupation with form produced the extra-refined, extra-lilting, sensuous type of rhyme and meter which relied for its appreciation more on the senses than on sense. Some of the poets sought to synthesize their form with their content, or rather to fuse both together making one inseparable whole; that is, they became symbolists. By its very nature, symbolism tended to be exclusive, esoteric, unworldly. It was a sign of the times, as the writings of Chekhov were a sign of the times, but it was not very sharply to be distinguished from the symbolism of the remainder of the continent, and not distinctively Russian.

The writer who best reflected the European moods of introspection and futility at the end of the century, although all his major works were written in the early part of this century, was

Leonid Andreyev (1871-1919). He fell under a strong influence of Schopenhauer's pessimism, and found no way out of the suffocating mire of Russian life, confirming the hopeless dictum "thus it has been, thus it will be." In *Zhizn' Cheloveka* (*The Life of Man*), Andreyev suggests that life is purposeless, senseless, and transitory, as well as full of suffering. We come to this earth we know not why, we depart we know not whither, we live we know not for what purpose, and we suffer all the time. It is a typical reaction of a petty-bourgeois intellectual in the period after the unsuccessful revolutionary outbreak of 1905. *Anathema* poses the old question raised in Dostoevsky's *Crime and Punishment* and in Tolstoy's *Power of Darkness*, and offers the same answer. The question is, what is of the higher order of things, Mind or Love, and the answer is Love. The Mind, that is the human mind, is personified in a significant symbol, Anathema, who is seeking admission to the region which lies beyond the realm of human intelligence. He is forever denied entrance there, but Love is permitted to enter in the person of the ignorant but lovable David Leizer. Other aspects of disillusionment appear in *Professor Storitzyn*, in which the idealistic professor, like a modern Don Quixote, falls before the forces of brutality and the commonplace. And in the powerful bit of fiction *Krasnyi Smekh* (*Red Laugh*), Andreyev makes an attempt to discredit the patriotic fervor of the unsuccessful Russian-Japanese War.

INDUSTRIALISM AND DISCONTENT

Although there was little political change in Russia in 1894, when Alexander III died and Nicholas II ascended the throne, industrialization, which was to be productive of the great changes in the fabric of Russian life, was already under way. With the increase of industries, industrial employees, the so-called industrial proletariat, began to play an increasingly important rôle, the more so because Marxist, social-democratic propaganda found its way into the workingmen's circles. As early as 1883, George Plekhanov organized a group called *Osvobozhdenie Truda* ("Emancipation of Labor"), a social-democratic formation patterned on a German model. The two currents of revolutionary thought in Russia, as they emerged by the beginning of this century, were the Socialists-Revolutionists and the Social-Democrats. The Socialists-Revolutionists, or S.-R., were the offshoot of the People's Will, the terrorist organization of the Populists. They retained much of the ideology of People's Will and Populism, particularly the agrarian socialist ideas, fitted to the peculiar Russian land organization. In politics, they continued to believe in an agrarian revolution, and adhered to terrorism, that is, to the policy of assassinating undesirable government officials. The Social-Democrats, or S.-D., were Marxists. They believed in the industrial character of the impending revolution, and placed chief reliance in the emerging, though numerically weak, industrial proletariat; they opposed individual terror. In 1903, at the London Congress of the S.-D. Party, a split occurred in its ranks. The majority faction, the Bolsheviks, held out for a tightly knit professional revolutionary organization, while the minority faction, the Mensheviks, continued to favor a looser, liberal formation.

Meanwhile, there was discontent. After the unsuccessful Russo-Japanese War, as after the Crimean War half a century earlier, there was a great unrest and searching of the minds on the part of the Russian intelligentsia. The same old question arose: what good is autocracy if it can not even protect the country from the external foe? Directed by various revolutionary elements, a series of strikes and armed uprisings broke out which threatened, for a time, to upset the throne. Nicholas II saved his crown, for the time being, by granting the people a minimum of civil liberties embodied in the Constitution of October 30, 1905. The edge was taken off the revolution by these measures, but the discontented elements remained discontented. When it became evident that the first World War was being lost, many blamed the inefficiency of the government and its reluctance to call upon the democratic strata of society for coöperation. Early in 1917, food riots in Petrograd (St. Petersburg) quickly got out of hand, and developed into a full-fledged revolution. The Tsar and his government were deposed, and the nominal power was assumed by the Provisional Committee of the State Duma, which formed the Provisional Government (Vremennoye Pravitel'stvo).

Meanwhile, the rising industrialism was finding its reflection in literature. Since Pushkin, each epoch in literature is easily identified by three outstanding names. The first part of the nineteenth century was dominated by Pushkin, Gogol, and Lermontov. The second part is anchored around the names of Turgenev, Dostoevsky, and Tolstoy. Modern Russian literature is easily placed around three outstanding writers: Chekhov, Andreyev, and Maxim Gorky (pseudonym for Aleksei Peshkov—1868-1936). Of this trinity, Gorky served as the reflection of social-democratic and revolutionary moods. Gorky's rise coincides with the rise of the proletariat in Russia, even though his earlier writings deal more with *lumpenproletariat,* the "hobo proletariat," than with the workers.

Gorky's distinctive characteristic, apart from his working-class origin, was his cheerfulness, a new tone in Russian literature, particularly in the nineties. The Russian reading public, which had become accustomed to the minor key of Chekhov and kept either quietly smiling or quietly weeping with its beloved writer of the twilight, suddenly became aware of a raucous, full-throated voice that came from the bottom of Russian life. A new and unfamiliar character—nay, a hero—paraded across Russian literature, the hobo, the tramp. What was even more strange, this tramp was not apologizing for his presence either in literature or in life. Indeed, he was obviously proud of himself, and treating the rest of Russian population, both rich and poor, with pity and contempt. He was equally contemptuous of the official, the merchant, or the peasant, so long as they worked for their daily bread. Gorky of this period, early and middle nineties, appears as a spokesman for homemade Russian anarchism, only one step removed from hooliganism.

Gorky's early ideal is expressed in two "songs," "*Pesnia o Sokolie*" (*Song of the Falcon*), and *Pesnia o Burevestnike* (*Song of the Storm-Petrel*), beautifully written blank-verse poems. Both are battle-cries. The first ends with a line which became famous, "To the madness of the brave we sing our song!"; and the second ends with no less famous words, "Let the storm break out fiercer!" Later, when Gorky made his acquaintance with Lenin and other Social-Democratic leaders of Bolshevik persuasion, he changed his early anarchist attitude to that of the Social-Democrats. He did not become a fanatical Communist—there is some justification in support of the view that he never became a Communist at all—but he was the only one of the major writers who was of a respectably proletarian origin, and he was one of the very few writers who felt no marked hostility to the Bolshevik revolution.

In the period from the early nineties, until the Russo-Japanese War, Gorky's cheerful voice was contrasted with Chekhov's minor key. From 1905 to the outbreak of the War of 1914, it rang as a counterbalance to the pessimistic Andreyev. But his forte remained the portrayal of things as he knew them at first hand. That is why his best work is to be found in the early tramp stories, his several autobiographies (*My Childhood; In the World; My University Days*), and the play *On the Bottom* (also translated as *The Lower Depths, Down and Out,* etc.). This play is merely a series of scenes showing the lives of the members of the city proletariat, as well as the underworld, the people "on the bottom" of life.

A series of works and writers bobbed to the surface of literary life in Russia in the interim between the two revolutions, 1905 to 1917, but they are too numerous to be surveyed here, and many of them seem not very revealing for an understanding of the broad growth of Russian letters. Men like Alexander Kuprin (1870-1938) and Mikhail Artzybashev (1878-1927) were significant but scarcely typical. One of the best known is Ivan Bunin (1870-   ) who, curiously enough, is the only Russian writer ever to receive the Nobel Prize for literature, although the Prize was being awarded during the lifetime of Tolstoy, Chekhov, and Gorky. Bunin's prose is polished and technically competent, without much inner fire. He is not excited over anything and, one feels, he does not particularly love anything or anyone. A case in point is his long narrative, *Derevnia (The Village)*, published in 1911, in which with clinical precision and detached curiosity he observes the most revolting manifestations of life of a Russian village. His account is as detached as if written by a foreign observer of the Zulu tribe. Unlike Chekhov, Andreyev, or Gorky, Bunin created no mood, founded no school, and has no disciples.

THE SOVIET PERIOD

This is not the place to recount the steps by which the democratic elements represented in the Provisional Government lost control to the Bolsheviks and the mass of war-weary soldiers. With the triumph of the extremist elements late in 1917, the majority of the established writers emigrated as soon as they could conveniently do so. Later, in some instances much later, some of them returned. Thus, the Soviet phase of Russian literature is marked by the appearance of new, young writers, with a somewhat different outlook and a different attitude. Of the old-time writers, who remained with the Bolsheviks and their revolution, the most prominent was Gorky. His best and most significant works, however, had been written before the revolution. After the revolution, he gradually became a symbol, not to say a figurehead, of revolutionary writing. He was honored almost to the point of canonization, but it is among the younger writers that we must look for the new developments, when and if they manifest themselves.

On the whole, the Soviet period of Russian literature failed to produce anything of comparable significance to the literature of the previous epoch, particularly to the high-water mark of the nineteenth century. There were several reasons for that. First, the country has lived under the driving force of increasing industrial production, to the neglect of cultural values. Lenin's famous equation, "Electrification plus Soviet Power equals Socialism," enunciated in 1921 and under which the country has been managed, put the land of the Soviets under the compelling necessity of building up "electrification," that is, a powerful industrial machine. The most productive and vital forces of the country were drawn into industrial production rather than into the realm of fine arts or literature. Secondly, the tight regimentation of every phase of public life has had an adverse effect upon the inspiration and freedom of expression of the Soviet writers and would-be writers. It became not merely unpopular, but downright dangerous, to express thoughts and moods which might be construed as impeding the progress of industrial development, which, for a considerable part, has been carried out under the threat of impending, later actual, war. Thirdly, the methods of censorship and control over individual writers have become greatly refined and perfected, compared to the Tsar's regime. The examples of writers who were severely reprimanded and declared "enemies of the people" for their real or imagined ideological divergences from the "Party line" were too vivid to inspire anything but fear, a poor substitute for artistic inspiration. Some of the younger writers, who might be genuinely inspired by the Bolshevik ideals, are too inexperienced and too lacking in tradition to produce anything of literary significance, even though they are trying. The artificial demand for "proletarian literature" —whatever that term may mean—has had a doubly sterilizing effect upon literary effort. In the first place, it inhibited the development of form (style), for to continue in the tradition of the pre-revolutionary literature might be construed as a "bourgeois" preoccupation. In the second place, it became too dangerous to select the content, the subject matter, without first consulting proper authorities.

Despite this strait jacket, some first-rate work has been done. Mention here may be made of two writers. First, Aleksey Tolstoy

(1882-1944), who was a writer of note before the revolution. In 1918, he was violently opposed to the Bolsheviks and fled abroad. In emigration, he started his masterpiece *Khozhdenie po Mukam* (*The Road to Calvary*), also translated as *Darkness and Dawn*. It was to be a trilogy covering the period just before the revolution, the revolution itself, and the post-revolutionary epoch. When he came to portraying the actual revolution and the period immediately following, he decided that he needed a closer look at Russia to write intelligently. His attitude to the Bolsheviks mellowed into the acceptance of the revolution, and he was permitted to return to Russia. That was in 1924, and for two decades thereafter he continued to write in the Soviet Union. However, nothing he wrote since can compare with *The Road to Calvary*.

Mikhail Sholokhov (1902-   ) is the one writer who inspires hope for the eventual reëmergence of significant literature in Russia. He is almost entirely a Soviet product, and he is the author of what appears to date the most ambitious work of a Soviet writer, *Tikhii Don* (*The Quiet Don*). In some aspects, and with certain reservations, the work may be compared to Leo Tolstoy's *War and Peace*. It is the story of the people of the Don River region, which was known in pre-revolutionary Russia as *Oblast' Voiska Donskovo* (The Domain of the Don Army), and of the impact of the war and revolution on them. The author is honest in recording the reactions of his heroes, whether they point to the right or to the left—he was on occasion severely rebuked by Soviet critics for this "deviation"—and he possesses the first-hand knowledge of his people and milieu. *The Quiet Don* is the only Soviet literary work which can unblushingly take its place alongside the literary masterpieces of the past.

BIBLIOGRAPHY

BIBLIOGRAPHY

GRIERSON, Philip, *Books on Soviet Russia, 1917-1942*: A Bibliography and Guide to Reading (London, 1943).

Inventar biblioteki universiteta: Catalogus occusionum bibliothecae imperialis literarum universitatis (St. Petersburg, 1893).

Katalog ruskshikh knig biblioteki umperato rskovo St. Petersburg skovo universiteta (St. Petersburg, 1897-1902).

MOHRENSCHILDT VON, D. S., "Books in English on Russian Literature, 1917-1942," *The Russian Review*, vol. II (1942), pp. 122-128.

Russia: A Check List Preliminary to a Basic Bibliography of Materials in the Russian Language (Washington, 1944), pt. 1, Belles.

SCHMIDT, John J., *Russian Literature, Including Ukrainian* (Chicago, 1918).

Contains preface, table of contents, captions, author index, etc. in Russian and English.

VITNAM, A., *Vosem let russkoi khudozhestvennoi literatury, 1917-1925* (Moscow, Leningrad, 1926).

Other Slavic Literatures

JANEČEK, Blanche, "Bibliography of Czech Literature in English Translation," *Bulletin of Bibliography*, vol. XVI (1937), pp. 47-49, 70-71, 98, 111.

KERNER, R. J., *Slavic Europe: A Selected Bibliography in the Western European Languages* (Cambridge, Mass., 1918).

Incomplete and out of date.

STANOYEVITCH, Milivoy S., *Slavonic Nations of Yesterday and Today* (New York, 1925).

LITERARY HISTORY AND CRITICISM

AIKHENVALD, Iu I., *Siluety russkikh pisatelei* (Berlin, 1923).

ANICHKOVA, A. M. (Avinova), *La pensée russe contemporaine* (Paris, 1903).

Partial contents: Chekhov, Gorki, Korolenko, Tolstoy.

BARING, Maurice, *Landmarks in Russian Literature* (London, 1916).

BRANDES, Georg, *Impressions of Russia* (New York, 1889).

BRONSTEIN, L. D. (L. D. Trotsky), *Literature and Revolution*, trans. by Rose Strunsky (New York, 1925).

BRÜCKNER, Alexander, *A Literary History of Russia,* trans. by H. Havelock (London and Leipzig, 1908).

IVANOV, Razumnick Vasilevich, *Russkaya literatura ot semidesiatych godov do nashikh dnei* (Moscow, 1938).
Thirteen pages of bibliography.

KROPOTKIN, P. A., *Ideals and Realities in Russian Literature* (New York, 1925).
Twelve pages of bibliographical notes.

LEGER, Louis Paul, ed., *La littérature russe: notices et extraits de principaux auteurs depuis les origines jusqu'a nos jours* (Paris, 1892).

LUTHER, Arthur, *Geschichte der russischen Literatur* (Leipzig, 1924).

LVOV-ROGACHEVSKII, V. L., *Noveishaya russkaya literatura* (Moscow; 1925).
Thirty-three pages of bibliography.

MANDELSHTAM, R. S., *Khudozhestvennaya literatura v otsenke russkoi marksistskoi kritiki; bibliograficheskii ukazatel* (Moscow, 1928).

MASARYK, Thomas G., *The Spirit of Russia: Studies in History, Literature, and Philosophy* (London and New York, 1919), 2 vols.
Contains a good bibliography.

MILIUKOV, Paul, *Outlines of Russian Culture,* Michael Karpovich, ed., Valentine Ughet and Eleanor Davis, trans. (Philadelphia, 1942), 3 vols.
Often considered most authoritative. Part 2 concerns literature.

MIRSKY, Prince D. S., *A History of Russian Literature, from the Earliest Times to the Death of Dostoyevsky (1881)* (New York, 1934).

———, *Contemporary Russian Literature,* 1881-1925 (London and New York, 1926).

OLGIN, M. J., *A Guide to Russian Literature (1820-1919)* (New York, 1920).

OVSIANIKO-KULIKOVSKI, Dmitrii, Nikolaevich, ed., *Istoriia russkoi literatury, XIX Vieka* (Moscow, 1908-1911).

PERSKY, Serge M., *Contemporary Russian Novelists* (Boston, 1913).
Partial contents: Chekhov, Korolenko, Veresaev, Gorki, Andreyev, Merezhkovskii, Kuprin.

SLONIN, M. L., *Portrety sovetskikh pisatelei* (Paris, 1933).

SNOW, Valentine, *Russian Writers: a Bio-biographical Dictionary* (New York, 1946).
The period from Catherine II to the Revolution of October, 1917.

TKHORZHEVSKII, Ivan, *Russkaya literatura* (Paris, 1946), 2 vols., vol. 1, to Tolstoy and Dostoevski; vol. 2, to its date.

Other Slavic Literatures

CHUBODA, F., *A Short Survey of Czech Literature* (London, 1924).
A good cursory literary history.

Columbia Dictionary of Modern European Literature (New York, 1947).
DYBOSKI, Roman, *Periods of Polish Literary History* (London, 1923).
For the early years.
——, *Modern Polish Literature* (London, 1924).
There is no good history of Polish literature in English. These two works are probably the best of available references.
LEDBETTER, Eleanor E., *Polish Literature in English Translation* (New York, 1932).
NIEDERLE, Lubro, *Manuel d l'antiquité slave* (Paris, 1923-1926), 2 vols.
The best introduction to Slavic beginnings.
PTOCEK, Cyril J., *Ss. Cyril and Methodius, Apostles of the Slavs* (New York, 1941).
PYPIN, A. N., and SPASOVIC, V. D., *Geschichte der slavischen Literaturen* (Leipzig, 1884), 2 vols.
The standard work for readers of German.
RIEDL, Frederick, *A History of Hungarian Literature; Short Histories of the Literatures of the World Series*, no. 13 (London, 1906).
SELVER, Paul, *Czechoslovak Literature* (London, 1942).
TALVJ, Mrs. Robinson, *Historical View of the Languages and Literatures of the Slavic Nations* (New York, 1850).
Reputedly the best study in English.

ANTHOLOGY

BECHLOFER, Carl E., *A Russian Anthology in English* (New York, 1917).
BOWRA, C. M., *A Book of Russian Verse* (London, 1943).
Although brief, probably the best anthology of verse.
COURNOS, John, *A Treasury of Russian Life and Humor* (New York, 1943).
COXWELL, Charles F., *Russian Poems* (London, 1929).
DEUTSCH, Babette, and YARMOLINSKY, Avahm, *Modern Russian Poetry* (London, 1923).
Good biographical notes.
GUERNEY, Bernhard, *A Treasury of Russian Literature* (New York, 1943).
Very good.
NOYES, George R., *Masterpieces of Russian Drama* (New York and London, 1933).
Contains twelve plays, 1782-1921, with a bibliography.
REAVEY, G., *Soviet Literature: an Anthology* (London, 1933).
WIENER, Leo, *Anthology of Russian Literature from the Earliest Period to the Present Time* (New York and London, 1902-1903), 2 vols.
Contains much material not readily available elsewhere, and a good bibliography.

YARMOLINSKY, Avrahm, *A Treasury of Great Russian Short Stories* (New York, 1944).
This is perhaps the best edited of collections of short stories.

Other Slavic Literatures

COLEMAN, Marian Moore, *The Polish Land: An Anthology in Prose and Verse* (New York, 1944).
Perhaps the best for its area.

KIRKCONNELL, Watson, *The Magyar Muse: An Anthology of Hungarian Poetry* (Winnipeg, 1936).
The best for Hungarian verse.

MANN, Klaus, and KESTEN, Hermann, *Heart of Europe* (New York, 1943).

SELVER, Paul, *Anthology of Modern Slavonic Literature, in Prose and Verse*, with an introduction and literary notes (New York and London, 1919).

UNDERWOOD, Edna W., *The Slav Anthology* (Portland, Me., 1931).

TRANSLATION

Of the many and varied translations from the Russian, the most dependable on the whole are those by Constance Garnett, though it must be added that they are rarely if ever brilliant. Leo Tolstoy is best translated by his authorized biographer, A. Maude. Izabel Hapgood's translations, particularly those of Turgenev's works, are very bad.

GARNETT, Constance, *The Works of Anton Chekhov* (New York, 1929), 9 vols. in one.

——, *Feodor Dostoevsky, Novels* (New York, 1914-1922), 12 vols.

——, *The Works of Nicolay Gogol* (London, 1922-1928), 6 vols.

——, *The Novels of Ivan Turgenev* (New York, 1906-1921), 17 vols.

The Tolstoy Society, *The Works of Leo Tolstoy* (London, 1928-1937), 21 vols.

YARMOLINSKY, Avrahm, *The Works of Alexander Pushkin* (New York, 1936).

13

Latin American Literature

MADALINE W. NICHOLS
UNIVERSITY OF NEW MEXICO

Latin Americans who do not love norteamericanos *are inclined to say we have too little interest in our Southern neighbors and too little knowledge of them. For whomever these charges may be valid, they are not for* DR. MADALINE W. NICHOLS, *who holds the only doctoral degree awarded at the University of California in the general field of Latin American studies, and is the author of numerous works which have been translated into Spanish and Portuguese and cordially received south of the border, as well as in the United States. These include her doctoral dissertation on the gaucho, her biography of the Argentinian, Sarmiento, and a* Bibliographical Guide to Materials on American Spanish (*Harvard University Press*). *She has a wide teaching background* (*at Dominican College, Goucher, Duke University, the University of California at Los Angeles, Florida State University*), *and is presently at the University of New Mexico, which maintains an unusually lively interest in Latin America and Latin American studies.*

Latin American Literature

IN DESCRIBING Cuba in the journal of his sea voyage to that Orient he sought in the West, Columbus wrote that never had he beheld "so fair a thing." He had found "trees all along the river, beautiful and green and different from ours, with flowers and fruit each according to their kind, and little birds which sing very sweetly." Indeed all America was new and, most of all, its inexplicable inhabitants. Swift description followed. From the literature telling the wonders of the new land came—and still comes—one of America's main contributions to the literature of the world.

America was discovered, explored, and settled at a singularly propitious moment in literary expression. After the awakening of the Renaissance, the European world had turned startled eyes to the mysteries of the Orient; brave Portuguese mariners had challenged the unknown perils of a seemingly interminable African coast. It was a time when all marvels must have seemed possible, and those which had already found literary reflection in novels of chivalry and adventure soon proved to be no more strange than reality itself. The American Indian, with his robes made from the brilliantly colored feathers of tropical birds; the golden plated temples of Cuzco; the chocolate and tobacco and potato and corn; the macaw and weirdly spined iguana; the decorative motif of the feathered serpent and the mocking indecipherability of Mayan stelae; the heathenish painted books and the mysterious knots of the *quipu*; the architectural masses of the pyramid builders or such megalithic monuments as the fortress of Sacsahuaman—all fitted naturally into already familiar literary patterns. The unreal had merely become real. Real and unreal fused, and that fusion found its reflection in such literary masterpieces as the letters[1] of Hernán Cortés to the Emperor Charles V, Bernal Díaz del Castillo's *True History of the Conquest of New Spain*,[2] and the *Royal Commentaries*[3] of the Inca, Garcilaso de la Vega. And then, with fighting and death ever accompanying conquest, the story was also poured into the more heroic mold of the epic poem—it, too, a literary fashion of the day—to fashion Ercilla's *The Araucaniad*.[4]

COLONIAL LITERARY BEGINNINGS

But beside such outstanding literary portrayals of the new American scene and the rigors of conquest, America, in the long three-hundred-year colonial period, also made her contribution to the literature primarily designed to reveal human personality. Two names recall writers whose work has stood the test of time: that of Juan Ruiz de Alarcón, who still ranks as one of Latin America's best humorists, her only great playwright, and one of the great creators of character of all time; and that of the nun Sor Juana Inés de la Cruz, whose verse is enduringly human because she dared to write from her heart. Behind the curtain of Gongoristic expression and the baroque involutions of literary style, Sor Juana was a woman who felt as women do and wrote that feeling beautifully in words that accordingly will live.

Brazilian colonial literature, according to one Brazilian critic,

[1] *Five Letters* (1519-1526), trans. J. Bayard Morris (New York, 1925).

[2] Written in the mid-sixteenth century but not published until 1632. The edition quoted here was *The Memoirs of the Conquistador Bernal Díaz del Castillo. Containing a True and Full Account of the Discovery and Conquest of Mexico and New Spain*, trans. by John I. Lockhart (London, 1844), 2 vols.
See also, *The True History of the Conquest of New Spain*, trans. by Maurice Keatinge (New York, 1938).

[3] Published in 1609 and 1617. For translation, see *Royal Commentaries of the Incas*, trans. by Clements R. Markham (London, 1869-1871), 2 vols. [Publications of the Hakluyt Society, vols. 41, 45.]

[4] The three parts of *La Araucana* were published in 1569, 1578, and 1589. For translation, see *The Araucaniad*, trans. by Charles M. Lancaster and Paul T. Manchester (Nashville, 1945).
See also, *La Araucana, The Epic of Chile*, trans. by Walter Owen (Buenos Aires, 1945), pt. 1.

remained ever "unsoiled by the rough facts of life." Perhaps, indeed, "rough" facts found no proper reflection in the literature of the time, but Brazilian life in its more romantic aspects appears in two epic poems, *The Uruguay*, by José Basílio da Gama (1740-1795), and *Caramurú*, by Friar José de Santa Rita Durão (1722-1784), while the lyric poetry of Thomaz Antônio Gonzaga (1744-*ca*. 1807) has been called the best love poetry in the Portuguese language. Far closer to reality, however, was Brazil's satiric poet, Gregório de Mattos (1633-1696), who compares with the Spanish American Juan del Valle y Caviedes (1652-*ca*. 1695) from the viceroyalty of Peru.

The primarily descriptive literature of colonial times reflects all the proprietary thrill of discovery in new lands. It is in this vein that Columbus writes, and Cortés, and Bernal Díaz. They, personally, have found this new world and conquered in it, and it is good. Descriptions are graphic; the narrative proceeds with appropriate vigor.

From the purely literary point of view, however, Bernal Díaz del Castillo (1492-1584) contributed much more than his descriptions of New Spain and a straightforward narrative of its conquest. His words have left on the printed page the living characters of the old conquistador himself, of the leader he followed, and of the men with whom he served. Indeed, in literatures still strangely weak in character portrayal, the *True History* presents to world literature a whole gallery of characters who are today no less vitally alive because their prototypes once lived in the flesh rather than only in an author's imagination. There were many heroic men in those days of conquest, but it was the literary skill of Bernal Díaz that brought to a few of them their measure of immortality.

As for himself, one of the main interests of Bernal Díaz had ever been his own good name. First, as a soldier; then, as one who spoke truly; finally, as author. In this final respect, he wrote:

After I had completed this my history, two licentiates called upon me and begged permission of me to peruse it, in order that they might acquaint themselves better with the history of the conquest of Mexico and of New Spain . . . As ignorant persons, like myself, always learn something from men of learning, I gave it to them, but under the condition that they should neither add nor take anything away from it; as everything I had related was conformable to truth. When the licentiates had read through the whole of my work, one of them who was a great rhetorician, said he was astonished at the sharpness of my memory, that I should not even have forgotten one single circumstance of the many things that had taken place . . . With respect to the style of writing, both remarked that it was plain old Castilian, which was more agreeable at the time than those embellished sentences which are generally affected by historians; and that though my style was plain it was rendered beautiful by the truth which it contained. They were, however, of opinion that I had written too conspicuously about myself, in describing the battles at which I was present, and that I should have left this to others. I ought also, they said, to have quoted other historians to confirm my statements, instead of dryly saying: This I did, This happened to me; for, added they, I was only witnessing for myself.

Bernal Díaz then continued:

. . . With respect to the reproach they made me of having spoken too much in my own praise, and that all this self-praise would have come with a better grace from others, I desired them to bear in mind, that there are indeed certain virtues and excellent qualities which we ought never to praise in ourselves, but let our neighbours do it for us; but how is it possible for a neighbour to mention anything in the praise of another if he was not present at the battle with him? Are the sparrows, said I, to speak of it, who flew over our heads during the engagements? or the clouds, that floated on high? Who can speak better about it than we, the officers and soldiers, the men who themselves fought the battles? Your reproach, gentlemen, would have been very just, continued I, if in my history you had found that I had withheld the praise that was due to the officers and soldiers who were my companions in arms, and I had claimed all the honour to myself; but I have not even said so much in my own praise as I could, and indeed ought to have done; but I write that my name may not be forgotten . . . It should therefore be no matter of surprise to anyone, when I mention a few words about myself, in describing the battles at which I was present, that future generations may say: this Bernal Díaz del Castillo wrote, in order that his children and descendants might share in the praise of his heroic deeds. . . .

The key to the man's character lies in that final sentence, with all its eternally human appeal, for who, among all mankind, has not longed to leave behind some memory of his name?

Throughout the work there is this constant preoccupation with good repute. Bernal Díaz was ever generous in praise of his comrades and as jealous of their fame as of his own. His book was written not only in the humanly pathetic endeavor to leave to his children his own unblemished and honored name—since human justice had brought him few more worldly goods—but to leave a similar inheritance to the children of his old comrades as well. Father López de Gómara may indeed write an official history of the conquest, giving all the praise to Cortés, but Cortés did not conquer alone. In simple justice his fame should be bound with the fame of all. And so—after telling the wonder of all the brave deeds—Bernal Díaz writes the names of the humble men who followed their leader and fought, that all together they might win glory for king and Spain and God. And he tells, too, how those humble men died.

But after they died, Bernal Díaz gave them a new life. There were Diego de Ordas, he who dared to climb the volcano Popocatepetl; stout Alonso Hernández Puerto Carrero, who died so miserably in a Spanish prison; Father Olmedo, wise and shrewd and "a capital singer" besides; Juan Catalán, with his useful skill in "charming wounds" so that they marvelously grew well. Juan Velásquez de León passes with a bit of a swagger. A man of "elegant carriage and powerful stature," he had

a winning countenance; his beard looked majestic; a heavy gold chain hung from his shoulder in graceful folds, and sat well on this courageous and spirited officer.

Then came that young soldier "of astonishing courage," Cristóbal de Olea, who twice saved the life of Cortés and so finally lost his own.

He was twenty-six years of age when he joined our ranks. He was of middling stature; his limbs were strong and beautifully proportioned; his chest and shoulders broad; his face was full and cheerful; his hair and beard curly, his voice clear and strong.

Picture after picture flashes by, as with the subtle magic of his words Bernal Díaz brings his comrades back to life.

Such skill in characterization makes this book still unique in Latin American literature. Stylistically, it has many other merits. Bernal Díaz notes that wise men have said "that honesty and truth are the true ornaments of history" and he plans a book that shall be *true,* even as his title promises. He readily makes the reader identify himself with the conquerors and feel their wonder and their fear as they advance into a hostile and strange new land. The element of suspense is used with marvelous effectiveness in the narrative, which is, as well, rich in picturesque detail. Throughout, there are flashes of dry humor or the hearty belly laughter of such an occasional anecdote as that story of the braggart Salvatierra and how he lost his horse, at which the Spaniards "laughed and rejoiced as if nothing but mirth and pleasure awaited us . . . and we no longer gave it a thought we should have to fight a battle next day, and measure our strength with five times our numbers." Conquest was not all tragedy.

Toward the end of his book Bernal Díaz wrote, "And here I must relate something after the manner of a dialogue." He imagines that he speaks with "illustrious Fame" who asks what rewards have been granted to the conquistadores who escaped alive from all the great battles. In reply, Bernal Díaz tells of the malice and envy of those who have sought to cast their heroic deeds into oblivion, that Fame may not praise them according to their deserts. "Know then, O Fame, that of the 550 warriors who sailed with Cortés from Cuba, that there are now . . . only five of us alive. . . ." He then begs Fame to lift up her "excellent and honest voice, and resound" their deeds throughout the whole world. This, Fame promises that she will do.

Fame has kept her promise. The *True History of the Conquest of New Spain* now stands proudly on Spanish bookshelves beside that other great story of conquest, the *Don Quijote* of Miguel de Cervantes.

INTEREST IN THE INDIANS

In the writing of the Inca Garcilaso and of Ercilla the primary literary emphasis is turned from the deeds of the conquerors to the lives and manners of the Indians. This is particularly true of the *Royal Commentaries,* a primary source record of the Indian civilization of Peru, which the Inca Garcilaso de la Vega (1539-1616) wrote sometime between his departure from the country in 1560 and the publication of the first part of his book in 1609, in Spain. Himself the descendant of a Spanish captain and an Inca princess, the author wrote with authority. That the telling is smoothly and pleasantly done, makes his book a work of literary merit as well.

The change in point of view is even more definite in *The Araucaniad,* by Alonso de Ercilla y Zúñiga (1533-1594), who glorifies in epic form the fateful struggle of the Indian against the Spanish invader. Here the Indians almost become the heroes of the tragedy. In further contrast with the *True History,* interest turns to the consciously sought literary excellence of the verse quite as much as to the truth of the narrative or any psychological penetration into human character. The poetry, however, is beautiful; references to the native scene are picturesque and often of historical value, and the theme of the defense of their land by a brave people falls fittingly into the epic mold. Not the least of the modern charms of *The Araucaniad* is the long memory of its successful utilization in the literary revenge of a wrathful poet against his unreasonable military superior.

Brazilian literature also utilized the Indian in its colonial poetry, but with a significant difference from the Spanish American approach to the theme. Much of this difference is a matter of period, for the best epic poems that have come down from Brazilian colonial times belong to the eighteenth century. Indians are now far less realistic than those met in conquest times. *The Uruguay* (1769) may tell the struggle of Spain and Portugal against the Uruguayan Indians in 1756, but Lindoya, the beautiful Indian girl of the poem, dies in the most approved romantic style,[5] while in *The Araucaniad* there was no true heroine at all. The masculine Homeric tone of the Spanish epic dies away in the Brazilian into the softer melody of the romantic legends that were to follow early in the next century.

The epic poem *Caramurú* (1781) moves even farther from reality. Shipwrecked near Bahía, Diogo Alvares Correa meets and marries the Indian girl, Paraguassu. He then sails away with her to many adventures in Europe, where the bride becomes a Christian and is named Catherine after her new godmother, who is no less a person than Catherine de' Medici! After the couple return to Brazil, Paraguassu-Catherine renounces all rights to her Indian kingdom in favor of her new Christian sovereign, João III. Obviously the plot of this novel in verse relates it both back to the romance of chivalry and ahead to romanticism. As Arturo Torres Ríoseco has shrewdly noted,[6] the so-called "Indianism" of this poem "is no more genuine than the artificial chivalric atmosphere" of *The Araucaniad* or the "pseudo-Indianism" that was to come in the second half of the nineteenth century as one of the aspects of romanticism.

In contrast with the exuberance of these late Brazilian epics is the thoughtful return to the study of human personality found in the two great Spanish American authors of the seventeenth century—Juan Ruiz de Alarcón (*ca.* 1580-1639) and Sor Juana Inés de la Cruz (1651-1695). In the fashion ever typical of the olden conquistadores, modern Spanish critics seem to be conquering Alarcón for the literature of Spain. While his plays[7] were

[5] For a translation of the excerpt, "Death of Lindoya," see L. E. Elliott, in *Pan American Magazine*, vol. XXVIII (1919), p. 250.

[6] *The Epic of Latin American Literature* (New York, 1942), p. 221.

[7] Strangely, only one play by Juan Ruiz de Alarcón has been translated into English, *La Verdad Sospechosa*. See "The Truth Suspected," trans. by J. del Toro and R. V. Finney, in *Poet Lore*, vol. XXXVIII (1927), pp. 475-530.

Among other famous plays were *Las paredes oyen, Ganar amigos, El examen de maridos, Los favores del mundo, No hay mal que por bien no venga.* In all there were twenty-three plays. Carefully edited by Alarcón himself, they were published in two volumes in 1628 and 1634.

indeed written in Spain and while they were of an excellence that might well be envied by any national literature of any time, it may be remembered that Juan Ruiz de Alarcón was born in Mexico, that there he received most of his education, and that he had passed his thirtieth year before he finally left his native land. Certainly Mexico has her own valid claim to his work, even though Alarcón wrote, not specifically of Mexico, but of mankind. His plays are universal in their appeal. They belong to Mexican literature, to Spanish literature, and to the literature of the world.

There is no challenge to Mexico's claim to the work of Sor Juana,[8] though again—as in the plays of Alarcón—it achieved greatness through a portrayal of universal human truth rather than from the reflection of any native scene. Indeed, in literary fashion, Sor Juana's poetry seems more closely related to Spanish literature than were the plays of her famous countryman; therein, in the affectation of her time, lies the occasional weakness of her verse. But Sor Juana's native skill overcame the handicaps of Gongorist conceit and, when most deeply moved, she abandoned all false ornamentation. Because she loved, and wrote of a woman's love in all its self-sacrifice, sincerity and passion, but with a restraint, dignity, simplicity and directness indicative of its depth, her poetry gave expression to emotion that is of universal and eternal appeal. There have been few love poems in the world's literature that can compare with her sonnet "Esta tarde, mi bien, . . ." a sonnet, incidentally, for which no adequate translation into the English language seems as yet to have been made.[9]

That Sor Juana had the grace of humor, adds to the charm of

[8] See the edition of her *Poesías* by Ermilo Abreu Gómez (Mexico, 1940).

[9] Although Elizabeth Seldon has done an excellent translation of the first stanza, as quoted in Torres Ríoseco, *op. cit.*, p. 38. See also, T. Walsh, *The Catholic Anthology* (New York, 1932), p. 215.

For other examples of her love poetry, see "The Lost Love," as trans. by Peter H. Goldsmith, in *The Hispanic Anthology* (New York, 1920), pp. 357-359, and the "Redondillas" on the torment of love—"Este amoroso tormento."

such poems as the "Autorretrato en que se burla de los ripios" and in the lines "To her portrait." [10] That she pled for greater justice in man to woman, adds an unfortunate modernity to the appeal of one of her most famous poems—the "Redondillas . . . a la inconsecuencia de los hombres," [11] and to her autobiographical letter in prose to "Sor Philotea de la Cruz."

ROMANTICISM AND NATIONAL LITERATURES

The literary transition from the colonial period to nineteenth century romanticism is ideally marked by the *Marilia of Dirceu* (1792) by the Brazilian Thomaz Antônio Gonzaga. It was because of the poet's personal participation in the attempted rebellion of 1789 against the governor of the province of Minas Gerais that he was condemned to exile in Angola and separated from his Marilia. His book sings his love with an unrestrained expression of personal emotion which is as romantic as the poet's own political activity which anticipated the whirlpool of the revolutions that were to follow.

The distinctively national literatures of Latin America began with the independent existence of the Spanish American republics and the Brazilian Empire in the early nineteenth century. With freedom from old controls, the general world literary currents flowed into America where they had their own peculiar distortion. Here the slow rhythm of the great world movements presented a new and quicker beat in the tempo of American literature. Classicism, romanticism, realism and its natural daughter, Parnassianism, and symbolism—all find their distinctive expression in America. The world social revolution is there tele-

---

[10] For translation, see Beatrice Proske, in *Translations from Hispanic Poets* (New York, 1938), p. 220. This book is hereafter referred to as *Hispanic Poets*.

[11] Trans. by Peter H. Goldsmith, *Hispanic Anthology*, pp. 360-362; by Garrett Strange, *The Catholic Anthology*, pp. 215-216; and Alice Stone Blackwell, in her *Some Spanish American Poets* (Philadelphia, 1937), pp. 150-153.

scoped into a clearer pattern. The course of the American national literatures follows the warp of national history; its woof is in the fashion of the literary expression of the day. With his usual intuition, the great Argentine literary critic, Ricardo Rojas, has noted this double character of works of art in a modern world. The subject should come, he believes, from the real life of the individual or the social group to which he belongs; the manner of its expression, the literary technique, may well draw upon a study of world literature in order to progress in literary perfection.

The first reflection of America's new political freedom is found in the parallel literary freedom of romanticism. Liberty of every sort was in the air. Strangely, however, romanticism in America developed in a far more sober manner than was the case in Europe. Themes were more often drawn from the national scene as America studied herself rather than exotic foreign lands; escape from time was an escape into her own past. Because American romanticism ran so close to a new reality, it made its distinctive contribution. Again behind that contribution was the newness of America.

Yet America followed the traditional patterns of the new romantic school of writing. In Brazil, as in Europe, romanticism began with sentimentalism, to be followed by the later *mal du siècle* pose. As in Europe, it attempted a reconstruction of the past, with an emotional description of landscape and customs. Verses that were reminiscent of Lamartine were written by Domingos José Gonçalves de Magalhães (1811-1882), whose lachrymose poetry, like that of the French writers, often turned to religion for its consolation.

Brazilian romanticism was not all mere imitation; it conformed too naturally to the exuberance of the national temperament. In Antônio Gonçalves Dias (1823-1864), who even led the life of a true romantic and died, in the best romantic tradition, in a shipwreck, it produced the first great Brazilian poet. Like Lamartine, Gonçalves Dias told the beauties of nature; he differed from the French writer in his choice of a national, rather than a foreign, scene. Again, as Dr. Torres Ríoseco has noted,[12] his work is full of the vague nostalgic melancholy which is the traditional Portuguese *saudade* and which was so well represented in the famous "Song of exile."[13] Because of his *American Poems* (1846), he became known as the national poet of Brazil and the founder of the Indianist movement of that country.[14] Because of his attention to his country's social problem of slavery, he has also been called the first of Brazil's socially conscious poets.

Antônio de Castro Alves (1847-1871) followed this social trend indicated by Gonçalves Dias. Profoundly emotional, grandiose in the expression of that emotion, his eloquence reflected a turning from the mood of Lamartine to that of Victor Hugo. He and his followers are referred to as the *condoreira* school of poets; they are portrayed as soaring on the immensity of their grandiloquence, even as the Andean condor soars through the blue.[15]

In a final manifestation of changing romanticism, Manoel Antônio Alvares de Azevedo (1831-1852) and his followers represent a turning from the early melancholic interest in nature to an imitation of the French *mal du siècle* pose, with all its sentimental pessimism and disillusion.

In prose, romanticism in Brazil followed the French tradition of Chateaubriand with its sentimental regard for nature and its portrayal of the Indian as a "noble savage." The greatest of the romantic novelists—and the one most typical of the school—was José de Alencar (1829-1877). Such novels on the Indian theme as *The Guaraní* (1857) or *Iracema* (1865) illustrate the romantic

---

[12] Torres Ríoseco, *op. cit.*, p. 227.

[13] For translation, see L. E. Elliott, in *Pan American Magazine*, vol. XXIV (1916), p. 210. See also, "Marabá," trans. by A. B. Poore, in *Poet Lore*, vol. XV (Spring, 1904), p. 43.

[14] A noteworthy follower in this movement was Casimiro de Abreu (1837-1860).

[15] Torres Ríoseco, *op. cit.*, p. 230. Compare their work with that of the Argentine poet, Olegario Víctor Andrade (1839-1882), who in his famous poem, "The Condor's Nest," even utilized the condor specifically as a symbol. (Translation in Blackwell, *op. cit.*, pp. 314-327).

inteipretation of the Indian. But although *The Guarani* is an unlikely story of the spiritual love of an Indian for a white girl and *Iracema* that of an Indian maid for a Portuguese warrior,[16] the novels of Alencar are filled with beautiful pictures of Brazilian nature, and the telling is not without its special charm. And despite his romanticism, Alencar began a national trend to a utilization, in the novel, of the Brazilian scene in a manner far more realistic than the exotic portrayal of foreign lands found, for example, in Chateaubriand's *Atala*.

Another romantic writer who marks ever more clearly a transition towards realism, was Alfredo D'Escragnolle, Viscount Taunay (1843-1899). His masterpiece, *Inocência* (1882)[17] is the story of a young country girl betrothed by her father to a mature man for whom she feels only dismay and fear, while she is deeply in love with a young travelling "doctor" whom her father has casually invited into their home. The novel ends as the spurned lover murders his rival. Comic relief to the tragedy is sought in the character of another visitor in the home, a foreign naturalist who is wrongly suspected of dishonorable affection for the heroine. Despite all banality of such a plot, however, there is a charming freshness and simplicity in its telling. Romantic though they are, the characters appear alive, and there is evident realism in the description of a patriarchal society and its meticulous care of its women.

In Spanish America the romantic period was preceded by one of transition which lasted until 1830. Outstanding among the works of this time were, in prose, *The Itching Parrot* (1816)[18] by the Mexican José Joaquín Fernández de Lizardi (1774-1827), and the poetry of the Ecuadorian José Joaquín Olmedo (1780-1847), the Cuban José María Heredia (1803-1839), and the Venezuelan Andrés Bello (1781-1865).

---

[16] For translation of *Iracema*, see Sir Richard and Isabel Burton (London, 1886).

[17] Trans. by Henriqueta Chamberlain (New York, 1945).

[18] *El Periquillo Sarniento*, trans. by Katherine Anne Porter (New York, 1942).

Lizardi's *The Itching Parrot* was anything but romantic. A strangely late picaresque novel, it might far more logically have been expected in the colonial period when the picaresque genre was the literary fashion in Spain. It followed the standard plan of such novels, with the narrative of a series of loosely related episodes in the life of the main character. In its satire of Mexican society on the eve of independence, are the humor and realism typical of the picaresque. The novel reflected, however, the new political turmoil of its time, and in the long moralizing passages interspersed throughout the narrative the author expounds ideas on such subjects as pedagogy and social justice which reflect many a theory of the French encyclopedists.

The transitional poetry at first followed the European classical manner, but used American themes. It reflected political conflict, as in Olmedo's "La victoria de Junín; canto a Bolívar" (1825); it described the American scene, as in the poems by Heredia[19] and in Bello's "Silva a la agricultura de la zona tórrida." [20] In the melancholy of tone, however, and in the reflection of the poet's personal and emotional approach to his subject matter, this early national poetry was moving towards the romantic. Bello's self-confessed direct imitation of Victor Hugo, in his "La oración por todos," furnishes the definitive date of 1830 to mark a beginning of the new period.

America's outstanding example of the romantic novel—*María* (1867),[21] by the Colombian Jorge Isaacs (1837-1896)—illustrates the distinctive American emphasis upon a native scene. In traditional romantic fashion it tells the story of a frustrated and hopeless tragic young love. But in addition to the simple direct-

[19] Four of the most famous are included in the 1825 edition of his poetry. For translations, see "On the Temple Mound of Cholula," by Edna W. Underwood, in *West Indian Review*, vol. II (April, 1936), p. 42; "To the Sun," by Blackwell, *op. cit.*, pp. 486-491; "Hurricane" and "Ode to Niagara," both trans. by William Cullen Bryant and quoted in Alfred Coester's *Literary History of Spanish America* (New York, 1928), pp. 99-100 and 94-98.

[20] "The Agriculture of the Torrid Zone," trans. by T. Walsh, in *Hispanic Anthology*, pp. 390-394.

[21] Trans. by R. Ogden, as *Maria. A South American Romance* (New York, 1918).

ness of this ordinary plot, it carried the beautiful literary portrayal of a new Colombian scene and of the manners of Colombian society. The exuberance of romantic prose harmonizes with that of tropical nature. In the description of the Colombian scene, in the simplicity of the plot, and in the freshness of its telling, the tragedy comes close to reality.

Far more true, however, were the short prose sketches which Ricardo Palma called his *Peruvian Traditions*.[22] So personal in character that they have never been successfully imitated, these *Traditions* form one of the two great American contributions to the literature of romanticism. As Palma himself said of them when he gave his "recipe for writing traditions," they began with some episode of life in colonial Peru and then combined this dose of truth with quite a pleasant bit of lying. The little tales were light and merry; the telling was swift and humorous. Palma concluded: "The *tradition* is a popular tale, and it's not a popular tale; it's history, and it's not history." But while he thus willed a delicate problem to all the generations of library cataloguers, Ricardo Palma also left his own personal stamp upon a distinctive American gift to the literature of the world.

Outstanding names among the Spanish American romantic poets are those of the Argentine Esteban Echeverría (1805-1851), whose *Rhymes* (1837) contained the famous story in verse of "The Captive Woman"; Gertrudis Gómez de Avellaneda (1814-1873), best known for the sonnet written on leaving her native Cuba;[23] and the Uruguayan Juan Zorrilla de San Martín (1857-1931), whose poetic legend of *Tabaré* (1886)[24] possibly marks the height of that literary genre.

---

[22] Published in 10 vols. between 1872 and 1906. Many individual stories have been translated in *Inter America*. See vols. I-III, V-VII. See also, *The Knights of the Cape*, trans. by Harriet de Onís (New York, 1945).
[23] "Al partir." Trans. by Blackwell, *op. cit.*, pp. 490-491.
[24] Trans. by R. W. Huntington (Buenos Aires, 1934).

THE GAUCHO

But besides the general emotional glorification of native scene and theme which are typical of romanticism, Spanish American romanticism adopted as its own a similar glorification of a particular class of society. From the astoundingly immense body of works about this gaucho class has come one of Latin America's greatest works—the *Martín Fierro*[25] by the Argentine José Hernández (1834-1886). Though told in the traditional forms of Spanish verse and following the general romantic pattern, this poem remains as distinctively American as Palma's *Traditions*. Its folklore, the homely wealth of its proverbs and its *payadas*, or contests in verse, all have legitimate Spanish ancestry; but the scene, the life, and the tragedy are American.

Yet a single great masterpiece—even though it may be one of the leading works of all literary time—by no means defines the importance of gaucho literature in the world literary movement. The poem of *Martín Fierro* ends when its hero gives his parting advice to his sons and all then ride off on their several ways into the pampa and to the uncertain, undoubtedly tragic, fate awaiting a class of men for whom society no longer had a place. But the social usefulness of the gaucho literary theme was far from done. Thousands of works—many of them utter trash from the literary point of view but many also of superior worth—appeared, and still appear, on the gaucho theme. Realistically, the gaucho may have been a criminal character busily engaged in the illegal work of smuggling cattle hides to traders across the Brazilian frontier, but the freedom and independence of gaucho life have become accepted as the norm of life in the Plata lands. In that acceptance, the gaucho progressed from police court blotter into literature. And gaucho literature has played a predominant rôle in the modern acceptance of the gaucho ideal of independence;

[25] For an excellent translation, see Walter Owen, *The Gaucho Martín Fierro* (New York, 1935). The poem appeared in two parts: *Martín Fierro* (1872) and *The Return of Martín Fierro* (1879).

Italian immigrants to the Plata have become identified with their new countries, have been spiritually nationalized as it were, largely through its force. Literature has become dynamic.

To be sure, much of it could hardly be classed as "literature" at all. The popular theatre in Argentina grew from circus riding acts to which were added, first, such gaucho "props" as a scene of costumed gauchos, seated on cattle skull "chairs" about a fire and singing their gaucho songs. The fancied arrival of the police gave occasion for a display of riding skill before an appreciative audience of connoisseurs. Then dialogue was added—a dialogue already pleasantly familiar in that it came from a popular novel by Eduardo Gutiérrez (1853-1890)—to give the first gaucho play, *Juan Moreira* (1886).[26] That the original novel and the resultant play were of scant literary merit are factors of relative unimportance. The gaucho theatre was a people's theatre, widely accepted because it responded to a popular feeling to which it gave expression. The heroic gaucho days might indeed be gone, but the audiences wistfully seemed to feel that the shadow of the gaucho's poncho lay upon them. His ideals were theirs. They, too, were bravely independent in their new land; at one with its spirit.

Not all of this literature was trash, however, and not all was directed towards the lower classes of society. The aristocracy, as well, accepted the gaucho ideals, and a parallel literature reflected that acceptance on a high literary plane. The *Martín Fierro* may be the only work to merit listing among the limited number of the world's great books, but many a gaucho work stands high in the ranks of national literature.

In general it may be said that gaucho literature follows two

---

[26] While by no means the original play, a translation of the Juan Moreira theme in dramatic form may be found in *Juan Moreira*, by Silverio Manco, as trans. by J. S. Fassett in E. H. Bierstadt's edition of *Three Plays of the Argentine* (New York, 1920).

A similar dramatization of the Santos Vega theme occurs in the same collection. (Luis Bayón Herrera, *Santos Vega*, trans. by J. S. Fassett.)

For more information about this little-known development of the popular theatre in Plata lands, see Madaline W. Nichols, "The Argentine Theatre," *Bulletin Hispanique*, vol. XLII (1940), pp. 39-53.

literary themes: the Santos Vega theme or that of Juan Moreira. Santos Vega was a *payador*, a singer who engaged in contests of extemporaneous composition in verse. Famous for his success, he eventually met defeat at the hands of a mysterious rival, who then strangely disappeared with a flash of flame and odor of sulphur. Santos Vega died from the shame of his defeat. Over a thousand titles bear witness to the popularity of this theme, to which the poets Bartolomé Mitre (1821-1906) [27] and Rafael Obligado (1851-1920) [28] gave the best literary expression.

As for Juan Moreira, he also represents the tragedy of defeat. Gaucho usefulness passed, along with the wild cattle he had hunted. The breeding of stock for use beyond any mere utilization of their hides, made any cattle hunter an economic liability rather than an asset—albeit an illegal one—to society. The gaucho was then faced with the unpleasant alternative of a voluntary abandonment of his wild nomadic life of personal freedom and a return to a soberly law-abiding existence as peon serving on the newly fenced estancias, or of the involuntary abandonment that necessarily followed when he was sent off to jail or drafted into the army. Juan Moreira typifies the gaucho in this period of his personal crisis. Unjustly persecuted by the authorities, he is joined by a sympathetic friend, and together they fight their battle to win justice from a hostile world. Their fate is inevitable; the tragedy lies in their hopeless, but courageous, struggle against it.

In the *Martín Fierro* the two themes of Santos Vega and Juan Moreira are interwoven. Fierro has his difficulties with local authorities at home and with the military command after he has

[27] Mitre's "Pampa Harmonies" were included in the *Rhymes* published in 1854. The poem specifically entitled "Santos Vega" dated from 1838; for a translation of excerpts, see *Inter America*, vol. V (1921).

Other famous gaucho poems by Mitre—though with no direct use of the Santos Vega theme—were "El ombú en medio de la pampa," "El pato" (on a gaucho game still popular in Argentina), and "El caballo del gaucho." For a translation of the latter poem, see Alice McVan, *Hispanic Poets*, p. 183.

[28] For translations, see Blackwell, *op. cit.*, pp. 348-379.

been drafted into the army on the Indian frontier. He escapes only to find that his family has been equally the victim of persecution after his departure from home. He finds a friend to share his sorrows and his battles. He takes part in a *payada*, like any legitimate heir of Santos Vega. He hands on to his sons such accumulated wisdom as age and experience have brought. In short, this work synthesizes the gaucho theme; its artistic expression makes for greatness. It is distinctively American.

While Santos Vega was pure romance, it is the more realistic shade of Juan Moreira that glides through any works portraying a gaucho in his unequal fight against society. As the romantic literary fashion gave way to realism, the gauchos of the better novels become more sharply defined, authentic characters, such as those found in the excellent novels *Ismael* (1888) by the Uruguayan Eduardo Acevedo Díaz (1851-1921) and *Ramón Hazaña* (1932) by his son, or in *Don Segundo Sombra* (1926)[29] by the Argentine Ricardo Güiraldes (1886-1927). And—now verily a ghost—it is Juan Moreira's spirit which haunts the plays of the Uruguayan Florencio Sánchez (1875-1910).[30]

But besides the gaucho works that turn on the two main themes of that literature, there are also primarily descriptive works. In verse, the long poem *Faust* (1870),[31] by Estanislao del Campo (1834-1880) is most notable; in prose, the famous descriptions of gaucho types in the *Facundo* (1845)[32] by Domingo Faustino Sarmiento (1811-1888), and many of the short stories by Roberto

[29] Translated as *Shadows on the Pampas*, by Harriet de Onís (New York, 1935).
[30] The plays of Florencio Sánchez have not been translated into English as yet. Among them, the best are: *Barranca abajo*, *La gringa*, and *M'hijo el dotor*.
[31] Trans. by Walter Owen (Buenos Aires, 1943).
[32] First published under the cumbersome title of *Civilización y barbarie. La Vida de Juan Facundo Quiroga*, the book rapidly became known as the *Facundo*, and Sarmiento himself so referred to it. For translation, see Mrs. Horace Mann, *Life in the Argentine Republic in the Days of the Tyrants, or Civilization and Barbarism* (London, 1868). A brief selection from the book, "The Private Life of Facundo," is included in *Tales from the Argentine*, Waldo Frank, ed. (New York, 1930), pp. 125-151; trans. by Anita Brenner.

Payró (1867-1928). Perhaps the masterpiece of such description occurs in "The death of a gaucho," [33] by the versatile poet Leopoldo Lugones, who here wrote in realistic prose the very real rôle in war of the gaucho of romance.

Indeed, realism is often close at hand, in the best tradition of old Spain, in all the writing on the romantic gaucho theme. It is found at the very beginning in Echeverría's brutal prose description of the *Slaughterhouse* (1840). [34] It is found as well in the novels of rural society by the Uruguayan Carlos Reyles (1868-1938). In Payró's story of "Laucha's marriage" and in his novel about the *Amusing Adventures of the Grandson of Juan Moreira* (1910), realism has progressed until no true gauchos are left; no naturalistic novel could portray greater degeneration of the gaucho type, even to the breath of old world cynicism which now blows coldly through the telling.

REALISM AND EXPERIMENTATION

As the romantic fashion passed, American literature turned either toward realism or toward an experimentation with literary technique. These two currents were presently reflected in the regional novel, culminating in the novel of class struggle, and in the movement known as "modernism." Of the two, the first was authentically American; the second had deeper roots in Europe.

The beauty of modernism was fundamentally a beauty of sight or sound; not of thought or feeling. Writers might, indeed, draw inspiration from the American scene—as, for example, in the poetry of the Peruvian José Santos Chocano—but in general their chief interest was in musical expression, in imagery, in an enlarged vocabulary, in the technique of literary composition.

[33] Anita Brenner's translations of two stories by Payró—"Laucha's Marriage" and "The Devil in Pago Chico" and her translation of "The Death of a Gaucho" by Lugones are included in Frank, *op. cit.*, pp. 1-76, 153-178, and 79-102.
[34] *El matadero.* Trans. by Angel Flores, in *New Mexico Quarterly*, XII (1942), 389-405.

Themes were frequently artificial, as the poets turned for inspiration to classic Greece, to the France of Versailles, to the Orient, to Scandinavian legends; or as they shut themselves away from all reality in a world of their own creation. Inspiration for new literary techniques came from sources as diverse as the old Spanish poets (Berceo, Quevedo, and Góngora), the Roman Catholic liturgy, a searching through foreign literatures. Above all, modernists turned to the French Parnassians and symbolists, seeking a synthesis of the sculptural qualities of Parnassian verse with symbolist word music. The swan became the symbol of the new school of writing; beauty was its ideal.

But a search for beauty of expression is a legitimate literary aim, and while modernism is not noted for having added depth to literature, it furthered an astonishing development of literary technique and produced some of the world's most beautiful poetry. Poems of the Nicaraguan Rubén Darío (1867-1916), the Colombian José Asunción Silva (1865-1896), and the Mexican Amado Nervo (1870-1919) merit comparison with those of any land and any time, while such poets as the Cuban José Martí (1853-1895) and Julián del Casal (1863-1893), the Mexican Manuel Gutiérrez Nájera (1859-1895), the Bolivian Ricardo Jaimes Freyre (1872-1933), the Peruvian José Santos Chocano (1875-1934), the Uruguayan Julio Herrera y Reissig (1875-1910), the Colombian Guillermo Valencia (1873-1943), the Guatemalan Rafael Arévalo Martínez (b. 1884), and the Argentine Leopoldo Lugones (1874-1938) and Enrique Banchs (b. 1888), all rank high among the national literatures of the world.[35] Their poetry was not only a matter of technical experi-

---

[35] The best single book of translations of the work of all these modernist poets is G. Dundas Craig's *The Modernist Trend in Spanish-American Poetry* (Berkeley, 1934). See, also, Blackwell, *op. cit.*

Among the most famous individual poems of modernism are: Darío's "Symphony in Grey Major," trans. by Alice McVan in *Hispanic Poets*, pp. 245-246; "To Marguerite Debayle," trans. *ibid.*, pp. 247-250, and by Blackwell, *op. cit.*, pp. 192-197; "Sonatina," trans. by J. P. Rice, in *Hispanic Anthology*, pp. 598-601; "Song of Autumn in Spring," trans. by T. Walsh, in *Hispanic Anthology*,

mentation, for each of these poets has left the imprint of his own distinctive human personality upon his work; as the greater among them matured, they tended to turn from the artificiality of foreign themes to an increasing preoccupation with the American scene. Finally, the Mexican Enrique González Martínez (b. 1871) suggested "wringing the neck" of their symbolic swan and a frank return to reality.[36] The poetic development of the greatest modernist of them all, Rubén Darío, typifies in the succession of his most notable books, this trend toward greater intensity, depth, sincerity. From *Azul* (1888), through *Prosas Profanas* (1896) and *Cantos de vida y esperanza* (1905), to *El Canto Errante* (1907), Darío illustrates not only maturing technical virtuosity, but a greater interest in man—the American man—his problems and his soul.

The modernist movement found its reflection in prose, as well as in verse. Again Darío leads with the exquisite cosmopolitan beauty of his "Death of the Empress of China," [37] to be followed in Mexico by the delightful stories of Gutiérrez Nájera and Amado Nervo, in Cuba by those of Martí, in Colombia by those of Silva, in Venezuela by the *Tales in Color* (1898) of Manuel Díaz Rodríguez (1868-1927), in Uruguay by Horacio Quiroga (1879-1937) with his charming little story of "The parrot that lost its tail," and in Guatemala by the sharply etched portraits of *Mr. Monitot: The Animals of the Tropics* (1922) and the

---

pp. 602-606; and "To Roosevelt," trans. by E. C. Hills, in *Hispanic Anthology,* pp. 595-598.

Silva's "Day of the Dead," trans. by Blackwell, *op. cit.,* pp. 404-413, marks the influence of Poe, while his "Nocturne," trans. by Alice McVan, in *Hispanic Poets,* pp. 205-206, is one of the best known of all modernist poems.

For a useful bibliographical guide to other translations of modernist verse—and of all Latin American literature as well—see W. K. Jones, *Latin American Writers in English Translation* (Washington, D.C., 1944).

[36] "Then Twist the Neck of This Delusive Swan," trans. by John P. Bishop, in *An Anthology of Contemporary Latin American Poetry,* Dudley Fitts, ed., (Norfolk, Conn., 1942), pp. VIII-IX.

[37] Trans. by Charles B. McMichael, in *Short Stories from the Spanish* (New York, 1920). Also included in this collection are other stories from those which Darío printed in *Azul:* "Veil of Queen Mab" and the naturalistic "The Box."

famous story of "The Man Who Resembled a Horse," [38] by Arévalo Martínez.

The trend away from the cult of pure beauty and towards a new interest in the social problems of America was marked in modernist prose more perfectly than in modernist verse. In fact, this interest is encountered from the very beginning with Martí, whose whole life's work was oriented toward the social end of Cuba's freedom, and a similar social interest occurs in the work of the great Peruvian writer, Manuel González Prada (1848-1918). It is the remarkable essay, *Ariel* (1900),[39] by the Uruguayan José Enrique Rodó (1872-1917), however, which marks the height of this social tendency attained by prose of consciously sought technical perfection. Because it set a pattern of Latin American thought and because of its now strangely modern emphasis upon the distinctive contributions of the nations of the new world to a new and better civilization for them all, *Ariel* is a book which merits thoughtful reading today, as well as continued appreciation of the perfection of its literary style.

THE TREND TOWARD REGIONALISM

Besides its turning to modernism, Spanish American romanticism also turned toward realism in novels which were generally regional in character. Realism was no sudden development; it had occurred in the details of even the most violently romantic literature. But as a distinct literary movement it may be said to have entered literature in Spanish America, as in Spain, by way of the

[38] For translation of stories by Arévalo Martínez, see "The Man Who Resembled a Horse," in *New Directions. 1944* (Norfolk, Conn., 1944); and "The Panther Man," trans. by Victor S. Clark, in *Living Age*, vol. CCCXXI (1924), pp. 1005-1011 and 1046-1052. The story by Quiroga is included in the translation of his *South American Jungle Tales* (*Cuentos de la selva*, 1918), trans. by A. Livingston' (New York, 1940).

The *Cuentos frágiles* (1883) and *Cuentos de color de humo* (1898) by Gutiérrez Nájera, the scattered stories which Nervo and Martí contributed to various reviews, Silva's *De sobremesa* (1926), and the *Cuentos de color* (1898) by Díaz Rodríguez have not been published as yet in English translation.

[39] Trans. by F. J. Stimson (Boston, 1922).

articles of customs, with their detailed concentration upon the
local scene, either directly or by implication through comparison
with happier lands. Notable among the collections of such
articles are those of Chile's "Jotabeche" (José Joaquín Vallejo,
1811-1858) and Guatemala's José Milla (1822-1882).

As for the novel, it followed the pattern of European regionalism, with a parallel late turning to a naturalism which, in
America, never went to the extremes found in the work of the
French founders of that school. The new realism reflected the
preoccupation with American society and American problems
already glimpsed in the later modernist poetry. In literary technique, however, the contrast is remarkable, for the new novels
pay scant tribute to beauty of style. It is the social significance of
the subject which is now important. Service—not self-expression
or pure beauty—is the new aim; novelists suddenly have a mes-
sianic mission to right humanity's wrongs. The novel becomes
the vehicle of a social message; its strength lies in the validity
of that message and in a kind of surging force coming from its
documentation of the world's injustice to man. It is a class novel,
and while to date it has produced no great literary characters, it
yet gives expression to the suffering of inarticulate masses of
people. For this very reason, perhaps, Latin America's modern
novel will prove to be her greatest gift to the world. Its contribution is in the dimension of depth which it brings to literature.
While it is authentically American, the novel is universal as
well as regional in its appeal, because suffering is everywhere. It
corresponds neatly to the world's modern class struggle.

Again, it is the social novel as a whole that is of literary importance, rather than the individual books. This is even more true
than was the case with the gaucho literature, which, in the
Martín Fierro, produced a work which could represent the movement in world literature, and with modernism, which was epitomized in Rubén Darío. No single great novel worthy to stand
with the great works of all time has yet come from Latin America.
Here the American contribution consists of a large number of

superior works, in constant reiteration of the fundamental problem of social conflict and the humanitarian urge to right social wrongs. Problems are local problems, regional. And so the Argentine Manuel Gálvez (b. 1882) writes of *The Normal School Teacher* (1914), who might be as anonymous as the title of his book but who yet typifies her class; the Mexican Federico Gamboa (1864-1939), in his *Santa* (1903), portrays a prostitute who seems more type than individual character; and the Cuban Carlos Loveira (1882-1928) writes of *Juan Criollo*. Among other outstanding novels of social conflict are *Martín Rivas* (1862) [40] and *El roto* (1920), by the Chileans, Alberto Blest Gana (1830-1920) and Joaquín Edwards Bello (b. 1888); *The Man of Gold* (1920) [41] and *Doña Barbara* (1929) [42] by the Venezuelans, Rufino Blanco Fombona (1874-1944) and Rómulo Gallegos (b. 1884); *The Eagle and the Serpent* (1928) in which the Mexican Martín Luis Guzmán (b. 1887) [43] tells of Pancho Villa and the Revolution; and such novels of the urban proletariat as *The Wharf* (1933) and *Baldomera* (1938) by the Ecuadorian Alfredo Pareja y Díez Canseco (b. 1908), or of life in the rice fields on the hot coast lands of Ecuador as described by Enrique Gil Gilbert (b. 1912) in *Our Daily Bread* (1943).[44]

A most important manifestation of class struggle is reflected in the so-called "Indianist" novel. Not only does it describe the sufferings of a distinctively American class, but insofar as the absorption of the Indian into the social body is the basic modern problem of such countries as Mexico, Guatemala, Ecuador, Peru, and Bolivia, it corresponds to the actuality of Latin American society. It presents, as well, the common problem of all societies which face a necessary assimilation of great masses of people.

This class novel began in Mexico when Mariano Azuela (b. 1873) wrote *The Under Dogs* (1916) [45] and told the story of

[40] Trans. by Mrs. Charles Whitham (New York, 1918).
[41] Trans. by Isaac Goldberg (New York, 1920).
[42] Trans. by R. Malloy (London, 1931).
[43] Trans. by Harriet de Onís (New York, 1930).
[44] Trans. by Dudley Poore (New York, 1943).
[45] *Los de abajo*, trans. by E. Munguía, Jr. (New York, 1929).

the Indian's uncomprehending participation in the Revolution. Other Mexican writers of Indianist novels are Mauricio Magdaleno (b. 1906) and Miguel Angel Menéndez (b. 1905), who have written of the sorrows of the Otomí Indians (*El resplandor*, 1937) [46] and of the Coras (*Nayar*, 1940).[47] Stylistically best of all, even in its use of a nameless hero as a class personage, is *The Indian* (1935) [48] by Gregorio López y Fuentes (b. 1895). With its leading characters symbolically blinded by the all-powerful white man, the contrast between the power of the subject and the restraint and smoothness of the literary style make *The Indian* one of the best books of all Latin American literature and, possibly, the single book which may best represent the Indianist novel to the world.

From Ecuador have come such a diversity of novels of social protest that this national literature best typifies the whole movement. Representative of its specifically Indian phase are the novels by Demetrio Aguilera Malta (b. 1909), whose *Don Goyo*[49] appeared in 1931, Jorge Icaza (b. 1906), who published *Huasipungo* in 1934, and José de la Cuadra (1903-1941), whose *Los Sangurimas* (1934) was one of the best of the lot. Here the force of the novel lies in the brutal tragedy of a seemingly hopeless conflict. Crudities of style match, perhaps unconsciously, the crudities of life itself.

In strange contrast, no adequate protest has come as yet from the prose of another great Indian land, Guatemala, where literature often seems divorced from life. In this respect modern prose remains true to the national pattern, for Guatemala's best literary works have paid scant homage to the Indian as a valued part of that nation's strength. The *Traditions of Guatemala* (1845) by José Batres Montúfar (1809-1844), the prose *Crónicas* which Enrique Gómez Carrillo (1873-1927) wrote in Europe at the

---

[46] Trans. as *Sunburst*, by Anita Brenner (New York, 1944).
[47] Trans. by Angel Flores (New York, 1942).
[48] Trans. by Anita Brenner (Indianapolis, 1937).
[49] Trans. by Enid E. Perkins, in *Fiesta in November*, an anthology, Angel Flores and Dudley Poore, eds. (Boston, 1942), pp. 120-228.

turn of the century, and the poetry and prose of Rafael Arévalo Martínez in the twentieth century, are all more cosmopolitan than national. In modern poetry, however, Miguel Angel Asturias (b. 1899) has broken this tradition of racial isolationism in his beautiful poem, "The Indians come down from Mixco." [50]

In contrast with Guatemala, Bolivia has one of the most powerful of all the works of Indianist literature in her *Race of Bronze* (1919), by Alcides Arguedas (1879-1946).

Finally, in Peru, the last of these countries in which the Indian forms such an important part of society, Ciro Alegría (b. 1909) has utilized the novel most effectively as a medium of social protest. Though preceded by the poet Chocano in the utilization of the Indian theme, Alegría broke completely with the romantic attitude found in the earlier verse treatment. His three novels—*The Golden Serpent* (1935), *Hungry Dogs* (1939), and *Broad and Alien is the World* (1941) [51]—are realistic. Distinctively Peruvian in the portrayal of Indian life on the puna or in the eastern valleys dropping down to the tropics and in the portrayal of the Peruvian scene which, in *The Golden Serpent*, becomes so alive that the Marañón river itself becomes almost a character in the novel, these works are among the best of their class.

And *The Golden Serpent* belongs not only to the Indianist novel, but also to another class of Spanish American literature in which man's fight is predominantly not with man but with nature. In this respect, it competes with some of the best of all Latin American prose, including the famous snake stories, *Anaconda* (1921) and *The Return of Anaconda*[52] by Uruguay's Horacio Quiroga, and the novels *The Vortex* (1924) [53] by the

---

[50] For translation, see Donald Walsh, in Fitts, *op. cit.*, pp. 140-141.

[51] Two of these novels have been trans. by Harriet de Onís: *The Golden Serpent* and *Broad and Alien is the World* (New York, 1943 and 1941, respectively).

[52] Published in *Los desterrados* (1926). Trans. by Anita Brenner, in Frank, *op. cit.*, pp. 237-268. See also, Quiroga's story "The Fugitives," as trans. by Drake de Kay, in Flores and Poore, *op. cit.*, pp. 398-408.

[53] *La Vorágine*, trans. by E. K. James (London, 1935).

Colombian José Eustacio Rivera (1889-1928) and Rómulo Gallegos' *Canaima* (1935), in both of which the tropical forest becomes the leading character.

Brazil, like Spanish America, also made its turn from romanticism to a realistic consideration of social problems. Here the novelists were ahead of the poets, and as in Spanish America, the articles of customs and the regional novel marked the way. Brazilian realistic preoccupation with the *sertanejo* roughly parallels the Argentine and Uruguayan shifting from a romantic to a realistic treatment of the gaucho class, while the racial phase of class conflict quite expectedly turns in Brazil from the Indian to the Negro, though with an absence of much of the bitterness found in the Indianist literature of Spanish America. Notable differences between the Brazilian novel and the Spanish American are the greater Brazilian emphasis on character portrayal and the more frequent recurrence of humor.

Despite the isolated forerunner in the realist novel—the *Memoirs of a Sergeant* (1854-55), by Manoel Antônio Almeida (1830-1861)—the transition from Brazilian romanticism to realism as a literary movement may be said to date from the work of a man who was primarily famous as a poet. In *The Posthumous Memoirs of Braz Cubas* (1881) and *Dom Casmurro* (1900), Joaquim María Machado de Assis (1839-1908) pioneered in the writing of realistic prose; because of the profundity of his treatment of character, he has been called Brazil's first psychological novelist as well. And yet the critic, Veríssimo, writes that despite the undoubted Brazilianism of Machado de Assis, that author had "none of the characteristics of his race. He had a sense of balance, he hated exhibitionism, he was discreet, and he abominated verbosity. In a land of eloquent extroverts

. . . he was an introvert without the love of eloquence or color." [54]

There was little of the ironic discretion of Machado de Assis in the novels of the next outstanding Brazilian author of the late nineteenth century. Aluízio Azevedo (1857-1913) was more a naturalist than a realist, although he interpreted naturalism in the sober Hispanic fashion rather than after the manner of Zola. His novel, *The Mulatto* (1881) is best known for its treatment of the question of race barriers in Brazil. *A Brazilian Tenement* (1890),[55] however, is quite possibly a better novel, not only for its descriptions of a changing community, but also for its creation of the notable character of João Romão, who may well compare with Blanco Fombona's "Man of Gold."

The single, autobiographical novel, *Athenaeum* (1888) by Raul Pompeia (1863-1895) turns back from naturalism to the more authentic realism of the national tradition. Bitter and ironical in style, it is the story of the sufferings of a boy in a boarding school. Critics have classed the book among the ten best works of Brazilian literature because of its expression of an obviously personal emotion and the excellence of the realistic descriptions of the stupidity of the director and the cruelty of the pedagogical methods of his school.

From the turn of the century come two other books of importance in Brazilian literary history; one of them is of importance in world literature as well. The first of these works, *Canaan* (1901),[56] was a thesis novel by José Pereira de Graça Aranha (1868-1931). In it, two German immigrants endlessly expound their none too original ideas on the topic of the mixing of races in Brazil and the resultant new society. In regard to action, the plot reaches its height in the lurid account of the manner in

[54] Erico Veríssimo. *Brazilian Literature* (New York, 1945), pp. 67-68.

Unfortunately neither of these novels by Machado de Assis has been translated into English. Three short stories, however, are included in the *Brazilian Tales*, Isaac Goldberg, ed. (Boston, 1921).

[55] Trans. by Harry W. Brown (New York, 1928).

[56] Trans. by M. L. Lorente (Boston, 1920).

which some pigs eat up the new-born son of the hapless heroine. Accused of its murder, the young woman thereupon becomes a symbol of the cruelty of man, a cruelty as intense in the new world as in the old. Enthusiastic critics of this novel have noted the book's "incomparable" descriptions of landscape and native customs, but its value will doubtless prove to be mainly historical, for *Canaan* marks a step in the turning of the Brazilian novel to Brazilian problems.

An infinitely more important book—undoubtedly the greatest in Brazilian literature—was *Rebellion in the Backlands* (1902) [57] by Euclydes da Cunha (1866-1909). Compared by the critic Pedro Henríquez Ureña with the equally celebrated Argentine work, Sarmiento's *Facundo*, it focusses Brazilian attention on the *sertanejo* class, even as Argentine attention was turned to the. gaucho. Like the *Facundo*, the book is not a novel. Its story is simple. The book tells of a rural mystic named Antonio Conselheiro, of the fanatic multitude that followed him to settle in the northern hinterland known as the sertão, and the final complete annihilation of the lawless community by the forces of the federal government. The hopeless bravery of the Counsellor's followers made the tragedy of the historical event and gives an epic quality to its telling. But aside from its historical and human aspects, the work is famous for its marvelous descriptions of the sertão, its people, and their relation to their environment. A new sobriety and scientific accuracy entered Brazilian literature with this book; there was integrity in the scholarship of its author.

While modern Brazilian novels are still too close in time for an adequate appreciation of the trends which the literary genre will follow, it is obvious that the leading writers of creative prose in modern Brazil—Monteiro Lobato, Lins do Rego, Amado, Veríssimo, and Rachel de Queiroz—are, first of all, regionalists. First in point of time, José Bento Monteiro Lobato (b. 1883) wrote such short stories of regional interest as those in the collection *O Urupês* (1918).[58] José Lins do Rego (b. 1901) is the

[57] *Os Sertoes*, trans. by Samuel Putnam (Chicago, 1944).
[58] See *Brazilian Short Stories*, Isaac Goldberg, ed. (Girard, Kansas, 1925).

novelist of the Northeast and famous for his Sugar Cane cycle in which he told of the life on the great sugar plantations that he knew so well from his own childhood and youth. Among those novels about the sufferings of the people, their habits and customs, and the rural tasks, *The Moleque Ricardo* (1935) is one of the best, in its consideration of the social problems involved as the Negro leaves the plantation for the city. In *Pedra Bonita* (1939), Lins do Rego leaves the cycle, to turn back to the problem of religious fanaticism in the sertão which had so intrigued Euclydes da Cunha, even as it does Rachel de Queiroz (b. 1910) today in her *O Quinze*. As for Jorge Amado (b. 1912), his interest is in Bahía. Among the best of his novels are *Jubiabá* (1935) and *Sea of the Dead* (1936), which belong to the literature about the Negro, and *The Violent Land*,[59] which tells a "Wild West" kind of struggle for control of the land where the cocoa grows.

Erico Veríssimo (b. 1905) is an exception to the general trend, for although he has been called the novelist of the city of Porto Alegre, there is little real regionalism in his work. His interest lies in the portrayal of character. Two of his novels, *Cross Roads* (1935) and *The Rest Is Silence* (1946) [60] illustrate his literary technique, which consists in showing characters drawn together by chance for a little while, only to be separated again as their lives go their several ways. In *Cross Roads*, the lives observed are those seen by Professor Clarimundo, who says: "I live in a suburban street whose focal point is the window of my room. And what do I see? Always the same daily sight, the same identical and monotonous scenes." This is the incorrect conclusion which the book has been vigorously disproving. Similarly, *The Rest Is Silence* relates the lives of the people who happened to witness the suicide of Yanya Karewska as she jumped from the appropriate thirteenth floor of the Empire Building in Porto Alegre. Un-

[59] *Sea of the Dead*, trans. by Donald Walsh, in Flores and Poore, *op. cit.*, pp. 384-397; *Terras do sem fim*, trans. by Samuel Putnam as *The Violent Land* (New York, 1945) is one of the best novels from Brazil.
[60] Both trans. by L. C. Kaplan (New York). A third novel by this author, *Consider the Lilies of the Field*, was published in 1947 (New York).

happily, all these lives portrayed by Veríssimo are tragic or drab; his characters vary the monotony in the circumstances of their tragedy and in their reaction to it, as they either fight against Fate or surrender to it. The literary technique is basically artificial and eventually palls; characters are pictured, rather than developed. The tone is one of a sophistication which relates it to modern Brazilian verse.

In its evolution from romanticism Brazilian poetry showed greater diversion from the general Latin American pattern than did Brazilian prose. Like the poetry of Spanish America, it followed the European fashions, first that of the Parnassians with their emphasis upon form and later that of the symbolists whose primary interest was in sound. But nonetheless there is a profound difference between the Brazilian ultraism that is a rational development of Parnassianism and symbolism and related to the modern world movement known as "vanguard" literature, and the Spanish American preliminary creation of modernism.

Again it is Machado de Assis, a pioneer in poetry even as he had been in prose, who illustrates overlapping poetic tendencies and marks the turn from romanticism to Parnassianism. Combining romantic melancholy with the preoccupation with form characteristic of the Parnassian, he modernized Brazilian poetry. To that poetry he brought as well his personal qualities of a deep, though skeptical, understanding of man and a penetrating sense of humor, both of which he expressed with the perfection of the Parnassian.

Among the Brazilian Parnassians, three names are of especial note—those of Alberto de Oliveira (1857-1937),[61] Raymundo Correa (1860-1911),[62] and Olavo Bilac (1865-1918).[63] With these writers, poetry turned from the intimate confession of the

[61] Some of Oliveira's poetry may be found in the *Pan American Magazine,* in translations by L. E. Elliott, vol. XXIV (1917), p. 211; XXVII (1918), 46, and by L. P. Hill, XXVII, 98.
[62] See "Saudade," trans. by Frances E. Buckland, in Torres Ríoseco, *op. cit.,* p. 235.
[63] An excerpt from one of the most popular of Bilac's poems, "Emerald hunter," is trans. by T. Walsh, in *Hispanic Anthology,* pp. 572-577.

romantic to impersonal description or to narrative. Interest no longer necessarily centered on Brazil. And yet Oliveira, though never a popular poet, was still truly Brazilian in his melancholy sensibility. Correa, known as a "landscape painter," expressed his feeling for nature in verse rich in imagery and charming in its spontaneity though sophisticated in poetic technique. The third poet, Olavo Bilac, was the most typically Brazilian in his voluptuous love of color and music and image and in that vague nostalgia which the Portuguese know as *saudade*. He became the greatest of the Brazilian Parnassians and one of the leading poets in the Portuguese language.

Towards the end of the nineteenth century, the inevitable reaction against Parnassianism appeared in Brazil, as it had elsewhere. Poets became bored with a poetry of mere description and form. To express once more their intimate feelings, they turned to symbolism with its vague suggestions and its music. Brazil's outstanding symbolist was João da Cruz e Souza (1862-1898), a Negro poet from Santa Catarina.

HAITI, AND TRENDS IN MODERN PROSE

Although Haiti is one of the Latin American republics, her literature has been largely forgotten in the literary histories of Latin America. Surely the beauties of the Haitian landscape, as well as the strong rhythmic sense of the Negro, the quick flash of his emotional intensity, his tropic sensuality, his love for color, his spontaneity and the profundity of a long history of suffering, might—with all logic—be expected to produce great poetry. Yet little is known about what has been written.[64]

Great novels may also be expected. Reputedly the best, to date,

---

[64] See Edna W. Underwood's *The Poets of Haiti, 1782-1934* (Portland, Me., 1934). Translations of poems by Duraciné Vaval (b. 1879), Emile Roumer (b. 1903), and Jacques Roumain (b. 1906), done by Donald Walsh, John P. Bishop, and Langston Hughes, respectively, may be found in Fitts, *op. cit.*, pp. 446-447, 488-489, and 278-281.

See also, Mercer Cook, "Trends in Recent Haitian Literature," *The Journal of Negro History* (April, 1947), pp. 220-231.

is *Gouverneurs de la Rosée*, by Jacques Roumain (1906-1944), whom Haitians regard as their greatest novelist. It is *Canapé-Vert* (1944) [65] by Philippe Thoby-Marcelin (b. 1904) and Pierre Marcelin, which is best known abroad, however, since it won the second Latin American prize novel contest. While this novel bears comparison with the best from all Latin America in its literary technique and the artistic utilization of native material, its essential greatness lies in the atmosphere of tragic intensity, as its humble little characters become the pawns of an inscrutable and merciless Fate, because they are, first of all, the victims of their own superstitious beliefs. And so Judge Dor loses his proud position as a kind of combination rural justice of the peace and sheriff, because he knew the hopelessness of trying to make the city authorities realize that he had done nothing to stop his dog when it went mad because of his belief that in that case its evil spirit would have entered his own body. Such fear might be horribly real to him, but to city folks it would be unintelligible. Similarly, another of the book's many characters, Aladin, re-membered his desire to kill Florina, the girl he had loved, and the man to whom she had turned her affection, but

. . . in his honesty of heart he had always pushed [this desire] aside knowing it wasn't a Christian idea, but the suggestion of one of those ancient bloody loas [gods] of Africa, relegated to forgetfulness by the softened manners of the good black people of Haiti. It reappeared some-times to avenge itself with implacable fury for this impious abandonment.

In this book the old African gods get their revenge through the atavistic beliefs of the Haitian people. Any resistance against belief is hopeless, and the tragedy of the characters is portrayed in the novel with the somber intensity of the olden Greek trage-dies of man in his struggle with the gods.

While it may be too close in time for an accurate estimate of current trends, much of modern Latin American literature seems to be following the European patterns of literary style away from

[65] Trans. by Edward Larocque Tinker (New York, 1944). Another novel by the same authors—*La bête du Musseau*—has been trans. by Peter C. Rhodes as *The Beast of the Haitian Hills* (New York, 1946).

American reality. Yet, in a sense, sophistication in itself is true to Latin America; many of her writers are cosmopolitan individuals who are far more close in spirit to the foreign lands in which they have lived for many years than to the lands of their birth. At their best, they use all the new continental literary techniques to tell the new story of America.

This was true of Teresa de la Parra (1891-1936), who in *The Memories of Mamá Blanca* (1929), gave one of the best illustrations of a work which is at once profoundly national in its portrayal of a distinctively Venezuelan life and yet European in the perfection and the daring simplicity of its literary style. She brought to Latin American literature a new wholesomeness and absence of pretense; she brought also her feminine charm, grace, and humor. One of the few Latin American writers to have created literary characters real enough to be remembered, Teresa de la Parra employed in that creation a smoothness of literary technique reflecting with constant naturalness the France which the author knew so well.

The Mexican José Rubén Romero (b. 1890) also combines a sophisticated simplicity of style with the portrayal of his native land to become one of the best and most authentic of the modern novelists. From the early *Desbandado* (1934), with its excellent realistic tale of the Revolution as it swept through a Mexican town, to his famous picaresque *Futile Life of Pito Pérez* (1938) [66] and the *Anticipation of Death* (1939), with its imaginative description of the sensations of death and its delicious mockery of the author's contemporaries as he enjoys their enforced eulogies at his funeral, Romero shows himself to be Mexican, and not merely a stylist.

Some of the best writing in Latin America, however, has brought little or no reflection of the American scene; its greatness must depend either on perfection of style or creation of character. *The Glory of Don Ramiro* (1908) [67] by the Argentine Enrique

[66] Trans. by Joan Coyne, in Flores and Poore, *op. cit.*, pp. 303-367.
[67] Trans. by L. B. Walton (New York, 1924).

Rodríguez Larreta (b. 1875) and *The Spell of Seville* (1935) [68] by Carlos Reyles are Spanish rather than American. In *Brother Ass* (1922),[69] Eduardo Barrios (b. 1884) has created a character one might have expected from almost any other land save his sober, practical Chile. Even the humor of this book is not American; it is the sly, cynical humor of Europe. Other prose examples of this influence of modern Europe are to be found in the writing of Eduardo Mallea (b. 1903) of Argentina, Pedro Prado (b. 1886) of Chile, and José Revueltas (b. 1914) of Mexico.[70] In *The Shrouded Woman* (1938) and *The House of Mist* (1947),[71] María Luisa Bombal (b. 1910) also writes with all the technical perfection which she learned in France. While there is little of her native Chile in her writing, her smooth cosmopolitanism comes naturally from her own life, and since her interest is in the creation of character, her work rings true. Human personality knows no bonds of nationality.

The sophistication characteristic of many modern Latin American novels is even more obvious, if possible, in modern Latin American poetry. Proceeding from that preoccupation with form and sound and poetic technique that had led Spanish America to develop modernism, Brazil, in the twentieth century, created her own distinctive modernism, known as ultraism. Officially proclaimed by Graça Aranha and supported by the poet and critic Ronald de Carvalho (1893-1935), ultraism was designed to free poetry from the bonds of reality. Distinguishing characteristics were its daring use of metaphor, greater variety of image association, free syntax, free verse.

Despite the extremes to which this movement soon went, it

[68] *El embrujo de Sevilla,* trans. as *Castanets,* by Jacques LeClercq (New York, 1929).

[69] Trans. by R. Selden Rose and Francisco Aguilera, in Flores and Poore, *op. cit.,* pp. 488-608.

[70] See Mallea's *Fiesta in November* (1938), trans. by Alis de Sola, in Flores and Poore, *op. cit.,* pp. 11-119, and *Bay of Silence* (1940), trans. by Stuart Grummon (New York, 1943).

Stone Knife by Revueltas has been published in a translation by H. R. Hays (New York, 1947).

[71] New York, 1947.

produced some excellent poets, among whom the most notable were Carvalho, Manoel Bandeira (b. 1886), and, finally, Jorge de Lima (b. 1895),[72] whose poem, "The Negress Fulô," is perhaps the most famous single poem to have come out of the movement. Although the ultraists planned to go beyond (hence, *ultra*) reality, the best poets of the school have nevertheless been able to reconcile the new poetic fashion with an authentic interpretation of Brazilian life.

Obviously the exaggerations of the ultraist movement were bound to lead to reaction. Jorge de Lima and Murilo Mendes (b. 1902) have now turned toward mysticism; Augusto Frederico Schmidt (b. 1906) and Carlos Drummond de Andrade (b. 1902)[73] are illustrating in their verse a new social trend that corresponds to the social emphasis of the modern novel.

TRENDS IN POETRY

In Spanish America poetry follows the two main trends already noted in the novel—one, a trend toward the greater native realism; the other, a reflection of the world "vanguard" movement, which parallels Brazilian ultraism. A notable illustration of the "social" poetry that utilizes art for the service of mankind is the poetry using the Negro as its theme. Here the outstanding Spanish American poet is Nicolás Guillén (b. 1904),[74] himself a mulatto. Protesting the injustice faced by the Negro, he words that protest in the wild beating of the rhythms of the race.

Another phase of the modern poetry that bears its message of truth is to be found in the astoundingly personal self-revelation in

[72] For translations, see Dudley Poore, in Fitts, *op. cit.*, pp. 128-135, 108-123, and 62-81. See also "Songs," trans. by Ruth Anderson, in *Hispanic Poets*, p. 197, and the stanzas from "The Negress Fulô," trans. by Frances Buckland, in Torres Ríoseco, *op. cit.*, pp. 239-240.

[73] For translations, see Dudley Poore, in Fitts, *op. cit.*, pp. 84-85 (Mendes), and 164-171 (Drummond de Andrade).

[74] "A Little Anthology of Afro-Cuban Poetry" is included in *New Directions*, 1944. Among the translations of poems by Guillén are those by H. R. Hays, in his *Twelve Spanish American Poets* (New Haven, 1943), pp. 220-237, and in Fitts, *op. cit.*, p. 244-261, translations by Hays, Fitts, and Langston Hughes.

the work of a group of women poets: the Uruguayan Delmira Agustini (1887-1914) and Juana de Ibarbourou (b. 1895), the Argentine Alfonsina Storni (1892-1938), and Chile's Gabriela Mistral (pseudonym of Lucila Godoy Alcayaga, b. 1889).[75] Because their poetry is subjective and often unrestrained, it brings to Latin American literature a long delayed expression of feminine emotion. Gabriela Mistral, however, transcends her own personal emotions when she directs her poetry into the expression of her sympathy for the weak and the oppressed— particularly for children. Combining the best in feminine sensitivity with the actuality of the social problems of her time, she well merited her Nobel Prize for the excellence of her work. With Gabriela Mistral, poetry is no mere literary exercise. One interesting personal manifestation of her poetic skill is to be found in her *Themes of the Clay* and *Poems of the Home*, where things, as well as people, acquire souls to be regarded with sympathetic understanding. Here Gabriela Mistral is at one with the pantheism of the Indian and furnishes one of the best illustrations of an authentic Americanism.

Of the many names that might be given to illustrate the trend of modern poetry toward realism—in addition to those of the poets who have expressed the emotions of distinctive classes of

[75] Of the work of these Spanish American poets, that of Delmira Agustini remains to be translated.

For translations of poems by Juana de Ibarbourou, see Blackwell, *op. cit.*, pp. 448-449; translations by Beatrice Proske and Elizabeth Trapier, in *Hispanic Poets*, pp. 261-264; and Rolfe Humphries, in Fitts, *op. cit.*, pp. 478-481.

Jessie Wendell and Alice McVan have translations of poems by Alfonsina Storni, in *Hispanic Poets*, pp. 192-194; see also, Donald Walsh, Richard O'Connell, and Rolfe Humphries, in Fitts, *op. cit.*, pp. 506-513; Craig, *op. cit.*, pp. 220-225; and Blackwell, *op. cit.*, pp. 386-391.

Among the many translations of poems by Gabriela Mistral are those by Craig, *op. cit.*, pp. 194-205, and Blackwell, *op. cit.*, pp. 236-279. See also, R. Gill, in *Hispanic Anthology*, pp. 735-736; Alice McVan, in *Hispanic Poets*, pp. 199-200; and, in Fitts, *op. cit.*, pp. 38-43, those by Muna Lee and Donald Walsh.

A Brazilian parallel to this Spanish movement is represented by the poetry of Cecília Meirelles, which still awaits a translator into English.

society—that of Carlos López (b. 1883) [76] of Colombia is possibly the most notable; similarly, that of the Argentine Jorge Luis Borges (b. 1899) [77] can best represent the vanguard movement of which he is the acknowledged leader.

While the many names of undoubtedly superior Spanish American poets are of changing and uncertain classification without the perspective that comes from time, there seems to be no doubt that the name of Pablo Neruda (pseudonym of Neftalí Reyes, b. 1904) [78] belongs among those of the great writers of modern times. Much of his early poetry may well be forgotten; it might better have been left in the literary exercise book where it belonged. But then Pablo Neruda went to Spain and became personally acquainted with war and the challenge of a defense of freedom. Emotion then went deeper than any vicarious stimulation of the senses, and at last Pablo Neruda really began to write. The cheap dross of a coarse, adolescent sensationalism gave way to the surpassing beauty of a rich expression of human emotion. To be sure, all the early literary experimentation proved its effectiveness in this later work, once Neruda had found themes worth the writing. His poem on "Death" is one of the best to be found in any literature. In it an astounding technical skill in a new use of language gives expression to a profound and universal human emotion. The dimension of depth has finally been added to Latin American verse; in that dimension, and in the sublimation of its expression, is the true greatness of poetry as well as the greatness of all literature.

[76] For translations, see T. Walsh and William G. Williams, in *Hispanic Anthology*, pp. 711-714; Alice McVan, in *Hispanic Poets*, p. 212; Hays, *op. cit.*, pp. 52-63; and Donald Walsh, in Fitts, *op. cit.*, pp. 198-205.

[77] See Hays, *op. cit.*, pp. 120-137; Craig, *op. cit.*, pp. 244-247; and Robert Fitzgerald, in Fitts, *op. cit.*, pp. 52-61. One of the best poems by Borges is "The guitar" (See Craig).

[78] Translations in Hays, *op. cit.*, pp. 242-265; Craig, *op. cit.*, pp. 226-235; Hays, Fitts, and Angel Flores are the translators of the poems in Fitts, *op. cit.*, pp. 302-315. See also Angel Flores, "Selected Poems," in *New Directions, 1944*, and his translation of *Residence on Earth* (Norfolk, Conn., 1946).

THE ESSAY AND LITERARY CRITICISM

But depth—profundity—is a dimension all too seldom found in any literature. It is a dimension of maturity; for that reason, perhaps, it would seem unreasonable to have expected it as yet from the new national literatures of Latin America. Against all reasonable expectation, however, that very measure of depth is found in two kindred Latin American literary manifestations—the essay and literary criticism. Here literature has "come of age." From Ecuador's Juan Montalvo (1832-1889) [79] through Rodó [80] to the work of the modern Mexican writers Alfonso Reyes (b. 1889) and José Vasconcelos (b. 1881) [81]—to name only two among many—the essay is one of Latin America's great contributions to world literature. Unfortunately, little is as yet known about it, for essays have been largely buried in unavailable periodical literature.[82] There is no adequate study of this literary field.

In the allied field of literary criticism, however, we are better informed. Again Rodó led, with the remarkable essays on Montalvo and Rubén Darío included in his *Five Essays* (1915), while from the vantage points of Paris and Madrid, the Venezuelan

[79] See translation of "On Pichincha," in *Pan American Bulletin*, vol. LXVIII (1934), pp. 208-209.

[80] "Ariel" was included in the volume *Cinco ensayos* (Madrid, 1915). The famous essay on "Bolívar," also from this volume, was translated anonymously in the *Pan American Bulletin*, vol. LXIV (1930), pp. 1390-1406. See also, *Motives of Proteus*, trans. by Angel Flores (New York, 1928).

[81] For an example of the writing of Reyes, see "Modern Poetry of America Hispana," trans. by Waldo Frank, *Nation*, vol. CLII (March 29-April 5, 1941), pp. 376-379, 411-412.

An essay by Vasconcelos, "Latin America, an Interpretation and a Prophecy," was published in *Living Age* (May 1, 1927).

[82] Periodical literature will apparently remain almost completely unknown until the bibliographical guide prepared by S. E. Leavitt, *et al.*, is finally published. See, however, the annotated bibliographies of the articles on literature appearing in the leading Argentine review, *Nosotros—A Bibliography of Articles in Nosotros: General Literary Criticism Exclusive of Hispanic American Literature*, Publications of the Institute of French Studies, Columbia University (New York, 1935) and *Bibliografía Hispánica: Revista "Nosotros," Artículos sobre literatura hispanoamericana*, Instituto de las Españas, Columbia University (New York, 1937)—both by M. W. Nichols and L. B. Kinnaird.

Blanco Fombona, the Chilean Francisco Contreras (1877-1933), and the Peruvian Ventura García Calderón (b. 1887) [83] surveyed the broad field of Latin American letters. Santiago Argüello (1871-1946) [84] of Nicaragua published one of the best studies of modernism, and in his *Literary Currents in Hispanic America*, Pedro Henríquez Ureña (1884-1946) of the Dominican Republic demonstrated anew that he was one of Latin America's best literary critics of all time.[85] The Argentine Ricardo Rojas (b. 1882) is the author of the remarkable interpretative essay, *Eurindia* (1924), as well as one of the best of all histories of a national literature.[86] In his *Epic of Latin American Literature*, the Chilean Arturo Torres Ríoseco (b. 1897) has published the best popularly written, and yet scholarly, survey of Latin American literature. Among Brazilian critics, the work of Erico Veríssimo is well known and his little volume, *Brazilian Literature*, furnishes a useful modern guide to the field.[87] Strange to say, the best reference work on Spanish American literature, the best general survey of Latin American thought, and the best historical interpretation of the colonial period are the work of three North American scholars, Alfred Coester (b. 1874), William R. Crawford (b. 1898), and John Crow (b. 1906).[88]

Other fields in which Latin American letters have shown surprising strength are those of bibliography and philology.[89]

[83] See such works as *Grandes escritores de América (Siglo XIX)* (1917) and *El modernismo y los poetas modernistas* (1929) and the 'nterpretative study, *La evolución política y social de Hispano-América* (1911), by Blanco Fombona; *Les écrivains contemporains de l'Amérique Espagnole* (1920) and *L'esprit de l'Amérique Espagnole* (1931), by Contreras; and *Del romanticismo al modernismo* (1910) and *Semblanzas de América* (n.d.), by Ventura García Calderón.

[84] *Modernismo y modernistas* (Guatemala, 1935).

[85] Boston, 1945.

[86] *La literatura argentina* (Buenos Aires, 1917-1922).

[87] New York, 1945. See also, Isaac Goldberg, *Brazilian Literature* (New York, 1922).

[88] *The Literary History of Spanish America* (New York, 1928); *A Century of Latin American Thought* (Cambridge, Mass., 1944); and *The Epic of Latin America* (New York, 1946).

[89] Among many names which might be given to illustrate the wealth of this field are those of Juan María Gutiérrez of Argentina and José Toribio Medina of Chile (for bibliography), while the names of Andrés Bello and Rufino José Cuervo may represent the philologists.

BY WAY OF SUMMARY

But there are equally astounding weaknesses in Latin American literature. Of these, the greatest is the novel's relative failure to have studied character, despite all the Latin emphasis on the importance of personality. Its characters are shadowy figures, quickly glimpsed in passing, and usually without development or depth. In general, too, the novel has shown a too obvious straining to attract attention by the use of the extraordinary; too often its success is only *de scandale*. Similarly, in poetry, while the writers have shown surpassing skill in the creation of beauty, they have often been found lacking in sincerity and depth, and the same sensationalism appears in much of the ultra-sophistication of modern verse written in a language of symbols that only the initiate can understand. As for the theatre, there have been no plays that are of interest from the standpoint of any contribution they may make to the world's literature.[90]

A final weakness—particularly of Spanish American literature —has been its undue seriousness. There are, of course, honorable exceptions. Alarcón and Caviedes, in the colonial period; Palma, Batres, and Milla among the romantics; and, in later times, Eduardo Barrios, Jenaro Prieto (1880-1946), Rafael Arévalo Martínez, and Carlos López are names that come instantly to mind. In this respect the relative emergence of the Chileans is remarkable in view of the seriousness generally attributed to the writers of that nation. Also notable is the change encountered in the humor of the twentieth century, with its new bitterness. The poetry of López and the character sketches of Arévalo Martínez are not exactly kind; as for *Brother Ass,* by Barrios, and Prieto's *Partner,*[91] both end in far from humorous death. One might

[90] Similarly, there have been few good biographies to have come from Latin American literature. Aside from short biographical essays, the most outstanding biography is Mitre's *History of San Martín* (1888); for a condensed translation, see William Pilling, *The Emancipation of South America* (London, 1893).

claim that both the desire to attract attention and the solemnity of their literatures were characteristics of an insecure adolescence, if the equally youthful Brazilian literature did not present such a striking contrast to the Spanish American in the sanity of its humor and in the comparatively greater interest in the creation of character.

Perhaps it may seem unreasonable to expect as yet any important gifts from the Latin American literatures to the body of world literature. After the long quiet of a three-hundred-year period in which colonial literature tended to mirror that of Spain and Portugal, those republics began an independent existence in the early nineteenth century, only to become at once involved in bloody civil wars which, in some cases, still continue. As Ricardo Rojas has noted, it took Europe centuries to produce a Homer and a Dante, a Shakespeare and a Hugo, a Cervantes, a Goethe, and a Tolstoy. He feels that it is absurd to measure New World literature by the creation of the Old. But, absurd or not, it is precisely by such a standard of world literary achievement that the American literatures must be measured, just as it is only from the background of the literature from which they came that the great masterpieces, when they appear, are seen in proper perspective.

In America, that background—if it be of value—must come from a deep sounding of the national conscience. American literatures must reflect distinctive national scenes, people, customs, thought patterns; or they must create literary characters so profoundly human that they transcend nationality. For any national literature to have a "gift" for the world, it must bring something new, give more profound or beautiful expression to some universal human experience, illustrate technical skill of a superior order of precision or beauty, or create character. These are characteristics of maturity, and America is young. America's literary

---

Entirely different in type was Sarmiento's *Provincial Recollections* (1850) with its incidental account of the life of the author's mother, which is one of the few good character portrayals in all Spanish American literature.

* *El socio*, trans. by Blanca de Roig and Guy Dowler (London, 1931).

strength is still to be found in her newness—even as it was in the time of Bernal Díaz. She has a new story to tell.

But despite all obstacles, America has brought her gifts to the world's literature, and some of her works merit serious consideration to a rank among the best. From colonial times the *True History* of Bernal Díaz and from romantic times the *Martín Fierro* of Hernández and the *Traditions* of Palma, are original and timeless in their human appeal. And just as the portrayal of a distinctively American social class culminated in the *Martín Fierro* and in the later *Rebellion in the Backlands* by Euclydes da Cunha, so the modern regional novel of class strife is a literary movement of great promise; it has already brought many an outstanding novel and may logically be expected to lead to one that will be truly great when Latin American writers personalize the social conflict in a truly great human character. The essay can hold its own with the best that Europe has brought; bibliography and philology are equally strong. In poetry, Latin America had, in Rubén Darío and José Asunción Silva, poets who rank with any in the creation of pure beauty, and many another poet deserves serious consideration, even when judged by the most severe world literary standards. And while they are still too close at hand for any proper perspective, the poetry of Gabriela de Mistral and Pablo Neruda marks an advance in profundity and in poetic creation which seem to bring to those poets a deserved place among the great writers of all lands and times.

BIBLIOGRAPHICAL NOTE

Contributors have been asked to append to their chapters brief bibliographical notes which will offer introductory guidance to the reader ambitious to explore the literature discussed. This note will be restricted to works which may be generally useful.

For general bibliography, any but professional research workers are likely to find the readiest extensive help in the catalogues of the great libraries, especially of the Library of Congress and the British Museum. Useful for literature as well as general reference is Isadore Gilbert Mudge, *Guide to Reference Books*, 6th ed. (Chicago, 1936); supplements, Mudge and C. M. Winchell (Chicago, 1925-1947), 4 vols. The best one-volume bibliography of world literature now available is Hanns W. Eppelsheimer, *Handbuch der Weltliteratur von den Anfängen bis zum Weltkrieg* (Frankfurt am Main, 1937); as its title suggests, it continues only to the first world war, and it is damaged for readers of English by the bibliography of translations being restricted largely to works in German. For strictly comparative studies, the standard bibliography is Fernand Baldensperger and Werner P. Friederich, *Bibliography of Comparative Literature*, University of North Carolina Studies in Comparative Literature (Chapel Hill, N.C., 1950). Although it is a mine of comparative research, for any but scholars it is damaged by indiscriminate inclusion of much superseded material, and by an organization which makes it awkward for inexperienced users. Both books are likely to be superseded in part for general use in this country by the forthcoming *Guide to Comparative Literature*, a critical bibliography to be published by the American Library Association, presumably in 1952, which will be directed toward readers of English, and will have the advantage of expository and critical comments. It

491

will include a general bibliographical introduction with emphasis upon world literature, a selected but extensive bibliography of translations into English from all languages; bibliographies of studies of the relationships between literature and other fields; and bibliographies of studies of influences from abroad upon British and American literature. For more detailed bibliographies, see Mudge, above.

There is no satisfactory history of world literature, and the useful works are too numerous to list here. Perhaps the best survey by countries is the *Handbuch der Literaturwissenschaft* (Berlin, 1923 —), incomplete but extending to twenty-three volumes by 1941. Two works edited by Joseph Twaddell Shipley are useful though uneven; *Dictionary of World Literature* (New York, 1943); *Encyclopedia of Literature* (New York, 1946), 2 vols. Excellent within its limits is the *Columbia Dictionary of Modern European Literature*, Horatio Smith, ed. (New York, 1947). *The Encyclopaedia Britannica* is of course standard for general reference in English; those who are not impeded by the languages will find the great foreign encyclopedias useful, works like the German *Brockhaus' Konversations-Lexikon* (Leipzig, 1934) 20 vols., supplement, 1935; the Italian *Enciclopedia italiana di scienze, lettere ed arti* (Rome, 1929-1948) 36 vols.; the Spanish *Enciclopedia universal ilustrada europeo-americana* (Barcelona, 1905-1933) 70 vols.; the French *La Grande Encyclopédie: Inventaire raisonné des sciences, des lettres, et des arts* (Paris, 1886-1902) 31 vols. There are important encyclopedias, though they are generally briefer, in the lesser-known languages. Slanted toward English and American literature, but useful for critical concepts is William Flint Thrall and Addison Hibbard, *A Handbook to Literature* (New York, 1936).

INDEX